T0367160

GENEALOGIES OF ORIENTALISM

# Genealogies of Orientalism:
## *History, Theory, Politics*

EDITED BY EDMUND BURKE III

AND DAVID PROCHASKA

University of Nebraska Press | Lincoln and London

Publication of this book was supported by the University of Illinois at Urbana-Champaign Research Board.

© 2008 by the Board of Regents of the University of Nebraska. All rights reserved.

*Library of Congress Cataloging-in-Publication Data*
Genealogies of orientalism : history, theory, politics /
edited by Edmund Burke III and David Prochaska.
p. cm.
Includes bibliographical references and index.
ISBN 978-0-8032-1342-5 (pbk. : alk. paper)
1. Orientalism—History. 2. Postcolonialism. I. Burke,
Edmund, 1940– . II. Prochaska, David.
DS61.85.G46 2008
303.48'2182105—dc22
2008002929

Set in Minion by Kim Essman. Designed by A. Shahan.

# CONTENTS

## *Part 3 | Power*

# ILLUSTRATIONS

# PREFACE

This book began as a conventional conference volume, the sort of symbolic object that signifies that all the authors collected within its covers had a really good (or at least productive) time and were pleased to be in one another's company for the duration of the conference. It has broadened and deepened into a truly extraordinary intellectual and mutually enriching collaboration between the two editors. We wish here to celebrate the wonderful no-holds-barred debates that gradually found focus in the introduction to the present collection and the selection of the essays included here.

Our hope is that it provides a needed supplement to the Anglocentric orientalism of Edward Said and the South Asian subaltern historians. The history of European empire is not just the history of the British Empire writ large. This book, by asserting the alternative (mostly unknown) Francocentric orientalist tradition of Sartre, Fanon, and the Algerian critics of colonial forms of knowledge seeks to inspire other historians of other empires to provide more complex and historically grounded understandings of the multiple cultural encounters that made the modern world. It would be a mistake, we think, to view European empire as only giving rise to a singular homogenized discourse on the other. Rather, we note that specific colonial encounters produced historically distinctive orientalist "takes" on the other, and arose from rather different metropolitan anxieties and histories, themselves changing over time in response to the changing dynamics of world history. It is our conviction that the making and unmaking of empires and civilizations over the past several centuries unfolded not just in response to the laying on of imperial trips, but also in response to unforeseen (and sometimes unseen) collaborations and resistances.

The idea for this book derives from a conference at the University of California, Santa Cruz, in fall 1993. The title of the conference, "Beyond Orientalism," betrays the era's misplaced confidence that it might be possible politically if not epistemologically to transcend the limits of a discourse. Since the conference was held soon after Gulf War I (1991), you might ask: What were you thinking? Many years later it has become clear that while Edward Said's *Orientalism* continues to inspire arguments, conferences, books, and articles, we are in no sense in a postorientalist era. Or a postimperial era, for that matter. Orientalism continues; the need for a more adequate critique of orientalism continues as well.

As historians, we have long believed that it is not enough to theorize orientalism; we must also understand its specific histories. As a step in this direction the essays in this book seek to provide a more complex and historical genealogy of orientalism than has hitherto been available; they chart some histories of the critique of orientalism. A present-day politics of anti-imperialism more than ever requires an adequate understanding of the historical as well as the discursive ways knowledge and power continue to shape the world in which we live. The essays here provide a series of notable explorations of the cultural and political work done by orientalism written by leading scholars.

As a "science of society," nineteenth-century orientalism claimed to provide a total description of non-Western societies yoked to the needs of European empire. While empires of course had existed from time immemorial, what was new about the discourse of orientalism was that it provided both a science and an ideology of conquest and domination. Orientalism structured the mental worlds of imperialist policy makers and newspaper tabloid editors. As kitsch and camp, it soon scrambled existing ideas of the exotic, while providing new models of the modern and the antimodern seen through the lens of highly gendered and racist concepts—West/non-West, black/white, civilized/uncivilized, active/passive, male/female—through which the world is perceived. Today, orientalism still structures our ways of thinking about the world, and how we Americans in particular justify morally our interventions around the globe.

|   |   |   |

In the course of developing this book we have incurred many debts, both personal and professional; we are happy to acknowledge them here. In particular the editors are grateful for the support of the Center for Cultural Studies at the University of California, Santa Cruz, which provided the seed money for the spring planning meeting that preceded the 1993 "Beyond Orientalism" conference. Generous support for the conference itself was provided by the University of California Humanities Research Institute (UCHRI), and former director Patricia O'Brien. In addition, we thank the University of Illinois for research support, plus a publication subvention.

We'd like next to thank the individuals who helped make this book a reality even when they may not have thought so. (We invite them and others here unnamed who were involved in different stages of this project to share with us in the sweetness that is long delayed gratification.) At the head of this list are the original conference co-organizers together with Burke, namely, historians Dilip Basu (UC Santa Cruz) and Takashi Fujitani (currently UC San Diego). Their intellectual energy, friendship, and commitment helped make it a success. James Clifford, the founding director of the Center for Cultural Studies, played a crucial role in development of the conference proposal and helped us secure funding from UCHRI, and we thank him here. Finally, we'd like to express our gratitude to the conference participants and discussants.

Terry dedicates this book to his daughter, Garance, from whom he has learned much, most of it happily.

David dedicates this book to his daughter, Natalie (namesake of another historian): would that she were growing up into a world less instead of more orientalist, but at least she knows that some of us are doing all we can (yelling at the top of our voices).

GENEALOGIES OF ORIENTALISM

# Introduction: Orientalism from Postcolonial Theory to World History

EDMUND BURKE III and DAVID PROCHASKA

Orientalism is over. Or so some stoutly maintain. Unfortunately, the rumors of its demise have been greatly exaggerated. In the post-9/11 United States, the debate over orientalism is far from over. Indeed, in many ways it has just begun. Although orientalism, the philologically driven discipline of the study of Asian languages, no longer exists as such, orientalism as discursive practice linking culture and power is more important than ever. Today the United States peers at the Middle East through orientalist spectacles. Their special properties miraculously filter out historical context and complexity, the better to spotlight the supposedly essential cultural features of Middle Eastern culture that make "them" hate "us." Seen through an orientalist lens, causality is reversed, and morality is readily assigned to the Good Guys.

If we trace the genealogy of the critique of orientalism, we can now see that the publication of Edward Said's *Orientalism* (1978) marked a paradigm shift in thinking about the relationship between the West and the non-West. Said sought to untangle the ways in which Western political, literary, and scholarly representations of the Middle East were fatally inflected by political power. In demonstrating that Michel Foucault's ideas could be brought to bear upon the representation of Middle Eastern cultures and societies in European thought, Said coupled his critique of European discourse on the Middle East to issues of representation generally, demonstrating that Western discourse on the Middle East was linked to power, trafficked in racist stereotypes, and continually reproduced itself. In naming this discourse "orientalism," Said performed a major political as well as intellectual service and made it available to all who had been seeking an effective means of intellectually opposing the canon in its various disciplinary manifestations. Subsequent work by Said and other scholars has deepened and extended, as well as contested, his original vision (Ansell-Pearson, Parry, and Squires 1997; Ashcroft and Ahluwalia 1999; Bové 2000; Said 1993; Sprinker 1992). There is a broader stake for us here as well. Because Said's book became one of the foundational texts not only in the field of orientalism but in the larger field of postcolonial studies and cultural studies, much of the argument we develop in this introduction can be applied to these other fields of inquiry as well (Loomba 2005; Grossberg, Nelson, and Treichler 1992; Young 1990).

Thanks to the scholars of the first generation of the critique of colonial forms of knowledge—Edward Said and those inspired by him (including ourselves)—questions of the role of colonial representation in shaping the discourse of imperialism have assumed an important place on the academic agenda. The critique of orientalism launched by Said's book has thus far proven most fruitful to scholars based in literary theory, as a result of which, history has been de-emphasized. These scholars have primarily focused their critique at the level of epistemology and metacommentary on the discourse of orientalism, where they have indeed made a vital contribution. However, despite important achievements in theorizing orientalism as a discourse and some notable work that explores specific instances of how it shaped and was shaped by colonialism, the critique of colonial representations appears increasingly abstract and disengaged with both its own history as well as the specific colonial histories that it seeks to explain. We believe it is time not only to reevaluate the achievements of the critique of orientalism, but also to recognize some of its weaknesses.

As historians with a stake in the complex issues raised by the critique of colonial forms of knowledge, we contend that while colonial representations have been theorized, they have yet to be adequately historicized. More tellingly, *Orientalism* and the works inspired by it have failed to consider the political contexts in which it arose. A knowledge of this history can help us to understand what was lost in the move to view orientalism primarily as a discursive intervention. We accept that the critique of orientalism has had implications for the ways we understand colonialism and its relationship to the Enlightenment. Colonial representations were instrumental in shaping the culture worlds inhabited by colonizers and colonized because those representations were deeply infused with power. However, by presenting orientalism as the discourse of power by which imperialism rationalized itself to itself, justifying its domination while distorting the image of the colonized,

Said in effect imported the very dichotomies between powerful, active colonizers and passive peoples he otherwise sought to refute. This essentially Foucauldian insight is scarcely adequate to explain the relationship between "the West" and "the Rest." By homogenizing and totalizing the Enlightenment (viewed primarily as a discourse of power) and evacuating history, this approach leaves us stuck in the same old binaries it purports to reject.

The essays in this book propose an alternative approach to the critique of colonial representations advanced by Said and some of those inspired by him. Our basic premise is that further progress in the understanding of how both colonial forms of knowledge and colonial cultures operated requires a deeper engagement with the historical contexts in which they developed (as at least some works in this field assume). We accept that the discourse of orientalism shaped the culture of colonialism in diverse ways. But we disagree that the discourse of orientalism was alone in so doing. Theoretically informed but deeply committed to inscribing themselves in the histories they survey, the authors of the chapters in this book suggest that a deeper historicization of the contexts and contents of colonial representations can help us reimagine the relationship between the West and colonialism. This volume is thus about the need for historicizing both the critique of orientalism and its place in the history of the human sciences over the past thirty years.

In this introduction we seek to accomplish several things. First, in an effort to evaluate Said's achievement, we present a brief historiographical review of the field since *Orientalism* was published, and seek to identify the limitations of Said's original insights, as well as how they have continued to inform scholarship on orientalism and postcolonialism. We ask: What has become of the critique inspired by Said over the past thirty years? What has it enabled us to see more clearly, and what topics has it occluded? Said's book provides a place from which to evaluate the impact of the so-called linguistic and cultural turns both on the wider intellectual field, as well as the field of orientalism from the standpoint of history. To this end, in the pages that follow we seek to locate Said's critique in the larger context of the transformation of the intellectual field in Britain, France, and the United States in the 1950s and 1960s, especially in the move from social history to the linguistic and cultural turns.

To appreciate the precise character of Said's intervention, we must next seek to insert it in the political and intellectual contexts in which it appeared. To this end, we ask: What was the state of the critique of colonial forms of knowledge prior to 1978? How did it manifest itself in Britain, France, and the United States? How did *Orientalism* differ from the works it ultimately displaced? In what ways, despite its undeniable achievement, might we see its appearance as representing an intellectual and political regression? To respond to these questions, we trace the genealogy of the critique of colonial forms of knowledge in Britain, France, and the United States from the mid-1940s to the late 1970s. We'll discover that *Orientalism* did not emerge from nothing, but rather was linked to a deep history of anti-imperialist thought and activism in the metropole as well as in the colonies. Following this critical review, we turn to a presentation of the essays included in this volume.

### History and Postcolonial Studies

One place to start such a review is to ask: Where does the critique of orientalism fit into the larger transformation of the human sciences since the 1950s? As a result of the interventions of Michel Foucault, Jacques Derrida, and other poststructuralist thinkers, the organization of knowledge was transformed and its epistemological premises questioned. Central to these changes was a profound shift in the categories of culture, power, and history, which underwent a meltdown as disciplinary canons were overthrown. Thus anthropologists, for whom culture was a central term, had previously conceived of cultures as homogeneous, stable, and clearly bounded. Historians had operated with a sense of the pastness of the past shaped by empiricism; the facts, once discovered, would speak for themselves. Power had previously been held to reside in states and governments or in economic and social structures. Neither diffuse nor impermanent, it "had an address," that is, an institutional point of attachment to society. In the aftermath of the transformations of the past thirty years, each of these previously stable categories underwent a profound shift. We'll briefly discuss each in turn, before returning to the question of where the critique of orientalism fits into this turbulent period of intellectual and cultural change.

In retrospect, we can see that *Orientalism* involved two distinct intellectual operations. The first was Said's appropriation of Foucault's re-visioning of Enlightenment science as deeply invested in the project of control. Here Foucault's work on institutions like the prison, the school, the medical clinic, and the asylum provided instances of how knowledge and power were fused in Enlightenment thought and practice (Foucault 1961/1965, 1963/1973,

1975/1979). The second operation involved revealing the racist implications of the Enlightenment. Said argued that European representations of the non-West were deeply imbricated in the discourse of imperialism, while his harnessing of continental poststructuralist theories to post–Vietnam War era liberation politics constituted a major move that gave opponents of the established literary canon enormous critical power. Here, precisely, *Orientalism* had its greatest impact. This permitted him to argue that orientalism was a European discourse of control and domination of the non-West.

The advantage for Said (1983: 178–225) in adopting Foucault's methodology was the apparent rigor it lent his analysis (discourse as omnipotent) and how it enabled him to weld together text (knowledge) and context (power). This made clear the functioning of the binary logic of orientalism, as well as its deeper roots in European culture. However, this operation entailed some significant intellectual losses. As we will see in the next section, the older Marxist critique was more complex and historically engaged. Not only did it accord a larger role to social structural context, but it also claimed to provide an explanation for nationalism and resistance.

Ours is emphatically not a narrow disciplinary reaction. On the one hand, even as literature specialists assumed the lead in orientalism and postcolonial studies, they negotiated their own "historical turn," notably in the form of the so-called new historicism, and moved considerably away from primarily formalistic analyses of texts (Gallagher and Greenblatt 2000; Greenblatt 1991; Veeser 1989, 1994). We discuss later Said's criticism of Derridean deconstruction and situate his more historically minded approach within the field of literary studies at the same time as we position him vis-à-vis historians by qualifying his use of "history." On the other hand, we emphasize how variously historians have responded to literary studies generally and to *Orientalism* specifically. A widespread reaction to the postcolonial challenge generally has been to assert history's continuing relevance and then proceed to conduct business as usual. But the problem is that asserting the continued importance of history cannot substitute for demonstrating exactly where and why a historical perspective is intellectually efficacious.

What do we mean when we call for the historicization of the critique of orientalist forms of knowledge? For us this entails three distinct but related operations. First, we seek to relocate the critique of orientalism in the wider history of the human sciences, that is, after the linguistic and cultural turns. Only by doing this will we be able to evaluate both its accomplishments and its weaknesses. A second operation is also necessary, namely, the insertion of the object of study (and its author) into its political and intellectual fields. (We borrow the concept of fields from Pierre Bourdieu, whose work has provided a stimulus for some of the reflections developed here. We return to Bourdieu and how he can help us later in this essay.) Third, because there has been a tendency by some authors influenced by Said to see orientalism as a uniquely Western phenomenon, we insist that a more adequate historicization of orientalism necessarily implies the reinscription of the colonial moment in the context of world history, and not just that of the West. We return to this point later. Why are we so insistent on a full and adequate historicization of the critique of orientalism? Far from being over ("Done that"), the critique of orientalism has much to offer scholars interested in questions of history and theory, knowledge and power, and the relations between metropoles and colonies. But for this rethinking to yield its fruits, there must be a careful rehistoricization of orientalist texts and contexts in the multiple fields in which they exist. The section that follows is an attempt to perform this operation for the critique of orientalism.

We begin by reconsidering from the standpoint of the discipline of history the paradigm shift known as the linguistic or more generally the cultural turn. In the early 1970s history was in the methodological forefront of the human sciences, led by the Annales school in France and the "new social history" in Britain and the United States (P. Burke 1990; Dosse 1987/1994; Hexter 1972/1979). Even as Geertzian cultural anthropology began exerting its influence within the social sciences in the 1980s, history continued to be in the intellectual ascendancy (Geertz 1973, 1983; Hunt 1989). But things were rapidly changing. Developments in linguistic philosophy, including semiotics, structuralism, and poststructuralism, were already beginning to transform the human sciences, starting with literary theory. As deconstruction and postmodernism took hold in the late 1980s and 1990s, the linguistic and cultural turns became ascendant. It is in this intellectual field that orientalism and postcolonial studies emerged, transforming in turn the human sciences. In the critique of orientalism and postcolonial studies that has ensued, the linguistic and deepening cultural turns have been the main driving intellectual force (Bonnell and Hunt 1999; Jay 1993b: 158–166; McDonald 1996; Rabinow and Sullivan 1979/1987; Toews 1987).

At this point it is useful to state our own position on the relationship between society and culture, history and literature, contexts and texts, which we summarize as follows. Nonhistorians like Said turn to history either for specific information about a historical topic, or for knowledge a particular historical approach provides. In the latter case, any given historical approach already entails (even if only implicitly) a way of modeling history, and thus involves choices about competing intellectual approaches, such as cultural versus social history, or discursive versus social structural approaches. Historians who view new historicist literary critics—to consider only those literature specialists closest to historians—as not "historical" enough usually argue that they commit the fallacies of "culturalism" and "textualism." The culturalist fallacy is to construe the historical context as a cultural system, which social historians find impoverishing. The textualist fallacy considers the relationship between texts and the cultural system so construed as "intertextual," that is, as a relationship between a literary text and a cultural "text." The textualist fallacy is faulted, therefore, for being doubly reductive: first it reduces the social to a function of the cultural, and then it further reduces the cultural to the status of a "text."

The key issue, as we have been insisting throughout this discussion, turns on the relationship between texts and contexts, culture and society: Are they relatively autonomous, or does one or the other function as an independent causal variable? Historians who criticize new historicists (and others) usually argue that they privilege literary texts over historical contexts, idealism over materialism. We reject the view that cultural products are primary and in some sense determine their historical contexts, but we also reject as equally reductive the reverse argument: that the historical context is necessarily determinative and that cultural artifacts simply mirror or reflect this context. In keeping with much recent work in history and postcolonial studies, we contend instead that both literary texts and historical contexts are relatively autonomous, entwined dialectically, and mutually constitutive of each other.

It is here that we come to Said's use of history (or uses, as his position evolved over time, and a discussion of the sequences is instructive). First, we can observe that compared to the many literature specialists who adopt one or another formalist approach to literary texts, Said paid relatively greater attention to context, to what goes on outside the text, an approach he glossed as "worldly criticism" (Said 1983). Thus, he ranged himself squarely against deconstruction, for example, according to which "there is nothing outside the text." He criticized literary theory for having "retreated into the labyrinth of 'textuality'" and observed that "textuality has therefore become the exact antithesis and displacement of *what might be called history*" (3–4, emphasis added).

But what exactly is that which "might be called history"? We argue that for Said, "history" actually amounts to the "history of literary criticism." Note in the following passage the slippage that occurs from the former to the latter: "This insensitivity to *history* spoils the very matter being anthologized; *history* is irrelevant. . . . These distortions stem in part from a peculiar disorder in modern criticism itself. As a discipline, *criticism has given very little notice to its history* as a discipline" (Said 1983: 149, emphasis added). Moreover, the payoff for Said in doing the history of literary criticism is that "if we could have accounts by critics of what led them to a given project, why and how they fashioned the project, how they undertook its completion and in what context, we would have opportunities for future study of a very important sort" (153–54). But, again, Said has no theory for how such information relates either to individual texts, or to the history of criticism, or to the relationship between literary texts and historical contexts.

Consonant with this position is Said's preference for Foucault over Derrida, which is based on his view that Derrida deals with texts, while Foucault engages power, history, and context (Said 1983: 144). Said generally failed, however, to consistently apply Foucault's method. He stressed the discursive context, but, as James Clifford has pointed out, he also sought to restore the preeminent position of the canonical author. "In attempting to derive a 'discourse' from a 'tradition,' Said abandons the level of cultural criticism proposed by Foucault and relapses into traditional intellectual history" (Clifford 1988: 268). Part of Said's relapse "into traditional intellectual history," of reinscribing individual authors in a historical tradition, is that in doing so, he fell back on a biographical, even psychological explanation to account for motivation and in the process moved even further away from a historical, contextual approach (Said 1983: 153).

Later, in his *Culture and Imperialism*, Said jettisoned Foucauldian discourse (as his method for connecting texts and contexts, literature and history) and substituted what he termed "contrapuntal analysis" (Said 1993: 32, 51, 66–67, 318). In fact, contrapuntal analysis was not a theory but a metaphor or figure Said used to describe his reading practice, a metaphor that derived from his experience as a pianist where he practiced it more literally (Said 1991: 102). He employed it first to characterize his personal experience of exile, and only later as a metaphor for his approach as a literary critic (Prochaska 2000).[1] We can note that just as Said did not theorize his use of contrapuntal, so, too, he did not engage new historicism as a theoretical practice and the stakes involved in its approach to the relationship between literary texts and historical contexts.[2] We may conclude by saying that Said is interested in history as a body of information efficacious for fleshing out the context of a literary work, but he does not self-consciously employ historical models or theories on the historical data he uses. Within literary studies he employs a more historical approach than his more formalist colleagues, but within historical studies most historians, including us, argue that he failed to sufficiently historicize the discourse of orientalism (Said 1978, 1993). If we examine the political and intellectual context in which Said wrote, the stakes and consequences of his move away from history appear even more vividly.

### The Critique of Orientalism: A Historical Genealogy

We turn next to a historical genealogy of the critique of orientalism as a colonial form of knowledge. The critique of orientalism itself has a history that is not limited to the history of the British Empire, although generally this is what its history is taken to be. What was the critique of orientalism before the appearance of Edward Said's book? The question, and the answers to it, help us both to historicize Said's work and to understand how he innovated, and where he built on the work of others. An exploration of the genealogies of the study of colonial discourse also helps frame some of the larger objectives of this volume: to understand the world historical contexts in which orientalism flourished (as well as that in which the critique of orientalism might also take root), and in the process to encourage new reflection on the areas of weakness as well as the strengths of Said's contribution.

What, to begin with, was orientalism? In the primary sense of the term, orientalism referred to the academic discipline based on the philological study of original texts in Asian languages which flourished in the late eighteenth century and the nineteenth century. As one stream of Enlightenment thought, it sought to uncover the allegedly essential features of civilizations possessing developed writing systems through the critical philological study of their allegedly central cultural texts.[3] Prior to the emergence of the social sciences, orientalism derived its prestige from its claim to be the "science of society," by which Asian civilizations and peoples might be understood and classified according to their level of development. In the nineteenth century's division of academic labor, orientalists adopted as their field the study of societies with writing systems, and those without writing became the province of the emergent discipline of ethnology. Scholarly work on orientalism in this primary sense was the principal subject of Said's work. The essays in part 1 provide an overview of the British and French traditions of textual orientalism.

In the same period orientalism came to acquire a second meaning, as a term referring to the romantic and exoticizing impulse of nineteenth-century European artistic culture. In the nineteenth century orientalist representations of supposedly exotic cultures became commonplace themes in art, literature, and music. Many leading artists (and many not so leading ones), including Mozart, Flaubert, and Delacroix (to mention but three), made extensive use of orientalist settings, motifs, and tropes in their work. Since the publication of Said's book, and especially his *Culture and Imperialism* (1993), the critical study of orientalism as culture has received a new impetus and has become a major area of research. A host of studies have been produced that span subjects from Hollywood movies to high culture, including art, architecture, colonial expositions, dance, music, opera, and photography. The essays in part 2 direct our attention to some of the key contributions in the exploration of orientalism and culture.

Finally, with twentieth-century nationalist movements of decolonization, orientalism acquired a third meaning when some nationalist activists and scholars argued that the scholarly discipline of orientalism could not be understood apart from the circumstances of its production, namely, Western imperialism. Thus was born the debate over orientalism, a debate that occurred primarily in the French-speaking world around the issue of Algerian independence, where it initially presented itself as a struggle "to decolonize history" (E. Burke 1995). Yet neither Said nor the other scholars of the first generation seemed aware of this struggle. Only in his *Culture and Imperialism* did Said even mention the role of Frantz Fanon. Why is this so? To pose this question is to begin to realize that *Orientalism* and the works inspired by it have failed to consider the political contexts in which they arose. The critique of orientalism has forgotten its own history, which is rooted in the anti-imperialist struggles of the past century.

Anti-imperialism was an increasingly powerful political force in the decades between the end of World War II and the publication of *Orientalism*. Opposition to European empire in Asia, Africa, and Latin America importantly shaped the politics of the postwar world, both in the metropolitan centers and in the former colonies. In this process, the leading role was played by Third World nationalisms. Among the chief arenas of conflict were the independence struggles in India, Palestine, Ghana, the Congo, Suez, southern Africa, Algeria, and of course Vietnam. It was the Vietnam War, in particular its American phase (1964–75), that led to unparalleled levels of mobilization throughout the world, especially in the United States and other industrialized countries. This political mobilization was matched by the emergence of anti-imperialism as a cultural and intellectual force in the period. Thus we may usefully ask: How were critiques of imperialist thought framed before, thanks to Said, the term "orientalism" became available? Which disciplines were most affected? The essays in part 3 explore the complex imbrications of orientalism, imperialism, and nationalism.

To gain a sharper sense of the stakes involved and the possibilities of "unthinking" imperialism at the time, we briefly consider in parallel the British and French traditions of the critique of imperialist culture. In each case we examine first the conditions that shaped the political field in which contestation over empire existed, before taking up the question of intellectual field. For Bourdieu, from whom we borrow the concept of intellectual field, the *champ scientifique* is constituted by the grid of intellectual and scientific influences that act on and are reflected in intellectual products and artistic works. The political field, the *champ politique*, encompasses the larger political and social context that a particular intellectual product occupies (Bourdieu 1976, 1977, 1984/1993). We begin with a consideration of the critique of imperialism in Britain and the United States.

### The British and U.S. Critiques of Imperialist Thought

Opponents of British colonialism in the 1950s and early 1960s did not lack detailed critiques of British rule, but stressed denunciations of imperialism as a system linked to capitalism or general critiques of racism in the colonial situation, rather than a critique of colonial representations as such (Kiernan 1969; Mason 1953).[4] In their rereading of colonial histories produced by Europeans, nationalist critics of European empire replaced colonial and racist representations of their societies with nationalist ones. But they were unable to see either colonialism as a discursive system, or colonial forms of knowledge as situated knowledges (which is where Said's book was such a stimulus to further thought and analysis). When a theorized critique of British colonialism in India eventually did appear, it was not during the Indian freedom struggle, but more than a generation later, with the emergence of the Indian Subaltern Studies Group in the 1980s. (We return to this topic in the conclusion.) In the United States, the critique of imperialism was poorly developed prior to the emergence of a movement in opposition to the Vietnam War. While there were some currents of opposition on the Left, the general post-1945 mood stressed material success and conformity.

By the late 1960s the radicalization of politics and thought in both Britain and the United States, fueled by the Vietnam War and the development of the civil rights movement, gave rise to movements for social and political change. When the critique of colonial forms of knowledge emerged in both countries, however, it was largely limited to the discipline of anthropology, which was particularly exposed because of the entangled histories of anthropology and empire. Most critics were strongly influenced by currents of Marxist and anti-imperialist thought (Anon. 1968; Fabian 1983; Hymes 1972; Stocking 1968/1982; Wolf 1970). They concluded that anthropology was fatally impregnated with racist and colonialist attitudes, and that such standard anthropological tropes as "the primitive" were merely the theoretical masks of this underlying ideology. The other discipline open to radical currents of thought was history. Although influenced by Marxism (in the form of the "new" social history) and the nationalist critique of imperialism (especially the histories of Third World countries), history as a discipline adhered to the nation as the appropriate frame for analysis and fetishized written sources. Both tended to limit the impact of radical critiques that crossed national boundaries. As for literature, it was at this time coming under the influence of poststructuralism. Moreover, the theorization of race and gender as categories of analysis was just beginning to emerge in the 1970s.

Efforts to broaden the critique of colonialism and imperialism beyond anthropology to encompass history and other disciplines failed to take hold in Britain and the United States during the 1960s and 1970s for several reasons. Rather than raise troubling questions about the situated character of all knowledges, anti-imperialist Western historians in the 1950s and 1960s tended to reinscribe nationalist rewritings of history as their own. Questions about the politics of representation—Who owns colonial history, nationalists or Europeans?—were not yet on the intellectual agenda (E. Burke 1998b). Lacking a more philosophically grounded critique, particularly a theory of representations, anti-imperialist Marxists in Britain and the United States were unable to transcend the politics of anti-imperialism and antiracism or to develop a critique of the antihumanist political tendencies within progressive nationalisms. Nonetheless, Marxist critiques of imperialism possessed some important advantages over the discursively based critiques that came along with *Orientalism*, because they were in some respects better able to imagine the mental world of imperialism as shaped by complex world historical processes.

Two works that exemplify this phase of the critique are Talal Asad's *Anthropology and the Colonial Encounter* (1973) and Bryan Turner's *Marx and the End of Orientalism* (1978). The contributors to Asad's volume sought to move beyond the ritual denunciation of colonial social science and engage the historical contexts in which it had flourished. In his introduction Asad (1973: 16–17) noted that anthropology was a child not only of the Enlightenment, but also of unequal power relations between the West and the non-West. He called into question the uses to which anthropological knowledge had been put and noted that anthropological declarations of political neutrality had had important consequences, including the inability of the field to study the colonial system as such. Anthropology was not just the reflection of colonial ideology, Asad argued, but as a product of an inherently ambiguous and often contradictory bourgeois consciousness, it was capable of developing more complex and historically situated understandings of its own history and its relationship to colonialism.

Turner's book was an intervention in the field of Middle Eastern studies that was linked in some ways to the activities of the so-called Hull group of progressive scholars, including Asad and Roger Owen.[5] Published the same year as *Orientalism*, it anticipated certain of Said's main themes. Without once using the word "discourse" or invoking the work of Foucault, Turner was the first to argue that Middle Eastern area studies was linked to the orientalist study of art, literature, history, and religion (6). At the same time, he responded to debates within 1970s British Marxism sparked by the introduction of Althusserian interpretations of Marx concerning precapitalist formations (Hindess and Hirst 1975; Wolf 1982). For Turner, Marx's assumptions that history proceeded in stages, that Europe was at the leading edge of progress, and the efforts to distinguish an Asiatic mode of production derived from the penetration of Marx's thought by orientalist categories and assumptions. It was the Hegelian (and orientalist) epistemological limitations of Marxist thought about the Middle East that needed to be queried, so Turner argued. Although *Marx and the End of Orientalism* shows that something was in the air, and may help to explain why Said's book was so rapidly taken up, it remained fundamentally linked to Marxist structuralist thought. This suggests that British and American Marxist thought alone would have been unlikely to achieve Said's intellectual breakthrough. But what of the critique of imperialist thought in France? Here the situation was more complex but, as we'll see, also rather different.

### The French Critique of Imperialist Thought

Because the history of the intellectual critique of colonialism in France is less well known than in the case of Britain, we provide a more detailed account here, beginning with the political field. The decolonization of the French Empire, especially the struggle over Algeria, produced a prolonged debate that questioned both the contents of French colonial *science* and the nature of the colonial relationship. Because the Algerian War involved not a distant colonial territory but a part of France itself, the intellectual struggle within France was far more bitter than debates spawned by the end of the British Empire or by Vietnam in the United States (D. C. Gordon 1964, 1971; Le Sueur 2001; Schalk 1991; Sorum 1977).[6] It is one thing to relinquish control over a foreign territory, quite another to yield part of what is considered national territory. The French debate over Algeria came in the midst of the turmoil over decolonization in Southeast Asia, sub-Saharan Africa, and the Maghreb, and badly split both political Left and Right. But mobilization was slow to emerge because of the success of defenders of empire in portraying the struggle as one over France itself, widespread racist attitudes toward colonial peoples in France, and restricted media coverage of the war. Until late in the game, large majorities within the major political parties, from the communists on the left to the Gaullists on the right, supported holding onto *l'Algérie française*, while the cause of independent Algeria received support from a small coalition of ex-Resistance fighters, nationalists, and leftist Catholic intellectuals.[7] Support for the Front de Libération Nationale (FLN) remained, however, a minority position in France until the eve of Algerian independence.

As the Algerian struggle grew more intense, the cultural battle widened. Algerian intellectuals and their French allies launched a no-holds-barred attack on colonial history and social science (Vatin 1983). Unlike in Britain and the United States, the critique of colonial knowledges in France embraced a larger intellectual field, encompassing not only anthropology, but also history and the social sciences generally. Inspired by Sartre's example, young Third World intellectuals like Albert Memmi (1957/1965) and Frantz Fanon (1952/1967, 1961/1968) wrote biting critiques of colonial racism in the late 1950s. Sartre's journal, *Les Temps modernes*, became a major venue for colonial critique. Portions of Fanon's brilliant counterethnography *A Dying Colonialism* (1959/1965) first appeared there as well as the work of Algerian nationalist historians Mostefa Lacheraf (1965) and Mohamed C. Sahli (1965), who demolished the colonial historiography of Algeria and argued for the necessity of "decolonizing history." Leftist Catholic publications, in particular *Esprit* and *Témoignage chrétien*, were also important venues for intellectual attacks on colonialist thought (Mandouze 1961, 1998). In "Orientalism in Crisis" Anouar Abdel-Malek (1963), a francophone Egyptian Marxist scholar, broadened the critique to colonial knowledge more generally in an article that influenced later commentators, including Said (Tibawi 1963, 1979).

The most important work by far to come out of the French decolonization struggle was, however, Frantz Fanon's *The Wretched of the Earth* (1961/1968). Simultaneously an anti-imperialist militant's manual and a scathing analysis of colonialism as a system of racist violence and oppression, *The Wretched of the Earth* systematically challenged the assumptions of colonial social science and presented a brilliant counteranalysis (E. Burke 1976). Contesting the view that the French simply practiced colonization as *mise en valeur* in Algeria, Fanon emphasized the harshness of French colonialism as an across-the-board project of mental and material domination. At the same time, however, he did not consistently distinguish between the Algerian case and the rest of the Third World he generalized about. The slippage from Algeria to the Third World generally led Fanon to emphasize violence, a Manichaean all-or-nothing struggle, which was more characteristic of settler colonialism in Algeria than European colonialism elsewhere (Fanon 1961/1968: 40–42, 84, 86, 88–89, 93–94; Prochaska 1990/2004).

Very much influenced by Fanon were later critiques by Philippe Lucas (1969) and Jean-Claude Vatin (Lucas and Vatin 1975), Gerard Leclerc (1972), and Jean Copans (1975). The decolonization struggle continued to haunt

French culture into the early 1970s, when *Les Temps modernes* published two separate double issues on the theme of "Anthropology and Imperialism" (nos. 253–54 and 299–300, 1970–71). While it may be surprising to some, nothing like the breadth and amplitude of the French critique can be found in the English-speaking world. After a period of relative neglect, today a new generation of scholars is discovering Fanon and the French legacy of the critique of colonial forms of knowledge (Alessandrini 1999; Bhabha 1994: 40–65; Gibson 1999; L. R. Gordon, Sharpley-Whiting, and White 1996).

Let us assess the French critique of colonial knowledge up to this point, beginning with the political field. The ambiguous legacy of the anti-Nazi Resistance was politically crucial for the way it legitimized struggles against foreign occupation and provided a ready-made political vocabulary (resisters and collaborators) for understanding anticolonial nationalism. One indication of this link was the publication of Henri Alleg's *La Question* (1958/2006) by the formerly clandestine resistance publisher, Editions du Minuit. Alleg's condemnation of the systematic use of torture in Algeria by the French authorities helped to build opposition to the war among the French public (Branche 2001; Le Sueur 2001).[8] In short, the political instability of the Fourth Republic, the Cold War atmosphere of contestation, Soviet support for Third World nationalism, and the fact that Algeria was juridically part of France all worked together to heighten the feeling, especially on the Right, that the fate of France itself was at stake in Algeria. This political context figures importantly in understanding why the French critique went further than that in Britain and the United States.

Turning to the intellectual field, we see that although the dominant intellectual influence was anti-imperialist Marxism, as in Britain and the United States, a number of specifically French determinants were also present. Postwar French thought was profoundly shaped by the broad context of underlying philosophical contestation of Cartesian rationalism, including a suspicion of the faculty of sight, together with a fascination with the ethical position of the Other, or *l'autrui* (Jay 1993a; Poster 1975, 1989).[9] From different angles the thought of philosophers such as Sartre, Merleau-Ponty, Emmanuel Levinas, and Vladimir Jankélévitch, as well as anthropologists like Claude Lévi-Strauss all converge (Descombes 1979/1993; Dosse 1997). Out of this broad intellectual ferment was eventually to come critical theory and poststructuralist thought and critical theory. Although Sartre's (1968) engagement on behalf of anticolonial nationalists did the most to legitimize support for Algerian independence in France and Europe more generally, others also played important roles. In retrospect, it is significant that although Foucault's first works were published in the early 1960s (Foucault 1961/1965, 1963/1973, 1966/1970, 1969/1972), their relevance to the critique of colonial forms of knowledge was mostly unsuspected at the time. The future lions of deconstruction mostly chose to sit out this round.

The state of the question in the mid-1970s emerges clearly in *Le Mal de voir* ("The Difficulty in Seeing"; Moniot 1976). The result of a 1974 conference organized by Africanist Henri Moniot and a younger generation of scholars drawn from a variety of disciplines and areas of specialization, including Africa, Asia, the Americas, and the Arab world, the conference included established anticolonial intellectuals such as Jean Chesneaux and Maxime Rodinson. *Le Mal de voir* showcased the work of scholars who had been directly involved in Algeria, notably Pierre Bourdieu and Fanny Colonna, that reconsidered the legacy of the French ethnology of colonial Algeria. The conference volume provides a window into the French critique of colonial knowledge in the mid-1970s similar to that provided for Britain by Asad (1973), although the French critique was more far-reaching. It evidenced a deep concern with problems of representation and foregrounded the importance of historicizing the production of colonial forms of knowledge. *Le Mal de voir* is intellectually dominated by Bourdieu (Calhoun, LiPuma, and Postone 1993; Robbins 1991). Although a significant proportion of his sociological work concerned Algeria, Bourdieu wrote about his Algerian experience only rarely (Bourdieu 1980/1990: 3, 1987/1990: 23; Mudimbe 1993). Because of his impressive productivity, it is easy to forget that he taught at the University of Algiers during the Algerian War and continued to do research there, some of it in collaboration with Algerian scholars, until 1970.

Bourdieu's contribution to *Le Mal de voir* theorizes from the vantage point of the sociology of knowledge the position of individual intellectuals in the context of the political and intellectual fields they occupied in their society. As defined previously, the intellectual field, or *champ scientifique*, refers to those intellectual and scientific influences on a given intellectual product. The political field, or *champ politique*, encompasses the larger political and social context of a particular intellectual work (Bourdieu 1976, 1977, 1984/1993). As sociological categories, fields constitute useful tools for performing a sociology of knowledge, as we do here. To place the political field in relation to the intellectual field forces scholars to pose questions that generally go unasked. Yoking the fields in tandem works in particular against presentism, against anachronistic readings, because the logic of fields links the intellectual field with the political field contemporaneous with it. Similarly, Said's (1993: 96) contrapuntal analysis avoids what he terms the "rhetoric of blame," but this is not intrinsic to the contrapuntal analytic. Mapping the positions of intellectuals on both grids is more efficacious, for example, than Foucault's less specific concept of knowledge/power. Finally, it is important to note that the idea of fields works well for France, where it is relatively straightforward to institutionally locate intellectuals in an empirical manner: *agregé* or not, *grandes écoles* or not, and positions held.

Although Bourdieu's notion of fields is efficacious for conducting a sociology of knowledge, it is not without problems as a philosophy of knowledge. As a typology, fields have no inherent explanatory power, nor does Bourdieu explain how they are linked. The concept of fields implicitly assumes a level of rationality difficult to square with the often directionless nature of quotidian life. Moreover, the concept assumes that individual acts and utterances neatly fall into one or another discrete field, an assumption that poststructuralism and postmodernism show cannot be sustained. Although conceptual alternatives to fields have been proposed (Fish 1980: 320–21; Jay 1993b: 158–66; Kuhn 1962; Lyotard 1979/1984; Miller 1985), especially "interpretive communities," the key point is that all such concepts underscore the situatedness of knowledge, including orientalist knowledge, in a way rarely done prior to *Orientalism*. Thus, we retain the notion of fields here, employing it as a heuristic device.

In the present context, we find Bourdieu's sociological approach of intellectual and political fields more useful than Said's biographical-cum-psychological approach to authorial "position." One preliminary conclusion that clearly emerges from this review is the relatively greater methodological sophistication of the French tradition of the critique of orientalism, especially in work concerning Algeria and the Maghreb, as opposed to the British and American critiques of imperialism, which were imbued with what can now be seen as an undertheorized Marxism.

Let us now pause to recall the historical contexts on the eve of the publication of Said's book, looking first at the intellectual field, then at the political field. The critique of imperialist thought was no longer an urgent intellectual project in Britain, with the exception of Turner and a few others in the Hull group. In the United States, while the anticolonial struggle had provoked broad intellectual questioning of colonial knowledges (notably in anthropology), by 1978 this had not led to a break with the established progressive, Marxist-derived language of anti-imperialism and antiracism. Barring the emergence of a new intellectual paradigm such as that eventually brought about by the linguistic turn, academic Marxism was definitively stalled. It was insufficiently powerful to develop a broadly appealing critique of patriarchy, race, and culture (on all of which points Marxism had strayed but little from Marxist orthodoxy). Instead, the end of the Vietnam War and the waning of the social and political struggle over decolonization was a period in which intellectual energies were shifting in other directions in Britain and the United States.

In retrospect we can see that the years around 1978 were a political watershed as well. Externally, with the end of the Vietnam War, Third World progressive nationalism and solidarity appeared poised for further victories, while in the United States, the civil rights and antiwar coalition remained for the moment intact. To many observers, progressive Arab nationalism seemed on the verge of triumph in the Middle East, and the Palestine Liberation Organization (PLO) was at the apex of its power. But things were about to change. Abortive revolutions in Afghanistan and Lebanon, the 1979 Islamic revolution in Iran, the 1982 Israeli invasion of Lebanon, and the subsequent expulsion of the PLO from Beirut were soon to completely reshape the Middle Eastern political context. Meanwhile, the rise of Margaret Thatcher in Britain and of Ronald Reagan in the United States marked the end of a political era. In a twinkling, Third World nationalism was finished, along with the Marxist critique of imperialist thought. This is where the fate of *Orientalism* is drenched in irony. By the date of its publication, the political and intellectual contexts in which it had been conceived were already in the process of transformation. Although *Orientalism* played a key role in stimulating these changes, this possibility was entirely unforeseen by its author.

In this context we can now more clearly evaluate the historic achievement of Said's book. On the one hand, by seeing orientalism as a discourse, Said opened a new (incipient) post-Marxist cultural space of contestation and (as we have seen) forged political as well as intellectual links between feminists and peoples of color at home and abroad. On the other hand, at the political level, in abandoning the Marxist critique of imperialism, he also abandoned historical explanations of imperialism. And by conceiving of orientalism as the manifestation of imperialism at the discursive level, Said made it difficult to explain where nationalism came from, and undermined the agency of colonized peoples. For if orientalism was viewed as a hegemonic discourse, in what space could resistance arise? At its best, the pre-1978 Marxist critique of imperialist thought was aware of the situatedness of colonial knowledges, complex in its analysis of orientalist representations and their connections to power, and morally clear in its opposition to imperialism. In this respect, it provided a more successful and historically engaged critique than the concept of "orientalism" that replaced it. However, despite the pertinence of its analysis, the Marxist critique was unable to move beyond its relative academic isolation to transform the intellectual field because the emergent strands of cultural critique found no home within the confines of the Marxist critique. Though much was gained with the move to discursive analyses of orientalism, an awareness of the complex genealogy that we have just reviewed teaches that much was lost as well when the Marxist critique of imperialist thought was abandoned. Finally, the discursive interconnections between orientalism and nationalism that were (ironically) opened by Said's 1978 book were poorly understood in the 1970s (a point developed further by the essays in part 3). Not only was the conceptual and theoretical language for discussing nationalism as a discourse unavailable until after the maturing of the critique launched by Said, but it was all but impossible to enunciate criticisms of progressive Third World nationalisms.

Having described the multiple political and intellectual contexts in which Said's book intervened and the historiographical record it has left, we are now ready to turn to a consideration of the essays included in this book. For convenience, we have grouped the essays that follow under the headings of "History," "Culture," and "Power." These categories map the larger discursive dimensions of the critique of orientalism, and remind us of the larger intellectual context in which it occurred. This is of course a heuristic device. Crucially, all three vectors shaped the context of action (though not all to the same degree).

The essays in the first section, "History," provide a more complex and historically situated genealogy for the critique of orientalism. Counter to the approach taken by Said and those who have followed him, which has assumed the essential similarity of the British and French colonial experiences, we insist on their difference. This is in part because of the divergent cultural forms taken by Enlightenment narratives in the two countries (which in turn were somewhat differently deployed in the colonial world). In part it has to do with the differences in the divergences between the two modal colonial societies: India for the British Empire, Algeria for the French Empire. Finally, it also has to do with the divergence of their respective histories of decolonization. The essays by David Ludden and Bernard Cohn discuss India, and those by Edmund Burke and Fanny Colonna focus on the Maghreb.

The next two sections contain essays that continue our focus on the Middle East and India, even as they broaden to the rest of Asia. The essays by Julia Clancy-Smith and Jenny Sharpe in part 2, "Culture," explore the entanglements of history, gender, and orientalism in Algeria and India. Much important work has been done on artistic representations of colonial subjects. David Prochaska examines the complex place of colonial photography in contemporary India and Algeria. Zeynep Çelik and Leila Kinney present a skeptical ethnography of one aspect of Parisian culture, the representations of Islamic culture in world's fairs, and they trace the imbrications of popular culture between the metropole and the colonies.

In part 3, "Power," we take up the ways colonialism reimagined the world and consider how orientalism and power came to define it. Nicholas Dirks and Ella Shohat explore the complex interrelationship of orientalism and nationalism even as they reframe the South Asian and Middle Eastern comparison. Our final two essays, by Arif Dirlik and Alan Christy, explore the complex appropriations of the new technologies of power by East Asian societies in their efforts at self-imagining as modern states. Broadening our focus beyond the Middle East and South Asia, these chapters consider how power/knowledge questions have played themselves out in the quite different histories of China and Japan.

### Orientalism and History

Although Said discussed the work of several French orientalists (de Sacy, Renan, Massignon) at length, and despite the prestige of French scholarship on the Middle East in the nineteenth century, it is the British model of orientalism that is normative for him. No doubt, the central role that Britain played in the twentieth-century history of the Middle East is key. The fact that many of the most influential studies of orientalism published after Said have taken the British Raj as their subject has helped reinforce this tendency and given it a colonial Indian twist. As a result we have come to accept a model of orientalism that takes the British colonial experience as the standard. We suggest instead that the orientalist representations took distinctively different shapes depending on the cultures of the colonizer and the colonized. At another level, we note that Said described the discourse of orientalism as basically homogeneous—as a European discourse that transcended the differences between European colonial empires. But upon reflection once again we see that in fact it is British orientalism (and not some abstract European discourse) that he has in mind.

Though there is no denying Said's point of the homogeneity of orientalist discourse in certain respects, the essays in part 1 provide a more complicated genealogy for the discourse of orientalism than that which we get in *Orientalism*. Building on the immediately preceding discussion of the British and French critiques of imperialist thought, these essays draw attention to the differences in the British and French colonial experiences. Although the orientalisms each produced may have overlapped at the discursive level, they nonetheless diverged in some important ways as well. Here it is necessary to recall that the different political and cultural settings of the Enlightenment project sparked rather different internal cultural struggles within Europe. Thus, for example, the church-state conflict that so divided France has no counterpart in British history. Similarly, the British experience of race, starting with their representation of the Irish, differed profoundly from the ways race was experienced in France. If we expand our field of vision, we can observe that modernity etched rather different cultural fault lines in each society, and that the axes of cultural struggle around which modernity emerged also differed. In the effort to problematize and contest the unwitting homogenization of orientalism, two cases recommend themselves as especially paradigmatic: India and Algeria. Each was central to the development of a distinctive orientalist discourse. And protracted liberation struggles in each site provoked intense political and cultural mobilizations, ultimately leading to profound transformations of their respective metropolitan intellectual fields. The contrasting essays in part 1 help to demonstrate that the critique of orientalist forms of knowledge was well advanced prior to the publication of *Orientalism*.

In Britain and the United States, the principal focus for the development of the critique of colonial representations was India, and David Ludden's essay "Orientalist Empiricism: Transformations of Colonial Knowledge" provides a good overview of the way the critique unfolded with respect to British India. Drawing on the sophisticated language of critique developed in the

1980s and early 1990s, Ludden takes pains to establish the connections between the history of political power in South Asia and knowledge, especially European, about India from the colonial era to the present. He provides a coherent and theoretically informed narrative of the ways British orientalists and imperial officials collaborated and struggled over the representation of Indian society that is all the more effective because of the care he takes to historicize the different moments of colonial knowledge about India from the late eighteenth to the mid-twentieth century, rather than treat successive transformations of British knowledge as a seamless web.

In his survey of the development of British Indology, Ludden traces the sequence leading from the empiricist orientalism of William Jones and Thomas Munro under the Company Raj (1750–1820) to its reformulation by the Utilitarians (James Mill and others) in the first half of the nineteenth century, and its eventual incorporation into social theory under the Victorian empire. As Ludden explains, Mill's role was central. Critical of the romanticism of the orientalists, he viewed India as an object to reform, a site for Utilitarian experiment. Marx later drew on Mill in his own writings on India, which emphasize Britain's historical role as the bearer of the dialectic to the subcontinent. This line of argument has more recently exposed him to the charge that he, too, was an "orientalist" (Said 1978: 153–56; Turner 1978). After Mill, British authority concerning the empirical realities of India became hegemonic. In the construction of an essentialized India, two key orientalist tropes predominated: the supposedly autonomous Indian village, and religious conflict between Hinduism and Islam, the latter of which provided the analytic grid for the later construction of communalism. By 1850, British orientalism consistently viewed traditionalism as woven into the local institutions that conditioned social life. However, it remained profoundly ambivalent about the legacy of Hinduism. While orientalists saw Hinduism as a sister civilization to Europe, a great civilization in its own right, they also saw it as the chief source of Indian moral degeneration. Finally, in an ironic involution, Ludden argues that the epistemological power of British orientalism was appropriated by Indian nationalists such as Tagore, Gandhi, and Nehru.[10] Thus Indian nationalist authors accepted the orientalist view that European materialism had corrupted a timeless and spiritual India. How orientalism was imbricated with nationalism is an important theme that is discussed further in part 3 of this book.

Bernard S. Cohn's essay "The Command of Language and the Language of Command," provides a complex reading of the unfolding of British orientalism in India. Cohn problematizes the relationship between two moments of British orientalism: the precocious virtuoso orientalist studies of Indian languages in the years before 1820, and the remarkable banality and racial stereotyping of British Indology in the years after 1830. He traces the evolution of British orientalism from the textualism of Sir William Jones and his collaborators to the empiricism of the imperial mapping of the peoples and cultures of India, and the ways these transformed Indian realities as well as European understandings of India. His discussion of the compilation of a Sanskrit/English dictionary and the mapping of the languages of India reveals the surprising ways in which British presuppositions about what a language is, where one leaves off and another begins, were inflected by power. Cohn contrasts the remarkable first generation of East India Company orientalists, who lived an Indian lifestyle, learned Indian languages, and had "the command of language," and the post-1830 generation, who retreated to the British drawing room, content to give orders in "kitchen Hindi," "the language of command," and no longer were willing to accommodate to Indian realities. Although this essay adopts a very Foucauldian reading of the development of British orientalism in India, most of Cohn's work explored other dimensions of colonial knowledge. Well before Said and Foucault, his essays constituted an archaeology of colonial forms of knowledge in India in which he mapped the ways the British mentally "created" colonial India and endowed it with meaning. Cohn's concept of "colonial forms of knowledge" has the clear advantage of historical specificity, against the one-size-fits-all world of discursive analysis (even as amended to permit counterdiscourses). Because Cohn primarily wrote essays rather than books, and most of his papers appeared in specialist journals, the importance of his work was not widely known outside of the India field (Cohn 1987, 1996).[11] For Cohn, colonial history was not something already known, but a strange world requiring excavation.

In contrast to the history of British orientalism in India is the example of French North Africa. How did the French represent the Maghreb, and with what consequences? The essay by Edmund Burke III, "The French Tradition of the Sociology of Islam," provides a parallel overview of the colonial Maghreb to that afforded by Ludden for India. He argues that the French elaboration of the sociology of Islam was produced in three eras: the Egyptian period (1798–1828), especially the *Description de l'Égypte* (Bourguet,

Lepetit, Nordman, and Sinarellis, 1998; Prochaska 1994); the Algerian period (1830–70); and the Moroccan period (1900–1930). Most important was the Algerian period for "it was through an Algerian lens that Frenchmen viewed other Islamic societies" (E. Burke, this volume). In Algeria the sociology of Islam consisted of three strands: the tradition of the Arab Bureaus, the civilian amateurs, and the academics. Yet the intellectual field of the sociology of Islam in Algeria was "frankly marginal" to sociology in France, whether one thinks of Comte, Durkheim, Mauss, or Lévi-Strauss, due to the power of the political field (Valensi 1984). Although in the initial decades of military conquest the Arab Bureaus constituted significant sites of intellectual production, by 1870, with the advent of the civilian-dominated Third Republic, they were eclipsed politically by the European settlers (Prochaska 1990/2004). Settler intellectual production centered among scholars of the *École d'Alger*. Through their ties to colonial Algerian politicians, and the dominant role played by these politicians in the *parti colonial* in Paris, these scholars wielded disproportionate influence in France. The dominance of settler stereotypes of North Africans, or what Burke calls the "colonial vulgate," reduced French ethnography to a fossilized remnant of its former self by the eve of the Algerian revolution in 1954. What use is French colonial ethnography? Burke argues that its facts cannot be separated from its theories, because "the facts themselves derive from the theory, their very factness certified by it." Thus the strands of the French tradition of the sociology of Islam together constitute a Foucauldian discourse.

The final essay in this section is Fanny Colonna's probing discussion of the work of several French ethnographers of colonial Algeria in the light of Bourdieu's fields, "Scientific Production and Position in the Intellectual and Political Fields: The Cases of Augustin Berque and Joseph Desparmet." It begins with the question How does the position of an individual in the intellectual and political fields of his or her time explain the pertinence (or lack thereof) of his or her scholarship (Colonna, this volume; Colonna and Brahimi 1976)? She contrasts the work of two little-known authorities of the early twentieth century: Augustin Berque and Joseph Desparmet. Berque, a high-up administrator of *affaires indigènes*, was marginal in the intellectual field but central in the political field, from which vantage point he produced a series of important sociological studies on the changing social structure of colonial Algeria, while Desparmet was marginal to both the intellectual field and the political field. Both produced ethnographic work of great impor-

tance though neither was a prominent figure in the world of Algerian scholarship. Colonna seems to imply that the more marginal to the mainstream
of a field, the greater the lasting insights. Yet she explicitly argues against
drawing such a conclusion by briefly invoking a third case, that of Émile
Masqueray, who was at the center of both the intellectual and the political
fields in Algeria in the 1880s and 1890s (Colonna 1983a). It is useful to know
that in her choice of Berque and Desparmet as cases to study, Colonna went
against the grain of 1970s Algerian historiography, which tended to assign
merit to Algerian perspectives and blame to French colonial scholars. With
Colonna, therefore, we reach a new level of penetration in the critique of
colonial thought. One is tempted to see her personal involvement in the Algerian struggle as in some ways making possible her more finely calibrated
evaluation of the situatedness of colonial knowledges. Colonna was born in
colonial Algeria and was one of the handful of French settlers to side with
the FLN during the war and to take Algerian citizenship in 1962. Although not
widely known outside of North Africanist circles, she has produced a body
of work that cumulatively performs for Algeria intellectual work analogous
to that of Cohn for India (Colonna 1975, 1987, 1995).

### Orientalism and Culture

A central aspect of the changes of the past thirty years has been the transformation of our understandings of culture. In place of a model of cultures as
"thick description" (Geertz 1973, 1983), in which individuals act as a function
of common understandings of deeply rooted bundles of symbolic meaning, we have come to think of cultures as patchy and contingent, or possessing what William Sewell (2005: 169) terms "thin coherence," incomplete
scripts that enable us to get through the day, but not always without incident.
Whereas cultures were previously viewed as timeless essences or homogeneous fields, now we have come to see them as continually being invented,
challenged, and reinvented (Hobsbawm and Ranger 1983). Cultures are always also partial stories that ignore the continual existence of a problematic
hybridity. Above all, as we have learned from Foucault (and Gramsci), they
are fields of struggle in which meanings are always contested (though not
always the same ones or in the same ways). The work of Raymond Williams
(1977) in particular has helped us to understand that culture derives from
a politics of cultural production in which cultures are viewed both as the

product of particular interests and as constituting the meanings by which consent is enforced or opposed.

Despite its important political and intellectual achievements, *Orientalism* failed to account for (except obliquely) the ways in which the discourse of orientalism deployed the categories of gender and race. Since 1978, the theorization of racial and ethnic difference has emerged as crucial to discussions of the representation of colonial societies and their role in discursively shaping the culture of colonialism. Race has been extensively theorized in the U.S. field, though generally not with a view toward the meanings of discourses on race outside of the North American context. Among those with an eye to the broader ways race has been deployed, members of the so-called Birmingham school of cultural studies have been in the forefront, notably Paul Gilroy and Stuart Hall (Gilroy 1993; Gilroy, Grossberg, and McRobbie 2000; Morley and Chen 1996). U.S. feminist scholars have sought to theorize links between race and gender, and to instantiate the ways both have been powerfully shaped by the particular political contexts in which they emerged (Frankenberg 1993). Studies of the culture of colonialism by scholars, most of whom work on South Asia, have emphasized the ways race and gender profoundly etched the divisions of colonial society, naturalizing the understandings of both colonizer and colonized of how and where each one fit, a highly gendered product of Western superiority (Cooper and Stoler 1997; Dirks 1992; Stoler 1995, 2002). The undoubted theoretical achievement of this literature, however, has not come without a cost. The effort to develop large theorizations of the colonial experience risks overwhelming the evidence, flattening more complex efforts to understand the multiple historical contexts of actually existing colonialisms. The more deeply historicized essays in this section provide a set of alternative strategies that collectively explore the relations between orientalism and culture.

Colonial culture in the sense of visual culture, literature, and the performing arts has been powerfully reshaped by a new awareness of the politics of representation. By demonstrating the extent to which the European representations of others (the orientalist gaze) have derived from and were shot through with the fact of European dominance, Said challenged aesthetic theories that had unproblematically posited the West as the ground of culture. This permitted him and us to see how Western literature, art, photography, dance, and other fascinations with the exotic all took place under the sign of Western dominance. As a literary critic Said was in the end primarily interested in deepening our understandings of the way high culture was shaped by the fact of Western dominance. This is the burden of both *Orientalism* and *Culture and Imperialism* (1993). But Said's work paid much less attention to the culture of colonialism, to how orientalism, viewed as the construction of otherness and difference, fused with projects of rule and domination to constitute the culture of colonialism. Before introducing the selections included in this volume on orientalism and culture, we turn briefly to the larger theoretical contexts and debates, the better to clarify the reasons for our choices.

Although Said discusses women and gender in *Orientalism*, notably in the section on Flaubert in Egypt (1978: 186–90), his approach largely ignores the salience of gender in colonial representations of the other that has become a central aspect of the post-Saidean critique of orientalism. Yet the confluence of gender with orientalism and postcolonial studies has produced an outpouring of work influencing gender studies far beyond the chronological and geographical boundaries of colonialism *per se* (Abu-Lughod 1998; Burton 1994, 1999; Chaudhuri and Strobel 1992; Clancy-Smith and Gouda 1998; Midgley 1998; Pierson and Chaudhuri 1998; Stoler 1995, 2002; Strobel 1993). In an example that we discuss further below, Gayatri Spivak's (1988) "Can the Subaltern Speak?" constitutes both a canonical work in the literature on gender and imperialism, and a response to the lack of gender in Said.[12] Delineating differences within male-female difference not only adds nuance to our understanding concerning the imbrication of gender and orientalism, but also demonstrates how certain groups such as colonial women were doubly colonialized.[13] In addition, some authors, such as Mrinalini Sinha (1995), have turned their attention to masculinity. Sinha has described the construction of male identities in colonial India as, on the one hand, the "effeminate" Bengali among colonized Indians and, on the other, the "manly" Englishman among British colonizers.

In discussions of gender and colonialism two sites in particular have attracted attention: the harem and *sati* (widow burning). Scholarly work on the harem and its place in gendered constructions of colonial culture has yielded a range of important studies that challenge the modern patriarchal orientalist gaze. Historians and literary critics have contextualized the joint family, the seclusion of women, and perceptions of gender power imbalances, among other aspects of the harem, from a variety of different viewpoints (Apter 1999; Peirce 1993). But attention to the place of the harem in colonial representations has thus far not provoked a debate over the ways gender in colonial societies was represented and theorized. The intellectual linkages between orientalism and gender are, however, even more direct in feminist studies of *sati*. Here the work of Spivak and Lata Mani is of special interest, as it brings to the fore issues that are central to this volume (Hawley 1994; Loomba 1993; Mani 1998; Spivak 1999; Yang 1989).

"Can the subaltern speak?" Spivak (1988) asked in a foundational text in postcolonial studies, to which she replied, in effect, that no, she could not. Spivak's essay constituted as well an oblique response to the lack of gender in *Orientalism*, a Derridean *supplément* to its absence in Said.[14] Her essay directly challenged the assumptions of social historians (in this case, the Indian Subaltern Studies Group) that it is possible to recover the voices of poor and powerless groups. On the contrary, she insisted, subalterns, especially subaltern women, cannot speak (in historical texts), and all claims to the contrary amount, in effect, to disguised acts of historical ventriloquism, since historians write from a field of power that is not that of subalterns. Thus her discussion of *sati* constituted part of a larger argument about poststructuralism, in which she sided with Derrida rather than Foucault. As opposed to Foucault, "Derrida marks radical critique with the danger of appropriating the other by assimilation. He reads catechesis at the origin" (308). Here Spivak resisted what she viewed as the temptation to see herself as an Indian woman similar to subaltern Indian women, and to appropriate thereby subaltern women, that is, to claim a similarity, and therefore a shared understanding, that did not in fact exist.[15] Instead of similarity with the potential for assimilation and the attendant risk of appropriation, Spivak underscored difference. With Derrida, therefore, she "marks catechesis at the origin" of her understanding of subaltern women. In this sense "the subaltern cannot speak." Or rather, the subaltern can speak; it is just that we cannot make out what she is saying. Instead of uncovering subaltern speech, Spivak employed Derridean deconstruction to deny the possibility of history. Or, more precisely, she constructed her argument by progressively narrowing her purview from "subaltern" to "women" to "*sati*" so that the *sati* implicitly emerged as the worst-case scenario for recovering the subaltern's voice. While we may agree with Spivak that ultimately anything like *the* representation of the subaltern is epistemologically impossible since any historical representation is a representation of the past rather than the past itself, we argue that *a* representation or series of representations of the subaltern, partial though they may be, are indeed possible.

Lata Mani's (1992, 1998) influential work took a more historically engaged (though ultimately also discursive) approach to the question of representing *sati*. By posing a series of questions, Mani usefully complicated Spivak's theorizations: "Which groups constitute the subalterns in any text? What is their relationship to each other? How can they be heard to be speaking or not speaking in any given set of materials? With what effects?" (1992: 403).[16] While the debate over *sati* was allegedly about the status of women, Mani's larger argument was that the discourse on *sati* exemplified the refiguration of tradition in colonial India. Thus, the debate over *sati* was "a modern discourse on tradition" in which Indian women were "neither subject, nor object, but ground" of the debate. Although she did not explicitly refer to this discourse as "orientalism," it is the internal logic of orientalism that she delineated when she pointed out that both British colonial officials and the Indian male elite "agreed that scripture overrode custom, that explicit scriptural evidence had greater weight than evidence based on inference and that, in general, the older the text the greater its value" (1987: 145). Thus Mani returns us to Hobsbawm and Ranger's (1983) invention of tradition and to Cohn's (1996) enterprise regarding the construction of India as a discursive object. To Spivak's question "Can the subaltern speak?" Mani responds in effect, No, but I think I can hear her. Although "it is difficult to know how to interpret these accounts [of *sati*]," Mani nonetheless concluded that "the volition of some widows can justifiably be seen as equal to the resistance of others" (1987: 129).[17] That is, she refused to read texts on *sati* as texts only of oppression, but held open instead the possibility of multiple meanings and intentions.

In her essay in this volume on Isabelle Eberhardt, "The 'Passionate Nomad' Reconsidered," Julia Clancy-Smith substitutes just such a social historical approach for a discursive one. In a frankly revisionist account, Clancy-Smith demythologizes Eberhardt as someone undeserving of the esteem she enjoys among postcolonial and feminist critics (Abdel-Jaouad 1993; Hamdy and Rice 1994). Where some see Eberhardt as exemplifying a postcolonial and feminist sensibility *avant la lettre*, Clancy-Smith locates her as a white woman in a profoundly racist society and an "honorary male" with connections to men of privilege. To make her case, Clancy-Smith takes a primarily historical rather than literary tack. From Clancy-Smith's perspective, few if any recent studies examine Eberhardt within the "proper historical perspectives" of late nineteenth-century European orientalism and French settler colonialism in Algeria. Clancy-Smith contends that Eberhardt, having arrived in Algeria "already imbued with the Orientalist fable as told in Europe," viewed Algeria through orientalist lenses. Resituating Eberhardt in the context of settler colonialism in Algeria reveals her as less of "an anomaly or a social aberration" and more as "a collaborator in the construction of French Algeria." Eberhardt's gender transgression and sexual proclivities may have been related to acute manic depression, but Clancy-Smith scores Eberhardt for wielding "gender conflict" as her principal tactic of appropriating another culture, of using gender transvestism to "engage in cultural transvestism." In short, Eberhardt was an extreme example of "cultural hyphenation." Where literary critics tend to see proto-feminism, Clancy-Smith sees "gender conflict." Where others see proto-nationalism and a lively sympathy for Arabs and Islam, she discerns orientalism. And where postcolonial critics tend to value cultural hybridity, she devalues Eberhardt's "cultural hyphenation" and urges us to examine the Algerian colonial political context inhabited by Eberhardt (Clancy-Smith, this volume). In effect, we may say that though Eberhardt speaks loud and long to contemporary critics, it is a very different Eberhardt that Clancy-Smith hears.

That the choice is not a narrow disciplinary one between either a literary and textual or a historical and contextual analysis Jenny Sharpe makes clear in her essay, "The Unspeakable Limits of Rape," which combines both approaches in mutually reinforcing ways. Sharpe rethinks the coded historical messages in E. M. Forster's A *Passage to India* (1924/1984) by connecting changes in India between Forster's two visits to revisions Forster made in his novel. A *Passage to India* revolves around a discourse of rape that Sharpe, rather than treating it as an unchanging literary trope, historicizes by tracing rape from its origins in the 1857 uprising to the 1919 Amritsar massacre and later. Although Forster never explicitly refers to Amritsar, Sharpe links the Amritsar context to the novel's text by showing how Forster revised in particular the crucial scene in which Adela is allegedly assaulted in the Marabar caves. Through her reading Sharpe makes two primary contributions. First, she demonstrates the efficacy of using gender as a category of historical and literary analysis, for without understanding the gender relations involved between "superior race" British and "inferior sex" women we cannot understand how gender crosscuts colonialism in works such as A *Passage to India*. Second, she shows how melding literary and historical perspectives enriches Forster's text in the historical context of colonial India. Unlike Spivak, for whom colonialism becomes in effect the discourse of colonialism (Gates 1991: 466), Sharpe's position is that "if we are to study literature for its disruption of an ideological production [the discourse of rape] that prevents social change, we can no longer afford to restrict our readings to the limits of the literary text. Rather, we should regard the literature as working within, and sometimes against, the historical limits of representation."

For Sharpe, Forster's novel poses a problem that is "particularly vexing" for feminists: Which is the real crime, Adela's accusation or Aziz's alleged assault? This choice forces critics to defend either colonized male Aziz or colonizer female Adela, with the result that this "either/or decision (but neither both) has divided anticolonial criticism" of A Passage to India along gender lines. As a result, feminist interpretations of the novel generally "ignore the racial memory" that constitutes in fact the historical framework for the novel's theme of interracial rape. The problem, Sharpe concludes, is that "by deploying 'rape' as a master trope for the objectification of English women and natives alike, [literary critic Brenda] Silver produces a category of 'Other' that keeps the colonized hidden from history."

Sharpe simultaneously places the novel in the context of the trope of race. Again her move is to historicize, and not merely to theorize. She insists that Forster's novel be located in British colonial writings on the 1857 revolt, specifically the racial discourse on "brown-skinned men sexually assaulting white women in India." The event that revived the racial memory of 1857 in Indian colonial society was the British massacre of some 375 Indians at Amritsar in 1919, which she argues connected to apparently two discrete historical moments. It is "the shadowy presence of the [1919 Amritsar] massacre"—which occurred between Forster's two visits to India—that "haunts the novel," linking Forster's A Passage to India and Paul Scott's The Raj Quartet (1966–71/1976). In this manner Sharpe shows "literature as working within, and sometimes against, the historical limits of representation." It is precisely such "historical limits" or parameters of representation, to echo Bourdieu (1972/1977), that Sharpe's analysis illuminates (Sharpe, this volume). By asserting the specific political contexts in which Forster conceived and later wrote his novel, Sharpe invites us to consider that colonial discourses on race and gender themselves need to be historicized.

Turning next to visual culture, we may begin by noting that Said and his commentators initially paid scant attention to visual orientalism (Beaulieu and Roberts 2002; R. Benjamin 2003; Bohrer 2003; Grigsby 2002; Porterfield

1998). Thus, for example, although Jean-Louis Gérôme's *The Snake Charmer* (ca. 1870) appears on the cover of *Orientalism*, Said did not discuss it. Similarly, Said (1978: 92–94, 80–88) asserted that it is possible to discern a "textual attitude" toward the Orient in the works of orientalists such as William Jones in India and Napoleon in Egypt, but when he discussed the primary publication resulting from Napoleon's Egyptian campaign, the *Description de l'Égypte* (1809–28), he neglected entirely its more than three thousand engravings (Bourguet et al. 1998; Prochaska 1994).[18] These images constitute a formidable data bank of representations that might have been subjected to analysis, yet Said limited his analysis of the *Description* to a brief discussion of Jean-Baptiste-Joseph Fourier's historical preface (and to one paragraph at that!).

Let us take a leaf from Said's book, however, and by analogy to his "textual attitude," characterize an approach to visual culture by the "new art history" as one that detects a "visual attitude" that when applied to "Oriental" materials can be termed visual orientalism. One way to distinguish such an approach from earlier ones is to contrast vision and visuality, where "vision" refers to the physiological, biological, and psychological basis of sight, and "visuality" considers sight as a social and cultural construction with its own history of successive scopic regimes (Buci-Glucksmann 1986; Foster 1988; Jay 1993a). The "new art history" construes visual culture broadly for just such a "visual attitude" (W. Benjamin 1936/1969; Bryson 1983; Bryson, Holly, and Moxey 1994; Crary 1990; Krauss 1985; Krauss and Livingston 1985; Mirzoeff 1998, 1999; W. J. T. Mitchell 1994; Rouillé and Marbot 1986; Schwartz and Przyblyski 2004; Sekula 1986; Solomon-Godeau 1991; Squiers 1990; Tagg 1988; Taylor 1994). Within the field of visual culture we take visual orientalism to encompass the whole of visual production with an "oriental" referent, ranging from painting, architecture, and photography, to panoramas and theater design, to world's fairs, museums, and film (Alloula 1980/1986; Bohrer 2003; Çelik 1992; Crinson 1996; Grabar 1973/1987, 1978; Mitter 1977/1992; Pinney 1997, 2004; Prochaska 1990, 1991, 1994; Solomon-Godeau 1981). Interpreting orientalist works in terms of visual culture necessitates moving beyond a consideration of objects *per se* to their production and reception, or consumption, a theme we pursue below.

In her now classic essay, "The Imaginary Orient," Linda Nochlin (1983/1989) was one of the first to yoke together visual culture and orientalism. In an analysis of nineteenth-century French painting that moved beyond traditional art history, Nochlin discussed not only what was present in these orientalist paintings but also what was absent. She identified four major gaps or lacunae: the absence of history ("Time stands still"), the absence of "scenes of work and industry," the absence of Westerners despite their presence in the region, and "the apparent absence" of art where the striving for a "reality effect" unproblematically reflected "a preexisting Oriental reality" (35–37, 39; Barthes 1982/1984).[19] Interpreting orientalist painting as neither documentary realism nor Romantic exoticism, Nochlin usefully located such works "under the aegis of the more general category of the picturesque," which ranges from regional genre painting to the *National Geographic*. In a painterly counterpart to so-called "salvage ethnography," the picturesque records people and customs "on the brink of destruction" (Nochlin 1983/1989: 50–51; Clifford, Dominguez, and Minh-ha 1987). Nochlin's critical reading exemplified an approach to visual culture grounded in cultural studies, semiotics, and poststructuralism. She aimed, among other things, to decode these paintings' "strategies of concealment" (Nochlin 1983/1989: 57) just as Mani decoded the discourse on *sati* as a *de facto* male debate about colonial modernity.[20] More a suggestive reading than a definitive analysis of these paintings, Nochlin's essay helped push art history beyond canonical artworks to engage visual culture generally and visual orientalism specifically.

Yet critiques of orientalist artworks still are often based on arguments about realism, documentary, and positivism, which in turn are ultimately based on a theory of mimeticism (R. Benjamin 1997; MacKenzie 1995; Rosenthal 1982; Stevens 1984; Thornton 1983, 1985).[21] The relationship between realism as a genre and the "real" is problematic, however, and requires decoding mimetic fallacies, the differences between reality and its representations. For example, Timothy Mitchell (1988: 1–33) has demonstrated how world exhibitions employ strategies of staging, specularity, and reduced scale to achieve their realistic effects. Moreover, deconstructing cases of colonial realism parallels the approach to unpacking gender constructions discussed earlier.

An alternative approach employed in the essays here in varying degrees emphasizes, not the individual artwork, but the nexus or relations between producer, the object produced, and the object's reception by an audience. Considerations of production (producer, painter, photographer) range from issues such as means of reproduction and copies to imitation and translation. Considerations of the object (work, painting, photograph) involve iconography and aesthetic genres and their relations. Considerations of the viewer (audience, buyer, market) entail reception and circulation (Bohrer 2003; Richon 1985, 1989). It is in the producer-product-reception nexus that social, historical, and political power intersects with culture. As Cohn (1996: 77) pointed out, for example, unequal colonial power relations, especially in the nineteenth century, meant that a Western audience or market figured as more important than the producer or the work in determining "success."

To ask with the "new art history" how an art object works rather than what it means often leads beyond the object to its production and reception, but how exactly can we examine the nexus of producer, product, and reception?[22] David Prochaska's essay "Telling Photos" approaches this issue by discussing a photograph he took in India and a photograph he saw in Algeria. Instead of interpreting the photos per se, he focuses on their production and reception. His Indian acquaintances would not let him take the candid snapshot he intended, but instead took the opportunity to pose themselves as if for a formal studio portrait, which was simultaneously a public presentation of public selves. In Algeria his landlord had a police mug shot of a family relative with barbed wire in the background enlarged, framed, and displayed prominently in the family sitting room. This iconic representation of family history advertised to all the family's contribution to the Algerian Revolution, and at the same time legitimized their continued political and economic importance in contemporary Algeria. Whereas photographic history and analysis necessarily focus generally on photos in isolation, Prochaska demonstrates that the production of his photo in India and the reception or context of the photo he saw in Algeria are key to understanding the images themselves, that their meaning is tied inextricably to their conditions of production and reception.

Reception also plays a prominent role in "Ethnography and Exhibitionism at the Expositions Universelles," the analysis by Zeynep Çelik and Leila Kinney, who show that it was the Western audience for belly dance that ultimately determined its "exotic" nature. Belly dance in nineteenth-century France consisted of a hybrid construction "made in Paris" at least as much as it drew on "authentic" indigenous Islamic forms. Thus, Parisian belly dance reveals how exoticism employs realist modes to create a reality effect that is patently "unrealistic."

Çelik and Kinney's feminist analysis makes clear how orientalist and patriarchal attitudes combined to produce a hybridized Parisian belly dance that they situate in a larger sexual economy of female performers developing in the last third of the nineteenth century. Portrayed especially in the paintings of Edgar Degas and Henri Toulouse-Lautrec, "the ascendance of the eroticized female performer" is exemplified by two individuals. First is Rachel Bent-Eny, who, although referred to as "La Belle Fathma" after the Prophet Mohammed's daughter, was actually an Algerian Jew who gained fame at Parisian world's fairs. Çelik and Kinney's ironic conclusion underscores the performer's hybrid background and her allegedly "authentic" performance. "Fathma already was a star attraction by the time she performed at the 1889 exhibition, presumably as evidence of the indigenous culture of Tunisia, rather than of Paris, as she had become." Second is Louise Weber, better known as "La Goulue," who at the height of her fame in 1895 built an onion-domed booth with a crescent-and-star insignia and façades painted by Toulouse-Lautrec, where she performed a supposedly "Moorish" dance. Louise Weber's career demonstrates how orientalism and eroticism were imbricated in these popular entertainments (Young 1995).

In a final twist that counters reductive colonizer/colonized dichotomies, Çelik and Kinney point out that the invention in Paris of a hybrid belly dance occurred precisely at the time that the dance was dying out in places like Istanbul, where it was replaced partly by Parisian-style dances performed in Parisian-style clubs. Although the authors do not pursue it, the transnational circulation of cultural models raises the question of exactly how what we may term "modernist exoticism" functioned in places like Istanbul (Savigliano 1995). Çelik and Kinney conclude that such hybrid situations "cannot be grasped by squaring two pairs of oppositions, between man and woman and colonizer and colonized," as a reductive Saidean reading would have it. They go to the heart of the matter when they query, "Who is the other when La Goulue interprets the [Moorish] dance of La Belle Féridjée? And who is in which position when [Parisian] Suzanne performs for an audience in Istanbul, in a place called *Le Café du Luxembourg*?" (This volume).

### Orientalism and Power

A third important arena to be affected by the intellectual changes of the 1980s and 1990s is power. Previously power was understood as structural; the power of European states, armies, and economies forge new contexts in which peoples and cultures might exist and contend: the world market, the modern state, European colonial empires. Marx and Weber were the theorists who most persuasively analyzed power in these senses. More recently, drawing on the works of Foucault and Gramsci, we have come to understand power in a second sense, that is, as a discursive system. In this view power is an omnipresent vector that defines cultures and helps to determine the histories that organize cultural meanings (not always successfully). For Foucault and those influenced by him, modernity in all its aspects is inseparable from the development of new cultural technologies for the control and domination of human populations. Social statistics, public health measures, urban planning (what Foucault referred to as "bio-power") are examples of how the modern state sought to exercise power. Enlightenment thought has been seen as the driving force of the discourse of modernity (Foucault 1975/1979: 198; 1976/1978: 143; Rabinow 1989). Because of its focus on deploying technologies of knowledge and power, neglecting difference and homogenizing society under its unflinching gaze, many authors in this tradition have regarded the export of the European Enlightenment around the globe under the auspices of colonialism as nothing short of a catastrophe. (Whether this approach is adequate is a question to which we'll return below.) The aspect of orientalism and power that preoccupies us in this context is the connections between orientalism and nationalism. The four chapters in this section suggest some of the important intellectual gains that have resulted from pursuing this relationship.

Said gave us a world in which orientalism constituted a totalizing system of domination that structures and controls the relationship of the West and the non-West. Given the logic of his argument, where then does nationalism come from? To the extent that orientalism functions as a Foucauldian discourse, there is little or no room for resistance in the guise of nationalism. Contra Bhabha (1994: 66–84), who identified a fundamental instability at the center of orientalism, Said, following Foucault, lacked a theoretical basis for incorporating nationalism-as-resistance into orientalism. Instead, it took Said (1993: 191–281) another and different book to take up nationalism. In *Culture and Imperialism* he focused on key writers (George Antonius, C. L. R. James), but, as in *Orientalism*, the source of nationalism implicitly lay in the deep refusal of the non-West to accept the stereotypes of orientalist thought, that is, in the upwelling of what could be termed a primordial national essence. Since, however, the idea that cultures are guided by their essences is a presupposition of orientalist thought, this possibility must be excluded at least explicitly. In short, Said failed to adequately historicize the relationship of orientalism and nationalism and left us thereby with no sat- isfactory way of accounting for the origins of nationalism.

In Benedict Anderson's (1983) influential theory of nationalism, nations are "imagined communities" rather than entities determined by sociological characteristics of language, race, and religion. His most suggestive formula- tion is that of "print-capitalism," the fortuitous combination of capitalism and printing that occurred first in early modern Europe. To this "vernacular" European nationalism Anderson adds two others: "creole" (Americas) and "official" (Russian). What characterizes all three is that once formed, they are "modular," that is, ready for export to Africa and Asia, where in the twentieth century they can be adopted wholesale. Nowhere, however, did Anderson spell out in detail how his "modular" nationalist models interact with cur- rents such as orientalism in particular societies to produce specific national- isms. Indeed, the question of orientalism is of little interest to him.

This prompted Partha Chatterjee (1993: 5) to ask Anderson what we asked Said, namely, "If nationalisms in the rest of the world have to choose their imagined community from certain 'modular' forms already made available to them by Europe and the Americas, what do they have left to imagine?" Chat- terjee began by noting an inherent contradiction in nationalist discourse, be- cause it "reasons within a framework of knowledge whose representational structure corresponds to the very structure of power [European] national- ist thought seeks to repudiate" (Chatterjee 1986/1993: 38). Building on the insights of Abdel-Malek (1963), Chatterjee crucially distinguished between the "problematic" and the "thematic" of orientalism. "The problematic in nationalist thought is exactly the reverse of that of Orientalism," for where "Orientals" are passive historical objects in the latter they constitute active historical agents in the former (Chatterjee 1986/1993: 38). But at the level of the thematic, nationalism employs the same essentialist conceptions as ori- entalism, distinguishing "the East" from "the West."

Here we relate both orientalism and nationalism to the heritage of En- lightenment thought, from which both derive. As the nineteenth-century science of culture, orientalism claimed through the study of key texts to be able to capture the essence of particular civilizations while revalorizing and systematizing their ethnic pasts and imagining a world of ethnic nations. Nationalism does much the same. Both are progressive and secular narra- tives that see human history unfolding in a series of stages, regard nonmod- ern traits as survivals of an earlier age, and assume that religion is fated to be outmoded (E. Burke 1998b). The essays by Nicholas Dirks and Ella Shohat below problematize and historicize in differing ways the imbrication of orientalism and nationalism rather than assuming, as do many postcolonial theorists, that the latter is the antidote to the former.

Nicholas Dirks's "Orientalist Counterpoints and Postcolonial Politics: Caste, Community, and Culture in Tamil India" demonstrates this interrelationship by examining how, in the context of postcolonial south India, the idea of the Dravidian, once viewed by British orientalists as the repository of pre-Aryan Indian traditions, has been appropriated by some Hindu nationalists as the symbol of Hinduness. Dirks delineates the discursive context in which orientalist categories of Aryan, Brahman, non-Brahman, and Dravidian emerged under colonialism and their successive transformations down to the present. A Scottish missionary, Rev. Robert Caldwell, first developed the view of Dravidians as essentially autonomous culturally, linguistically, and racially from the Sanskrit-speaking Aryan Brahmans, whom he saw as colonizers. A noted Tamil philologist, Caldwell recast the Aryan/Dravidian division of the early Europeans in racial terms, while reversing the orientalist low valorization of Dravidian culture. Caldwell's views were developed into a critique of Aryan influence by other British orientalists and officials based in south India toward the end of the nineteenth century. Thus the Dravidian renaissance of the twentieth century, when it came, built on the problematic legacy of orientalist racializing.

Dirks's essay raises important issues about the relationship between postcolonial politics and orientalist forms of knowledge. He argues that caste in contemporary south India has become both stronger and more "colonial" in defiance of the ongoing political struggle between the Congress Party and its rivals within India. In south India contemporary Tamil nationalist proponents of Dravidianism have recuperated the nineteenth-century narrative invented by Christian evangelical missionaries, according to which the historical subjection of non-Brahman Dravidian peoples was based on the Aryan conquest of Dravidian southern India.

This raises a host of unsettling questions. Is caste the badge of a retrograde communalist politics (as well as an orientalist invention)? If so, it is progressive to oppose it. But is this still the case if opposing it means supporting Hindu fundamentalism? Is the Congress Party progressive if, through its opposition to caste, it also supports the regional dominance of south India by the north through an alliance with southern anti-Brahmanism? The roots of contemporary Tamil separatism and Dravidianism must be excavated in the successive layers of social and political meanings preserved in the language of caste rather than viewing caste as evidence of a primordial cultural stratum. Tamil nationalism emerged in post-Independence India as a counternationalism over and against the Indian freedom struggle whose genealogies refer to a history of collaboration and appropriation. Dirks's historicization of this process reveals that from the perspective of southern India, the other is not only Europe, but also the Brahman, the North Indian, the Aryan, and the Congress Party government. For Dirks, orientalism and nationalism are imbricated in a complex double mimesis in which Europe and the Brahman are both cast as the other against whom identity must be defined.

From Aryan-Dravidian relations in India we turn to the complex and politically charged relationship of Arab and Jew in the modern Middle East. Like the parallel British representations of India, orientalist constructions of the Middle East were based on a series of binaries: West/East, modern/traditional, Jew/Arab. Orientalism and nationalism have both sought to fix identities and social boundaries. In her essay "Taboo Memories and Diasporic Visions: Columbus, Palestine, and Arab Jews," Ella Shohat seeks to destabilize interpretations of modern Middle Eastern history that posit Jews and Arabs as antonyms; she is struck not so much by the fixity and homogeneity of national identities in the region as by their fragility. Modern nation-states have imposed coherent national identities, but this has occurred against a historical background of colonial partitions, forced amalgamations, and ethnic cleansings. Situating her essay against the background of the 1492 quincentenary and the ethnogenesis of modern Spain and Israel/Palestine, Shohat, an Israeli of Iraqi Jewish origin, focuses on Sephardic Arab Jews known in Israel as Mizrahim. She reminds us of the historical legacy of hybridity and contingency which in fact informed the experiences of Arab Jews, and seeks thereby to undo the contemporary policing of national and ethnic boundaries between Jews and Arabs.

Ultimately, Shohat aims to challenge Zionist claims for a universal narrative of Jewish victimization that erases the specific histories of Middle Eastern Arab Jewish communities. According to the Zionist narrative, Israel figures as West and Palestine as East, while the identity of Judeo-Arab communities constitutes a paradox. Shohat uncovers the ambivalence of Zionist founder figures toward both Europe and the East. Europe was the home of anti-Semitism and exile as well as the ideals of European civilization; the

East was the site of Judaic origins and the longed-for homeland as well as of backwardness. In unraveling this story, she compares U.S. and Zionist historiographies and links the Puritan "errand into the wilderness" of the American national narrative with the parallel Zionist narrative of redemption of the land. In both settlers fought to free themselves from British imperialism; in both the indigenous peoples are positioned as the chief obstacle in the drama of redemption. In a particularly challenging comparison, Shohat suggests that the Arab Jews occupy the place of the African American slaves, since they were originally brought to Palestine to perform the menial labor that European Jews would not or could not do.

Shohat returns to the larger frame of the quincentennial celebrations in the final section of her essay. While Palestinians commemorate the loss of their country, Sephardi Jews are forbidden to nourish memories of connections to their lost Middle Eastern homelands. The de facto collaboration of Israel and some Arab governments under the sanction of the Western colonial powers produced an "exchange of populations" in which Middle Eastern Jews and Palestinian exiles changed places. By examining the Middle East question from the standpoint of the Arab Jews of Israel, Shohat puts into play the shared histories of cultural interaction in the Mediterranean region, and the ways in which European orientalist views helped shape the national discourses of the region's nation-states.

Scholars of China and Japan initially refused to engage the Saidean critique even more than Middle East specialists, imbued as they were with a sense of the East Asian experience as singular (Minear 1980). Sinologists generally viewed China as "the Middle Kingdom," a millennial civilization set off from others that stigmatized outsiders as barbarians (Fairbank 1968; Fairbank, Reischauer, and Craig 1973). That non-*Han* minorities may view the history of China as different from the history of the *Han* was not considered. Similarly, scholars of Japan tended to claim that Japan's historical experience was unique and resisted applying the approach of *Orientalism* to Japan. By the 1990s, however, some students of China and Japan began to reevaluate the pertinence of the critique of colonial forms of knowledge to the East Asian situation (Barlow 1993; Dirlik 1993; Lowe 1991). True, East Asian societies did not experience formal colonial empire, these scholars argued, but applying the tools of critique to the examination of the relations of culture and power appeared to shed considerable light on East Asian realities. Precisely because the East Asian historical experience differs in important respects from that of India and the Middle East, it constitutes a useful site where Said's theory can be essayed more broadly.

The critique of colonial forms of knowledge can also help us understand how China and Japan have come to modernity. In both countries local scholars constructed complex genealogies of their respective nations, deriving both from indigenous thought as well as from the work of Western writers. More generally, we may say that although orientalism constitutes one among many "othering" discourses, its geographical referent is the main characteristic that distinguishes it from other areas of history and postcolonial studies (Gringeri 1997; Miller 1990, 1998). Translating texts ultimately entails "translating" cultures; translation lies, of course, at the heart of the discipline of orientalism. Promoted as the science of society in the nineteenth century, philology sought in words and their meanings the key to cross-cultural understanding (Boon 1990; Olender 1992; Rafael 1988/1993; Reig 1988). Philologists claimed to have discovered the essential basis of civilizations through the study of key texts. In the hands of gifted orientalists like William Jones, Max Müller, and Silvestre de Sacy, this approach resulted in complex and illuminating discoveries (E. Burke 1995; Halbfass 1981/1988). But with the establishment of European hegemony, the exigencies of colonial rule increasingly displaced sophisticated and historically situated interrogations of significant texts. This is a central point made by Bernard Cohn in his essay included here. Orientalist writings tended increasingly to collapse civilizations into one or another of their allegedly essential features: caste for India, Islam for the Middle East, Confucianism for China. As we have seen, Cohn glossed this shift as one emphasizing cultural sophistication ("the command of language") to one reflecting colonial power politics ("the language of command"). An aspect of colonial discourse, translation returns us, therefore, to issues of realism, signs and correspondences, and metonymy discussed earlier.

In "Chinese History and the Question of Orientalism" Arif Dirlik uses the politics of cultural representation in the China field to rethink the epistemological issues implicit in Said's approach and to extend the critique beyond *Orientalism*. Is orientalism an autonomous product of Euro-American development which is then projected onto the world? Or is it a product of an unfolding relationship between Euro-Americans and Asians that required the complicity of the latter to endow it with plausibility? Is it a thing or a relationship? These questions open up a parenthesis in the Saidean epistemology of orientalism. In lieu of Said's model of a relationship between "active" Europeans and "passive" Orientals, Dirlik characterizes orientalist texts in China as a joint product of Euro-American orientalists and their Chinese interlocutors. Thus, for example, while Confucianism was historically the ideology of Chinese state elites, and seventeenth-century Jesuit missionaries first developed the Western discourse on "Confucianism" as emblematic of Chinese civilization, twentieth-century Chinese elites have in effect appropriated this discourse for their own purposes. These complex appropriations and reappropriations take us far from Saidean notions of orientalism, for many supposed Asian traditions, Dirlik reminds us, "turn out upon closer examination to be 'invented traditions,' the products rather than the preconditions of contact between Asians and Europeans."

This argument has important implications for the way we conceptualize the relationship between orientalism and nationalism. When modern nationalism emerged in the twentieth century in China it was in part as a response to Western imperialism, but it also involved reductive because metonymic orientalist images of the Chinese past. As Chinese elites circulated abroad, they came in contact with and subsequently drew on the images, concepts, and imaginative geography of orientalism in their own reformulations of the Chinese nation in the 1920s and 1930s. With the emergence of Chinese nationalism and an independent China, the power relationship that had been a condition for the emergence of orientalism has shifted, but ironically orientalism itself has not disappeared. Rather, "the very transformation of power may have culminated in the reification of Orientalism at the level of a global ideology" (Dirlik, this volume). Thus, the so-called Confucian revival of the early to mid-1990s was the joint product of American futurologists such as Herman Kahn and sociologists like Peter Berger eager to see in Confucianism a positive force in capitalist modernization, plus East Asian intellectuals such as Tu Wei-ming anxious to provide a global and deterritorialized ideology to postcommunist Asian societies. Instead, Dirlik views orientalism not as a product of European modernity but as a product of the encounter between Europeans and non-Europeans in the world's "contact zones," sites of colonial encounter characterized by mediation and exchange as well as domination (Pratt 1992). In short, nationalists and orientalists were both products of the contact zone, a space where metonymic cultural representations both positive and negative flourished.[23]

Dirlik concludes with a searching examination of contemporary Chinese intellectuals who traffic in essentialisms such as "Chineseness" partly in response to the heterogeneous forces of globalization and partly due to the shifting location of power within China and between China and the rest of the world. For Dirlik, the development of a new Asian assertiveness, for example, the "Confucian revival," signals the emergence of different versions of capitalist modernity. Capitalism and not Eurocentrism constitutes the chief characteristic of modernity, Dirlik argues, and therefore the road to reconceptualizing modernity as global and more than the history of the West alone lies in the proper historicization of both orientalism and nationalism.

Turning from China to Japan, we note first the emerging literature on the connections between knowledge and power in post-Meiji Japan. Carol Gluck (1985) first drew attention to the ways Meiji statesmen self-consciously sought to forge a "modern Japan" while at the same time inventing a "traditional Japan." Fear of social conflict drove Japanese elites to develop "Meiji ideology," a construct of an essentialized Japanese culture grounded in concern for morals, proper behavior, good citizenship, and loyalty to the emperor. Gluck demonstrated that Meiji borrowings from Europe were only one side of a coin, the reverse of which was the retrospective invention of traditional Japan from a heterogeneous cultural heritage that was well rooted in the Han, the local terrains ruled by *daiymo* lords.

Because her subject was Meiji ideology, Gluck did not directly engage the central argument of *Orientalism*, nor did the Japan field for the most part find the approach to the relations between power and representations of alterity to be relevant to the Japanese experience (Minear 1980). More recently, Takashi Fujitani (1998) has brought newer methods of cultural history to bear on the reflexive relationship between Europe and Japan in a study of modern Japanese nationalism and its embodiment in cultural artifacts. Focusing on the Meiji period (1868–1912), Fujitani examines ceremonials such as imperial weddings and funerals to explore what visual symbols and rituals reveal about monarchy, nationalism, city planning, discipline, gender, memory, and modernity. In the process he exposes the complex cultural appropriations out of which Meiji Japanese ideology emerged. Fujitani's work reflects a fuller engagement with theories of cultural representation deriving from the critique of colonial forms of knowledge.

More directly relevant is Stefan Tanaka's (1993) work, which traces the ways in which *Shina*, the Japanese construction of an essentialized Confucian China ideologically positioned as the past of Japan, served as the source for such quintessentially Meiji innovations as the 1890 Imperial Rescript on Education and the creation of state Shinto. As Tanaka details, the venture was fraught with peril. By yoking Shinto ideology to Confucianism, post-Meiji intellectuals risked implying that Japan was culturally derivative of China, clearly a contradiction for an ideological strategy that sought to emphasize Japanese distinctiveness. To ensure that there was no misunderstanding, one group claimed on the basis of some shared cultural features that the Japanese people originated in Melanesia and migrated to the Japanese islands in antiquity. As a result Okinawa, the southernmost Japanese prefecture, was identified as a potential locus of historic Japaneseness and spurred a series of ethnological investigations that sought to link strands of Okinawan culture to Japanese culture.

Alan Christy argues in his essay in this book, "Profiteering Women and Primitive Communists: Propriety and Scandal in Interwar Japanese Studies of Okinawa," that because of its liminal position in the Japanese imaginary—neither fully part of Japan nor fully other, but in some complicated way both—Okinawa provides a strategic lens through which to assess the self-fashioning of twentieth-century Japan. Christy's essay usefully complicates our understanding of power/knowledge relationships in the emergence of what might be called Japanese orientalism, that is, the discourse on the Okinawan cousin/other, which had implications for how Japanese nationalism might be conceived. Multiple contexts have shaped the cultural struggles in the Japanese semicolony of Okinawa during the twentieth century. Previously the kingdom of Ryūkyūs had been a tributary of imperial China, its elites profoundly Sinified culturally. Following its annexation by Japan in 1879, it quickly became a site for the debates over Japanese origins referred to earlier. Christy excavates early twentieth-century Japanese ethnological investigations of Itoman, a community in southern Okinawa, to demonstrate that debates about the "true" character of Itoman, and implicitly Okinawan, society constituted complex Japanese attempts to culturally appropriate Okinawa.

### From Postcolonial Theory to World History

A central theme of this introduction (and of the essays in this volume) is that the critique of orientalism is far from exhausted. The essays included here argue collectively that orientalism was a far more complex phenomenon than many have suspected, homogeneous neither culturally nor over time, and deeply embedded in the collective reimaginings that were (and are) nationalism. They also enable us to see the complex ways in which modern cultures have drawn on orientalist representations as well as indigenous self-representations. However, as we have also argued, in important ways the critique (at least at the theoretical level) has increasingly arrived at an impasse. For the critique to prosper, it must now make a historical turn, and rethink the way modernity is theorized as well as historicized. Both are necessary. On the one hand, scholars influenced by postcolonial theory, convinced that there is no master narrative that cannot be destabilized, resist engagement with world history because of the latter's residual teleology and resistance to the linguistic and cultural turns. World historians, on the other hand, resist postcolonial theory because of its abstract conceptual approach and its historically ungrounded theorizations. As we argue below, both need to recognize the validity of one another's approach. The critique of orientalism, by opening up new theoretical and historical perspectives, is in the process of transforming itself again.

First, let's reprise the political and intellectual history that underlies our discussion so far. We've argued that the critique of orientalism must be viewed as a manifestation of the linguistic and cultural turns. Where Foucault had distinguished the discursive bases of modernity within the West, Said pointed out that the fact of European dominance was inseparable discursively from its deep Eurocentrism and power-laden character. Whereas Foucault's work opened up the study of the discursive bases of power in modern Europe, Said's book directed the critique outward to the discursive roots of the modern world. He argued that by producing the intellectual grid through which Europe saw the rest of the world, the discourse of orientalism sustained and justified European dominance. At the same time, his critique stripped Western dominance of its moral authority, and exposed the Eurocentrism in most Western accounts of the origins of modernity. What happened next was that the critique of orientalism provided the missing piece of the puzzle, making it possible to link the critique of imperialist thought with other ongoing projects of critique (feminist studies, ethnic studies, and queer studies). Postcolonial studies was the result. With its emergence, it was possible for the first time to theorize the ways race and power shaped the modern world, linking the fates of peoples of the ex-colonial world and those of the internal minorities within the West. However, the effects of especially the linguistic turn (and thus of the critique of orientalism) did not stop there. They soon led to the contesting of all homogeneous and foundationalist narratives, which ran the risk of leading away from an engagement with history.

The essays in this volume point toward one possible solution. We earlier invoked a useful distinction made by William Sewell between culture and Geertzian "thick description" and what he terms "thin coherence" (Sewell 2005: 152–68). Historically, orientalism as an outgrowth of Enlightenment thought tended to construct an essentialized or "thickly" coherent Orient based on alleged "primordial essences." Thick description generates homogeneous narratives, and stands outside history. To view culture as "thinly" coherent is to move beyond orientalist views of the Middle East. Where an orientalist view of Islamic culture based on "primordial essences" is congruent with a general view of culture as "thickly" coherent, the essays in this book reflect more a view of culture as "thinly" coherent. Çelik and Kinney demonstrate the hybrid French and Islamic construction of Parisian belly dance. Shohat shows how Sephardic Arab Jews disrupt Zionist narratives of Arab versus Jew. Prochaska documents how Indian photographer Lala Deen Dayal employed different photographic styles to cater to different Indian and European communities. Rather than "active" Europeans and "passive" Chinese, Dirlik characterizes orientalist texts in China as a joint coproduction hammered out in colonial contact zones.

The view of culture as possessing "thin coherence" links us with the linguistic turn (including deconstruction and other critical practices) insofar as such practices also assume that the coherence of symbol systems is "thin." Deconstruction "demonstrates over and over that what are taken as the certainties or truths of texts or discourses are in fact disputable and unstable" (Sewell 2005: 167). What is "disputable and unstable" are precisely those constitutive elements of contestation and difference that make a culture's coherence "thin." As we've seen, Said and *Orientalism* are tied directly to Foucault and poststructuralism, because Said took the poststructuralist critique in a postcolonial direction and trained it on orientalism as a situated knowledge.

The essays in this volume exemplify in varying degrees a poststructuralist sensibility combined with a "thinly" coherent concept of culture. Such an approach continues and also takes in new directions Said's original insights. Cohn's "investigative modalities" correspond to Foucault's discourses. This introductory essay plus those by Colonna and Burke all employ Bourdieu's notion of fields to situate orientalism. Colonna gauges the contributions of Berque and Desparmet by locating them in their respective intellectual and political fields. Burke considers the French tradition of the sociology of Islam as a Foucauldian discourse in which the facts cannot be separated from the theories but derive from the theories that in turn verify their facticity. Collectively, they take us from the critique of orientalism to those colonial forms of knowledge that were hammered out interactively in colonial contact zones.

There is a second direction in which the further development of the critique of orientalism may lead us: toward a rehistoricization of the place of Europe in world history (and not just to the further critique of Eurocentrism). Although it is now clear that colonial culture was more complex than previously figured, it makes little sense to debate whether colonial modernity was comparative or derivative. Rather, it was shaped by all the world historical contexts (as well as the outcomes of specific histories of contestation and appropriation) in which it was embedded. By locating modernity as derivative of European culture, rather than of the prior history of all of humanity, postcolonial theory inadvertently reproduces the same binaries of the West and the Rest it sought to overthrow. This leads to some strange history. In effect, postcolonialism sees the Rest (portrayed as the repository of authenticity) as untimely ripped from a supposed Edenic state by the predatory West, fueled by capitalism and the Enlightenment. Despite recent laudable efforts to "deprovincialize Europe" (in the phrase of Dipesh Chakrabarty, 2000), a retheorization of the place of Europe in global modernity by itself cannot lead us out of the impasse in which we find ourselves currently. We must rethink the way modernity is theorized as well as historicized. In world historical terms, there is but one modernity, though it may have taken a variety of cultural forms in response to the specific historical experiences of individual societies.

Refiguring the history of modernity, including the Enlightenment-derived narrative of orientalist history, entails rethinking the relations between world regions and world cultures. Throughout the essays in this volume, the authors contest the tendency historically to configure the "Orient" reductively and bracket it off as different and antithetical to the West. We have seen how such essentializing strategies were part and parcel of the Enlightenment's view of non-Western cultures. For example, Cohn urges that metropole and colony be placed in the same "unitary field of analysis" (Cohn 1996: 4; Cooper and Stoler 1997). More radically, Ella Shohat and Robert Stam (1994) call for a "relational approach" that focuses on the conflictual hybrid interplay of communities within and across borders, rather than segregating historical periods and geographical regions into neatly fenced-off areas of expertise. They stress the horizontal and vertical links threading communities and histories together in a conflictual network, in an effort to transcend some of the politically debilitating effects of disciplinary and community boundaries. In an essay not included here, Burke (1998a) eschews a perspective that views Islam as a bounded and closed social and cultural system, and argues instead that to fully understand the history of Islamist movements we must situate Islam in a world context and recognize the multiple ways the Middle East is connected to rather than closed off from other world regions.

The critique of orientalism is not just about the non-Western other, but is also about the historical self-fashioning of the West itself. The West itself (accepting for the moment the premises of this shopworn intellectual construct) also engaged in large-scale acts of appropriation, mostly unacknowledged, of cultural innovations from outside the region: gunpowder, the compass, the sternpost rudder, and printing, among other notable examples. It was quite as active in developing representations of itself as of others. Indeed, we can say that Western civilization is the form of auto-orientalism by which the West represented itself to itself, a form of self-blinding quite as destructive ultimately as any orientalist representation of a non-Western society. In response to orientalist essentialisms, the critique of orientalism has insisted increasingly on the heterogeneous and often hybrid character of non-Western societies, their internal variety and difference. It has until recently denied difference to European societies, grounding its analysis of the Enlightenment in such homogeneous categories as Western modernity. This seems increasingly implausible. The way out requires not more and better theory, but a deeper historicization of European history. One likely result of this process will be to help us disaggregate Western modernity, and to become more alert to its different forms within Europe. As modernity etched rather different cultural fault lines in each European society, the sites of cultural struggle also differed. Here it is well to recall that not only non-Western societies were affected. The same processes also tossed Western societies upside down, sparking contrasting internal cultural struggles within Europe. And they did so in ways that bring out the differences among

European states. Thus the sites of cultural struggle differed within Europe, as did the ways in which the rise of the state and the emergence of a world economy were experienced. The divisive conflict between church and state in France has no counterpart in British history; likewise, the British experience of race differed significantly from that of France (E. Burke 2001). What's true for Britain and France is true for other European states, each of which had somewhat different relationships to the Enlightenment and the democratic and industrial revolutions, which tended to shape somewhat different orientalisms, and thus imperial histories. Finally, while both Britain and France were profoundly affected by decolonization and the linguistic turn, they were affected differently. As a result, the forms assumed by the critique of colonial forms of knowledge differed as well.

A comparative and interactive approach to the history of modernity takes us away from high theory and toward a more fine-grained, more historically situated understanding of the contexts in which orientalism existed, as well as the facts and representations of orientalist and other discourses of Western dominance. Ultimately, a reconsideration of orientalism leads us to rethink the Enlightenment from a world historical point of view. Put differently, it leads us to rethink the place of the West in the long-term history of humanity. In calling for the insertion of the history of modernity in world history, we must recognize that it will have to be a different world history from the one that exists now. The refusal of world history to develop a theoretical understanding of modernity, that is, a way of theorizing it, has blunted its persuasiveness and left it vulnerable to charges that it too remains stuck in the West-and-the-Rest model. It needs to move beyond its own narrative—world history as the rise of the West, or as a history of civilizations, or as some version of world systems theory. After some notable advances in thinking the history of modernity in world terms, the post-9/11 terrain has seen a regrettable regression toward civilizationist narratives. If a case can be made for the historicization of the critique of orientalism, then an equally powerful case can be made for a more philosophically adequate theorization of modernity in world history. Atheoretical world historians, whose attachment to largely unexamined and putatively empirical explanations can only seem touching (if not politically dangerous), have much to learn from the linguistic and cultural turns. This is where the critique of orientalism launched by Said, and the linguistic and cultural turns more generally, can help. The new world history has made it possible for the first time to begin to see the history of humanity whole and entire—and the place of modernity within it—but it has yet to be theorized. Here is a task worthy of the next generation of scholars.

We conclude where we began. The critique of orientalism is not over. Indeed, it is not even past. In the post-9/11 era, the "war on terrorism" and the Iraq war have acquired a discursive power to shape the political field akin to the phase of high imperialism in the nineteenth and twentieth centuries. The absence of debate over the colonial character of the American presence in Iraq, and the Middle East more generally, is one telling index of the invasion of the intellectual field by the political field. So, too, is the extent to which the discourse on terrorism has come to suffuse political discourse generally. Thus, the extent of Israeli dominance over the Palestinian people has reached an all-time high, leading to levels of economic deprivation among Palestinians never before observed, yet the colonial context of the Israeli occupation of Palestine is almost entirely occluded by the discourse on "terrorism." The land question that underlies the Arab-Israeli conflict is banished altogether from political discourse. Unless proven otherwise, Palestinians are presumptively considered terrorists. More broadly, such is the overwhelming power of the discourse on terrorism that the complex realities of 1.2 billion global Muslims can scarcely be admitted, let alone discussed. Linked to this is the unprecedented concentration of media into the hands of a few extremely wealthy and powerful individuals and institutions that helps ensure that deviant opinions are marginalized. In this regard, it is not surprising that to claim the existence of an Israel lobby powerfully influencing and directing American foreign policy is met with vehement criticism. Taken together, the hegemony of the discourse on terrorism and on Muslims is an act of self-blinding perhaps unique in the modern era. It shapes perceptions, channels discussion, and forestalls critique. In a Bourdieuian sense, the political field has truly swamped the intellectual field. No, the study of colonial forms of knowledge is not just an esoteric academic pursuit. It is crucial to the political and intellectual future of the United States, of the United States in the world.

### Notes

1. "Instead of the partial analysis offered by the various national or systematically theoretical schools, I have been proposing the contrapuntal lines of a global analysis, in which texts and worldly institutions are seen working together" (Said 1993:

318). "Texts and worldly institutions . . . working together" is how Said connected culture and imperialism, culture and society. However, applying his contrapuntal approach does not improve on Foucauldian discourse analysis, because Said did not think through sufficiently the theoretical implications of his mostly unreflective practice. Thus he placed what remains at base a formalist approach that privileges canonical texts and authors—Jane Austen, Albert Camus—alongside a contextual or discursive approach in which he mined history for bits and pieces of data to flesh out the imperial contexts of his literary texts (80–97, 169–85). But the central difficulty is that the principle of selection—which data to include and exclude—is not spelled out, and this is because Said did not consider the historiographical stakes, the competing views of rival "schools" or approaches, involved in choosing this or that historical datum. Thus Said laid his contrapuntal readings side by side, but ultimately canonical texts and imperial contexts were not connected logically or theoretically.

2. What is significant here is not the connection between Said's contrapuntal approach, for example, and new historicism, but the lack of connection. On the one hand, Said was critical of "cults like post-modernism, discourse analysis, New Historicism, deconstruction, neo-pragmatism" because of their "astonishing sense of weightlessness with regard to the gravity of history" (Said in Ansell-Pearson, Parry, and Squires 1997: 8). On the other hand, the key is that Said was a practicing literary critic, not a literary theorist. Interviewed in the early 1990s, he stated, "I simply lost interest in literary theory about ten years ago. . . . I watched with some interest and eagerness the emergence of something called the New Historicism, its peak and its now apparent sliding into an orthodoxy. . . . I still don't quite know what it is" (Said in Sprinker 1992: 247–48).

3. Although Islamic science and philosophy attracted the interest of such scholars as Roger Bacon and Leibniz, earlier Western studies of Islam had been marked by Christian precommitment. Voltaire and Montaigne utilized Muslim locales to develop utopias and dystopias the better to criticize European governments and propose reforms.

4. Kiernan was a member of the British Communist historians group (Cornforth 1978).

5. A British Marxist sociologist of religion, Turner had earlier written *Weber and Islam* (1974). The Hull group is briefly discussed in Said (1978: 325, 327).

6. Misremembered by Judt (1998).

7. Opponents of empire included the Catholics Emmanuel Mounier (editor of the monthly review *Esprit*) and novelist François Mauriac, and resistance heroes Jean Daniel, editor of *Le Nouvel Observateur*, Sartre, and (more ambiguously) Camus. Although some French academics distinguished themselves in the de-

colonization struggle, none held important positions in the French university system or in the larger French intellectual field.

8. In France a major debate emerged, especially during 1998–2002, concerning torture in Algeria. For an overview, see, among others, Prochaska (2003b) and the references cited there.

9. For a different view, see Judt (1998).

10. In the original published version of this essay, Ludden discusses further British orientalism and the emergence of Indian nationalism.

11. His first collection (Cohn 1987), published by Oxford University Press in India, was not widely distributed outside the subcontinent. Cohn's Chicago colleagues anthropologist George Stocking (1968/1982, 1983–96, 1987, 1992, 1995), who pioneered the history of British and American anthropology, and Ronald Inden (1990), whose genealogy of Indology was inspired by Cohn, provided the supportive intellectual context in which his work could develop.

12. From the 1980s on some feminists, influenced in particular by poststructuralism, adopted an approach that emphasized difference instead of an "add and stir" approach, according to which women's experience was recovered and added to male experience (much as the "new social history" recuperated workers' and peasants' experience). Rather than gender difference dissolving as women's experience was uncovered, gender in this latter view was considered a relationship centered on male/female difference. "Male" was defined in relation to "female" and vice versa. It is important to note that although employed less frequently, such a view of gender as a system of relations can be applied, *mutatis mutandis*, to racial and ethnic and colonizer/colonized differences.

13. By the early 1980s it was no longer possible to consider "women" as an undifferentiated historical category; women of color emerged as different from white women. The moment during "second wave" feminism when women of color began to bracket themselves off from women treated globally constituted a crucial breakthrough. At least in the United States minority discourses were now distinguished ranging from African American and Asian American to Latino/a and Chicano/a and Native American.

14. We intentionally use Derrida's notion of *supplément*, the addition of which points up a lack or element missing in what was there before, because the Spivak essay also constitutes a demonstration of her preference for Derrida (1967/1976: 141–64), which replies to Said's predilection for Foucault. Similarly, the work of Bhabha can be situated as a response to Said's *Orientalism*. This is explicitly the case in "The Other Question," but in addition the enormously suggestive figures proposed in "Mimicry," "Sly Civility," and "Signs Taken for Wonders" can all be connected to Bhabha's arguments regarding the instability of the colonial subject

discussed at length in the former essay, and thus related to Bhabha's (1994: 66–122) response to *Orientalism*.

15. In an excellent discussion of the subaltern studies school, Rosalind O'Hanlon (1988) makes a similar point.

16. Mani (1992: 403) concludes that "rephrasing the questions in this way enables us to retain Spivak's insight regarding the positioning of women in colonial discourse without conceding to colonial discourse what it, in fact, did not achieve—the erasure of women."

17. The thrust of Mani's argument is to question at the level of discourse the mostly discursive practices of British and Indian males alike who emphasized Brahmanic scriptural discourse over daily practice and everyday ritual. Though much of Mani's most striking counterevidence comes from daily practice, she did not systematically inquire into this practice. In fact, she explicitly eschewed such a social historical approach. "This is not a social history of *sati*. I am not concerned here with what the practice of *sati* meant to those who undertook it" (Mani 1987: 123).

18. By "textual attitude," Said signaled texts that create knowledge and reality, that is, a Foucauldian discourse. "Such texts can *create* not only knowledge but also the very reality they appear to describe. In time such knowledge and reality produce ... what Michel Foucault calls a discourse" (Said 1978: 94).

19. Although Nochlin does not cite him, her argument resembles deconstruction insofar as her absences correspond to Derrida's notion of *supplément*.

20. Nochlin's essay was written originally as a response to an exhibition of orientalist paintings (Rosenthal 1982). To understand the stakes involved, compare her essay with the exhibition catalogue in which the curator, Donald Rosenthal, invoked Said only to dismiss him: "For Said, Orientalism ... is a mode of thought for defining ... the presumed cultural inferiority of the Islamic Orient ... a part of the vast control mechanism of colonialism. . . . In this study, French Orientalist painting will be discussed in terms of its aesthetic quality and historical interest, and no attempt will be made at a re-evaluation of its political uses" (9). Responding to this exact passage, Nochlin (1983/1989: 34) countered, "In other words, art-historical business as usual. Having raised the two crucial issues of political domination and ideology, Rosenthal drops them like hot potatoes."

21. Note that both Said (1978: 72) and Bhabha (1994: 70–71) identify realism as the prevalent strategy of representation in colonial discourse.

22. For another approach, see Haskell (1987: 175–85).

23. Dirlik's consideration of the Chinese encounter with imperialism and the subsequent emergence of nationalism in China reframes Said's questions about power and representations. As Dirlik suggests, orientalist tropes such as "Confucianism" derive from complex cultural encounters in the contact zone. If we

envision the contact zone as a field of power in which the power dynamics are always changing, then an examination of the particular configuration at a particular historical moment may help explain the valence of a particular cultural representation, for example, the differing meanings and uses of terms such as "Confucianism," "caste," and "Islam" as shorthand notations for particular civilizational entities, nations, or social formations.

## References

Abdel-Malek, Anouar. 1963. "Orientalism in Crisis." *Diogenes* 44: 103–40.

Abdel-Jaouad, Hedi. 1993. "Isabelle Eberhardt: Portrait of the Artist as a Young Nomad." *Yale French Studies* 83: 93–117.

Abu-Lughod, Lila. 1985. *Veiled Sentiments: Honor and Poetry in a Bedouin Society.* Berkeley: University of California Press.

———, ed. 1998. *Remaking Women: Feminism and Modernity in the Middle East.* Princeton NJ: Princeton University Press.

Ahmad, Aijaz. 1992. *In Theory: Classes, Nations, Literatures.* London: Verso.

Alessandrini, Anthony. 1999. *Frantz Fanon: Critical Perspectives.* New York: Routledge.

Alleg, Henri. [1958] 2006. *La Question.* Lincoln: University of Nebraska Press.

Alloula, Malek. [1980] 1986. *The Colonial Harem.* Minneapolis: University of Minnesota Press.

Althusser, Louis, and Étienne Balibar. 1970. *Reading Capital.* New York: Pantheon Books.

Anderson, Benedict. 1983. *Imagined Communities: Reflections on the Origin and Spread of Nationalism.* New York: Verso.

Anon. 1968. "The Social Responsibility of Anthropology." Forum. *Current Anthropology* 9: 391–435.

Ansell-Pearson, Keith, Benita Parry, and Judith Squires, eds. 1997. *Cultural Readings of Imperialism: Edward Said and the Gravity of History.* New York: St. Martin's Press.

Apter, Emily. 1999. *Continental Drift: From National Characters to Virtual Subjects.* Chicago: University of Chicago Press.

Aruri, Naseer, and Mohammad A. Shuraydi, eds. 2000. *Revising Culture, Reinventing Peace: The Influence of Edward Said.* Brooklyn NY: Interlink Publication Group.

Asad, Talal, ed. 1973. *Anthropology and the Colonial Encounter.* London: Ithaca Press.

Ashcroft, Bill, and Pal Ahluwalia. 1999. *Edward Said: The Paradox of Identity.* New York: Routledge.

Atil, Esin. 1987. *The Age of Sultan Suleyman the Magnificent.* New York: Abrams.

Ausserasses, Paul. 2001. *Services Spéciaux Algérie 1955–1957.* Paris: Perrin.

Ballantyne, Tony. 2002. *Orientalism and Race: Aryanism in the British Empire*. New York: Palgrave Macmillan.

Barlow, Tani E., ed. 1993. *Colonial Modernity*. Durham NC: Duke University Press.

Barthes, Roland. [1982] 1984. "The Reality-Effect." In *The Rustle of Language*. New York: Hill and Wang.

Bates, Robert H., V. Y. Mudimbe, and Jean O'Barr, eds. 1993. *Africa and the Disciplines*. Chicago: University of Chicago Press.

Bayoumi, Moustefa, and Andrew Rubin, eds. 2000. *Edward Said Reader*. New York: Vintage.

Beaulieu, Jill, and Mary Roberts, eds. *Orientalism's Interlocutors*. Durham NC: Duke University Press, 2002.

Benjamin, Roger, ed. 1997. *Orientalism: Delacroix to Klee*. London: Thames and Hudson.

———. 2003. *Orientalist Aesthetics: Art, Colonialism, and French North Africa, 1880–1930*. Berkeley: University of California Press.

Benjamin, Walter. [1936] 1969. "The Work of Art in the Age of Mechanical Reproduction." In *Illuminations*. New York: Schocken.

Bhabha, Homi. 1989. "Location, Intervention, Incommensurability: A Conversation with Homi Bhabha." *Emergences* 1: 63–88.

———, ed. 1990. *Nation and Narration*. New York: Routledge.

———. 1993. "Beyond the Pale: Art in the Age of Multicultural Translation." In *1993 Biennial Exhibition*, ed. Thelma Golden and Elisabeth Sussman. New York: Whitney Museum of American Art.

———. 1994. *The Location of Culture*. New York: Routledge.

Bohrer, Frederick N. 2003. *Orientalism and Visual Culture*. New York: Cambridge University Press.

Bonnell, Victoria E., and Lynn Hunt, eds. 1999. *Beyond the Cultural Turn*. Berkeley: University of California Press.

Boon, James A. 1990. *Affinities and Extremes: Crisscrossing the Bittersweet Ethnology of East Indies History, Hindu-Balinese Culture, and Indo-European Allure*. Chicago: University of Chicago Press.

Bourdieu, Pierre. [1958] 1962. *The Algerians*. Boston: Beacon Press.

———. 1963. *Travail et travailleurs en Algérie*. Paris: Mouton.

——— (with Abdelmalek Sayad). 1964. *Le Déracinement: La crise de l'agriculture traditionnelle en Algérie*. Paris: Editions de Minuit.

———. [1972] 1977. *Outline of a Theory of Practice*. New York: Cambridge University Press.

———. 1976. "Conditions sociales de la production scientifique." In *Le Mal de voir. Ethnologie et orientalisme: politique et épistemologie, critique et autocritique*, ed. Henri Moniot. Cahiers Jussieu no. 2, Université de Paris VII. Paris: Collection 10/18.

———. 1977. "Le champ scientifique." In *Actes de la recherche en sciences sociales*. Paris: Service des publications de la Maison de l'Homme.

———. [1977] 1979. *Algeria 1960: The Disenchantment of the World; The Sense of Honour; The Kabyle House or the World Reversed*. New York: Cambridge University Press.

———. [1980] 1990. *The Logic of Practice*. Stanford: Stanford University Press.

———. [1984] 1993. *Sociology in Question*. Thousand Oaks CA: Sage Publications.

———. [1987] 1990. *In Other Words: Essays towards a Reflexive Sociology*. Stanford: Stanford University Press.

Bourguet, Marie-Noëlle, Bernard Lepetit, Daniel Nordman, and Maroula Sinarellis, eds. 1998. *L'Invention scientifique de la Méditerranée: Égypte, Morée, Algérie*. Paris: Éditions de l'École des Hautes Études en Sciences Sociales.

Bové, Paul, ed. 2000. *Edward Said and the Work of the Critic: Speaking Truth to Power*. Durham NC: Duke University Press.

Branche, Rafaëlle. 2001. *La Torture et l'armée pendant la guerre d'Algérie, 1954–1962*. Paris: Gallimard.

Breckenridge, Carol A., and Peter van der Veer, eds. 1993. *Orientalism and the Postcolonial Predicament: Perspectives on South Asia*. Philadelphia: University of Pennsylvania Press.

Bryson, Norman. 1983. *Vision and Painting: The Logic of the Gaze*. New Haven CT: Yale University Press.

Bryson, Norman, Michael Ann Holly, and Keith Moxey, eds. 1994. *Visual Culture: Images and Interpretations*. Hanover NH: University Press of New England.

Buci-Glucksmann, Christine. 1986. *La Folie du voir: De l'esthétique baroque*. Paris: Editions Galilee.

Burchell, Graham, Colin Gordon, and Peter Miller, eds. 1991. *The Foucault Effect: Studies in Governmentality*. Chicago: University of Chicago Press.

Burke, Edmund, III. 1973. "The Image of the Moroccan State in French Ethnological Literature: A New Look at the Origin of Lyautey's Berber Policy." In *Arabs and Berbers*, ed. Ernest Gellner and Charles Micaud. London: Duckworth.

———. 1976. "Frantz Fanon: A Retrospective Review." *Daedalus* 105: 127–35.

———. 1984. "The Institutionalization of Sociology in France: Its Sociological and Political Significance." *International Social Science Journal* 36: 643–55.

———. 1995. "Orientalism." In *Encyclopedia of the Modern Islamic World*. New York: Oxford University Press.

———. 1998a. "Orientalism and World History: Representing Middle Eastern Nationalism and Islamism in the Twentieth Century." *Theory and Society* 27: 589–607.

———. 1998b. "Theorizing the Histories of Colonialism and Nationalism in the Arab Maghrib." *Arab Studies Quarterly* 20: 5–19.

———. 2001. "The Terror and Religion: Brittany and Algeria." In *Colonialism and the Modern World*, ed. Gregory Blue, Martin Bunton, and Ralph Croizier. White Plains NY: M. E. Sharpe.

Burke, Peter. 1990. *The French Historical Revolution*. Stanford: Stanford University Press.

Burton, Antoinette. 1994. *Burdens of History: British Feminists, Indian Women, and Imperial Culture, 1865–1915*. Chapel Hill: University of North Carolina Press.

———, ed. 1999. *Gender, Sexualities, and Colonial Modernities*. New York: Routledge.

Calhoun, Craig, Edward LiPuma, and Moishe Postone, eds. 1993. *Bourdieu: Critical Perspectives*. Chicago: University of Chicago Press.

Carlier, Omar. 1995. *Entre Nation et Jihad: Histoire sociale des radicalismes*. Paris: Presses de la Fondation nationale des sciences politiques.

Carlier, Omar, Fanny Colonna, and Radouane Aïnad-Tabet. 1988. *Lettrés, intellectuels et militants en Algérie, 1880–1950*. Algiers: Office des publications universitaires.

Caton, Steven C. 1999. *Lawrence of Arabia: A Film's Anthropology*. Berkeley: University of California Press.

Çelik, Zeynep. 1992. *Displaying the Orient: Architecture of Islam at Nineteenth-Century World's Fairs*. Berkeley: University of California Press.

Chakrabarty, Dipesh. 2000. *Provincializing Europe: Postcolonial Thought and Historical Difference*. Princeton NJ: Princeton University Press.

Chatterjee, Partha. [1986] 1993. *Nationalist Thought and the Colonial World: A Derivative Discourse?* Minneapolis: University of Minnesota Press.

———. 1993. *The Nation and Its Fragments: Colonial and Postcolonial Histories*. Princeton NJ: Princeton University Press.

Chaturvedi, Vinayak, ed. 2000. *Mapping Subaltern Studies and the Postcolonial*. New York: Verso.

Chaudhuri, Nupur, and Margaret Strobel, eds. 1992. *Western Women and Imperialism: Complicity and Resistance*. Bloomington: Indiana University Press.

Clancy-Smith, Julia, and Frances Gouda, eds. 1998. *Domesticating the Empire: Race, Gender, and Family Life in French and Dutch Colonialism*. Charlottesville: University of Virginia Press.

Clifford, James. 1988. *The Predicament of Culture*. Cambridge MA: Harvard University Press.

———. 1997. *Routes: Travel and Translation in the Late Twentieth Century*. Cambridge MA: Harvard University Press.

Clifford, James, Virginia Dominguez, and Trinh T. Minh-ha. 1987. "Of Other Peoples: Beyond the 'Salvage' Paradigm." In *Discussions in Contemporary Culture*, ed. Hal Foster. Seattle: Bay Press.

Cixous, Hélène. [1975] 1986. *The Newly Born Woman*. Minneapolis: University of Minnesota Press.

Cohn, Bernard S. 1984. "The Past in the Present: India as Museum of Mankind." Unpublished manuscript.

———. 1987. *An Anthropologist among the Historians and Other Essays*. Delhi: Oxford University Press.

———. 1993. "Genealogies of Power: Imperial Routes in the Imperial Center." Unpublished manuscript.

———. 1996. *Colonialism and Its Forms of Knowledge*. Princeton NJ: Princeton University Press.

Colonna, Fanny. 1975. *Instituteurs algériens (1883–1939)*. Algiers: Office des publications universitaires.

———. 1983a Introduction to *La Formation des cités chez les populations sédentaires de l'Algérie* by Émile Masqueray. 1886. Aix-en-Provence: Édisud.

———. 1983. *Les Spécialistes de la mediation: Naissance d'une classe moyenne au Maghreb*. Oran, Algeria: CRIDSSH, Université d'Oran.

———. 1987. *Savants paysans: Elements d'histoire sociale sur l'Algérie rurale*. Algiers: Office des publications universitaires.

———, ed. 1991. "*Sciences sociales/Sociétés arabes.*" Special issue, *Peuples Méditerranéens* 54–55.

———. 1995. *Les Versets de l'invincibilité: Permanence et changements religieux dans l'Algérie contemporaine*. Paris: Presses de la Fondation nationale des sciences Politiques.

Colonna, Fanny, and Claude Haim Brahimi. 1976. "Du bon usage de la science coloniale." In *Le Mal de voir. Ethnologie et orientalism: Politique et épistemologie, critique et autocritique*, ed Henri Moniot, Cahiers Jussieu no. 2, Université de Paris VII. Paris: Collection 10/18.

Colonna, Fanny, and Zakya Daoud, eds. 1993. *Être marginal au Maghreb*. Paris: CNRS Editions.

Cooper, Frederick. 2005. *Colonialism in Question: Theory, Knowledge, History*. Berkeley: University of California Press.

Cooper, Frederick, and Ann Laura Stoler, eds. 1997. *Tensions of Empire: Colonial Cultures in a Bourgeois World*. Berkeley: University of California Press.

Copans, Jean. 1975. *Anthropologie et imperialisme*. Paris: Maspero.

Cornforth, Maurice, ed. 1978. *Rebels and Their Causes: Essays in Honour of A. L. Morton*. London: Lawrence and Wishart.

Crary, Jonathan. 1990. *Techniques of the Observer: On Vision and Modernity in the Nineteenth Century*. Cambridge MA: MIT Press.

Crinson, Mark. 1996. *Empire Building: Orientalism and Victorian Architecture*. New York: Routledge.

Davis, John. 1996. *The Landscape of Belief: Encountering the Holy Land in Nineteenth-Century American Art and Culture*. Princeton NJ: Princeton University Press.

Derrida, Jacques. [1967] 1976. *Of Grammatology*. Baltimore: Johns Hopkins University Press.

———. 1998. *Monolingualism of the Other; Or, the Prosthesis of Origin*. Stanford: Stanford University Press.

Descombes, Vincent. [1979] 1993. *Modern French Philosophy*. New York: Cambridge University Press.

Dirks, Nicholas, ed. 1992. *Colonialism and Culture*. Ann Arbor: University of Michigan Press.

Dirlik, Arif, ed. 1993. *What Is in a Rim? Critical Perspectives on the Pacific Region Idea*. Boulder CO: Westview Press.

———. 1997. *The Post-Colonial Aura: Third World Criticism in the Age of Global Capitalism*. Boulder CO: Westview Press.

Dosse, François. [1987] 1994. *New History in France: The Triumph of the Annales*. Urbana: University of Illinois Press.

———. 1997. *History of Structuralism*. 2 vols. Minneapolis: University of Minnesota Press.

Dunn, Ross E., ed. 1999. *The New World History*. New York: Bedford Books.

Edwards, Elizabeth, ed. 1992. *Anthropology and Photography, 1860–1920*. New Haven CT: Yale University Press.

Edwards, Holly, ed. 2000. *Noble Dreams, Wicked Pleasures*. Princeton NJ: Princeton University Press.

Fabian, Johannes. 1983. *Time and the Other: How Anthropology Selects Its Object*. New York: Columbia University Press.

Fairbank, John King, ed. 1968. *The Chinese World Order*. Cambridge MA: Harvard University Press.

———. 1982. *Chinabound: A Fifty Year Memoir*. New York: Harper and Row.

Fairbank, John King, Edwin O. Reischauer, and Albert M. Craig. 1973. *East Asia*. Boston: Houghton Mifflin.

Fanon, Frantz. [1952] 1967. *Black Skin, White Masks*. New York: Grove Press.

———. [1959] 1965. *A Dying Colonialism*. New York: Grove Press.

———. [1961] 1968. The *Wretched of the Earth*. New York: Grove Press.

Fish, Stanley. 1980. *Is There a Text in This Class? The Authority of Interpretive Communities*. Cambridge MA: Harvard University Press.

Forster, E. M. [1924] 1984. *A Passage to India*. New York: Harcourt Brace.

Foster, Hal, ed. 1988. *Vision and Visuality*. Seattle: Bay Press.

Foucault, Michel. [1961] 1965. *Madness and Civilization: A History of Insanity in the Age of Reason*. New York: Random House.

———. [1963] 1973. *The Birth of the Clinic: An Archeology of Medical Perception*. New York: Random House.

———. [1966] 1970. *The Order of Things: An Archeology of the Human Sciences*. New York: Random House.

———. [1969] 1972. *The Archeology of Knowledge*. New York: Random House.

———. [1975] 1979. *Discipline and Punish: The Birth of the Prison*. New York: Random House.

———. [1976] 1978. *The History of Sexuality. Volume 1: An Introduction*. New York: Pantheon.

Frankenberg, Ruth. 1993. *White Women, Race Matters: The Social Construction of Whiteness*. Minneapolis: University of Minnesota Press.

Fujitani, Takashi. 1998. *Splendid Monarchy: Power and Pageantry in Modern Japan*. Berkeley: University of California Press.

Gallagher, Catherine, and Stephen Greenblatt. 2000. *Practicing New Historicism*. Chicago: University of Chicago Press.

Gates, Henry Louis, Jr. 1991. "Critical Fanonism." *Critical Inquiry* 17: 457–70.

Geertz, Clifford. 1973. *The Interpretation of Cultures: Selected Essays*. New York: Basic Books.

———. 1983. *Local Knowledge: Further Essays in Interpretive Anthropology*. New York: Basic Books.

Gibson, Nigel C., ed. 1999. *Rethinking Fanon: The Continuing Dialogue*. Amherst NY: Prometheus Books.

Gilroy, Paul. 1993. *The Black Atlantic: Modernity and Double Consciousness*. Cambridge MA: Harvard University Press.

Gilroy, Paul, Lawrence Grossberg, and Angela McRobbie, eds. 2000. *Without Guarantees: In Honour of Stuart Hall*. New York: Verso.

Gluck, Carol. 1985. *Japan's Modern Myths: Ideology in the Late Meiji Period*. Princeton NJ: Princeton University Press.

Godlewska, Anne. 1988. *The Napoleonic Survey of Egypt: A Masterpiece of Cartographic Compilation and Early Nineteenth-Century Fieldwork. Cartographica* monograph 38–39, no. 25.

Gordon, David C. 1964. *North Africa's French Legacy, 1954–1962*. Cambridge MA Harvard University Press.

———. 1971. *Self-Determination and History in the Third World*. Princeton NJ: Princeton University Press.

Gordon, Lewis R., T. Denean Sharpley-Whiting, and Renée T. White, eds. 1996. *Fanon: A Critical Reader*. Cambridge MA: Blackwell.

Grabar, Oleg. [1973] 1987. *The Formation of Islamic Art*. New Haven CT: Yale University Press.

———. 1978. *The Alhambra*. Cambridge MA: Harvard University Press.

Graham-Brown, Sarah. 1988. *Images of Women: The Portrayal of Women in Photography of the Middle East, 1860–1950*. New York: Columbia University Press.

Greenblatt, Stephen. 1991. *Marvelous Possessions: The Wonder of the New World*. Chicago: University of Chicago Press.

Grigsby, Darcy Grimaldo. 2002. *Extremities: Painting Empire in Post-Revolutionary France*. New Haven CT: Yale University Press.

Gringeri, Richard. 1997. "The Sun Kings: A History of French Anthropology in the Imperial Age, 1900–1960." Unpublished manuscript.

Grosrichard, Alain. 1979. *Structure du sérail: La fiction du despotisme asiatique dans l'occident classique*. Paris: Seuil.

Grossberg, Lawrence, Cary Nelson, and Paula Treichler, eds. 1992. *Cultural Studies*. New York: Routledge.

Guha, Ranajit, ed. 1997. *A Subaltern Studies Reader, 1986–1995*. Minneapolis: University of Minnesota Press.

Guha, Ranajit, and Gayatri Spivak, eds. 1988. *Selected Subaltern Studies*. New York: Oxford University Press.

Guha-Thakurta, Tapati. 1992. *The Making of a New "Indian" Art: Art, Aesthetics and Nationalism in Bengal, 1850–1920*. New York: Cambridge University Press.

Halbfass, Wilhelm. [1981] 1988. *India and Europe: An Essay in Understanding*. Albany: State University of New York Press.

Hamdy, Karim, and Laura Rice, eds. 1994. *Isabelle Eberhardt: Departures (Selected Writings)*. San Francisco: City Lights Books.

Harlow, Barbara, and Mia Carter, eds. 1999. *Imperialism and Orientalism: A Documentary Sourcebook*. Malden MA: Blackwell.

Haskell, Francis. 1987. "A Turk and His Pictures in Nineteenth Century France." In *Past and Present in Art and Taste: Selected Essays*. New Haven CT: Yale University Press.

Hawley, John Stratton, ed. 1994. *Sati: The Blessing and the Curse*. New York: Oxford University Press.

Hexter, J. H. [1972] 1979. "Fernand Braudel and the *Monde Braudellien* . . ." In *On Historians*. Cambridge MA: Harvard University Press.

Hindess, Barry, and Paul Q. Hirst. 1975. *Pre-Capitalist Modes of Production*. Boston: Routledge & Kegan Paul.

Hobsbawm, Eric, and Terence Ranger, eds. 1983. *The Invention of Tradition*. New York: Cambridge University Press.

Hourani, Albert. 1991. *Islam in European Thought*. New York: Cambridge University Press.

Howe, Kathleen Stewart. 1994. *Excursions along the Nile: The Photographic Discovery of Ancient Egypt*. Santa Barbara CA: Santa Barbara Museum of Art.

Hunt, Lynn, ed. 1989. *The New Cultural History*. Berkeley: University of California Press.

Husain, Asaf, Robert Olson, and Jamil Qureshi, eds. 1984. *Orientalism, Islam and Islamists*. Brattleboro VT: Amana Books.

Hyam, Ronald. 1990. *Empire and Sexuality: The British Experience*. Manchester, England: Manchester University Press.

Hymes, Dell, ed. 1972. *Reinventing Anthropology*. New York: Pantheon.

Inden, Ronald. 1990. *Imagining India*. Cambridge MA: Blackwell.

Jameson, Fredric. 1991. *Postmodernism, or, The Cultural Logic of Late Capitalism*. Durham NC: Duke University Press.

Jay, Martin. 1993a. *Downcast Eyes: The Denigration of Vision in Twentieth-Century French Thought*. Berkeley: University of California Press.

———. 1993b. *Force Fields: Between Intellectual History and Cultural Critique*. New York: Routledge.

Johnson, Richard. 1986–87. "What Is Cultural Studies Anyway?" *Social Text* 16: 38–80.

Jones, Eric. 1987. *The European Miracle: Environments, Economies and Geopolitics in the History of Europe and Asia*. New York: Cambridge University Press.

Judt, Tony. 1998. *The Burden of Responsibility: Blum, Camus, Aron, and the French Twentieth Century*. Chicago: University of Chicago Press.

Jullian, Philippe. 1977. *The Orientalists: European Painters of Eastern Scenes*. Oxford: Phaidon.

Kennedy, Dane. 1996a. "Imperial History and Post-Colonial Theory." *Journal of Imperial and Commonwealth History* 24: 345–63.

———. 1996b. *The Magic Mountains: Hill Stations and the British Raj*. Berkeley: University of California Press.

Kennedy, Valerie. 2000. *Edward Said: A Critical Introduction*. Malden MA: Polity Press.

Kiernan, Victor G. 1969. *Lords of Human Kind*. Harmondsworth, England: Penguin.

Kopf, David. 1969. *British Orientalism and the Bengal Renaissance*. Berkeley: University of California Press.

Krauss, Rosalind. 1985. *The Originality of the Avant-Garde and Other Modernist Myths*. Cambridge MA: MIT Press.

Krauss, Rosalind, and Jane Livingston. 1985. *L'Amour fou: Photography and Surrealism*. New York: Abbeville.

Kuhn, Thomas S. 1962. *The Structure of Scientific Revolutions*. Chicago: University of Chicago Press.

Lacambre, Geneviève. 1995. *Les Oubliés du Caire: Chefs d'oeuvre des musées du Caire*. Paris: Association Française d'Action Artistique, Musée d'Orsay, and Réunion des Musées Nationaux.

Lacheraf, Mostefa. 1965. *L'Algérie: Nation et société*. Paris: Maspero.

Lacoste, Yves, André Prénant, and André Nouschi. 1960. *L'Algérie, passé et présent: Le cadre et les étapes de la constitution de l'Algérie actuelle*. Paris: Editions sociales.

Lant, Antonia. 1992. "The Curse of the Pharaoh, or How the Cinema Contracted Egyptomania." *October* 59: 86–112.

Laurens, Henri. 1987. *Les Origines intellectuelles de l'Expedition d'Égypte: L'Orientalisme Islamisant en France (1698–1798)*. Paris: Isis.

Lebovics, Herman G. 1992. *True France: The Wars over Cultural Identity, 1900–1945*. Ithaca NY: Cornell University Press.

Leclerc, Gerard. 1972. *Anthropologie et colonialisme: Essai sur l'histoire de l'africanisme*. Paris: Fayard.

Le Sueur, James. 2001. *Uncivil War: Intellectuals and Identity Politics During the Decolonization of Algeria*. Philadelphia: University of Pennsylvania Press.

*Les Temps modernes*. 1970–71. "Anthropologie et imperialisme." Nos. 253–54, 299–300.

Lewis, Bernard. 1993. "The Question of Orientalism." In *Islam and the West*. New York: Oxford University Press.

Lewis, Reina. 1995. *Gendering Orientalism: Race, Femininity, and Representation*. New York: Routledge.

Lockman, Zachary. 2004. *Contending Visions of the Middle East: The History and Politics of Orientalism*. New York: Cambridge University Press.

Loomba, Ania. [1991] 1994. "Overworlding the 'Third World.'" In *Colonial Discourse and Post-Colonial Theory*, ed. Patrick Williams and Laura Chrisman. New York: Columbia University Press.

———. 1993. "Dead Women Tell No Tales: Issues of Female Subjectivity, Subaltern Agency and Tradition in Colonial and Postcolonial Writings on Widow Immolation in India." *History Workshop Journal* 36: 209–27.

———. 2005. *Colonialism/Postcolonialism*. 2nd ed. New York: Routledge.

Lowe, Lisa. 1991. *Critical Terrains: French and British Orientalisms*. Ithaca NY: Cornell University Press.

Lucas, Philippe. 1969. *Frantz Fanon: Négritude et nationalisme*. Paris: Thèse 3ème cycle.

Lucas, Philippe, and Jean-Claude Vatin. 1975. *L'Algérie des anthropologues*. Paris: Maspero.

Lyotard, Jean-François. [1979] 1984. *The Postmodern Condition*. Minneapolis: University of Minnesota Press.

Macfie, Alexander Lyon, ed. 2000. *Orientalism: A Reader*. New York: New York University Press.

———. 2002. *Orientalism*. Edinburgh: Pearson Education.

MacKenzie, John M. 1995. *Orientalism: History, Theory and the Arts*. Manchester, England: Manchester University Press.

Mammeri, Mouloud. 1955. *The Sleep of the Just*. Trans. Len Ortzen. Boston: Beacon Press.

———. 1965. *L'Opium et le baton*. Paris: Plon.

———. 1982. *Les Isefra, poèmes de Si Mohand-ou-Mhand*. Paris: Maspero.

———. 1991. *Culture savante, culture vécue: Études, 1938–1989*. Algiers: Association culturelle et scientifique TALA.

Mammeri, Mouloud, and Tassadit Yacine-Titouh. 1992. *Amour, phantasmes et sociétés en Afrique du Nord et au Sahara: Actes du colloque international des 14–15–16 juin 1989*. Paris: L'Harmattan, AWAL.

Mandouze, André. 1961. *La Révolution algérienne par les Textes*. Paris: Maspero.

———. 1998. *Mémoires d'outre-siècle: D'une resistance à l'autre*. Paris: V. Hamy.

Mani, Lata. 1987. "Contentious Traditions: The Debate on *Sati* in Colonial India." *Cultural Critique*, no. 7: 119–56.

———. 1992. "Cultural Theory, Colonial Texts: Reading Eyewitness Accounts of Widow Burning." In *Cultural Studies*, ed. Lawrence Grossberg, Cary Nelson, and Paula Treichler. New York: Routledge.

———. 1998. *Contentious Traditions: The Debate on Sati in Colonial India*. Berkeley: University of California Press.

Mani, Lata, and Ruth Frankenberg. 1985. "The Challenge of Orientalism." *Economy and Society* 14: 174–92.

Mannheim, Karl. [1929] 1936. *Ideology and Utopia*. New York: Harcourt, Brace.

Mason, Philip [Philip Woodruff, pseud.]. 1953. *The Men Who Ruled India*. 2 vols. London: Jonathan Cape.

McDonald, Terrence J., ed. 1996. *The Historic Turn in the Human Sciences*. Ann Arbor: University of Michigan Press.

Melman, Billie. 1992. *Women's Orients: English Women and the Middle East, 1718–1918*. London: Macmillan.

Memmi, Albert. [1957] 1965. *Colonizer and Colonized*. New York: Orion.

Metcalf, Thomas. 1989. *An Imperial Vision: Indian Architecture and Britain's Raj*. Berkeley: University of California Press.

———. 1995. *Ideologies of the Raj*. New York: Cambridge University Press.

Midgley, Clare. 1998. *Gender and Imperialism*. New York: Manchester University Press.

Miller, Christopher. 1985. *Blank Darkness: Africanist Discourse in French*. Chicago: University of Chicago Press.

———. 1990. *Theories of Africans: Francophone Literature and Anthropology in Africa*. Chicago: University of Chicago Press.

———. 1998. *Nationalists and Nomads*. Chicago: University of Chicago Press.

Minear, Richard H. 1980. "Orientalism and the Study of Japan." *Journal of Asian Studies* 39: 507–17.

Mirzoeff, Nicholas, ed. 1998. *The Visual Culture Reader*. New York: Routledge.

———. 1999. *An Introduction to Visual Culture*. New York: Routledge.

Mitchell, Timothy. 1988. *Colonizing Egypt*. Berkeley: University of California Press.

———. 2002. *Rule of Experts: Egypt, Techno-Politics, and Modernity*. Berkeley: University of California Press.

Mitchell, W. J. T. 1994. *Picture Theory*. Chicago: University of Chicago Press.

Mitter, Partha. [1977] 1992. *Much Maligned Monsters: History of European Reactions to Indian Art*. Chicago: University of Chicago Press.

Mohanty, Chandra Talpade. [1988] 1994. "Under Western Eyes: Feminist Scholarship and Colonial Discourses." In *Colonial Discourse and Post-Colonial Theory*, ed. Patrick Williams and Laura Chrisman. New York: Columbia University Press.

Moniot, Henri, ed. 1976. *Le Mal de voir. Ethnologie et orientalisme: politique et épistemologie, critique et autocritique*. Cahiers Jussieu no. 2, Université de Paris VII. Paris: Collection 10/18.

Morley, David, and Kuan-Hsing Chen, eds. 1996. *Stuart Hall: Critical Dialogues in Cultural Studies*. New York: Routledge.

Mudimbe, V. Y. 1988. *The Invention of Africa: Gnosis, Philosophy, and the Order of Knowledge*. Bloomington: Indiana University Press.

———. 1993. "Reading and Teaching Pierre Bourdieu." *Transition*, no. 61: 144–60.

Nair, Janaki. 1992. "Uncovering the Zenana: Visions of Indian Womanhood in Englishwomen's Writings, 1813–1940." In *Expanding the Boundaries of Women's History*, ed. Cheryl Johnson-Odim and Margaret Strobel. Bloomington: Indiana University Press.

Nochlin, Linda. [1983] 1989. "The Imaginary Orient." In *The Politics of Vision*. San Francisco: HarperCollins.

O'Hanlon, Rosalind. 1988. "Recovering the Subject: Subaltern Studies and Histories of Resistance in Colonial South Asia." *Modern Asian Studies* 22: 189–224.

Olender, Maurice. 1992. *The Languages of Paradise: Race, Religion, and Philology in the Nineteenth Century*. Cambridge MA: Harvard University Press.

Peirce, Lesley. 1993. *The Imperial Harem: Women and Sovereignty in the Ottoman Empire*. New York: Oxford University Press.

Pierson, Ruth Roach, and Nupur Chaudhuri, eds. 1998. *Nation, Empire, Colony: Historicizing Gender and Race*. Bloomington: Indiana University Press.

Pinney, Christopher. 1997. *Camera Indica: The Social Life of Indian Photographs*. Chicago: University of Chicago Press.

———. 2004. *"Photos of the Gods": The Printed Image and Political Struggle in India*. London: Reaktion.

Pomeranz, Kenneth. 2000. *Great Divergence: China, Europe and the Making of the Modern World Economy*. Princeton NJ: Princeton University Press.

Porter, Dennis. 1986. "Orientalism and Its Problems." In *The Politics of Theory*, ed. Francis Barker, Peter Hulme, Margaret Iversen, and Diane Loxley. Colchester, England: University of Essex Press.

Porterfield, Todd. 1998. *The Allure of Empire*. Princeton NJ: Princeton University Press.

Poster, Mark. 1975. *Existential Marxism in Postwar France: From Sartre to Althusser*. Princeton NJ: Princeton University Press.

———. 1989. *Critical Theory and Poststructuralism: In Search of a Context*. Ithaca NY: Cornell University Press.

Pouillon, François. 1997. *Les deux vies d'Etienne Dinet, peintre en Islam*. Paris: Balland.

Prakash, Gyan, ed. 1995. *After Colonialism: Imperial Histories and Postcolonial Displacements*. Princeton NJ: Princeton University Press.

———. 1999. *Another Reason: Science and the Imagination of Modern India*. Princeton NJ: Princeton University Press.

Pratt, Mary Louise. 1992. *Imperial Eyes: Travel Writing and Transculturation*. London: Routledge.

Prochaska, David. 1990. "The Archive of *Algérie imaginaire*." *History and Anthropology* 4: 373–420.

———. [1990] 2004. *Making Algeria French: Colonialism in Bône*. New York: Cambridge University Press.

———. 1991. "Fantasia of the *Photothèque*: French Postcard Views of Colonial Senegal." *African Arts* 24: 40–47.

———. 1992. "'Disappearing' Iraqis." *Public Culture* 4: 89–92.

———. 1994. "Art of Colonialism, Colonialism of Art: The *Description de l'Egypte* (1809–1828)." *L'Esprit Créateur* 34: 69–91.

———. 1996. "History as Literature, Literature as History: Cagayous of Algiers." *American Historical Review* 101: 670–711.

———. 1999. "Writing Colonial Algeria." In *The Sphinx in the Tuilleries and Other Essays in Modern French History*, ed. Robert Aldrich and Martyn Lyons. Sydney: University of Sydney Press.

———. 2000. "Edward Said: The Contrapuntal Self." Unpublished manuscript.

———. 2003a. "The Other Algeria: Beyond Renoir's Algiers." In *Renoir in Algiers*, ed. Roger Benjamin. Exhibition catalogue. New Haven CT: Yale University Press.

———. 2003b. "This Is Now, That Was Then: *The Battle of Algiers* and After." *Radical History Review*, no. 85: 133–49.

———. 2004. "*Untitled (2004)*." In *Beyond East and West: Seven Transnational Artists*, by David O'Brien and David Prochaska. Exhibition catalogue. Seattle: University of Washington Press.

———. 2007. "Returning the Gaze: Orientalism, Gender, and Yasmina Bouziane's Photographic Self-Portraits." In *Modern Art and the Idea of the Mediterranean*, ed. Vojtěch Jirat-Wasiutyński. Toronto: University of Toronto Press.

Rabinow, Paul. *French Modern*. Cambridge MA: MIT Press, 1989.

Rabinow, Paul, and William M. Sullivan, eds. [1979] 1987. *Interpretive Social Science: A Second Look*. Berkeley: University of California Press.

Rafael, Vicente. [1988] 1993. *Contracting Colonialism: Translation and Christian Conversion in Tagalog Society under Early Spanish Rule*. Durham NC: Duke University Press.

Reig, Daniel. 1988. *Homo orientaliste: La langue arabe en France depuis XIXe siècle.* Paris: Maisonneuve.

Richon, Olivier. 1985. "Representation, the Despot and the Harem: Some Questions around an Academic Orientalist Painting by Lecomte-du-Nouy." In *Europe and Its Others*, ed. Francis Barker, Peter Hulme, Margaret Iversen, and Diana Loxley. Colchester, England: University of Essex Press.

———. 1989. "The Imageless Sanctuary: Piazzi Smyth, the Pyramid, and Photography." *Block* 15: 32–42.

Robbins, Derek. 1991. *The Work of Pierre Bourdieu.* Boulder CO: Westview Press.

Rodinson, Maxime. 1987. *Europe and the Mystique of Islam.* Seattle: University of Washington Press.

Rosenthal, Donald. 1982. *Orientalism: The Near East in French Painting, 1800–1880.* Rochester NY: Memorial Art Gallery of the University of Rochester.

Rouillé, André, and Bernard Marbot. 1986. *Le Corps et son image: Photographies du dix-neuvième siècle.* Paris: Contrejour.

Sahli, Mohamed C. 1965. *Décoloniser l'histoire : Introduction à l'histoire du Maghreb.* Paris: Maspero.

Sahlins, Marshall. 1981. *Historical Metaphors and Mythical Realities.* Ann Arbor: University of Michigan Press.

———. 1985. *Islands of History.* Chicago: University of Chicago Press.

Said, Edward. 1978. *Orientalism.* New York: Random House.

———. 1979. *The Question of Palestine.* New York: Random House.

———. 1981. *Covering Islam.* New York: Pantheon.

———. 1983. *The World, the Text and the Critic.* Cambridge MA: Harvard University Press.

———. 1991. *Musical Elaborations.* New York: Columbia University Press.

———. 1993. *Culture and Imperialism.* New York: Random House.

———. 1994. *The Politics of Dispossession: The Struggle for Palestinian Self-Determination, 1969–1994.* New York: Random House.

———. 1999. *Out of Place: A Memoir.* New York: Knopf.

———. 2000. *Power, Politics and Culture: Interviews with Edward Said.* New York: Pantheon.

———. 2001. *Reflections on Exile and Other Essays.* Cambridge MA: Harvard University Press.

Sangari, Kumkum, and Sudesh Vaid, eds. 1990. *Recastng Women: Essays in Indian Colonial History.* New Brunswick NJ: Rutgers University Press.

Sartre, Jean-Paul. 1968. Preface to The *Wretched of the Earth*, by Frantz Fanon. New York: Grove Press.

Savigliano, Marta. 1995. *Tango and the Political Economy of Passion.* Boulder CO: Westview.

Schalk, David. 1991. *War and the Ivory Tower*. New York: Oxford University Press.

Schwab, Raymond. [1950] 1984. *The Oriental Renaissance: Europe's Rediscovery of India and the East, 1680–1880*. New York: Columbia University Press.

Schwartz, Vanessa, and Jeannene M. Przyblyski, eds. 2004. *The Nineteenth-Century Visual Culture Reader*. New York: Routledge.

Scott, Paul. [1966–71] 1976. *The Raj Quartet*. New York: William Morrow.

Sekula, Allan. 1986. "The Body and the Archive." *October* 39: 3–64.

Sewell, William H, Jr. 2005. *Logics of History: Social Theory and Social Transformation*. Chicago: University of Chicago Press.

Sharpe, Jenny. 1991. "The Unspeakable Limits of Rape: Colonial Violence and Counter Insurgency." *Genders* 10: 25–46.

———. 1993. *Allegories of Empire: The Figure of Woman in the Colonial Text*. Minneapolis: University of Minnesota Press.

Shohat, Ella, and Robert Stam. 1994. *Unthinking Eurocentrism: Multiculturalism and the Media*. New York: Routledge.

Sinha, Mrinalini. 1995. *Colonial Masculinity: The "Manly Englishman" and the "Effeminate Bengali."* Manchester, England: Manchester University Press.

Solomon-Godeau, Abigail. 1981. "A Photographer in Jerusalem, 1855: Auguste Salzmann and His Times." *October* 18: 91–107.

———. 1991. *Photography at the Dock*. Minneapolis: University of Minnesota Press.

Sorum, Paul Clay. 1977. *Intellectuals and Decolonization in France*. Chapel Hill: University of North Carolina Press.

Spivak, Gayatri. 1985a. "The Rani of Sirmur." In *Europe and Its Others*, ed. Francis Barker, Peter Hulme, Margaret Iversen, and Diana Loxley. Colchester, England: University of Essex Press.

———. 1985b. "Three Women's Texts and a Critique of Imperialism." *Critical Inquiry* 12: 43–61.

———. 1987. *In Other Worlds: Essays in Cultural Politics*. New York: Methuen.

———. 1988. "Can the Subaltern Speak?" In *Marxism and the Interpretation of Culture*, ed. Cary Nelson and Larry Grossberg. Urbana: University of Illinois Press.

———. 1999. *The Critique of Postcolonial Reason*. Cambridge MA: Harvard University Press.

Sprinker, Michael, ed. 1992. *Edward Said: A Critical Reader*. Cambridge MA: Blackwell.

Squiers, Carol, ed. 1990. *The Critical Image: Essays on Contemporary Photography*. Seattle: Bay Press.

Stevens, MaryAnne, ed. 1984. *The Orientalists: Delacroix to Matisse. European Painters in North Africa and the Near East*. London: Weidenfeld and Nicolson.

Stocking, George. [1968] 1982. *Race, Culture, and Evolution: Essays in the History of Anthropology*. Chicago: University of Chicago Press.

———, ed. 1983–96. *History of Anthropology*. Vols. 1–8. Madison: University of Wisconsin Press.

———. 1987. *Victorian Anthropology*. New York: Free Press.

———. 1992. *The Ethnographer's Magic and Other Essays*. Madison: University of Wisconsin Press.

———. 1995. *After Tylor*. Madison: University of Wisconsin Press.

Stoler, Ann Laura. 1995. *Race and the Education of Desire: Foucault's History of Sexuality and the Colonial Order of Things*. Durham NC: Duke University Press.

———. 2002. *Carnal Knowledge and Imperial Power: Race and the Intimate in Colonial Rule*. Berkeley: University of California Press.

Strobel, Margaret. 1993. "Gender, Sex, and Empire." In *Islamic and European Expansion: The Forging of a Global Order*, ed. Michael Adas. Philadelphia: Temple University Press.

Strobel, Margaret, and Cheryl Johnson-Odim, eds. 1992. *Expanding the Boundaries of Women's History*. Bloomington: Indiana University Press.

Sweetman, John. 1988. *The Oriental Obsession: Islamic Inspiration in British and American Art and Architecture, 1500–1920*. New York: Cambridge University Press.

Tagg, John. 1988. *The Burden of Representation: Essays on Photographies and Histories*. Amherst: University of Massachusetts Press.

Tanaka, Stefan. 1993. *Japan's Orient: Rendering Pasts into History*. Berkeley: University of California Press.

Taylor, Lucien, ed. 1994. *Visualizing Theory: Selected Essays from V.A.R., 1990–1994*. New York: Routledge.

Thompson, E. P. 1978. *The Poverty of Theory and Other Essays*. New York: Monthly Review Press.

Thornton, Lynne. 1983. *The Orientalists: Painters-Travellers, 1828–1908*. Paris: ACR Edition.

———. 1985. *Women as Portrayed in Orientalist Painting*. Paris: ACR Edition.

Tibawi, Abdelatif. 1963. "English-Speaking Orientalists: A Critique of Their Approach to Islam and Arab Nationalism." *Muslim World* 53: 185–204, 298–313.

———. 1979. "Second Critique of English-Speaking Orientalists and Their Approach to Islam and the Arabs." *Islamic Quarterly* 23: 4–8.

Toews, John E. 1987. "Intellectual History after the Linguistic Turn." *American Historical Review* 92: 879–907.

Tucker, Judith E. 1985. *Women in Nineteenth Century Egypt*. New York: Cambridge University Press.

Turner, Bryan. 1974. *Weber and Islam*. London: Allen and Unwin.

———. 1978. *Marx and the End of Orientalism*. London: Allen and Unwin.

Valensi, Lucette. 1984. "Le Maghreb vu du Centre: Sa place dans l'école sociologique française." In *Connaissances du Maghreb: Sciences sociales et colonisation*, ed. Jean-Claude Vatin. Paris: Editions du CNRS.

Vatin, Jean-Claude. 1983. *L'Algérie politique: Histoire et société*. 2nd ed. Paris: Fondation nationale des sciences politiques.

———, ed. 1984. *Connaissances du Maghreb: Sciences sociales et colonization*. Paris: Editions du CNRS.

———, ed. 1991. *D'un Orient l'autre: Les métamorphoses successives des perceptions et connaissances*. 2 vols. Paris: Editions du CNRS.

Veeser, H. Aram, ed. 1989. *New Historicism*. New York: Routledge.

———, ed. 1994. *New Historicism Reader*. New York: Routledge.

Viswanathan, Gauri. 1989. *Masks of Conquest: Literary Study and British Rule in India*. New York: Columbia University Press.

Waardenburg, Jean-Jacques. 1963. *Islam dans le miroir de l'Occident*. Paris: Mouton.

Williams, Raymond. 1977. *Marxism and Literature*. New York: Oxford University Press.

Wolf, Eric. 1970. "Anthropology on the Warpath." *New York Review of Books*, November 19: 26–35.

———. 1982. *Europe and the People without History*. Berkeley: University of California Press.

Yang, Anand. 1989. "Whose Sati? Widow Burning in Early 19th Century India." *Journal of Women's History* 1: 8–33.

Young, Robert. 1990. *White Mythologies*. New York: Routledge.

———. 1995. *Colonial Desire: Hybridity in Theory, Culture and Race*. New York: Routledge.

# 1 | HISTORY

# 1 | Orientalist Empiricism

## Transformations of Colonial Knowledge

DAVID LUDDEN

Uncertainty about what constitutes truth underlies the pursuit of knowledge and logically entails critical scrutiny of the means by which some representations of reality and not others become established as true. In this endeavor, the veracity of statements about reality is not at issue so much as their epistemological authority, their power to organize understandings of the world. In this vein, I join authors in this volume to pursue a proposition derived from Edward Said: There is knowledge constituted as truthful by the authority of a system of representations called "orientalism," which arose from and bolstered European supremacy.

Michel Foucault provides a point of departure for many authors in this volume, as he does for Said (1978: 23). Said recognizes that Foucault's method is deficient for historical studies because "the individual text or author counts for very little" (23). Thus Foucault can conjure discursive formations in history but cannot write their histories, having blinded himself to dynamics of creation, tension, contest, and change. Said (1984, 1986) only partially liberates himself from Foucault. Seeing orientalism in descriptive, literary terms, he makes provocative associations among texts that constitute orientalism and dynamics of European power. But the particulars that connect histories of imperialism and knowledge are missing. In this essay, I consider connections between histories of political power in South Asia and knowledge about Indian tradition. Though my goal is not a critique of Said, I do conclude that by detaching his chosen texts from history, in the manner of Foucault, Said has lost sight of the politics that reproduce the epistemological authority of orientalism today.

Orientalism

Said conflates three formations of "orientalism" that have very distinct relations to colonial power. Most narrowly, orientalism is a field of scholarship
with a distinct academic genealogy and tradition. I designate only specialists
in this field as "orientalists." Most broadly, orientalism is a vast set of images
in scholarship, painting, literature, and other media—a sprawling formation
in which the works of William Jones, orientalist painters, Rudyard Kipling,
and Henry Kissinger mingle in a multimedia text that conjures the essences
of the East. This constitutes orientalism for Edward Said. Between these two
extremes—the first formation being small and defined rigidly by scholarly
norms, the other being huge and defined loosely by the implications of its
imagery—there is a third formation: a venerable set of factualized statements
about the Orient, which was established with authorized data and research
techniques and which has become so widely accepted as true, so saturated by
excess plausibility (Ludden 1988/1990), that it determines the content of assumptions on which theory and inference can be built. This body of knowledge did originate in part in the work of orientalists, but it grew far beyond
their scope by contributions from other authorities. Now shared and disseminated within a multicultural world, where many disciplines add to its
authority (Abdel-Malek 1963), this last formation—orientalism as a body of
knowledge—is the subject of this essay.

The three formations of orientalism overlap and share historical space.
They all presume a fundamental divide between East and West and observe
the East through Western epistemologies in cognitive relation to the West.
That they have common substance defined by a single attitude toward the
East and common links to Western domination is an argument Said makes,
but I do not. For, despite a history that unites them, they have separate histories that account for their distinctive substance and interactions with power.
Orientalists, for instance, played a more distinct, powerful role in the production of official colonial knowledge about India before 1830 than after.
By 1830, Parliament and political economy provided independent authority for the determination of truths about the "real" India. By 1880, imperial government and European social theory were arguably more important
than were orientalists for the production of orientalist images like those in
Kipling's work, as well as for the authority of conventional wisdom about
India, such as that enshrined in census reports and ethnological tradition

(Cohn 1983, 1989). By 1900, high imperialism, social Darwinism, and scientific racism gave orientalism meanings quite contrary to orientalist scholarship (Stepan 1982).

For Said, imperialism is inherent in orientalism. Knowledge is power. But this begs many important questions: How does orientalism support imperialism? How does imperialism explain the substance of orientalism in different world areas? How has orientalism survived and even thrived in a world of nation-states and national movements? By separating knowledge and power (which Said does not do, following Foucault), we can address issues like these and historicize orientalism more effectively. By locating forces at work in the production of orientalism, we can show how its reproduction has transformed its composition and political meanings over time. Doing so, we find orientalism much more diverse and vital than Said makes it out to be.

Orientalism as a body of knowledge about India dates back to classical antiquity and has many early-modern precursors (Halbfass 1988; O'Leary 1989). But eighteenth-century European expansion in India generated qualitatively new knowledge. Much of it served instrumental functions for capitalist, military, and administrative expansion by the English East India Company. Yet methods to produce this knowledge were not specific to India, nor was its substance understood to be dictated by utility. Even the most instrumental knowledge, produced to sustain technologies of colonial rule—what I will call colonial knowledge—was produced under the Enlightenment rubric of objective science. Additions to knowledge about India were understood as scientific discoveries whose veracity was based on methodologies authorized by scientific standards of the day. Orientalism as a body of knowledge drew material sustenance from colonialism but became objectified by the ideology of science as a set of factualized statements about a reality that existed and could be known independent of any subjective, colonizing will. Thus detached epistemologically from politics by a culture that objectivized the world as a collection of scientific observations with universal validity, orientalism floated free of its original moorings; it could, therefore, serve diverse political purposes and receive new sustenance from many quarters. By 1900, it was even deployed against European dominance by Indian nationalists. Its substance also changed with time: because it ordered knowledge about India in relation to the West, orientalism changed substantively through the production of new "facts," with advances in science and changing structures of world power.

## Colonial Knowledge

Foundations of orientalism lie in the transition to Company rule in India, circa 1770–1820, when producing new knowledge about India was bound tightly with political patronage. As Company territory grew, centralization became a policy imperative; as the Company became a ruling power, its autonomy decreased (Spear 1978: 85–86). Intellectual labor became implicated in struggles to subordinate Company to Parliament, Indian provinces to Calcutta, and districts to provincial capitals. The centralization that accompanied colonial expansion involved the subordination of many intermediaries, "partners in empire," and "loose cannons" who had been critical for the Company in earlier decades but were now seen as detrimental (Furber 1948/1970; Kling 1976; Nightingale 1970; Sutherland 1952/1962). The fathers of orientalism in India furthered colonial centralization by subordinating the Indian intelligentsia to English epistemological authority.

Beginning in 1784, the year that Pitt's India Act was passed and the Asiatic Society of Bengal founded, and increasingly with reforms under Lord Cornwallis in the wake of Burke's denunciations of Company Raj (Furber 1987), new attention was paid to Indian intermediaries who stood between the Court of Directors and Indian subjects (Stein 1989). To subordinate these men, Europeans had to appropriate knowledge that was locked away in the minds of Indian commercial, judicial, military, and revenue specialists. By appropriating knowledge toward this end, Europeans discovered India for themselves, in their own terms, by converting knowledge from native sources into English-language forms that were systematic, scientific, and accessible to means of truth testing that were becoming the pride of European culture (Adas 1989). In addition, military operations and political centralization required that data that had never been produced by Indian rulers be generated and controlled by government; such data constituted new facts for the creation of orientalism as a body of knowledge. Colonialism reorganized India politically and empirically at the same time, and the two reorganizations supported one another.

The works of James Rennell, William Jones, and Thomas Munro show how military expansion and political centralization implicated colonial knowledge. Rennell joined the Royal Navy in 1756 at age fourteen and went to the Philippines with Alexander Dalrymple at age twenty. He had been surveying harbors for the Royal Navy when the Company, in 1763, hired him to survey routes from Calcutta to the Bay of Bengal. He became Surveyor General of Bengal the next year; when he left India, in 1777, he literally put India on the map with his comprehensive *Map of Hindoostan*, whose accompanying *Memoir* appeared in three editions, the last in 1793. This compendium was not superseded for decades and was possible, Rennell says in the preface to his *Memoir*, because so few geographical facts were known when he began his work. He says also that he abandoned revising the *Memoir* because data multiplied too rapidly with the expansion of Company power and that the market for his work arose from public curiosity in England stimulated by Company wars.

The lithograph adorning Rennell's map symbolizes the progress of geography during Rennell's career. It shows the surveyor's and mapmaker's tools on the ground and European civilians in the shadow of Britannia, as she receives texts from Brahmans, one text being labeled "Shastas" (*shastras*), Hindu law books. The gesture linking Britannia and the central Brahman figure seems ambiguous and could be seen to depict a gift being made to him by Britannia. But Brahmans in a queue with arms full of texts wait to give, not receive. And the temple tower behind Britannia presents her as a goddess/queen receiving gifts from suppliants who bear offerings/tribute. They offer knowledge, that special gift of India's literati, so critical for Britannia's transformation from conquering to ruling power (Bayly 1988; Dirks, 1993). The lithograph thus represents European merchants and surveyors dependent on Britannia's might, through which they gain knowledge from a supplicant India. The irony is that even as the lithograph represents the power of Britannia and pays homage to her from the vantage points of science and commerce, it implies that natives, especially Brahmans, hold knowledge that she needs. To loosen that grip became a political goal for Company Raj for the advancement of science and commerce. With military victories, more English surveyors marched into the interior every year. Observation and measurement by Englishmen supplanted "secondhand," "hearsay," and "traditionary" native accounts. In 1808, Rennell measured progress in surveying by looking back to the 1770s; he said to a gathering of surveyors, "At that day we were compelled to receive information from others respecting the interior of the country, but in your time you *explored for yourselves*" (Phillimore 1954–56: frontispiece).

The shastras in Rennell's lithograph signify another branch of knowledge in which the Company sought to end its dependence on native experts. A letter from William Jones to Cornwallis proposing that Jones be commissioned to compile a "Digest of Hindu and Mohammadan laws" shows the importance of this project for colonialism. Penned in Calcutta in 1788, the letter reads like a grant proposal. It begins by arguing that civil law should accord with native practice, a principle enshrined in the 1781 Act of Settlement (Mukherjee 1968/1987: 117), with which Jones begins his proposal. He goes on to say that "the difficulty lies . . . in the application of the principle to practice; for the Hindu and Muselman laws are locked up for the most part in two very difficult languages, Sanscrit and Arabick, which few Europeans will ever learn." As a result, judges in Jones's day depended on native experts, and on his arrival in Calcutta as a judge, Jones "soon began to suspect the pandits [Hindu religious scholars] and maulavis [Muslim religious leaders]." In 1784 he wrote to Warren Hastings, "I can no longer bear to be at the mercy of our Pundits, who deal out Hindu law as they please" (Mukherjee 1968/1987: 118). His argument to Cornwallis—who once wrote, "Every native of Hindustan, I verily believe, is corrupt" (Spear 1978: 88)—proceeds accordingly: "If we give judgment only from the opinions of native lawyers and scholars, we can never be sure, that we have not been deceived by them. . . . My experience justifies me in declaring, that I could not with an easy conscience concur in a decision, merely on the written opinion of native lawyers, in any case in which they could have the remotest interest in misleading the court" (Cannon 1970, 2:795). Jones had devised "the obvious remedy for this evil" and communicated it to Burke and others before he left England. It is this plan that he submitted to Cornwallis for support:

> If we had a complete digest of Hindu and Mohammadan laws, after the model of Justinian's inestimable Pandects, compiled by the most learned of the native lawyers, with an accurate verbal translation of it into English; and if copies of the work were reposited in the proper offices of the Sedr Divani Adalat, and of the Supreme Court, that they might occasionally be consulted as a standard of justice, we should rarely be at a loss for principles at least and rules of law applicable to the cases before us, and should never perhaps, be led astray by the Pandits or Maulavi's [sic], who would hardly venture to impose on us, when their impositions might be so easily detected. (Cannon 1970, 2:795)

Jones then goes on to sketch a proper method for the project, estimate its cost, and modestly offer himself as "superintendent of such a work." His argument and offer were accepted. Jones could then seek what S. N. Mukherjee (1968/1987: 112) calls "his greatest desire": to become "the legislator of the Indians." To fulfill his desire required disciplined devotion to divulging secrets buried in difficult texts in languages "few Europeans will ever learn" (see Rocher, 1993). The requisite esoteric skills became the orientalists' hallmark, which Nietzsche subsequently criticized for its intellectual narrowness and which soon marginalized Indology as "it quickly became clear that the most interesting scholastic problems had no practical value at all" (Gaeffke 1990: 67, 69). But his language skill, his ability to systematize legal codes on Justinian principles, and the patronage of Cornwallis did give Jones real power in his day, enabling him to attempt a reversal of the power/knowledge relationship depicted in Rennell's lithograph. Through Jones, Britannia could generate knowledge of Hindu law that never existed before; she could give the "Shastas" to Indians who would rely on her for correct understanding of their own sacred texts and laws.

Jones saw this reversal of roles, its attendant subordination of "pandits and maulavis," and the power it gave him both as scientific achievement and as testimony to his dedication and intellect. He also saw it as a paternal generosity that would typify orientalists, as Wilhelm Halbfass indicates when he says of J. G. Herder, "His sympathy for the people of India became ever more apparent in his friendly and glorifying view of the 'childlike Indians'" (Halbfass 1988: 70; see Mojumdar 1976). Jones described his feelings in a letter to G. J. Spencer in 1791:

I speak the language of the Gods, as the Brahmens call it, with great fluency, and am engaged in superintending a Digest of Indian Law for the benefit of the twenty four millions of black British subjects in these provinces: the work is difficult & delicate in the highest degree & engages all my leisure every morning between my breakfast and the sitting of the court; the natives are charmed with the work, and the idea of making their slavery lighter by giving them their own laws, is more flattering to me than the thanks of the company and the approbation of the king, which have also been transmitted to me. (Cannon 1970, 2:885; emphasis in original)

Language learning also enabled Thomas Munro to perform a special role

in the production of colonial knowledge, also under the patronage of Cornwallis, who appointed him to assist another military officer, Alexander Read,
in administering the Baramahal territory ceded to the Company by Tipu Sultan in 1792. Cornwallis appointed these military men to perform this critical civilian duty on the frontiers of Company expansion in order simultaneously to subordinate Madras to Calcutta and native intermediaries to the
Company. Cornwallis distrusted Madras civilians because, as he reported to
the Court of Directors in 1792, few men under the governor of Madras "are
acquainted with country languages," so they

> are obliged, both from habit and necessity, to allow the management of
> their official, as well as their private business, to fall into the hands of du-
> bashes, a description of people in the Carnatic, who, with very few excep-
> tions, are calculated for being the most cruel instruments of rapine and
> extortion in the hands of unprincipled masters, and even of rendering . . .
> the most upright and humane intentions . . . perfectly useless to the in-
> terests of the company, and to the unfortunate natives who happen to be
> within the reach of their power and influence. (Stein 1989: 38)

Munro, appointed as revenue administrator, advanced his career for thirty
years by applying the "political principle of destroying any and all intermediary authority between the Company and the cultivator as the best assurance of the securing of control by the Company over its new dominions." He
sought "nothing less than the completion, by administrative means, of the
military conquest of the Baramahal" (Stein 1989: 59–60). From this arose the
authoritative construction of village India enshrined in the "ryotwari system,"
which became an essential element of orientalism as a body of knowledge.

## Politics and Empiricism

William Jones, Indologist and lawgiver, died in 1793, and Thomas Munro,
soldier and administrator, died in 1827. Their legacies grew from intellectual
constructions of India relative to Britain during the institution of that relationship as colonial. Though Munro died preoccupied by war in Burma, the
conclusion of the Maratha wars had eliminated the Company's last major
military threat. By 1820, "the acute moral crisis of a generation before—the
time of Burke's attack—had passed" (Stein 1989: 138). When Sir Thomas

was governor at Madras, fears of the French and revolution had also passed away, which had preoccupied Wellesley when he established the College at Fort William (Kopf 1969: 46–47) and which made Jones, whatever his own beliefs, "part of [a] revivified conservatism, which sought to define and defend British society in the terms employed by Burke" (Majeed 1990: 211). As the frontier days of colonial knowledge passed away, Company Raj became secure; pathbreaking discoveries became authoritative wisdom; innovative methods became systems. Jones fathered a discipline and Munro an administration.

Like Indian administrative politics, which remained split into provinces and departments but became ever more centralized, colonial knowledge remained divided into specialized compartments but became increasingly integrated as a body of knowledge by forces centered in London. Continuities across this transition and beyond reveal major political victories and long-term trends in the history of knowledge that built empirical certainty into orientalism. Among political victories, none is more critical than Munro's triumph in constructing *The Fifth Report on East India Company Affairs*, which made him an architect of the modern understanding of agrarian India (Stein 1989: 138–77). Among long-term trends, the most critical is the expanding scope of empiricism, which made colonial knowledge into a set of factualized statements about reality. Indology, revenue surveys, and commission reports came to share the same epistemological terrain with positivist knowledge about all societies, cultures, and political economies. Separate streams of knowledge about India could thus intersect and enrich one another, and facts from investigations in India could be integrated with facts from around the world in political economy and world history.

Empiricism embraced ever more of the world with the expansion of British power. Encyclopedic compendia like Malachy Postlethwayt's *The Universal Dictionary of Trade and Commerce* (1766) organized data from treaties, laws, travel accounts, histories, and technical manuals on productions and trades in one authoritative, fact-filled format; but much of the world was still missing, including India. In their day, Rennell and later surveyors like Hamilton Buchanan and Benjamin Heyne published accounts of Indian journeys, and their volumes went beside others of the same sort, like that by Joseph Townsend, a rector from Cornwall who published his account of a journey in the 1780s in France and Spain, advertising "particular attention to the agriculture, manufacture, commerce, population, taxes, and revenue."

Rennell also drew maps for Mungo Park's best-selling account of an expedition to Africa. Such works made the world visible and usable for British enterprise. They were of a piece with efforts in art and literature to render the world as a unified landscape for intellectual and material appropriation by English capitalism (Cosgrove 1984).

In the early nineteenth century, pieces of colonial knowledge generated by experts as diverse as Munro and Jones, on subjects as diverse as Hindu law and agrarian administration, became situated side by side within one empiricist epistemology, in which they could be integrated into a unified construction of India. Authoritative sources produced diverse types of data that became factualized and located in a unified empirical domain where they could be formed into verified statements about Indian reality. "Hindu law books" became understood as accounts of legal practice and therefore of actual law-abiding behavior and thus of religious norms that guided traditional life. These could then be combined with accounts of observed practice and of history and lore to demonstrate how Indians obeyed or violated norms in practice. In short, once the authority of colonial knowledge was established in its power over English-language understandings of India, its veracity escaped the political nexus portrayed in Rennell's lithograph. Freed from politics, authoritative knowledge about traditional India could be designed from virtually any collection of authoritative data.

The template for a lasting design was devised in Munro's time and became increasingly ornate and codified by the routinization of the colonial administration; as knowledge production was systematized, individual explorations gave way to routine reports, native informants became employees and subjects of the Raj, and journey literature gave way to official correspondence. By 1820, colonial knowledge had begun to emerge as authoritative, official wisdom, and orientalism to take definite shape as a body of knowledge.

We have no complete account of this process, and I cannot attempt one here. What I can do is illustrate how colonial knowledge generated authoritative "facts" that constituted traditional India within a conceptual template that would be progressively theorized within modern world history. These factualized representations of India became official wisdom. They were conventionalized and then fixed as a factual basis for inference and theory. Two vignettes illustrate how early colonialism produced two foundational ideas about traditional India: (1) India was "from time immemorial" a land of autonomous village communities in which (2) the force sustaining tradition was Hindu religion, with its complex social prescriptions, above all those pertaining to caste.

1. When Read and Munro went to Baramahal in 1792, their purpose was revenue collection. They found that by eliminating middlemen they could contract for revenue directly with village leaders. This was a major change in Company routines, and Read had to defend it to the Board of Revenue in Madras. From experience in Bengal and in Madras territories, the Board assumed that it would collect its revenue from zamindars (landholders) and contractors who would deliver revenue from the villages; indeed, in 1801, the Board confirmed erstwhile poligar (Telugu-speaking warrior clan) chiefs as zamindar landlords in Madras territories. But Read argued that collecting taxes directly from villagers enabled him to lower tax rates and to collect more taxes, though this raised the cost of tax collection, which led to vehement objections from the Board. Eliminating the middlemen between the Company and village taxpayers became a crusade for Munro. By 1811 he had collected revenue and information from several parts of South India, and his influence in London enabled him to organize evidence for submission to Parliament as it considered the Company's 1813 charter renewal. Evidence for the *Fifth Report*, which Munro effectively compiled, helped to prove his case, with data from Company experts, that the village had always been the basic unit of administration in India, and peasant rights in villages had been usurped by thieving middlemen and tyrants like Tipu Sultan. Thus, for its own interests and to protect the rights of the people, the Company should establish the village as the basic unit of administration.

Munro argued for and effectively proved traditions in which village headmen administered villages composed of peasant families who had always enjoyed the equivalent of private property rights, though these had been abrogated by rapacious tyrants, poligars, and renters. To accomplish his victory, Munro had to best competitors in Madras, above all Francis Ellis, who commanded evidence that might have won the day, were the matter to have been settled scholastically. But this was not to be (Stein 1989).

2. For surveyors and revenue collectors throughout South India, as for Rennell, Brahmans were the most influential native informants, and they became key figures in Company administration. Even so, until 1810, it seems that Britons in Company service viewed Brahmans essentially as specialists in a complex division of labor. Early lists of castes from southern territories normally transliterate and translate caste names with occupational labels

without ranking. By 1820, this pattern had changed; why, I cannot say exactly. But it seems that as the village became for the Company the foundation of Indian society, principles were needed for ordering that society without reference to political structures larger than the village. In principle, Munro's ryotwari system proposed that all citizen taxpayers were juridically equal; in practice, however, revenue collection and Company law rested on a logic of hierarchy, with the Company at the top adjudicating disputes based on precedent (Washbrook 1981). Company courts established precedents, but common law tradition required a logical basis for precedent in Indian society itself. Though Company officials collected evidence to confirm rights on the basis of charters from precolonial kings, this evidence was often inconvenient or lacking, and positivist law required logic to fill in the gaps left by its silences and exclusions.

Hindu law codes and caste prescriptions therein provided that logic. By 1820, legal and revenue proceedings are filled with cases and reports on the traditional, religiously based, social order of village society, self-regulated by caste and village panchayats (local councils), demanding recognition in Company governance and law. Caste lists by 1820 uniformly use *varna* (literally, "color") categories to rank *jatis* (subcastes ordered by occupation). By this time, of course, the Company was deeply embroiled in the administration of Hindu temples (Appadurai 1981). Hindu religion in the early nineteenth century was very much a part of Company Raj; the colonial construction of caste society in village India needs to be seen in this light (Bayly 1988). Practical experience proved and proved again that religion was the basis of social order in India.

These early moments in the making of colonial knowledge suggest how Company Raj produced factualized formulations that would populate orientalism as a body of knowledge. They also suggest the complex and contested, shifting role of native authority for Company experts who endeavored to establish truths about India. Though the distinctions between the intellectual work of Jones and that of Munro suggest a division like that which would later separate humanities from social sciences, it was the combination of these two streams of learning that created colonial knowledge and orientalism, by establishing epistemological privilege for European expertise deployed to establish concurrently the essential truth about India and policies for Indian governance. The utility of ideas about India for gover-

nance and their institutionalization by the state bolstered their epistemological authority.

Orientalism began with the acquisition of the languages needed to gain
reliable information about India. Indian languages became a foundation
for scientific knowledge of Indian tradition built from data transmitted to
Europeans by native experts. Rennell's lithograph illustrates that texts were
the most valued objects of transmission: properly studied, texts would reveal
the positive facts of Hindu legal doctrine. For collectors as much as judges,
precedent and principles of right were essential and could be positively determined from reputable witnesses through translation. Reliable evidence
with which to establish a factual basis for Company Raj thus came initially
from reputable natives whose authority was rooted in their expertise and
social status, as evaluated by Company authorities. Evidence from Brahman
pandits and other Indian elites was essential for sound knowledge on which
to base sound policies, and it established a bond between the Company and
Indian elites that was used to stabilize the colonial state within a conservative mold (Bayly 1988).

Empirically sound and useful knowledge about India was not to be found
only in classical texts. Even Jones himself indicates that properly constituted
European expertise was required to discover the real truth in texts. For Rennell and the others, only British experts could determine veracity and therefore sound knowledge for government. Surveyors took great pains to distinguish data *gleaned* from the accounts of natives from data *produced* by
direct observation; Munro necessarily used only evidence produced by collectors to establish the village as a traditional foundation of government. For
Rennell and Munro, the real India experts were those scientists and trained
administrators who worked and traveled in the countryside and absorbed
local information and observed local conditions—those incipient social scientists who created "hard" objective data in surveys and settlements for policy decisions based on facts and political economy. A stray Sanskrit quote
might be relevant here and there, but only to provide color for conclusions
based on "real" data. For Munro, as for James Mill and many others to follow, skepticism about native sources combined with opposition to policies
intended to preserve native elite privileges, associated with orientalists like
Jones and Ellis.

My two vignettes also suggest how politics influenced not only the kind
of data generated by Company expertise but also the logic of their integra-

tion into constructions of India. Colonial knowledge was seriously contested intellectual terrain. The Company collected data that could have been used to construct very different images of rural India (Ludden 1988/1990). But alternative formations were obscured and marginalized in Munro's lifetime by the political process that wielded authority in the production of knowledge about India. This authority was centered in London. Munro worked within complex webs of influence connecting European trends, British politics, Indian administration, and orientalism. His prose shows the influence of logical positivism and utilitarianism. But his work is also tinged with conservative ideas about hierarchy and is inconsistent by standards of contemporary philosophy (Stein 1989). His victories in intellectual contests to construct rural India were not those of an ideology or philosophy. They were political. His formulations became fixed as factual knowledge about Indian reality by establishing effective official wisdom for Company Raj. Victories in London made Munro judicial commissioner and then governor; his minutes became almost biblical in authority. His characterization of the village as "a little republic" dates from 1806. Published by Mark Wilks in 1810 during the campaign to shape *The Fifth Report*, it was by 1830 at the metaphorical heart of orientalism (Stein 1989). Its most famous formulation, in a minute by Charles Metcalfe read in 1830 as evidence for the Select Committee of the House of Commons on the Affairs of the East India Company, had a powerful influence on Karl Marx. It reads in part:

> The village communities are little republics, having nearly everything they want within themselves, and almost independent of any foreign relations. They seem to last where nothing else lasts. Dynasty after dynasty tumbles down; revolution succeeds to revolution; Hindoo, Patan, Mogul, Mahratta, Sik, English are all masters in turn; but the village communities remain the same. . . . If a country remain for a series of years the scene of continued pillage and massacre, so that villages cannot be inhabited, the scattered villagers nevertheless return whenever the power of peaceable possession revives. A generation may pass away, but the succeeding generation will return. The sons will take the place of their fathers; the same site for the village, the same position for the houses, the same lands, will be occupied by the descendants of those who were driven out when the village was depopulated. (Kessinger 1974: 25)

Metcalfe, like Munro, engaged fierce debates in Britain about colonial policy that rested on disputed facts about India and policy principles for Indian governance. Science and political disputation continued to work together in the formation of orientalism and within it to fix the essentially timeless self-reproduction of village India firmly in the modern mind. Although James Mill savagely criticized the East India Company in his *History of British India*, published in 1820, his work marshaled what he believed to be all necessary facts to show the necessity of British rule as a remedy for India's traditional tyranny and chaos, which the village had survived to enjoy Company protection.

## Theory and Empire

Mill's *History* represents a starting point for the theoretical repositioning of India in relation to Europe that attended the growth of industrial capitalism. India's political and cognitive relation to Europe changed dramatically in the process, and with it orientalism. Mill attacked orientalists and romantics and denied that anyone could reconstruct India's past from native myth and legend. He erased cultural traditions altogether from his understanding of India and Europe. For him the study of history and law was founded on rational philosophical principles with which both "Britain and India could be criticized and reformed" (Majeed 1990: 212). He disliked empire because it sustained aristocratic privilege, but he embarked on a systematic intellectual subordination of India to the universalist principles of European social theory that attended European imperial expansion and inscribed orientalism at the roots of modern social science. Mill—and subsequently Hegel, Marx, and Weber—did not merely elaborate orientalism as a body of knowledge; they transformed it and enhanced its vitality by theorizing India's changing relation with Europe.

Mill first theorized India within British imperial hegemony, but for him their connection was merely circumstantial: both Britain and India were places like any other for the conduct of government. India may have only suffered bad government, but this was not an explanation or a justification of empire; it was a condition to be rectified. Universal rationality, not history, put Britain and India in the same theoretical field. It just so happened that British officials could effect rational policies in India and in fact could do so more freely there than in Britain. For India was a tabula rasa, to be inscribed with rationality. Cultural and historical differences were irrelevant: "Indeed, it was crucial to the emergence of Utilitarianism as a rhetoric of reform to ignore any such distinction" (Majeed 1990: 222–23). Mill's *History* began the intellectual project of using orientalism to identify features of India that were necessary objects for rational policies of social reform. Just as Mill attacked orientalists for romantic attachments and for "aesthetic attitudes which underpinned . . . revitalized conservatism" (218), he reformulated orientalism into a body of knowledge that revealed oriental irrationality, for which good government was to be the cure.

Mill's attack on orientalists, his repositioning of India as an object of reform, and his reformulation of orientalism indicate how "the emergence of new political languages in Britain in the early nineteenth century was closely involved with the British imperial experience" (Majeed 1990: 222). But for the history of orientalism it is also critical that shipments of colonial knowledge back to Britain were continuously reconstituted and reauthorized by European political discourse. Empirical data and factualized statements about India entered European intellectual life through Parliamentary debates, books, newspapers, pamphlets, art, and universities. Such venues for disseminating and reproducing orientalism widened the scope for participation in the history of orientalism far beyond the halls of India House. In this setting, orientalism was shaped by forces having little to do with India. For instance, Mill's India was a platform for utilitarian studies that dovetailed with his cognitive psychology. Likewise, Hegel, Marx, and Weber had preoccupations unconnected to India that conditioned their ideas about its essential character.

Orientalism became a versatile component of political discourse in Europe, as political disputes about India in relation to Britain shaped understandings of both India and Europe. Jones and Mill informed Hegel's study of India (Halbfass 1988: 87). Parliamentary evidence for the Company charter renewal and news dispatches from India informed Marx's reports for the *New York Tribune* and his sketch of an Asiatic mode of production (Krader 1975; O'Leary 1989). Weber's later work drew on a huge body of orientalist scholarship. As the hearth of orientalism was moving increasingly into the universities, social sciences were developing within the legacy of Hegel, Marx, and Weber, who put India and Europe side by side in universal theories of history that made sense of each in their relation to one other.

European superiority became more theoretically pronounced in Europe as European supremacy became a dominant political phenomenon in the modern world. Beginning with Hegel, Europe's dynamism and historicity expressed Europe's primacy as a force in world history and India's at best secondary stature. For Marx and Weber, capitalism revealed and contextualized India's stagnant backwardness, which they explained using facts about traditional village economy, despotic governance, religiously based social life, and sacred caste divisions. The facts behind their theoretical formulations about India were not questioned. Established as facts by colonial knowledge and by their conventional authority in European political discourse, they were there as truths for theorists to use in making sense of the world. Orientalism became the template for knowing an oriental other in contradistinction to European capitalism, rationality, historicity, modernity, and powers of self-transformation.

As it became integrated theoretically into modern discourse on Europe's place in history, orientalism as a body of knowledge became more detached epistemologically from colonialism; it wielded power over understandings of the world grounded not only in conventional wisdom but in social theory. From this position, it would inform both modernization and Marxist theory in the twentieth century. This would not have been possible had not empirical reality in India been shaped on lines consistent with orientalism, so that "facts of life" apparent to the eye and institutional practices built into social experience in India would constantly verify perceptions of India guided by social theory. Colonial governance constructed this concordance between empirical evidence and social theory by weaving orientalism as a body of knowledge into the fabric of administration and law.

That the village constituted the basic unit of Indian social life became evident beyond critical questioning as government demarcated, bounded, surveyed, and studied villages, to make the village the basic unit of data collection and administration. Property rights and social order became officially grounded legally and textually in village traditions and village records. The village officer became the "keystone of the arch" of rural administration. Whatever its status in precolonial times, the village thus became the elemental unit of empirical and theoretical reference in British India through its construction as a unit of governance. Empirical evidence about the countryside based on village data and social theory positing village autonomy "from time immemorial" harmonized completely. The origin of this concordance in a colonial politics of knowledge—which had thrust Munro's theory of village India into social theory, on the one hand, and built an Indian system of village administration, on the other—became irrelevant for the authority of ideas about the status of village society in Indian civilization. In the twentieth century, the authority of these ideas increased further as they entered social science practice: first for economics, then for anthropology, village India became the elemental unit of empirical analysis and theory alike (Ludden 1988/1990).

Similarly, Indian political culture became institutionalized in religious terms that made the division of Indian society between Hindus and Muslims an iconic principle of governance. That this religious antagonism was the fundamental challenge to law and order—to the social tranquillity that benefited everyone—became conventional wisdom in Munro's lifetime, in part through the work of orientalists. But routine administrative practice produced data that accumulated over decades to bolster the concordance between theory and evidence pertaining to this fundamental division. A critical site for this construction of communalism was the writing of riot reports. To represent riots as communal, pitting Hindus against Muslims, became a routine solution to administrative problems posed by urban unrest (Pandey 1990). By selecting and excluding data, and by insinuating religious motives to crowds, official observers built a descriptive genre that evidenced unitary Hindu and Muslim communities fighting each other head to head in situations, such as the Banaras riots of 1809, where evidence abounded to show that various local groups confronted one another for various reasons and with various ends. This body of official evidence thus harmonized with the theory on which it was based and which it substantiated (Freitag 1989: 51–52). Orientalism as a body of knowledge informed this empirical genre by establishing the analytic grid for description and explanation and locating the origin of conflict in the essential character of Indian civilization.

In addition, as with the building of village India as the basic unit of social life, official evidence that substantiated India's essential communalism removed the colonial state as an explanation of realities reflected in authoritative data and empirical facts. The state could thus be represented as an impartial arbiter of communal disputes, an attitude enshrined in imperial historiography, where government always does its best to mediate conflicts between Hindus and Muslims that originate in the Muslim conquest and spoliation of Hindu India centuries before British rule (e.g., Spear 1978).

The imperial state thus represented itself both as the origin of authoritative knowledge about India and as the protector of all Indian people, striving to maintain order in the realms of knowledge and social life and to facilitate modernization in a fundamentally divided oriental society. Orientalism bolstered the authority of the state and was in turn sustained as a body of knowledge about that society that gave the imperial state confidence in selecting Indian representatives on religious grounds for inclusion in governance. That representatives should be officially recognized leaders of religious communities, and that the interests of those communities as expressed by these leaders should be balanced in government, became a natural means to articulate the state and society. It provided a logic to guide the imperial construction of local and then regional institutions of political representation after 1880 (Brown 1985). Built into institutional politics, theory and evidence of Hindu-Muslim conflict harmonized more completely and reproduced the authority of orientalism as effective knowledge in political practice.

The age of high imperialism thus transformed colonial knowledge and orientalism. Before 1850, the politics of Company Raj had turned statements about traditional India formulated in accord with British power into facts authorized by the epistemological powers of science. By 1850, factual foundations for orientalism as a body of knowledge were firm. After 1850, a second transformation involved constructions of theory and institutions on those foundations that wove orientalism deeply into social science and social experience. The ideas that the village constituted the basic unit of social order in India and that Indian civilization was built on religion became institutionalized and theorized so as to obscure their colonial origins, which became irrelevant to their authority.

In social theory, the orient served as the "other" to capitalist Europe. This defined Europe and capitalism as much as it did India. Thus, social science and political practice built on this foundation reproduced its authority without reference to its colonial origins, and did so, moreover, while the one theoretical principle informed actors on all sides of imperial struggles. In India, the colonial invention of tradition became irrelevant to experience of the village and communalism, once their traditionalism was built into institutions that conditioned social life. The evidentiary base for substantiating village and communal traditions arose from the same institutional practices. The empire made orientalism as a body of knowledge appear as a verified representation of reality by building it into both the construction of empirical evidence and the social experience of people in governance and education. Imperial bureaucracy produced empirical data of an ever more scientific and modern sort, a database so vast as to describe a reality of its own. Because the imperial bureaucracy defined reliable data, reliability became based on English training and imperial credentials commanded by a mass of technical specialists who gathered facts on economy, epigraphy, tribes, castes, religious practices, language, literature, and customs (Appadurai 1993). The reality of tradition arose from evidence, theory, administrative ideology, art, and literature that described India's subordination and England's supremacy, Europe's modernity and India's backwardness (Adas 1989; Bernal 1987; Cohn 1983; Fieldhouse 1981; Ludden, 1987; Moore-Gilbert 1986).

## States and Nations

Voices articulating orientalism thus multiplied and diversified across the colonial period. Factual formulations drawn from colonial knowledge gained authority by being theorized, institutionalized, and empirically substantiated. Yet from its birth on the frontiers of empire, the empirical construction of tradition served political functions. By 1880, it was woven deeply into the ideology of empire, capturing essences of South Asia in relation to Britain, to establish the fixity and timelessness of the essential India for intellectual manipulation by the imperial ruling class. And from Rammohan Roy to Bankimchandra Chattopadbyay, Rabindranath Tagore, Mohandas Gandhi, Jawaharlal Nehru, and beyond, orientalism as a body of knowledge informed the discourse of India's nationhood. For political discourse on both sides of the colonial encounter entailed the other. The colonial divide evolved as each side defined itself in relation to its "other" (Chatterjee 1986; Ludden 1992; Prakash 1990; Raychaudhuri 1988), and orientalism became a versatile component of national discourse, an authoritative base for India's self-definition. Both sides of the colonial divide were secure in the knowledge that village India had survived into modern times from ancient days, by its autonomous reproduction within a religiously prescribed caste society.

The role of orientalism in nationalism has not been studied adequately. But it seems evident that being grounded in a formulation of India in relation to Europe, orientalism contained vital elements for constructing national identity in India and in Britain alike. Vitality came from the longevity and the empirical and theoretical depth of these ideas, but also from their versatility in political debates conducted in the context of empire. The meaning and content of Indian "otherness" would be contested by nationalists, as they had been by Jones and Mill, Munro and Ellis, so that orientalism entered political rhetoric as a venerable set of analytic oppositions between Britain and India, with dispersed, fluid implications. Intellectuals in India never confronted a unified colonial construction of India, except when they devised it, and there was never a unified nationalist construction of India, except that devised by its proponents and their adversaries. Ideological terrain inscribed by orientalism provided rich ground for invention, wide ground for maneuver and opposition.

Foundational ideas established in early colonial decades, such as the religious basis of Indian social order, could be powerfully deployed for opposing purposes. This is sharply represented in successive editions of Mill's *History*, with editorial additions by Horace Hayman Wilson, the first professor of Sanskrit at Oxford, who defended Jones and criticized Mill. Wilson's preface to the fourth edition calls it "the most valuable work on the subject which has yet been published," but he then raves against its rash statements based on insufficient evidence and its "evil tendency" to depict Hindus as "plunged almost without exception in the lowest depths of immorality and crime," which is "calculated to destroy all sympathy between the rulers and the ruled." Wilson then ventures that "There is reason to fear that these consequences are not imaginary, and that a harsh and illiberal spirit has of late years prevailed in the conduct and councils of the rising service in India, which owes its origins to impressions imbibed in early life from the History of Mr. Mill." Wilson blames Mill for the growth among the impressionable youth who became colonial servants of feelings of "disdain, suspicion, and dislike" toward Indians "wholly incompatible with the full and faithful discharge of their obligations to Government and to the people" (Mill 1820/1968: viii; also Majeed 1990: 222).

Students who entered the colonial service, however, did not only read Mill. Racism became science (LaCapra 1991; Stepan 1982). Social Darwinism made poverty, weakness, and technological backwardness characteristic of all non-white peoples, who became degraded in the eyes of Europe (Adas 1989). In the 1850s Tocqueville "found it incomprehensible that the eighteenth-century Physiocrats should have had such an admiration for China" (Bernal 1987: 238). Whereas for orientalists the essence of India came from ancient family relations among the Indo-European languages, by Queen Victoria's death in

1901 the essence of India included prominently its religious irrationality and fractiousness. Thus orientalism as knowledge shifted meanings with India's changing relation to Britain, until the dominant fact, which made sense of all others—including subjective facts like imperial paternalism and liberal outrage, as well as disdain and distrust among colonial officers—ordering them all in a coherent discourse, was that India lived under the Crown.

Victorian empire also generated knowledge that could be used to defend Indian tradition in counterattacks against imperialism and its denigrations. Orientalists built a body of texts to document the grandeur of Indian culture. In the heyday of empire, Max Müller produced the *Sacred Books of the East*, which would number over fifty volumes, and argued in *India: What Can It Teach Us?* (1883) that Indian thinkers could edify all mankind. An imperial administrator, Alfred Lyall, even questioned the morality of imposing materialism on an inherently spiritual Indian people (Adas 1989: 351). At this juncture, Dadabhai Naoroji in the 1870s and Romesh Chandra Dutt in the 1890s began to nationalize orientalism by positing a British imperial assault on traditional India, employing colonial knowledge to criticize the Raj for impoverishing India. Like Mill, Munro, and imperial commissions, they used colonial knowledge to criticize colonial policy. As Wilson charged the liberal Mill with illiberal attitudes toward India, Naoroji castigated "un-British rule" and Dutt charged Munro with oppressive land taxation (Chandra 1966).

The nationalist critique inverted the imperialist claim to have brought India moral and material progress. Orientalism provided a framework for this effort. Dutt and Naoroji targeted oppressions heaped on formerly self-sufficient villages by imperial policy. Gandhi negated and inverted myths of Western superiority with his version of traditional Truth. Ideas that Gandhi used to conjure the essential India—with its ageless rural simplicity and moral continuity—came from the treasure chest of orientalism. Gandhi concludes *Hind Swaraj* (1909) with a list of "authorities"—including Naoroji and Dutt, but also Henry Maine's *Village Communities*—and "testimonies by eminent men," quotations from the likes of Müller, Frederick Von Schlegel, William Wedderburn, and Thomas Munro. Nehru's *Discovery of India* (1959) is a more systematic use of orientalism to craft a charter for nationhood. Nehru discovers a wise and ageless Indian nation, invaded, conquered, exploited, and divided over centuries of foreign rule, but still surviving in the essence of its traditions and still struggling for freedom. Nehru's *Discovery* is a journey toward national self-awareness; as he discovers India's identity in knowledge constituted by orientalism, he finds himself.

In nationalism we find the vitality of orientalism today. This conclusion is at odds with Said and suggests that his work inhabits a place inside the history of orientalism. For to imply, as he does, that orientalism sustains a body of false, colonial images of the East and its peoples leaves us with the implicit promise that a true image would be constructed if these peoples were free to render images of themselves. Such oppositional moments are many in the history of orientalism. Opposing claims to represent the real truth about the East and disputes over the authentic, authoritative voices and evidence that establish that truth animate orientalism historically. By presuming that there is to be found in the East a real truth about its self-existent peoples, Said employs the very positivist logic that gives orientalism life. And behind his back, nationalism has claimed authority over this truth and appropriated orientalism in the name of national self-representation. Today orientalism is most defensible on the ground that people in India and elsewhere believe its imagery to represent the truth about themselves.

### Note

A longer version of this essay appeared in Carol A. Breckenridge and Peter van der Veer, eds., *Orientalism and the Postcolonial Predicament: Perspectives on South Asia* (Philadelphia: University of Pennsylvania Press, 1993). Research was funded by the American Philosophical Society and The National Endowment for the Humanities.

### References

Abdel-Malek, Anouar. 1963. "Orientalism in Crisis." *Diogenes* 44 (winter): 103–40.

Adas, Michael. 1989. *Machines as the Measure of Men: Science, Technology, and Ideologues of Western Dominance*. Ithaca NY: Cornell University Press.

Appadurai, Arjun. 1981. *Worship and Conflict under Colonial Rule: A South Indian Case*. Cambridge, England: Cambridge University Press.

———. 1993. "Number in the Colonial Imagination." In *Orientalism and the Postcolonial Predicament*, ed. Carol A. Breckenridge and Peter can der Veer. Philadelphia: University of Pennsylvania Press.

Barrier, N. Gerald. 1974. *Banned: Controversial Literature and Political Control in British India 1907–1947*. Columbia: University of Missouri Press.

———, ed. 1976. *Roots of Communal Politics*. Columbia: University of Missouri Press.

Bayly, Christopher A. 1988. *Indian Society and the Making of the British Empire*. New Cambridge History of India. Vol. 2, part 1. Cambridge, England: Cambridge University Press.

Bernal, Martin. 1987. *Black Athena: The Afro-Asiatic Origins of Classical Civilization.* Vol. 1, *The Fabrication of Ancient Greece, 1785–1985.* New Brunswick NJ: Rutgers University Press.

Bhaskaran, S. Theodore. 1981. *The Message Bearers: Nationalist Politics and Entertainment Media in South India, 1880–1945.* Madras: Cre-A.

Brown, Judith M. 1985. *Modern India: The Origins of An Asian Democracy.* Delhi: Oxford University Press.

Cannon, Garland, ed. 1970. *The Letters of Sir William Jones.* 2 vols. Oxford: Clarendon Press.

Chandra, Bipan. 1966. *The Rise and Growth of Economic Nationalism in India: Economic Policies of the Indian National Leadership, 1880–1905.* New Delhi: People's Publishing House.

Chatterjee, Partha. 1986. *Nationalist Thought and the Colonial World: A Derivative Discourse.* London: Zed Books for the United Nations University.

Cohn, Bernard S. 1983. "Representing Authority in Victorian India." In *The Invention of Tradition,* ed. Eric Hobsbawm and Terence Ranger. Cambridge, England: Cambridge University Press.

———. 1989. "Cloth, Clothes, and Colonialism." In *Cloth and Human Experience,* ed. Annette B. Weiner and Jane Schneider. Washington DC: Smithsonian Institution Press.

Cosgrove, Denis. 1984. *Social Formation and Symbolic Landscape.* London: Croom Helm.

Dirks, Nicholas B. 1993. "Colonial Histories and Native Informants." In *Orientalism and the Postcolonial Predicament,* ed. Carol A. Breckenridge and Peter van der Veer. Philadelphia: University of Pennsylvania Press.

Farmer, Victoria L. 1997. "The Limits of Image-Making: Doordarshan and the 1989 Lok Sabha Elections." In *Nationalism, Democracy, and Development: State and Politics in India,* ed. Ayesha Jalal and Sugata Bose. Delhi: Oxford University Press.

Fieldhouse, D. K. 1981. *Colonialism, 1870–1945: An Introduction.* New York: St. Martin's Press.

Freitag, Sandria. 1989. *Collective Action and Community: Public Arenas and the Emergence of Communalism in North India, 1870–1940.* Berkeley: University of California Press.

Furber, Holden. [1948] 1970. *John Company at Work: A Study of European Expansion in India in the Late Eighteenth Century.* Cambridge MA: Harvard University Press. Reprint New York: Octagon Books.

———. 1987. "Edmund Burke and India." *Bengal Past and Present* 56 (1): 202–3; 56 (2): 163–75.

Gaeffke, Peter. 1990. "A Rock in the Tides of Time: Oriental Studies Then and Now." *Academic Questions* 3 (2): 67–74.

Habib, Irfan. 1963. *The Agrarian System of Mughal India (1556–1707).* Bombay: Published for the Department of History, Aligarh Muslim University, by Asia Publishing House.

Halbfass, Wilhelm. 1988. *India and Europe: An Essay in Understanding*. Albany: State University of New York Press.

Kessinger, Tom G. 1974. *Vilyatpur 1848–1968: Social and Economic Change in a North Indian Village*. Berkeley: University of California Press.

Kling, Blair. 1976. *Partner in Empire: Dwarkanath Tagore and the Age of Enterprise in Eastern India*. Berkeley: University of California Press.

Kopf, David. 1969. *British Orientalism and the Bengal Renaissance: The Dynamics of Indian Modernization, 1773–1835*. Berkeley: University of California Press.

Krader, Lawrence. 1975. *The Asiatic Mode of Production: The Sources, Development and Critique in the Writings of Karl Marx*. Assen, Netherlands: Van Gorcum.

LaCapra, Dominick, ed. 1991. *The Bounds of Race: Perspectives on Hegemony and Resistance*. Ithaca NY: Cornell University Press.

Lal, Deepak. 1988. *The Hindu Equilibrium. Vol. 1, Cultural Stability and Economic Stagnation, India, c. 1500 B.C.–A.D. 1980*. Oxford: Clarendon Press.

Ludden, David. 1986. "Historians and Nation States." *Perspectives, The American Historical Association Newsletter* 24 (4): 12–14.

———. 1987. "World Economy and Village India, 1600–1900: Exploring the Agrarian History of Capitalism." In *South Asia and World Capitalism*, ed. Sugata Bose. Delhi: Oxford University Press.

———. [1988] 1990. "Agrarian Commercialism in Eighteenth-Century South India: Evidence from the 1823 Tirunelveli Census." *Indian Economic and Social History Review* 25 (4): 493–519. Reprinted in *Merchants, Markets and the State in Early Modern India*, ed. Sanjay Subrahmanyam. Delhi: Oxford University Press.

———. 1990. Introduction to *Agricultural Production Regimes*, ed. David Ludden. Delhi: Oxford University Press.

———. 1992. "India's Development Regime." In *Colonialism and Culture*, ed. Nicholas B. Dirks. Ann Arbor: University of Michigan Press.

Majeed, J. 1990. "James Mill's 'The History of British India' and Utilitarianism as a Rhetoric of Reform." *Modern Asian Studies* 24 (2): 209–24.

Mill, James. [1820] 1968. *The History of British India*. Ed. Horace H. Wilson. 9 vols. New York: Chelsea House.

Mojumdar, M. A. T. 1976. *Sir William Jones, the Romantics, and the Victorians*. Dhaka, Bangladesh: Zakia Sultana.

Moore-Gilbert, B. J. 1986. *Kipling and "Orientalism."* New York: St. Martin's Press.

Moreland, William H. 1929. *The Agrarian System of Moslem India*. 2nd ed. Delhi: Oriental Books Reprint Corp.

Mukherjee, S. N. [1968] 1987. *Sir William Jones: A Study in Eighteenth-Century British Attitudes to India*. 2nd ed. Hyderabad: Orient Longman.

Müller, Friedrich Max. 1883. *India: What Can It Teach Us?* London: Longmans, Green.

Nandy, Ashis. 1983. *The Intimate Enemy: Loss and Recovery of Self under Colonialism.* Delhi: Oxford University Press.

Nehru, Jawaharlal. 1959. *The Discovery of India.* Ed. Robert I. Crane. Garden City NY: Anchor Books.

Nightingale, Pamela. 1970. *Trade and Empire in Western India, 1784–1806.* Cambridge, England: Cambridge University Press.

O'Leary, Brendan. 1989. *The Asiatic Mode of Production: Oriental Despotism, Historical Materialism, and Indian History.* Oxford: Basil Blackwell.

Pandey, Gyanendra. 1990. *The Construction of Communalism in Colonial North India.* Delhi: Oxford University Press.

Parenti, Michael. 1986. *Inventing Reality: The Politics of the Mass Media.* New York: St. Martin's Press.

Phillimore, R. H. 1954–56. *Historical Records of the Survey of India.* Dehra Dun, India: n.p.

Prakash, Gyan. 1990. "Writing Post-Orientalist Histories of the Third World: Perspectives from Indian Historiography." *Comparative Studies in Society and History* 32 (2): 383–408.

Raychaudhuri, Tapan. 1988. *Europe Reconsidered: Perceptions of the West in Nineteenth-Century Bengal.* Delhi: Oxford University Press.

Rennell, James. 1975. *Memoir of a Map of Hindoostan or the Moghul's Empire.* 3rd ed. Patna, India: N.Y. Publications.

Rocher, Rosane. 1993. "British Orientalism in the Eighteenth Century: The Dialectics of Knowledge and Government." In *Orientalism and the Postcolonial Predicament,* ed. Carol A. Breckenridge and Peter van der Veer. Philadelphia: University of Pennsylvania Press.

Said, Edward W. 1978. *Orientalism.* New York: Pantheon Books.

———. 1984. *The World, the Text, and the Critic.* Cambridge MA: Harvard University Press.

———. 1986. "Orientalism Reconsidered." In *Literature, Politics, and Theory: Papers from the Essex Conference, 1976–84,* ed. Francis Barker, P. Hulme, M. Iversen, and D. Loxley. London: Methuen.

Sen, Surendranath. [1925] 1976. *The Administrative System of the Marathas.* 3rd ed. Calcutta: K. P. Bagchi.

Sharma, Ram Sharan. 1980. *Indian Feudalism: c. 300–1200.* 2nd revised ed. Delhi: Macmillan Co. of India.

Spear, Thomas George Percival. 1978. *The Oxford History of Modern India, 1750–1975.* 2nd ed. Delhi: Oxford University Press.

Stein, Burton. 1989. *Thomas Munro: The Origins of the Colonial State and His Vision of Empire.* Delhi: Oxford University Press.

Stepan, Nancy. 1982. *The Idea of Race in Science: Great Britain, 1800–1960*. Hamden CT: Archon Books.

Sutherland, Lucy S. [1952] 1962. *The East India Company in Eighteenth-Century Politics*. Oxford: Clarendon Press.

Townsend, Joseph. 1791. *A Journey through Spain in the years 1786 and 1787, with Particular Attention to the Agriculture, Manufacture, Commerce, Population, Taxes, and Revenue of that Country*. 3 vols. London: C. Dilly.

Tully, Mark, and Satish Jacob. 1985. *Amritsar: Mrs. Gandhi's Last Battle*. London: Jonathan Cape.

Washbrook, David. 1981. "Law, State and Agrarian Society in Colonial India." *Modern Asian Studies* 15 (3): 649–721.

# 2 | The Command of Language and the Language of Command

BERNARD S. COHN

The records generated by the East India Company—in their published form found in series such as *The Letters Received from Its Servants in the East* and *The Fort William–India House Correspondence* and in manuscript records stored in the National Archives of India and the India Office Library and Records—are the primary sources utilized by all historians to reconstruct the facts of the British conquest of India and the construction of the institutions of colonial rule. These archival publications are a tribute to the extraordinary labors of thousands of employees of the Company who produced this seemingly endless store of information. These records are tribute in another sense of the word as well. To quote *Webster's Collegiate Dictionary* (1948), tribute is "a payment paid by one ruler or nation to another either as an acknowledgment of submission, or of the price of protection."

In this essay I argue that the tribute represented in print and manuscript is that of complicated and complex forms of knowledge created by Indians but codified and transmitted by Europeans. The conquest of India was a conquest of knowledge. In these official sources we can trace the changes in forms of knowledge which the conquerors defined as useful for their own ends. The records of the seventeenth and eighteenth centuries reflect the Company's central concerns with trade and commerce; one finds long lists of products, prices, information about trade routes, descriptions of coastal and inland marts, and political information about the Mughal Empire, and especially local officials and their actions in relation to the Company. Scattered through these records are mentions of names and functions of Indians who were employed by the Company or with whom it was associated, on whom the British were dependent for the information and knowledge to carry out their commercial ventures.

The anglicized titles of some of these functionaries include *akhund, banian* (trader or moneylender), *dalal, dubashi, gomastah, pandit, shroff,* and *vakil.* The titles varied with the location of the Company's factories, but the Indians bearing these titles all had specialized forms of knowledge, some about prices and values of currencies, the sources of specialized products, locations of markets, and the networks along which trade goods flowed; others knew about local and imperial governments, diplomatic and political rules, and the personalities of the rulers on whom the British were dependent for protection. All of these specialists were multilingual and had command of specialized languages necessary for the various levels of communication between foreigners and Indians. The dubashi of the Coromandel coast had his function embodied in his title, which means "two languages." In Bengal, the akhund, sometimes referred to as "Muhammadan school teacher," was employed in "composing, writing and interpreting all letters and writings in the Persian language."[1] The akhund was frequently trusted with diplomatic missions as well as with delivering letters and various documents to Mughal officials. Vakils were confidential agents who, like the akhunds, were frequently involved in negotiations with Indian officials and were not only Persian-using but had to be familiar with court formalities and personalities. They frequently advised the Company officials on courses of action in relation to the Company's continuing need to negotiate various legal and commercial matters with the Mughal state.

During the decade of the 1670s in Surat, the Company carried on repeated diplomatic negotiations with the Maratha ruler, Shivaji, seeking reparations for property lost in his attack on the Company's factory at Rajapur and seeking to establish trading rights in Shivaji's territories. The Company was well served during this period by a number of Indians, especially two brothers, Rama Shenvi, a Portuguese writer, and Narayan Shenvi, the Company's linguist.[2]

Almost from the inception of their trading efforts in India, the British had sought legitimacy and protection from Indian rulers, primarily the Mughal emperor. To this end in 1615 Sir Thomas Roe was dispatched to the Mughal's court jointly by the Company and James I to obtain a treaty or pact that would guarantee "constant love and peace" between the two monarchs.[3] Roe read the political world in which he found himself in terms of his own system of meanings; it was one that he thought compelled him to undergo a "thousand indignities unfit for a quality that represents a Kings Person," and in which he could not accomplish his ends "without base creeping and bribing." Roe was plagued by a lack of knowledge of Persian, the court language, and did not have anyone whom he thought he could trust to translate properly the letters he had brought from his king, which were to be presented to Jahangir. Roe complained to his employers, "Another terrible inconvenience that I suffer: want of an interpreter. For the Broker's here will not speak but what shall please; yea they would alter the Kings letter because his name was before the Mughals, which I would not allow."[4]

Roe employed as interpreters at various times during his stay at the court of Jahangir a Greek, an Armenian, an eccentric Englishman, and on at least one occasion an Italian who knew Turkish but no Persian. Roe spoke to this interpreter in Spanish, a language he had learned in the Caribbean; the Italian then would translate this into Turkish for an officer of Jahangir's court who knew both Turkish and Persian.[5]

The British realized that in seventeenth-century India Persian was the crucial language for them to learn. They approached Persian as a kind of functional language, a pragmatic vehicle of communication with Indian officials and rulers through which, in a denotative fashion, they could express their requests, queries, and thoughts, and through which they could get things done. To use Persian well required highly specialized forms of knowledge, particularly to draft the many forms of documents that were the basis of official communication throughout much of India. Persian as a language was part of a much larger system of meanings, which was in turn based on cultural premises that were the basis of action. The meanings and the premises on which the Indians constructed actions were far different from those of the British.

Europeans of the seventeenth century lived in a world of signs and correspondences, whereas Indians lived in a world of substances. Roe interpreted the court ritual of the Mughals in which he was required to participate as a sign of debasement rather than an act of incorporation in a substantive fashion, which made him a companion of the ruler. Relations between persons, groups, "nations" (qaum), and between ruler and ruled were constituted differently in Europe and India. The British in seventeenth-century India operated on the idea that everything and everyone had a "price." The presents through which relationships were constituted were seen as a form of exchange to which a quantitative value could be attached and which could be translated into a price. Hence, the cloth that was the staple of their trade was seen as a utilitarian object whose value was set in a market. They never seemed to realize that certain kinds of cloth and clothes, jewels, arms, and animals had values that were not established in terms of a market-determined price, but were objects in a culturally constructed system by which authority and social relations were literally constituted and transmitted.

Hindus and Muslims operated with an unbounded substantive theory of objects and persons. The body of the ruler was literally his authority, the substance of which could be transmitted in what Europeans thought of as objects. Clothes, weapons, jewels, and paper were the means by which a ruler could transmit the substance of his authority to a chosen companion. To be in the gaze or sight of one who is powerful, to receive food from or hear sounds emitted by a superior, was to be affected by that person.

Meaning for the English was something attributed to a word, a phrase, or an object, which could be determined and translated, at best with a synonym that had a direct referent to something in what the English thought of as a "natural" world. Everything had a more or less specific referent for the English. With the Indians, meaning was not necessarily construed in the same fashion. The effect and affect of hearing a Brahman chant in Sanskrit at a sacrifice did not entail meaning in the European sense; it was to have one's substance literally affected by the sound. When a Mughal ruler issued a *farman* or a *parvana*, it was more than an order or an entitlement. These were more than messages or, as the British construed them, a contract or right. Rather, they were a sharing in the authority and substance of the originator, through the act of creating the document. Hence in drawing up a document, a letter, or a treaty, everything about it was charged with a significance that transcended what might be thought of as its practical purpose. The paper, the forms of address, the preliminary phrases of invocation, the type of script, the elaboration of the terminology, the grammar, the seals used, the particular status of the composer and writer of the document, its mode of transportation, and the form of delivery—all were meaningful.[6]

The British mode of living in India provided cultural blocks to their acquisition of knowledge beyond their problem with language. From the middle of the seventeenth to the middle of the eighteenth centuries there were comparatively few covenanted servants of the Company. In 1665 there were one hundred Company officials in India,[7] in 1740 approximately 170;[8] in

1756, on the eve of the Battle of Plassey, there were 224.[9] The majority of the Company's servants lived in the cosmopolitan port cities, generally within the confines of their factories. Most of their social contacts were with other Europeans. The Indians who worked for them as domestic and commercial servants appear to have known some English or Portuguese, the coastal trade language of India. Most British found they could manage their affairs with these languages and with some knowledge of a pidgin version of "Moors," the lingua franca of India. Most of the Company servants lived for a limited time in India, some succumbing to disease or serving, as was the practice in the Company, for five years and then returning to Great Britain. The Europeans most likely to have known Indian languages well were the Portuguese, and "country-born" Europeans, many of whom were engaged in small-scale trading activities or found employment with the East India Company in subordinate positions. The directors looked with suspicion on this latter category, as they felt they were untrustworthy and likely to put their own interests ahead of those of the Company.

In 1713, when the Company wished to obtain a farman (royal order) from the Mughal Empire to reduce taxes on their internal trade in India and to make permanent a whole series of grants they had received at various times from the Mughal, they had no one in their Bengal establishment who knew sufficient Persian to carry out the negotiations, and had to depend upon an Armenian merchant for that vital function. John Surman, head of the embassy, eventually learned Persian, but not before their interpreter had led them into a number of difficulties. Their embassy was successful, but Surman died soon after his return to Calcutta and knowledge of Persian went with him.

It was not until the 1740s and 1750s that any significant number of officials of the Company knew any of the Indian languages, a result of more and more of them serving up-country in Company stations and having longer and longer careers in India. James Fraser, who was in the Surat establishment for nineteen years, learned Persian well enough to write a contemporary history of the court of Nadir Shah, based on a Persian account and "constant correspondence" with Persians and Mughals. He had learned his Persian from a Parsi, and had studied with a scholar who was famous for his knowledge of Muslim law in Cambay.[10]

In midcentury there were increasing numbers of British officials with knowledge of Persian and what the British termed "Indostan" or "Moors," as well as other "vulgar" languages of India. Warren Hastings had learned Persian and Moors while serving in Kassimbazar in commercial and diplomatic positions.[11] J. Z. Howell knew enough Bengali or "Indostan" to serve as judge of the zamindar's (landholder's) court in Calcutta and, at the time of the capture of Calcutta by Siraj-ud-daula, was translating into English an Indostan version of a "shastra" (sacred Hindu text). Those British immediately involved in the negotiations that led to the overthrow of the nawab of Bengal—William Watts, Henry Vansittart, and Luke Scrafton—were linguistically well enough equipped to outwit even such a canny political operator as Omichand. The architect of the Bengal revolution, Robert Clive, however, appears not to have known any Indian language except the Portuguese trade language, and he was dependent on his banian, Nubkissen, for translating and interpreting in his dealings with Indian rulers.[12] The British success at Plassey and the subsequent appropriation of the revenues of Bengal were to provide the impetus for more and more British civilians and military officers to learn one or more of the Indian languages.

### Indian Languages and the Creation
### of a Discursive Formation

The years 1770 to 1785 may be looked upon as the formative period during which the British successfully began the program of appropriating Indian languages to serve as a crucial component in their construction of the system of rule. More and more British officials were learning the "classical" languages of India (Sanskrit, Persian, and Arabic), as well as many of the "vulgar" languages. More importantly, this was the period in which the British were beginning to produce an apparatus: grammars, dictionaries, treatises, class books, and translations about and from the languages of India.[13] The argument of this essay is that the production of these texts and others that followed them began the establishment of discursive formation, defined an epistemological space, created a discourse (orientalism), and had the effect of converting Indian forms of knowledge into European objects. The subjects of these texts were first and foremost the Indian languages themselves, re-presented in European terms as grammars, dictionaries, and teaching aids in a project to make the acquisition of a working knowledge of the languages available to those British who were to be part of the ruling groups of India.

Some of these texts, such as Balfour's *Herkern* and Gladwin's *Ayeen*, were to be guidebooks—the one to the epistolary practice of professional scribes, the other to the administrative practices of the Mughal Empire. The translations of Dow and Davy of Persian chronicles were intended to be expositions of the political practices and the failures of the imperial predecessors of the British conquerors. Halhed's *Gentoo Laws* and Wilkins's *Geeta* were translations thought to be keys with which to unlock, and hence make available, knowledge of Indian law and religion held tightly by the "mysterious" Brahmans.

Seen as a corpus, these texts signal the invasion of an epistemological space occupied by a great number of diverse Indian scholars, intellectuals, teachers, scribes, priests, lawyers, officials, merchants, and bankers, whose knowledge as well as they themselves were to be converted into instruments of colonial rule. They were now to become part of the army of *babus*, clerks, interpreters, subinspectors, *munshis* (language instructors), *pandits*, *qazis*, *vakils*, schoolmasters, *amins*, *sharistadars*, *tahsildars*, *deshmukhs*, *darogahs*, and *mamlatdars* who, under the scrutiny and supervision of the white sahibs, ran the everyday affairs of the Raj.

The knowledge that this small group of British officials sought to control was to be the instrumentality through which they were to issue commands and collect ever-increasing amounts of information. This information was needed to create or locate cheap and effective means to assess and collect taxes, and maintain law and order; and it served as a way to identify and classify groups within Indian society. Elites had to be found within Indian society who could be made to see that they had an interest in the maintenance of British rule. Political strategies and tactics had to be created and codified into diplomacy through which the country's powers could be converted into allied dependencies. The vast social world that was India had to be classified, categorized, and bounded before it could be ordered. As with many discursive formations and their discourses, many of its major effects were unintended, as those who were to be the objects produced by the formation often turned it to their own ends. Nonetheless, the languages that the Indians spoke and read were to be transformed. The discursive formation was to participate in the creation and reification of social groups with their varied interests. It was to establish and regularize a discourse of differentiations that came to mark the social and political map of nineteenth-century India.

I have chosen to utilize a mode of exposition that is obviously influenced by the work of Michel Foucault. My effort will be to try to locate the kinds of questions his work directs us toward by rehearsing a history, much of which is familiar to students of India's past. It recounts some of the details of how the English, during the period from roughly 1770 to 1820, went about learning Indian languages, and how they developed a pedagogical and scholarly apparatus for this purpose. It does not aim to be complete, nor will it even deal with what might be thought of as its most important texts, its most famous leading figures, or its most important institutions, such as the College of Fort William and the College at Fort St. George.

## Persian: The Language of Indian Politics

A knowledge of Persian was needed immediately after the Battle of Plassey to recruit and train an Indian army and to develop a system of alliances and treaties with native independent princes and powers so as to protect "the rich and fertile territories" in Coromandel, upper India, and Bengal that the Company had conquered.[14] William Davy, who as a military officer in the Bengal army had found a knowledge of Persian highly lucrative, thought that the important job of translation could not be entrusted to Indian interpreters. In describing the talent needed for this important task, he wrote, "A Persian interpreter should not only be able to speak fluently in the language, but to read all such letters as he may receive, . . . to answer them with his own hand, if the importance of the subject, of which they treat should render it necessary. Otherwise the secret negotiations and correspondence of government are liable to be made public through the medium of the native Munchees, or writers, whom he will be obliged to employ and trust."[15]

Davy appears to have learned his Persian from a munshi, and without the aid of a Persian–English dictionary or grammar. The only dictionary of Persian then known was one in Latin by Franciscus Meninski, which was so scarce in India that Davy paid one hundred guineas for a copy he found in Calcutta in 1773. This was not much use to him, as Meninski, Davy thought, did not know Persian but did have an extensive knowledge of Turkish, on which he based his Arabic, Turkish, and Persian lexicon. The result, Davy felt, was that "words in one language, bearing a variety of significations, are given through the medium of words in another, having also various meanings, and many directly contradictory, were translated by words in a third, which in many significations, differs totally from both."[16]

There had been a chair in Arabic established at Oxford in the late seventeenth century and there were on the Continent a few scholars of Persian who, according to Sir William Jones, "had confined their studies to minute researches of verbal criticism." Jones further complained that the learned "have no taste, and the men of taste, have no learning." There was no patronage for literary and scholarly research on Oriental languages. Jones wrote that Meninski's work may have immortalized him as a savant, but it ruined him financially. Jones thought the Persian language "rich, melodious and elegant," with important works in poetry and history, which was due for a great interest now that India had become "the source of incredible wealth to the merchants of Europe."[17] Jones wrote, "The servants of the company received letters they could not read and were ambitious of gaining titles of which they could not comprehend the meaning; it was found highly dangerous to employ the natives as interpreters, upon whose fidelity they could not depend; and it was at last discovered that they must apply themselves to the study of the Persian language.... The languages of Asia will now perhaps be studied with uncommon ardour; they are known to be useful, and will soon be found to be instructive and entertaining."[18]

Sir William Jones's *Grammar of the Persian Language*, published in London in 1771, was very successful and went through six editions by 1804. Although it was recommended by the Court of Directors to their employees, they did not subsidize it, as they did many subsequent publications on Indian languages.

In constructing his *Grammar*, Jones was centrally interested in Persian poetry, and the descriptive statements on which the grammatical rules were based were "poetry composed in the Shiraz literary 'dialect' between the tenth and fifteenth centuries A.D."[19] The *Grammar* provided for its time a useful description of the phonology, morphology, and syntax of the language Jones was describing.[20]

Jones supplied his readers with advice on how to learn Persian, which was premised on the availability of a native speaker. The student should learn to read the characters with fluency and "learn the true pronunciation of every letter from the mouth of a native." Jones recommended using Meninski's dictionary but warned the learner that "he must not neglect to converse with his living instructor and to learn from him the phrases of common discourse."[21]

After six months, Jones recommended, the student should move on to reading "some elegant History or poem with an intelligent native." He should get his munshi to transcribe a section of the Gulistan or a fable of Cashefi, "the common broken hand used in India." In a year's time, the reader was assured, if he worked according to Jones's plan, he would be able to "translate and to answer any letter from an Indian Prince, and to converse with the natives of India not only with fluency but with elegance." However, if he aspires to be "an eminent translator," he will have to learn Arabic as well, "which is blended with the Persian in so singular a manner." Another benefit for the would-be official of the East India Company was a knowledge of "the jargon of Indostan, very improperly called the language of the Moors," which, Jones reports, "contains so great a number of Persian words that I was able, with little difficulty, to read the fables of Pilpai, which are translated into that idiom."[22]

The prestige of Persian as the best language for an ambitious cadet or junior writer continued into the early nineteenth century. Warren Hastings, who had lobbied unsuccessfully in 1765 for the establishment of a chair in Persian at Oxford,[23] vigorously argued that Persian and Arabic should be the keystone of the curriculum at the newly established College at Fort William:

> To the Persian language as being the medium of all Political intercourse the first place ought to be assigned in the studies of the Pupils; and as much of the Arabic as is necessary to shew the principles of its construction and the variations which the sense of the radical word derives from its inflections, to complete their knowledge of the Persian, which in its modern dialect consists in a great measure of the Arabic. . . . The Persian language ought to be studied to perfection, and is requisite to all the civil servants of the Company, as it may also prove of equal use to the Military Officers of all the Presidencies.[24]

Through the first fifteen years of the college, the Persian Department was the most prestigious and best supported. Those young officials who did well in Persian were frequently slated for the best beginning jobs, which often led to lucrative and influential positions in the central secretariat in Calcutta. In addition, it would appear that, as Persian and Arabic were the "classical languages" of India, they were worthy to be studied by gentlemen whose English education stressed the learning of the European classical languages, Latin and Greek, as the emblem of an educated man fitted thereby to rulership.

## Sanskrit: The Language of Indian Law and Lore

In India the other "classical" language, Sanskrit, was seen by the seventeenth- and eighteenth-century British as a secret language "invented by the Brahmins to be a mysterious repository for their religion and philosophy."[25] There was considerable curiosity about the religion of the Gentoos among the Europeans, and there had been scattered and discontinuous efforts to learn Sanskrit, particularly by Catholic missionaries in the seventeenth century, of which the British in the eighteenth century seemed unaware. James Fraser, J. Z. Howell, and Alexander Dow had all made unsuccessful efforts to learn Sanskrit. What knowledge the British had of the learning and religious thought of the Hindus came from discussions with Brahmans and other high-caste Indians, or from Persian or "Indostan" translations of Sanskrit texts.

John Z. Howell, who in his thirty years' experience in India had learned Persian, Bengali, and Indostan, wrote an extended account of the "religious Tenets of the Gentoos," published in 1767.[26] This account was based on an unidentified "Gentoo *Shastah*" (shastra), which he was translating at the time of Siraj-ud-daula's capture of Calcutta in 1756. At this time Howell lost "curious manuscripts" as well as a translation of a Hindustani version of a shastra. He also alluded to conferences with "many of the most learned and ingenious amongst the laity."[27]

Howell criticized all his predecessors' views that the Hindus were "a race of stupid and gross idolaters." Most of the more recent accounts of the Hindus, he argued, were by those of the "Romish communion," who had a vested interest in denigrating Hindus, as they wanted to convert them to Catholicism. Howell stigmatized Roman Catholic religious tenets as more idolatrous than those of the Hindus. He castigated not only "Popish authors" but also most others who had written only on the "exterior manners and religion" of the Hindus. The casual observer or traveler, Howell suggested, had to get beyond "his own ignorance, superstition and partiality" and the provincialism involved in thinking that anything "beyond the limits of their native land" was greatly inferior to their own. He castigated a travel writer as superficial:

His telling us such and such a people, in the East or West-Indies, worship this stick, or that stone, or monstrous idol; only serves to reduce in our esteem, our fellow creatures, to the most abject and despicable point of light. Whereas, was he skilled in the language of the people he describes, sufficiently to trace the etymology of their words and phrases, and capable of diving into the mysteries of their theology; he would probably be able to evince us, that such seemingly preposterous worship, had the most sublime rational source and foundation.

The traveller, who without these essential requisites, (as well as industry and a clear understanding) pretends to describe and fix the religious tenets of any nation whatever, dishonestly imposes his own reveries on the world, and does the greatest injury and violence to letters, and the cause of humanity.[28]

The motivation for the British in India to learn Sanskrit had a dual basis: at one and the same time there was a scholarly curiosity to unlock the mysterious knowledge of the ancients, and an immediate practical necessity fueled by Warren Hastings's plan of 1772 for the better government of Bengal. In writing to the Court of Directors explaining this plan, he stated that it would establish the Company's system of governance on a "most equitable, solid and permanent footing." The plan was based on "principles of experience and common observation, without the advantages which an intimate knowledge of the theory of law might have afforded us: We have endeavoured to adapt our Regulations to the Manners and Understandings of the People, and the Exigencies of the Country, adhering as closely as we are able to their ancient uses and Institutions."[29]

In Hastings's plan the theory was clear: Indians should be governed by Indian principles, particularly in relation to law. The practical question arose as to how the British were to gain knowledge of the "ancient uses and institutions." The answer was easy enough to state. The Hindus, Hastings averred, "had been in possession of laws which continued unchanged, from remotest antiquity." These laws, he wrote, were in the hands of Brahmans, or "professors of law," found all over India, who were supported by "public endowments and benefactions from every and all people." The professor received a "degree of personal respect amounting almost to idolatry."[30] In each of the criminal courts established, the qazi, *mufti* (Islamic law expert), and two *maulavis* (Muslim religious leaders) "were to expound the laws, and to determine how far the delinquents shall be guilty of a breach thereof." In the civil courts, "suits regarding inheritance, Marriage, caste and other religious usages and institutions, the Laws of the Koran with respect to Mahometans, and those of the Shaster with respect to the Gentoos shall be invariably adhered to."[31]

For officers of a commercial company it was clearly the laws that the civil courts were to administer that were most crucial, as they dealt with disputes "concerning property, whether real or personal, all cases of inheritance, marriage and caste; all claims of debt, disputed accounts, contracts, partnerships and demands of rent."[32] Through this plan, the Company's government was to become the guarantor of what Hastings and the other eighteenth-century British saw as the basic rights of Indians, oddly enough in a polity that was supposed to be despotic and hence without such rights.

In his discussion of his plans, Hastings was translating for a British audience theories and practices from one culture to another. India had an ancient constitution which was expressed in what came to be thought of as two codes, one Hindu and the other Muslim. Pandits were "professors," and some even came to be conceived of as "lawyers." For the demonstration of law there were also experts—qazis, or "judges"—who knew the appropriate codes to apply to particular cases. Following the current practice in Bengal, which was ruled by Muslims, the British accepted Muslim criminal law as the law of the land, but civil law was to be Hindu for Hindus and Muslim for Muslims. The decision of Hastings and the Council at Fort William was to have profound effects on the course of the judicial system in India.[33]

If the British were to administer Hindu law with the guidance and assistance of Hindu "law officers" (pandits), they had to establish some fixed body of this law, one that they hoped could become authoritative and that could be translated into English so that the judges would have some idea of the nature and content of this law.

In order to establish what the Hindu law was, Warren Hastings persuaded eleven of the "most respectable pandits in Bengal" to make a compilation of the relevant shastric literature. He appointed N. B. Halhed to supervise this compilation and to translate the resulting text into English.[34] Halhed described the manner in which the text was compiled and translated:

> The professors of the ordinances here collected still speak an original language in which they were composed. . . . A set of the most experienced of these lawyers was selected from every part of Bengal for the purpose of compiling the present work, which they picked out sentence by sentence

from various originals in the Shanscrit language, neither adding to, nor diminishing any part of the ancient text. The articles thus collected were next translated literally into Persian, under the inspection of one of their own body; and from that translation were rendered into English with an equal attention to the closeness and fidelity of the version.[35]

The compilation was known in Sanskrit as the *Vivadarnavasetu* (bridge across the sea of litigation). The manner in which the translation was made, and the authoritative nature of the compilation, came into question within the next fifteen years. Halhed had only a very limited knowledge of Sanskrit and depended on Bengali or Hindustani explanations of passages in the text by the pandits, which discussions were then abstracted into Persian by a munshi, and from this Halhed did the final translation into English.[36]

Sir William Jones, who had been appointed judge in the Supreme Court of Judicature in 1783, thought the *Gentoo Code* was like a Roman law digest, consisting of "authentic texts with short notes taken from commentaries of high authority." He praised the work as far as it went, but it was too diffuse, "rather curious than useful," and the section on the law of contracts was too "succinct and superficial." But if the Sanskrit text itself was faulted, the translation, he felt, was useless:

> But, whatever be the merit of the original, the translation of it has no au-
> thority, and is of no other use than to suggest inquiries on the many dark
> passages, which we find in it: properly speaking, indeed, we cannot call
> it a translation; for, though Mr. Halhed performed his part with fidelity,
> yet the Persian interpreter had supplied him only with a loose injudicious
> epitome of the original Sanscrit, in which abstract many essential passages
> are omitted. . . . All this I say with confidence, having already perused no
> small part of the original with a learned Pandit, comparing it, as I pro-
> ceeded, with the English version.[37]

On his arrival in Calcutta, Jones had no plans to undertake the study of Sanskrit; he complained to Wilkins, "Life is too short and my necessary business too long for me to think of acquiring a new language."[38] His curiosity about Indian thought and his role as a judge of the Crown Court in Calcutta, however, led him to undertake the task of learning Sanskrit. After he had been in India less than a year, Jones journeyed to Banaras, where he met maulavis, pandits, and rajas, among whom was Ali Ibrahim Khan, long regarded by the British as a distinguished scholar and judge. Jones had hoped to obtain from Khan a Persian translation of the "Dherm Shastr Menu Smrety," which was considered to be the authentic source of Hindu law. Although Khan obtained a Sanskrit text, Manu's *Dharmashastra*, the pandits refused to assist him in translating it into Persian.[39]

Jones became increasingly frustrated in having to depend on defective Persian translations of Hindu law books. He reported to William Pitt the Younger in February 1785 that he was almost "tempted to learn Sanskrit, that I may check on the pandits in the Court."[40] A month later he was complaining to Wilkins that "it was of the utmost importance that the stream of Hindu law should be pure: for we are entirely at the devotion of the native lawyers, through our ignorance of Sanskrit."[41] In September 1785 Jones had gone to Nadiya, a center of Sanskrit learning sixty miles north of Calcutta on the Hugli River, where he hoped "to learn the rudiments of that venerable and interesting language."[42] In October he was back in Calcutta with the "father of the University of Nadya," who, Jones explained, was not a Brahman but who had instructed young Brahman students in grammar and ethics. He would serve Jones's purpose as a teacher, as he lacked the "priestly pride" that marked his students.[43] A year later Jones could report that he was "tolerably strong in Sanskrit" and getting ready to translate a law tract ascribed to "Menu, the Minos of India."[44]

By October 1786, Jones had considerable confidence in his own knowledge of Sanskrit, for he was correcting his own court pandits' interpretations of legal texts by translating to his own satisfaction "the original tracts" on which they based their decisions.[45] He was now to go on to plan a much bigger project that he believed would free the British judges in India from dependence on what he thought was the venality and corruption of the Indian interpreters of Hindu and Muslim law. This was the exact counterpart of the effort a few decades earlier by the British to free themselves, through knowledge of Persian, from the akhunds, munshis, and kayasthas who translated and interpreted political documents. Jones now proposed to compile from the best available sources a digest of Hindu and Muslim law, which could then be translated into English and which would provide the European judges a "check upon the native interpreters." Jones wanted a means by which the "laws of the natives" could be preserved inviolate and the decrees of the courts made to conform to "Hindu and Mahomedan law."[46]

If the system that Jones hoped to see implemented was to succeed, it would require that several forms of knowledge become codified and public. The English judges and other officials would require access to what Jones and others believed at the time was "*the* Hindu and *the* Mahomedan law," which was locked up in the texts and the heads of pandits and maulavis. There had to be found a fixed body of knowledge that could be objectified into Hindu and Muslim law. This body of knowledge could be specified, set into hierarchies of knowledge, linearly ordered from the most "sacred" or compelling to the less powerful.

Jones and others had the idea that there was historically in India a fixed body of laws, codes, which had been set down or established by "law givers," which over time had become corrupted by accretions, interpretations, and commentaries, and it was this jungle of accretions and corruptions of the earlier pure codes that was controlled in the present by those Indians whom the British thought of as the Indian lawyers. An *ur*-text had to be found or reconstituted, which at one and the same time would establish *the* Hindu and Muslim law as well as free the English from dependency for interpretations and knowledge on fallible and seemingly overly susceptible pandits and maulavis. The task had also to be accomplished somehow by using the knowledge that their Indian guides, the mistrusted pandits and maulavis, seemed to monopolize. Jones, even before arriving in India, seemed to distrust Indian scholars' interpretations of their own legal traditions—a distrust that grew with experience in India. He wrote Cornwallis, the governor general, in 1788, that he could not with "an easy conscience, concur in a decision, merely on the written opinion of native lawyers in any case, in which they could have the remotest interest in misleading the court."[47] Jones wanted to provide the English courts in India, Crown and Company, with a sure basis on which they could render decisions consonant with a "true" or "pure" version of Hindu law. Then the pandits, Brahmans, and Indian "lawyers," Jones believed, henceforth could not "deal out Hindoo law as they please, and make it at reasonable rates, when they cannot find it ready made."[48]

In advocating his ambitious plan for a digest of Hindu and Muslim law, Jones deployed a discourse that made a direct connection between the British future in India and the late classical Roman past. In discussing his plans, he explained that his mode of proceeding would be that of Tribonian, the compiler of the Justinian code, with only "original texts arranged in a scientific method."[49] The main subject of the digests would be the laws of contract and inheritance and, as Jones was again and again to reiterate, these subjects were at the heart of the establishment of rights in property, "real and personal."[50]

Jones did not live to see the completion of his ambition to become the Tribonian of India, but to this day he stands in stone in St. Paul's Cathedral, a statue commissioned by the Court of Directors, dressed in a toga, with pen in hand and leaning on two volumes that are "understood to mean the Institutes of Menu."[51] Visual reminders of the British as Romans can still be found in the gardens of the Victoria Memorial, where we find Warren Hastings in the toga of a Roman senator, standing above a Brahman pandit with a palm-leaf manuscript, and a Muslim maulavi poring over a Persian manuscript.

### Classical Models and the Definition of the "Vulgar" Languages of India

N. B. Halhed, the translator of the *Gentoo Code* and author of the first English grammar of Bengali, drew heavily on analogies between the eighteenth-century English in India and the Romans. His grammar was part of a large project that would stabilize and perpetuate British rule in Bengal. The "English masters of Bengal," wrote Halhed in 1778, needed to add its language to their acquisitions, like the Romans, "people of little learning and less taste," who applied themselves to the study of Greek once they had conquered Greece. So the British in Bengal needed to cultivate a language that would be the "medium of intercourse between the Government and its subjects, between the natives of Europe who are to rule, and the inhabitants of India who are to obey." In addition, the English needed to know the language to explain "the benevolent principles" of the legislation that they were "to enforce."[52]

The British in late eighteenth-century Bengal found what was for them a complex language situation. Few of the British knew Bengali; rather, they used "Moors" and Persian in many of their transactions. This reflected the language use of many of their Indian associates and subordinates.

H. P. Foster, who produced an English–Bengali and a Bengali–English dictionary between 1799 and 1802, provided a hypothetical example of the results of dependence on Persian in the courts of Bengal at the time. A Dom—who, he informed his readers, is from "the lowest and most illiterate classes"—goes to a darogah, a minor police official, to make a complaint. According to Foster, the darogah's knowledge of Persian was restricted to reading *Tales of the Parrot*, a popular class book of the time. The Dom delivers his complaint in the "vulgar" dialect of Bengali, and gets it written down by the police official in "bad Bongalee in Persian characters with here and there a mangled Persian phrase." This document may then get translated into Persian, and finally, if the case makes its way up to the Nizamat Adalat, the documents that have accumulated are translated into English.[53] If the British learned Bengali, says Foster, it was because it was the language spoken around the major cities, such as Murshidabad, Dacca, and Calcutta, which were the "seats of foreign governments and the rendezvous of all nations," where the language spoken was much influenced by "Hindostanee of Moors," and this was the language that the British adapted as their "medium of communication" with the people of Bengal.[54]

William Carey observed that the Indian servant, personal and official, in speaking Bengali with Europeans "generally intermixes his language with words derived from the Arabic or Persian and with some few corrupted English and Portuguese words."[55] Carey warned his countrymen that dependence on poor interpreters and the continued use of the "jargon of Moors" limited their ability to deal directly with "men of great respectability" as well as the common folk of Bengal, who could "provide information on local affairs."[56]

The *Grammar* of the Bengali language that Halhed produced was organized in terms of European grammatical categories, the various chapters dealing with the parts of speech, elements and substantives, pronouns, verbs, words denoting attributes and relations, numerals, syntax, orthography, and versification. Halhed took pride in being the first European who related Bengali to Sanskrit: "The following work presents the Bengali language merely as derived from its parent Shanscrit," with all the words from the Persian and "Hindostanic" dialects expunged. He warned, though, that those who wanted to be accurate translators would have to study the Persian and "Hindostanic" dialects, "since in the occurrences of modern business, as managed by the present illiterate generation, he will find all his letters, representations and accounts interspersed with a variety of borrowed phrases or unauthorized expressions."[57] Halhed based his knowledge of Bengali grammar on "a pandit who imparted a small portion of his language to me" and readily "displayed the principles of his grammar."[58]

The speakers of pure "Hindostanic" are found in upper India and in western India, where they still use this language for purposes of commerce. Halhed drew an analogy between "Hindostanic" and Bengali:

> What the pure Hindostanic is to upper India, the language which I have here endeavoured to explain is to Bengal, intimately related to the Shanscrit both in expressions, construction and character. It is the sole channel of personal and epistolary communication among the Hindoos of every occupation and tribe. All their business is transacted, and all their accounts are kept in it; and as their system of education is in general very confined, there are few among them who can write or read any other idiom: the uneducated, or eight parts in ten of the whole nation are necessarily confined to the usage of their mother tongue.[59]

Halhed prefigured Jones's statement on the relation of Sanskrit to Latin and Greek. He was astonished "to find the similitude of Shanscrit words with those of Persian and Arabic, and even of Latin and Greek . . . in the main ground work of the language, in monosyllables, in the names of numbers, and the appellations of such things as would be discriminated at the immediate dawn of civilization."[60] He also commented that the "Hindostanic" dialect spoken over most of Hindostan proper was "indubitably derived from Shanscrit," with which it has exactly the same connection as the modern dialects of France and Italy with pure Latin.[61]

Another variety of "Hindostanic," wrote Halhed, was developed by the Muslim invaders of India, who could not learn the language spoken by the Hindus; the latter, in order to maintain the purity of their own tongue, introduced more and more abstruse terms from Sanskrit. The Muslims in turn introduced many "exotic" words from their own languages, which they superimposed on the "grammatical principles of the original Hindostanic." Halhed refers to this form of "Hindostanic" as a compound idiom that was spoken in Bengal by Hindus connected with Muslim courts. Those Brahmans and other well-educated Hindus "whose ambition has not overpowered their principles" continued to speak and write the pure form of "Hindostanic" and wrote it with Nagari characters rather than with the Arabic script.[62]

Halhed's introduction of the *Grammar* stands as a prime text that both summarizes and constitutes knowledge that the British were beginning to develop regarding Indian languages. It prefigures much that was to happen in the next thirty years. As a classically educated man, he was concerned to find general principles about Indian languages, and these were to be found in Sanskrit, the treasury of knowledge about India. Languages for the English were to be learned for practical reasons, but this was best done through some knowledge of the "classical" languages that underlay the contemporary dialects, jargons, vernaculars, and idioms.

Halhed's view that the languages currently spoken in Bengal and upper India were "fallen," "broken," or "corrupt" versions of some "pure," "authentic," coherent, logically formed prior language was one shared, of course, by his Hindu and Muslim instructors, who frequently were contemptuous of the spoken languages and favored the sacred and literary languages of Sanskrit, Arabic, and Persian.

### The Establishment of Hindustani as the
### British Language of Command

Until the late part of the eighteenth century, the British in India had done little to study systematically the wide variety of languages spoken in India. Portuguese, German, and Danish missionaries, as well as the Company's Dutch and French trade rivals, had produced grammars and dictionaries of one or another of the Indian languages. The British appear to have been ignorant of these efforts. The classifications of the Indian languages used by the British were vague and shifting, reflecting both geography and function. "Malabar" referred to the language spoken by fishermen and boatmen on both the Malabar and Coromandel coasts, and was by extension used as a label for the language spoken in what is today Tamil Nadu. "Gentu" or "Telinga" was found in what is Andhra, but was also widely diffused in south India, reflecting the presence as mercenaries of large numbers of Telingas in the south Indian armies. "Banian" was at times used to refer to Gujarati, reflecting the fact that many of the merchants on the west coast were Gujaratis. Calcutta, Bombay, and Madras were heterogeneous and polyglot cities. In the light of the political history of the seventeenth and eighteenth centuries, the British regarded Marathi, Persian, and "Moors" as important languages in south India.[63]

From their first exposure to the Mughal court, the British were aware of the central importance of the language spoken there and elsewhere in India. Reverend Terry, who accompanied Sir Thomas Roe, described the language thus: "The language of this Empire, I mean the vulgar, bears the name of it, and is called Indostan; it hath much affinitie with the Persian and Arabian tongue . . . a language which is very significant, and speaks much in a few words. It is expressed by letters which are different than those alphabets by which the Persian and Arabic tongues are formed."[64]

For the next two hundred years this language or variants thereof carried a bewildering variety of labels: Moors, Indostan, Hindoostanic, Hindowee, Nagreeo, and Koota. Most generally the British labeled it "Moors," and pejoratively referred to it as a jargon.[65]

In the period immediately after the Battle of Plassey, even before there were published grammars for this language, notes and manuscripts were circulating as aids for the Company's officers, particularly military ones, to acquire a working knowledge of it. The first grammar of Moors published in England was that of Edward Hadley, an officer in the Bengal army who had found it "impossible to discharge my duties . . . without a knowledge of the corrupt dialect" spoken by those troops he was to command. Hadley rejected the prevalent idea of the "Eastern Literate" that Moors was so irregular that it did not have a grammar. He demonstrated that the verbs in Moors were not declined as they were in Persian, and that its grammar was derived from some other language which, he speculated, was derived from India's northern invaders, the Tartars.[66] Hadley's grammar, revised by a number of authors, was to go through seven editions by 1809, at which time it was superseded by a series of works by John Borthwick Gilchrist, who is generally regarded as the creator of what was to become the British language of command in India—Hindustani.

In 1782, at the age of twenty-three, after studying medicine in Edinburgh, John Gilchrist arrived in Bombay, where he obtained an appointment as an assistant surgeon and was attached to a regiment in the Bengal army.[67] Gilchrist wrote that on his arrival at Bombay in 1782, "I instantly foresaw that my residence, in any capacity, would prove as unpleasant to myself, as unprofitable to my employers, until I acquired an adequate knowledge of the current language of the country, in which I was now to sojourn. I therefore sat resolutely down to acquire what was then termed as the *Moors*. . . . During the march with the Bengal troops under the command of Col. Charles Morgan from Surat to Futigurh, I had innumerable instances in every town and village we visited of the universal currency of the language I had been learning."[68]

Within two years Gilchrist had left the army and was settled in Faizabad, where he grew a beard and "assumed for a period the dress of the natives." Here he began an effort to prepare, with the assistance of several "learned Hindoostanees" (a term, he was careful to point out, that referred to Hindus and Muslims alike in upper India), a dictionary and grammar of their language.[69] His associates could not supply him with a dictionary of their language, so he began to extract from them viva voce every known word in their voluminous tongue. He did this by instructing his munshis to furnish him with every signification they could possibly attach to such words as *a*, *ab*, *abab*, *abach*, and so on. The syllables he wrote led the way to a "numerous tribe of words." He found this system of establishing a corpus for his dictionary too cumbersome and resorted to using Johnson's English dictionary. Gilchrist would explain the English term as best he could to the Hindustanis, who would then "furnish the synonymous vocables in their own speech."[70]

Gilchrist quickly discovered that his learned associates, rather than providing him with "the most easy, familiar and common words," would let their mind's eye roam for far-fetched expressions "from the deserts of Arabia, or they would be beating and scampering over the mountains of Persia." Others would search "in the dark intricate mines and caverns of Sanskrit lexicography." Not only did Gilchrist have difficulties with glossing, he kept insisting that there must be a written grammar of the language they were studying. His collaborators replied to his question with one of their own, asking "if it was ever yet known in any country that men had to consult vocabularies and rudiments for their own vernacular speech." Only after many inquiries did his colleagues produce a "Tom Thumb" performance, a *Khalig Baree*, which the Indians called a "vocabulary," but which Gilchrist slightingly referred to as "old meagre School vocabulary."[71]

What Gilchrist took to be the failure of his associates to take seriously their own vernacular speech, he attributed to the favorite British explanation of a conspiracy on the part of educated Indians to prevent the British from having access to the great mass of the Indian population. He theorized "that it is not at all improbable, that the cormorant crew of Dewans, Mootsuddies, Sirkars, Nazirs, Pundits, Munshis and a tremendous roll call of harpies who encompass power here see with jealous solicitude every attempt in their masters to acquire the means of immediate communication with the great mass of the people who those locusts of the land conceive their lawful prey."[72]

Why was Hindustani so badly studied, even ignored, by Gilchrist's European predecessors? Throughout the preface, he builds a complicated argument to answer this question. At base the problem was that the British labeled the language a "jargon," and conflated what Gilchrist began to call "Hindostanee" with what the majority of Europeans in India referred to as "Moors." Moors today would be termed a pidgin. Gilchrist thought of Moors as a "barbarian gabble [which] exists nowhere else but among the dregs of our servants, in the snip snap dialogues with us only. Even they would not degrade themselves by chattering the gibberish of the savage while conversing with or addressing each other in the capacity of human beings."[73]

### Gilchrist and the Definition of Hindustani

The Hindustani language has three levels or styles, which Gilchrist identified as the "High Court or Persian" style, the "Middle or Genuine Hindostanee" style, and the "vulgar of the Hinduwee."

The Court or Persian style is found in the elevated poems of Sauda, Vali, Mir Dard, and other poets. This is the "pompous and pedantic language of literature and politics," wrote Gilchrist, and it draws heavily on Arabic and Persian. The second level of Hindustani is what Gilchrist wanted to establish as the standard language, and it can be found in the elegy of "Miskeen, the satires of Sauda," and the translation of the articles of war. The third level, or the vulgar, is evidenced, Gilchrist wrote, "in Mr. Foster's translation of the Regulations of Government . . . in the greatest part of Hindostanee compositions written in the Nagaree character, in the dialect of the lower order of servants and Hindoos, as well as among the peasantry of Hindoostan."[74]

Gilchrist was very much aware that he was dealing with shadings, fluctuations, and a language that was evanescent. What made his task all the harder, he felt, was that those Indians, Hindu and Muslim, who professionally used languages and had a knowledge of them were dominated by what he felt was pedantry: "In a country where pedantry is esteemed [as] the touchstone of learning, the learned Moosulman glories in his Arabic and Persian. . . . The Hindoo is no less attached to Sunskrit and Hinduwee."[75]

Gilchrist explained the emergence and fixing of these language styles by constructing a history. He believed that before the "irruptions, and subsequent settlement of the Mossulmans there was a language spoken all over north India, referred to by Hindus as Brij Bhasa, a pure speech . . . the language of the Indian Arcadia." This language was referred to by the Muslims as "Hinduwee," the language of the Hindus. In his construction of a history of the Indian languages, Gilchrist compared Hinduwee to the language of the Saxons before their conquest by the French. Hinduwee, like Saxon, was then deluged by Arabic and Persian. After repeated invasions of Muslims, this resulted in the creation of the language that Gilchrist termed "Hindostanee." Muslims referred to this language as "Oorduwee" in its military form, "Rekhtu" in its poetical form, and "Hindee" as the everyday language of the Hindus.[76]

As a cover term for this language, Gilchrist chose the term "Hindostanee," which had a geographic referent, Hindustan. This could denote in the eighteenth century the whole of the South Asian peninsula or, in its more restricted sense, India north of the Vindhyas. Gilchrist intended through the use of the term "Hindostanee" to denote the contemporary spoken language of India, used by both Hindus and Muslims; he preferred it to labeling the language "Hindee," lest it be confused with Hinduwee, used exclusively by Hindus. For him it was a term like "British or European . . . a conciliating appellation for people in other matters very dissimilar, consequently the most applicable also to the grand popular connecting language of vast regions of the East."[77]

In Gilchrist's theory, Sanskrit, "the dead, sacred, mysterious tongue of the Hindoos," plays little part. He thought that Sanskrit was derived from Hinduwee, which was spoken over much of India before the Muslim invasions.[78] The other languages that he distinguished in north India were Bengalee, Rajpootee, and Poorbee (Bhoj Puri). He thought these languages were very different in both spoken and literary forms from the language he was classifying as Hindostanee. Other languages found in India included Dukhunee, the language spoken by Muslims in south India, Ooreea (Oriya), Mulwaree (Marwari), Goojaratee (Gujarati), Tilungee (Talinga, Telugu), and Kismeere (Kashmiri). These languages Gilchrist thought had been derived from Hinduwee, Brij Bhasha, or Bhakha. Gilchrist noted that the subdivisions of Indian languages were almost endless, with many local names. Some of the variations he thought of as varieties. Dukhunee and Punjabee were varieties of Hindostanee, whereas others, such as Bungal Bhasa, were specific dialects and, he implies, derived directly from the parent Hinduwee.[79]

Gilchrist theorized that there were "three grand indigenous languages which were to be found in India." Two were "orally current," Hinduwee and Hindostanee; the third was Sanskrit, "which really is the dead letter of civil and religious policy, is the consecrated palladium of science and the priest-craft among the Hindoos. The Hinduwee and Hindostanee have produced in the several kingdoms and states through which they range territorial varieties or dialects."[80]

The historical ordering of these three languages, Gilchrist speculated, was first Hinduwee, then Sanskrit, and most recently Hindostanee. Sanskrit was not a natural language but a "usurpation" on Hinduwee, a "cunning fabrication" of Hinduwee by "the insidious Bruhmans." The logic by which Gilchrist came to believe that Sanskrit was historically posterior to the Hinduwee was based on a general theory of language development. If Sanskrit was the original parent language of the other two, why is it so "inextricably perplexing" (by implication, to the Europeans), and why does its name imply that it is "polished or artificial"? He further wondered how such a language could be developed in "the earliest stages of civilization." The answer was that the cunning grammarians created Sanskrit out of a preexisting language that was the language of the folk themselves. From this folk language they constructed "a mystical, but splendid factotum factorum for the reception of the priest craft." The language of the priests was part of a conspiracy or plot, which resulted in the creation of a double yoke of "a mild despotism" and an "insatiable catholick religious persuasion." The language and its creators, the Brahmans, used their knowledge to enslave the Hindu population of India. The Brahmans he characterized as "a villainous priesthood" whose teachings are nothing but the "sonorous inarticulate bellowings of Brahmanical wolves."[81]

Gilchrist, with the publication of his *Dictionary* (which appeared in parts and with great difficulty), began to become more and more vociferous in his attacks on both Indian and British scholars of Indian languages, especially those who insisted that one or another of the Indian "classical" languages was the prerequisite for learning Hindustani. In 1799 Gilchrist wanted to establish an Oriental seminary in Calcutta to teach the newly appointed Company servants Hindustani. This was to replace the then current practice of granting Company appointees a Rs 30 allowance to enable them to hire a munshi to teach them the country languages. This system he deemed ineffective since few of the munshis spoke English and there were no adequate teaching materials. Simultaneously with the establishment of Gilchrist's seminary, the governor general, Lord Wellesley, had published a notification that starting on January 1, 1800, no civil servant "should be nominated to . . . offices of trust and responsibility until it shall be ascertained that he was sufficiently acquainted with the laws and regulations ... and the several languages, the knowledge of which is required for the due discharge of the respective functions of such offices."[82]

The seminary was quickly replaced by Lord Wellesley's ambitious plan for the College at Fort William, established in 1800, at which Gilchrist was appointed professor of Hindustani.[83] Here he supervised a staff of Indian scholars who were engaged in an extraordinary burst of scholarly, literary, and pedagogical activities directed toward making available to students at the college a corpus of works from which they could learn to read, write, and speak Hindustani.[84] At the college there was a distinct split in the European faculty, with some stressing the study of classical languages and others emphasizing the spoken languages. Gilchrist and William Carey led the spoken languages group. Each published "Dialogues" or phrase books to convey to the neophyte something of the flavor of the languages, as well as to introduce the young officials to the "manners and customs" of the Indians among whom they were going to work.[85]

Carey's *Dialogues* begins with a khansaman or sirkar talking with a European. The dialect is one in which there are mixed Persian, Bengali, and English phrases. The topics covered in this dialogue include phrases necessary to set up and run a household. The sahib learns how to berate his servants for slovenly attire and behavior. He learns brief commands to obtain food, requisites while traveling, and to have a garden laid out for his home. The rest of the work presents dialogues between various types of Indians: a Brahman talks in an elevated dialect about rituals and the family, and the sahib learns something about kinship terminology and the religious practices of Indians. There are also examples of the common talk of lower orders, fishermen and lower-caste women, whose dialect is characterized by Carey as the "greatest instance of literal irregularity." Carey compiled his work "by employing sensible natives" who composed dialogues "dealing with subjects of domestic nature." Sisir Kumar Das identifies the Bengali associates of Carey in this work as probably being Ram Ram Basu and Mrityunjay Vidyalamkar.[86]

Gilchrist published his first set of Hindustani conversations in 1798 in the *Oriental Linguist*. These were reprinted and revised in 1809 and 1820. In the 1809 version of the *Dialogues*, Gilchrist provides the young Englishman in India specific rules on how to talk with Indians, all of whom in his work seem to be servants.[87] The European must begin by learning how to get the native's attention, and this is accomplished by the command, "sunno." This, Gilchrist tells the reader, serves the function of putting the servant "on his guard." The commands issued should be as simple as possible, he advised; do not say "give me a plate," just utter the command "plate." The European should always use the imperative plural, "We want such and such." The asking of casual questions should be avoided since "the Hindostanee is too apt to conceive the most innocent of queries as only so many traps set to catch him in some villainy or other."

*Dialogues* covers the following topics: eating and preparation of food (31 pages); personal service, such as dressing and preparing for bed (18 pages); traveling, both locally and long distance (43 pages); sports and leisure activities (27 pages); the "memsahib" and her dealings with servants (only 7 pages); studying (14 pages); commercial transactions (13 pages); expostulating and abusing servants and eliciting information (13 pages); time and weather (5 pages); polite inquiries (2 pages); necessary military activities (5 pages); health, medicine, and consulting local doctors (40 pages, perhaps reflecting Gilchrist's original profession as a surgeon). The tone of the dialogues are mainly declamatory: "bring me this or that," "take everything away," "get the breakfast ready." The sahib, following Gilchrist's instruction, would quickly learn a considerable range of admonitions: "let me see them every morning on my table without fail, or I shall turn you off, as a good-for-nothing fellow"; "take care! or the House of Corrections will be your lot." Food sellers have to be constantly warned about the quality of the provisions. We get phrases like "the bread has sand in it." In almost all the dialogues the mishap, mistake, or stupidity of the Indian servant is the theme: soup is served without a spoon; food is either too hot, cold, thick, or thin. "In the future," the servant is told, "do not dress these Hindustanee dishes with so much spice, this tastes of nothing but pepper." The wine is never properly cooled.

The real disasters seem to strike when the sahib ventures forth. Walking only needs 21 phrases, but riding or going about in a carriage or palanquin requires 134. The sahib seems to get lost a lot, and servants are sent to make inquiries. While traveling everything seems to get misplaced, especially the wine. There are innumerable delays, people sleep when they should be working. But there are pleasures as well. The servant is sent off to find out from a local villager if there is game in the neighborhood; there is, but it turns out that it is dangerous to hunt there because of the large number of tigers. Orders have to be given to the local zamindar "to have his people beat up the game for us."

Language as command was not only a domestic or personal matter, but a matter of state. Lord Minto, in addressing the annual prize ceremony at Fort William College in 1808, explained to sixteen young officers that the nature of their relationship to Indians would be mediated by language: "You are about to be employed in the administration of a great and extensive country in which . . . the English language is not known. You will have to deal with multitudes; who can communicate with you, can receive your commands, or render an account of their performance of them; whose testimonies can be delivered, whose engagements can be contracted; whose affairs, only in some one or another of the languages taught at the College of Fort William."[88] The Englishman's honor and self-respect were also involved, as Minto echoed the statements of the Court of Directors and the governors general and language teachers for the previous sixty years on the evils of interpreters. Without proper knowledge of the language of the people they were ruling, there would arise an "unlimited dependence on native and subordinate officers, which inevitably leads to oppressive vexation, extortion, and cruelty towards our native subjects." Without the knowledge of languages, the European is delivered into a "helpless and dependent thraldom" of a native assistant. The officers' "fair fame" would be threatened, there would be public loss and calamity, and the officer would suffer individual shame and ruin.[89]

The Englishman needed not only to speak with grammatical precision, but had to learn to "manage his own language" in a manner most conducive to the execution of orders and the gratification of his own wishes on every occasion. Those who would follow Gilchrist's methods of teaching were assured that they would have the means to start their careers in India by making rapid progress in learning the vernacular and in doing so would acquire "local knowledge" and daily increase their "stock of general information." This Gilchrist contrasted with those who began with the study of the classical languages, who might find themselves diminishing "those intellectual powers, and that common sense which are frequently sunk under a heavy load of sheer pedantry and classical lore, very different indeed from real science and practical wisdom."[90] What emerges from reading Gilchrist is the image of the Englishman in India as the one who commands, who knows how to give orders and how to keep the natives in their proper place in the order of things through practical, not classical, knowledge.

The emphasis on the use of language as the key to understanding Indians, hence being able to control them, was stressed frequently in Lt. Col. John

Briggs's *Letters Addressed to a Young Person in India*, a book written in the form of letters by an old hand in India to two brothers, the elder in the military, the younger a civil servant.[91] Briggs sets out to instruct the civil servant in proper behavior. The elder brother, who has already been in India for a few years, has made all the mistakes, which the younger brother is to avoid. He fails to learn languages, gets into debt, selects the wrong type of servant, beats and abuses his servants, and generally makes a mess of things. In the letters to the young civilian, not only are the failures of the elder brother a constant reminder of what may happen to shame the individual but, more importantly, to shake the foundations of British rule in India. Briggs instructs his younger readers in these principles, as laid down by Maj. Gen. Sir John Malcolm:

> Almost all who, from knowledge and experience, have been capable of forming any judgment upon the question, are agreed that our power in India rests on the general opinion of the natives of our comparative superiority in good faith, wisdom, and strength, to their own rulers. This important impression will be improved by the consideration we show to their habits, institutions, and religion—by the moderation, temper, and kindness, with which we conduct ourselves towards them; and injured by every act that offends their belief or superstition, that shows disregard or neglect of individuals or communities, or that evinces our having, with the arrogance of conquerors, forgotten those maxims by which this great empire has been established, and by which alone it can be preserved.[92]

The only way to gain the knowledge and sympathy that Malcolm's instructions required was through the languages of the people. "The veil which exists between us and the natives can only be removed by mutual and kind intercourse." There might be kindly intercourse with the natives, but language was also the "channel of communicating your wants and of obtaining information," Briggs advised.[93] Knowledge of Indian languages was the means of gaining a more complex knowledge of the strange customs, codes, and rules of the Indians, who were in most instances docile, cooperative, and quite willing to obey the orders and commands of the sahibs, except when ignorance led the latter to offend the prejudices of the natives. The newcomer seemingly had to be instructed in the simplest and most obvious of distinctions, that between Hindus and Muslims. Gilchrist informed his readers that Muslims were larger, bearded, and more fierce and robust in appearance than Hindus. One had to learn how to distinguish the differences in dress by the way they tied their garments, by the form of hair style and turban, and above all by their names and their food habits.

Unlike Briggs and Malcolm, whose careers were amongst the peoples of central and western India—and hence who were instructing their juniors in proper behavior not only toward their Indian servants, domestic and civil, but toward learned men, chiefs, opulent bankers, and merchants and peasants—Gilchrist's image of Indian society seems to have been largely restricted to domestic servants and lowly assistants. No matter how one tried, apparently in Bengal there were occasions when even the most knowledgeable and even-tempered European would be driven "by the stupidity, perverseness, and chicanery" of natives to want to beat his servants. But, Gilchrist advises, "let the storm blow over" with a volley of abusive words directed at the miscreant.[94] The normal good manners of the European can be tested, according to Gilchrist, in all sorts of situations, for example when invited to a wealthy Indian's house for an entertainment. On such an occasion one should not condemn the music, dancing, and singing, or if a dramatic pantomime particularly offends the European's sense of modesty he should retire in silence rather than offer vociferous exclamations such as "beastly stuff." Quiet withdrawal in such situations, writes Gilchrist, "will do more to establish our superiority in breeding and morality."[95]

The European has to learn to insist on proper performance of the Indian's social and verbal codes in dealing with superiors. One should not let an Indian subordinate get away with behavior or speech that would be offensive not only to the European but to an Indian of superior quality. Gilchrist, like most Europeans in India, reduced what was and is an extremely sensitive, well-ordered, and complex system of deference and codes of demeanor that Indians follow to what for the Europeans were highly charged symbolic acts revolving around the wearing of various foot coverings.[96] Gilchrist explained that Europeans uncover their heads as a mark of respect, whereas Indians take off their slippers while performing worship in a mosque or temple or on entering a home or office. Yet he observes that natives "intrude on the British inhabitants of Calcutta and environs, without the slightest attention to this act of politeness, most scrupulously observed amongst themselves, as if they were determined to trample us under the pride of Caste, by evincing, that to a Hindoo or Moosulman alone, it was necessary to pay the common marks of civility or respect."[97] The wearing of shoes by Indians in the houses of Europeans was seen as part of a larger effort on the part of some Indians to establish equality or even superiority—not only in relation to Europeans but also with respect to other Indians, by appearing to be on a footing of equality with Europeans.

Indian languages, with their graded grammatical systems of polite forms and forms of various degrees of familiarity and respect, also could be a source of disrespect to the foreigners. For the unwitting Europeans in India, some servants and menials would use the singular pronoun in addressing the sahib. "It is rather surprising that servants and sipahees, etc., should be allowed to take such advantage of their master's ignorance of the language and customs of the country, as to *too* and *tera* them on every occasion: a liberty they dare not take with one another."[98] The insult of the use of familiar forms by the servant to the sahib was not just a personal insult but had a much greater consequence for the loss of dignity for his country and nation. Gilchrist stressed that the necessary knowledge of indigenous language and custom was not one of just the sahib getting proper respect; it also entailed the sahib avoiding unwittingly acting in a disrespectful manner toward the Indian.

Two issues arise related to Gilchrist's attempt to establish the British language of command. First, how well did the British learn this or any other Indian language? Second, how fixed did the standard that Gilchrist hoped to establish remain? Until the middle of the century there were recurrent complaints that the British lacked sophisticated knowledge of Hindustani, or Urdu as it became more generally called. F. J. Shore, who had considerable empathy with Indians and who was continually critical of both the policies of the Company's government and the behavior of his fellow countrymen toward Indians, ridiculed the level of knowledge of Hindustani that most "judges, magistrates and military officers" had attained even after a number of years' service in India. He likened their speech to the broken English of Frenchmen or Italians who are made objects of fun or contempt on the stage. This lack of capacity to speak properly, he felt, encouraged Indians to be equally slovenly or mannerless in their dealings with the sahibs. He cited a hypothetical case:

> Two or three English are out hunting or shooting; one of them who speaks broken Hindustanee, asks a peasant some questions relative to the sport: the native answers him in a careless way, perhaps without stopping his

work; and sometimes without even looking up from it, after the first glance; omitting, at the same time, the respectful terms of speech. Should another of the party, who can speak in a gentlemanlike manner, address the peasant, in an instant the latter will rise up, or stop his work, make a salaam, and reply in the most respectful language. Were the native asked by any one to whom he could speak freely, why he made such a difference in addressing the two gentlemen, his answer would be something to the following effect: "Two gentlemen! Do you call the first a gentleman; if so, why did he not speak like one? The second evidently was so, by his language, and I answered him as such."[99]

The Englishman with a limited grasp of Hindustani indeed received answers to his questions. The issue that Shore raises is not about communication of facts but about behavior and status, and I think this issue continued through much of the history of the British in India. There were obviously those British who spoke and understood the standard or even the literary registers of the varied languages of India, and hence could manage their official persona as Shore would have wished they did. I would speculate, however, that the majority knew only very restricted and specific codes, which were adequate to specified contexts such as running their households, dealing with their subordinates in the courts and offices, and in giving orders in the military.

The battle between the classicists and vernacularists in relation to Hindustani was to continue throughout the nineteenth century. Each new dictionary or grammar that would appear caused argumentation. The missionaries soon joined the officials of the Company, and questions of scripts and sources of borrowings for lexical items and for grammatical refinements became politically charged issues. In the 1860s, Indians, some of whom had added a sophisticated knowledge of English to their own "classical" education, began to argue, organize, and eventually to demand in the name of history and religion that the government favor one or another script and associated literatures.[100]

### British Power and Indian Knowledge

On the eve of the fiftieth anniversary of the founding of the Asiatic Society of Bengal, W. C. Taylor, in an address to the Royal Asiatic Society in London, declared that it was the British who in the last decades of the eighteenth century were responsible for the "literary treasures of Hindustan being opened up to the wonder and admiration of the world." He went on, like a twentieth-century counterpart in Great Britain or the United States, to appeal for funds to support continuing research and publication by linking the knowledge gained through the study of Oriental literature to success in "the pursuit of Oriental commerce." He clinched his argument by citing the aphorism "KNOWLEDGE IS POWER."[101]

In 1784 Warren Hastings had explicated for Nathaniel Smith, chairman of the Court of Directors, the relation of knowledge to power in the establishment of British rule in India:

> Every accumulation of knowledge and especially such as is obtained by social communication with people over whom we exercise dominion founded on the right of conquest, is useful to the state . . . it attracts and conciliates distant affections; it lessens the weight of the chain by which the natives are held in subjection; and it imprints on the hearts of our countrymen the sense of obligation and benevolence. . . . Every instance which brings their real character [i.e., that of the Indians] home to observation will impress us with a more generous sense of feeling for their natural rights, and teach us to estimate them by the measure of our own. But such instances can only be obtained in their writings and these will survive when the British dominion in India shall have long ceased to exist, and when the sources which once yielded of wealth and power are lost to remembrance.[102]

Hastings drew a contrast between the "benevolent and sympathetic interest" that the British had shown toward the Brahmans, the keepers "of the mysteries of their own learning," and the previous rulers, the Muslims, who had systematically derided the religion of the Hindus and who sought from their studies "arguments to support their own intolerant principles." Hastings believed that as a result of the conciliatory nature of British rule, the pandits were now "no less eager to impart their knowledge, than we are to receive it."[103]

Twenty years later Sir James Mackintosh, a Benthamite and legal reformer who was Recorder of Bombay, struck a somewhat harsher note in addressing the first meeting of the Bombay Literary Society. He urged his colleagues to "mine the knowledge of which we have become the masters." He went on to remind his listeners "that all Europeans who visit remote countries . . . are detachments from the main body of civilized men sent out to levy contributions and knowledge, as well as gain victories over barbarism."[104]

H. T. Colebrooke, in a letter to his father, described the ambivalence that characterized much of the British reaction to Indian culture: "The further our literary enquiries are extended here, the more vast and stupendous the scene which opens to us; at the same time that the true and the false, the sublime and the puerile, wisdom and absurdity, are so intermixed, that at every step, we have to smile at folly, while we admire and acknowledge the philosophical truth, though couched in obscure allegory and puerile fable."[105]

British studies of Indian languages, literature, science, and thought produced three major projects. The first involved the objectification and use of Indian languages as instruments of rule to understand better the "peculiar" manners, customs, and prejudices of Indians, and to gather information necessary to conciliate and control the peoples of India. The second project entailed what the Europeans defined as "discoveries" of the wisdom of the ancients, the analogy being to the restoration of Greek and Roman thought and knowledge in the fifteenth and sixteenth centuries. This was a European project, the end being to construct a history of the relationship between India and the West, to classify and locate their civilizations on an evaluative scale of progress and decay. The third project involved the patronage of institutions and religious and literary specialists who maintained and transmitted—through texts, writing, recitations, performances, painting and sculptures, rituals, and performances—that which the British conquerors defined as the traditions of the conquered. To appear legitimate in the eyes of the Indians, the British thought they had to demonstrate respect and interest in those Indians and institutions that were the carriers of the traditions.

There were to be consistent differences in the valuation of the three projects between the two centers of decision making. One was in London, where the Court of Directors represented the "owners" of the East India Company, and the Board of Control had been established by Parliament to exercise political control over the Company's affairs. In India there was a theoretically subordinate group of officials headed by the Governor General in Council and the governors of Bombay and Madras which supervised the functioning of the instrumentalities of colonial rule. Given the distance and time that separated London and India and the growing weight and power of senior civil servants, Calcutta, Madras, and Bombay frequently acted independently of the owners of the Company and the Home government.

London tended to put the question of language learning at the top of its priorities. The construction of "European" knowledge was increasingly left to semiofficial bodies such as the Asiatic Society of Bengal, and to professional scholars in the colleges and universities. The issues entailed in the construction of the legitimacy of the Company's rule through the preservation and patronage of Indian knowledge caused a political and epistemological battle between London and Calcutta over the allocation of resources, and a financial and moral battle about the forms of knowledge and the shape of institutions that could most effectively preserve and transmit their own and European thought.

### Education and the Preservation of the Past

In September 1780, a delegation of Muslims of "credit and learning" called on Warren Hastings to urge him to establish a madrassa for the instruction of young students "in Mahamadan law and other sciences."[106] The visit had been occasioned by the arrival in Calcutta of a famous teacher and scholar, Muiz-ud-din, whom the petitioners hoped the government would employ to direct the madrassa.[107] Hastings, in justifying the expenditure of the Company's funds to support a madrassa in Calcutta, painted a bleak picture of decaying remains "of these schools which could be seen in every capital, town and city of Hindustan." The Calcutta Madrassa, Hastings hoped, would preserve and further knowledge, provide training for future law officers of the Company, contribute to the "credit" of the Company's name, and "help soften the prejudices excited by the growth of British dominions."[108]

The madrassa, under the direction of Muiz-ud-din, appeared to have gotten off to a good start, with ninety students pursuing a wide range of studies. Within a few years, however, the maulavi was accused of mishandling Company funds, favoritism in appointments, and losing control over the students. A committee of British officials was appointed to supervise the administration of the college, the maulavi was dismissed, and the college was reorganized along European lines, although the subject matter studied remained Islamic.[109]

The Sanskrit College in Banaras had a similar history. The college owed its inception to the initiative of Jonathan Duncan, Resident in Banaras. He recommended that surplus revenue, expected to accrue to the Company from the Permanent Settlement of the Banaras zamindari, be applied to the establishment of "a Hindoo College . . . for the preservation and cultivation of Laws, Literature and Religion of that nation, at this centre of their faith." Such an institution, Duncan felt, "would endear our Government to the Native Hindoos." There were, he observed, "many private seminaries" for the study of various forms of Hindu learning, but as the Company's college would be the only "public" institution dedicated to this purpose, the reputation of the Company would be enhanced. In addition to its teaching functions, Duncan noted that as an institution it could without too much expense build a "precious library of complete and correct treatises . . . dealing with Hindoo religion, laws, arts and sciences."[110]

Perhaps influenced by the history of the madrassa, Duncan drew up a set of rules that made the Resident, acting on behalf of the governor general, responsible for the payment of stipends for those students being educated at government expense, the hiring and firing of faculty, and the dismissal of students. Duncan was to attend the quarterly examinations, at least in those subjects that were not considered sacred; for these he would appoint a committee of Brahmans who would examine students in the "more secret branches of learning." Within ten years of its founding, accusations of financial mismanagement and favoritism similar to those that had plagued the madrassa led to a more intensive British supervision of the Sanskrit College.[111]

The history of the British experiments with the Calcutta Madrassa and the Sanskrit College in Banaras is symbolic of wider issues entailed in the establishing of educational institutions under the colonial state. The British conceived of education as taking place in institutions, meaning buildings with physically divided spaces marking off one class of students from another, as well as teachers from students. There were to be fixed positions of professors, teachers, and assistants, who taught regular classes in subjects. The students' progress had to be regularly examined to measure their acquisition of fixed bodies of knowledge. The end of the process was marked by prizes and certification that attested to the students' command of a specifiable body of knowledge. Even with the undoubted goodwill and best intentions on the part of Duncan, Hastings, and others, a British metalogic of regularity, uniformity, and above all fiscal responsibility could not help but participate in the erosion and transformation of what the British wanted to preserve, that is, Hindu and Muslim learning.

The political project of enhancing the credit of the Company and the

British nation as the protector and preserver of indigenous knowledge was to lead them to become keepers of a vast museum that would, in turn, lead to providing definitions of what should be preserved, as well as to developing a program for locating and classifying the specimens to be maintained. The substance of Lord Minto's remarks on the decay of Indian science and literature was to echo throughout the nineteenth century:

> It is a common remark that science and literature are in a progressive state of decay among the natives of India. From every inquiry which I have been enabled to make on this interesting subject that remark appears to me but too well founded. The number of the learned is not only diminished but the circle of learning even among those who still devote themselves to it appears to be considerably contracted. The abstract sciences are abandoned, polite literature neglected and no branch of learning cultivated but what is connected with the peculiar religious doctrines of the people. The immediate consequence of this state of things is the disuse and even actual loss of many valuable books; and it is to be apprehended that unless Government interpose with a fostering hand the revival of letters may shortly become hopeless from a want of books or of persons capable of explaining them.[112]

Lord Wellesley, who had a magisterial and imperial vision of the Company's rule in India, conceived in 1800 a plan for the education and training of the young men appointed to the Company's civil service. No longer should these appointees be thought of as "agents of a commercial concern," he declared. They should be trained as "ministers and officers of a powerful sovereign." Wellesley, without the permission of the Court of Directors, established the College at Fort William to provide the education that he thought was required. He wrote to the Court of Directors that the education should impart a knowledge of "those branches of literature and science" such as was included in the education of persons "destined for high office in Europe." In addition, the young men required special instruction in the codes and regulations of the Company, as well as in the "true and sound principles of the British constitution." As they were to be the rulers of an alien race, they had to obtain "an intimate acquaintance with the history, languages, customs, laws and religions of India." As if this wasn't enough for a group of sixteen- and seventeen-year-olds, the college had to shape their moral character so they would be armed with the virtues of "industry, prudence, integrity, and religious sensibility" which would help them guard against the "temptations and corruptions" they would be exposed to because of the Indian climate and the "peculiar depravity" of the people of India. Their education, Wellesley claimed, had to form a natural barrier "against habitual indolence, dissipation, licentiousness and indulgence," which had marked the behavior of most of the employees of the Company.[113]

To accomplish this awesome educational project Wellesley planned a residential college where the young men's lives could be properly supervised. It was to be staffed by a European faculty of eight to ten who could teach Indian languages as well as the European curriculum. To set the proper tone, the vice provost was to be a clergyman of the Anglican faith. To teach the Oriental subjects fifty munshis were employed and divided into four departments: Sanskrit-Bengali, Arabic, Persian, and Hindustani. Each department had a European professor, a chief munshi, a second munshi, as well as subordinate munshis. The pay of the European faculty ranged from Rs 1,600 to Rs 500; for the Indian staff, the range was Rs 200 for the four chief munshis, Rs 100 for the second munshis, and Rs 60 for the subordinate munshis.[114] The duties of the munshis involved providing individual tutorials, preparing (in collaboration with the European professors) teaching materials, preparing and publishing grammars and dictionaries, as well as undertaking extensive projects in publishing "classic" works of Indian literature.

The Court of Directors, when they learned of the very ambitious plans, quickly cut back on the European part of the curriculum and barred the building of a residential college. Their central concern was with the college as a language-teaching institution. They did, however establish in England the East India Company's Training College at Haileybury for the education of their appointees to the civil service in India. Here the young men received an education in European subjects and some Indian language work.[115]

The College Council, which was the governing body of the College at Fort William, was estimated by the Court of Directors to have spent upwards of £40,000 to subsidize the editing, writing, and publishing of eighty-eight "Oriental works" in the period 1801 to 1812. The vast bulk of the funds was spent on works in or about Persian (Rs 110,000), Arabic (Rs 52,000), and Sanskrit (Rs 44,000). The Company informed their servants in Calcutta that any subsidized work should show "value and merit" in the teaching of languages. The Court complained of "the very heavy expense to which you have subjected us by the encouragement which seems to have been indiscriminately afforded to publications, several of which are very ill executed, or of no use as class books, nor are they in any other way objects which call for the patronage of your government."[116]

The Indian staff recruited for the college included a number of distinguished scholars, such as Mrityunjay Vidyalamkar from Midnapur and Maulavi Allah Daud from Lucknow. In addition several, such as Ram Ram Basu, Mir Amin, and Lalljilal from Gujarat, made major contributions to the prose literature of Bengali, Urdu, and Hindi. Some made a major scholarly and intellectual impact on their European counterparts. Mathew Lumsden, whose Persian *Grammar* was published in 1810, described Maulavi Allah Daud as "the great master under whom I have studied" and acknowledged his great debt to Daud's "knowledge and industry." Lumsden assured his European readers that though he was the author of the *Grammar*, "the more arduous task of supplying the information devolved . . . onto Daud."[117]

Lumsden's remark, I think, typifies the relations between Indian and British scholars who were engaged not only at the college but in other settings as well, transforming Indian knowledge into European information. The Indians were sources or "native informants" who supplied information, viva voce, in English or Indian languages; who collected, translated, and discussed texts and documents; and who wrote exegeses of various kinds that were classified, processed, and analyzed into knowledge *of* or *about* India.

As Das points out, in the college there were two separate categories: sahibs and munshis. There was indeed mutual learning going on, there was respect and some amicability in the relations between the two categories of persons, but it was the British who set the agenda and who had the authoritative voice in determining what was useful knowledge to be processed for the European projects: "The Indian scholar knew he was superior to his European Master in respect of Indian languages, [but] he was primarily an informant, a mere tool in the exercise of language teaching to be handled by others."[118]

The differences between the Indian scholars and their British counterparts were based on more than the social and political relations that had made the British dominant; there was a major epistemological gulf between the two cultures as well. Those British who sought to produce grammars, dictionaries, or translations of literary or "practical" works, such as law codes, frequently complained about the way in which Indian scholars worked and thought. C. P. Brown, who spent forty years working on Telugu, writes of working with Brahmans who nearly "shipwrecked" him with their pedantry.

He complained that the Brahmans valued only the abstract and abstruse and despised "all that is natural and in daily use."[119] He rebelled against their instructions to "learn by rote long vocabularies, framed in meter," while he was trying to construct his dictionary of Telugu. The Reverend Robert Caldwell claimed that the learning of "versified enigmas and harmonious platitudes" resulted in Indians developing a great capacity for patient labor and an accurate knowledge of details, but also prevented the development of a "zeal for historical truth" and the "power of generalization and discrimination."[120]

Developing a capacity for memorizing was part of the education that the British received as well. Brown complained of his pandits' demands to memorize, but also took pride in the fact that they thought he knew "the Bible, Shakespeare, and Milton by heart." What baffled the British most about the Indians' prodigious feats of memorization was that it appeared to them that the Indians did not know the meaning of what they had internalized so effectively.

A. D. Campbell found in Bellary district in 1823 that great attention was being paid in the schools to proper pronunciation of syllables of a "poetical" language but not to the meaning or construction of words in this language. He found that the teachers themselves could not "understand the purport of the numerous books which they had learn[ed] from memory." The result was that the students had a "parrot-like capacity to repeat, but not to understand what they had learned, they gained little from their education, as they did not have the means" to expand their general stock of useful knowledge.[121]

William Adam, in his reports on vernacular education in Bengal and Bihar, believed that the education in the local schools was "superficial and deficitive [sic]." Even at the Sanskrit colleges, at which grammar, law, rhetoric, literature, and logic were taught, following William Ward's assessment, few attained very high levels of knowledge, and only five out of one thousand students in the colleges knew anything of the philosophical systems of the Veda, even though they could chant from memory long passages in Sanskrit.[122]

One of the few Europeans of the early nineteenth century who was not dismissive of the Indian form of education based on memorization was Francis W. Ellis of the Madras civil service. Ellis, who had a career as judge and collector in south India, was one of the most accomplished and sensitive of the early orientalists.[123] Ellis was one of the founders of the Company's College at Fort St. George in 1812, which differed significantly in its purpose from the College at Fort William, since, in addition to training the British in south Indian languages, it also included the training of Indians in Hindu and Muslim law as part of its responsibilities. As in north India, the Company's courts administered Hindu and Muslim personal law, but in Madras they found that few of the south Indian Brahmans appeared to know the Dharmashastric literature. Ellis had drawn up a list of what he thought were the most useful and important compilations of Sanskrit works for the purpose of forming a "practical guide" for the administration of Hindu law in the Madras presidency. He recommended that these works be translated into Tamil verse for the use of the Hindu students in the college. He explained that only if they were translated into Tamil would they have any authority for the Indians. Ellis argued that "the mode of study prevalent among the natives of India [was] the best means of conveying the law." He went on to state that all knowledge and science in India, "from the lowest to the highest form of logic and theology," were acquired by "committing to memory technical verses." These memorized verses were like a taproot that the scholar or pandit could draw upon to "explain, illustrate or enforce dicta."[124]

What Ellis was pointing to was that the Indian mode of knowing and thinking was radically different from what the British assumed was the natural or normal form, and which they used as a standard by which they could adjudge Indian forms of knowledge as marred or inadequate, rather than different. Indian reasoning was based, Ellis wrote, on "the habit of their education," which rested on the memorization of "concentrated not diffuse knowledge," which was easier to comprehend in verse form. The use of Tamil in its verse form also would diminish the influence of the Brahmans, who were regarded with "jealousy" by the shudras (members of the lowest of the four main caste groups) in south India; the latter could now study law in their own language. It would also enable the pleaders in their courts to read the law and would serve a more impartial administration of justice. In addition, as the English judges were required to learn Tamil in Madras, they could discuss issues directly in a language common to themselves and their law officers.[125]

## Conclusion: The Reordering of the
## Nature of Indian Knowledge

The British conquest of India brought them into a new world which they tried to comprehend using their own forms of knowing and thinking. To the educated Englishman of the late eighteenth and early nineteenth centuries, the world was knowable through the senses, which could record the experience of a natural world. This world was generally believed to be divinely created, knowable in an empirical fashion, and constitutive of the sciences through which would be revealed the laws of Nature that governed the world and all that was in it. Unknowingly and unwittingly they had not only invaded and conquered a territory but, through their scholarship, had invaded an epistemological space as well. The British believed that they could explore and conquer this space through translation: establishing correspondences could make the unknown and the strange knowable.

At one level they found this could be done relatively easily and quickly through labels that served to locate the strange in a frame of reference with which they were familiar. Brahmans became "priests," and the *Kosha* of Amarasinha was a "Dictionary of the Sanskrit Language." Since all languages had a grammar, the commentaries on Indian languages could be turned into tools to enable the sahibs to communicate their commands and gather information. They found and utilized extraordinarily able guides, aides, and assistants who knew highly specialized forms of Indian knowledge and could be interpreters, sources, and transmitters of this knowledge to the new rulers. The Victorian successors to the first generation of scholars were more likely to describe their goals as "scientific and historical"; the wonders that had excited Jones, Wilkins, Halhed, and Ellis now had to be normalized and located in a discourse that would make India into a "case" of an earlier civilization, or a museum of ancient practices, from which earlier stages of universal world history could be recovered.

Sir William Jones, in his declaration of the relationship of Latin, Greek, and Sanskrit in 1785, provided the impetus for the development, largely by German scholars, of comparative philology, which in turn supplied the "scientific" model for the comparative study of law, religion, and society. The comparative method, as it became formalized in the middle of the nineteenth century, drew together many strands of eighteenth-century thought and scholarly practice. It promised answers to the persistent European quest for the origins of things. In its linguistic and literary forms it utilized techniques of the collation of texts in order to construct the original and pure versions that could then be used to establish a linear chronology. Europeans had utilized these critical methods of textual reconstruction to establish the documents, records, and texts by which they constituted their own "true" history. They were now prepared to give to the Indian the greatest gift they could give anyone—the Indians would receive a *history*.

The theory of language implicit in the comparative method is that there are "genetic" or "genealogical" relations among languages that have been determined to belong to a "family." It is posited that there was once a single, original language from which all the languages in the family descend. The establishment of the membership in the language family was based on the comparison of formal features, displayed lexically, syntactically, morphologically, and phonetically, in the language. The goal of the method was to establish a history; those features that appear from formal comparison as the most common in the family of languages were thought to be the most "authentic." The end of the exercise was the reconstruction of "the unrecorded languages of the past."[126]

The Reverend Robert Caldwell, a Church of England missionary in Tinnevelly, applied the methods that had been so successful in reconstructing the history of the Indo-European family of languages to the south Indian languages, which he labeled the Dravidian language family. Caldwell had two goals, the first being to add to European knowledge of the languages of the world and, in particular, to establish the significance of Dravidian in relation to other Indian language families. The other goal was to stimulate the "native literate" of south India "to an intelligent interest in the comparative study of their own languages." He noted, as had many British before, that Indians had long studied grammar, but in a regressive and unscientific way. They were more interested in mystifying the knowledge of languages than contributing to the "progressive refinement" of it, making it the means of clear communication. By studying the Dravidian languages comparatively the native literate would come to realize that "language has a history of its own which, throwing light upon all other history, would thereby be capable of rendering ethnology and archaeology possible."[127]

The power of the comparative method was that it enabled the practitioner to classify, bound, and control variety and difference. At a phenomenological level the British discovered hundreds of languages and dialects, and these could be arranged into neat diagrams and tables that showed the relationship of languages to each other. As with genealogies, which could represent all the members of a family or descent group visually as a tree with a root, trunk, branches, and even twigs, so could dialects and languages be similarly represented and grouped. Significantly, the trees always seemed to be northern European ones, like oaks and maples, and the British never seemed to think of using the most typical South Asian tree, the banyan, which grows up, out, and down at the same time.

The comparative method implied linear directionality: things, ideas, institutions could be seen as progressing through stages to some end or goal. It could also be used to establish regression, decay, and decadence, the movement through time away from some pristine, authentic, original starting point, a "golden age" in the past. The decline rather than the progress model came increasingly to be applied by the Europeans and some Indians to the textual traditions of India. In this view the present, because of the conquest, was seen as a period of dissolution and retrogression. This could be reversed by the re-establishment of "authentic" and pure versions of the great sacred works of the ancient Hindus.

C. P. Brown, in constructing a Telugu dictionary, after several false starts decided to establish his corpus of lexical items by standardizing several texts, one of which was *Manu Charitra*. He assembled a group of learned assistants and collected upward of a dozen manuscript versions of the texts. These manuscripts, he wrote, "swarmed with errors," which his assistants "adjusted by guess as they went along." Brown had copies made of each manuscript, leaving alternate pages blank with the verses numbered. He had a number of clerks with several copies of the manuscript in front of them, as well as three "professors," masters of grammar and prosody, both Sanskrit and Telugu. The verses were then read out, discussed by the pandits, with Brown deciding which version was correct, "just as a judge frames a decree out of conflicting evidence."[128]

Through this procedure, Brown was creating what he thought of as an authentic text. With the advent of printing in India, which was now developing along with the European ideas about how texts were constituted and transmitted, this was to have a powerful effect in standardizing the Telugu language and its literature. Implicit in this process were several European assumptions about literature. In European theory, texts have authors who create or record what had previously been transmitted orally or through writing. Before the advent of printing it was assumed that texts "swarmed with errors" because of the unreliability of the scribes, leading to the corruption of the original and pure version created by the author.

Europeans in the nineteenth century saw literature as being conditioned by history, with an author knowing and building on great works of thought that he or she, through an act of genius and originality, could affect. Kamil Zvelbil has argued that Indians do not order their literature in a temporal linear fashion, but rather by structure and type. Literature in India "has a simultaneous existence and composes a simultaneous order."[129] He has also pointed out that persons are constituted differently in India than in the West. In India they are less unique individuals and more incumbents of positions in a social order that existed before they did and will continue to exist after their deaths. Poets or writers before the nineteenth century, Zvelbil states, did not invent or create a poem or a literary work; rather, they could only express "an unchanging truth in a traditional form" and by following "traditional rules."[130]

The delineation of the cumulative effect of the results of the first half-century of the objectification and reordering through the application of European scholarly methods on Indian thought and culture is beyond the scope of this essay. The Indians who increasingly became drawn into the process of transformation of their own traditions and modes of thought were, however, far from passive. In the long run the authoritative control that the British tried to exercise over new social and material technologies was taken over by Indians and put to purposes that led to the ultimate erosion of British authority. The consciousness of Indians at all levels in society was transformed as they refused to become specimens in a European-controlled museum of an archaic stage in world history.

## Notes

1.  Sir Richard Temple, ed., *The Diaries of Streynsham Master, 1675–1680* (London, 1911), 1:446–47.
2.  D. V. Kale, ed., *English Records on Shivaji* (Poona, 1931), 195–96, 205, 266; Sir Charles Fawcett, ed., *The English Factories in India,* new series (London, 1936), 1:29, 69, 106.
3.  Sir William Foster, ed., *The Embassy of Sir Thomas Roe to India, 1615–19* (London, 1926), 129.
4.  Foster, *The Embassy of Sir Thomas Roe,* 100.
5.  Foster, *The Embassy of Sir Thomas Roe,* 130.
6.  Mohiuddin Momin, *The Chancellery and Persian Epistolography under the Mughals, from Babur to Shah Jahan* (Calcutta: Iran Society, 1971); Riazul Islam, *A Calendar of Documents on Indo-Persian Relations, 1500–1750* (Karachi: Institute of Central and West Asian Studies, 1979), 1:1–53.
7.  William Foster, *The English Factories in India, 1665–1667* (Oxford: Clarendon Press, 1925), 14.
8.  G. W. Forrest, ed., *Selections from the Bombay Records* (1887), 1:169–71; Madras Presidency, *Records of Fort St. George, Diary and Consultation Book, 1740* (Madras,

1931), 224–26; Peter Marshall, *East Indian Fortunes* (Oxford: Clarendon Press, 1976), 11.

9. Forrest, *Selections*, 2:202–9; Madras Presidency, *Records, 1740*, 85:209–303; S. C. Hill, ed., *Bengal in 1756–57* (London, 1905), 411–13.

10. James Fraser, *The History of Nadir Shah* (London, 1742), iii–vi; William Irvine, "Notes on James Fraser," *Journal of the Royal Asiatic Society* (1899): 214–20; L. Lockhart, *Nadir Shah* (London, 1938), 304–6.

11. For Hastings's language skills, see Peter Marshall, "Hastings as Scholar and Patron," in *Statesmen, Scholars and Merchants*, ed. Anne Whiteman, J. S. Bromley, and P. G. M. Dickson (Oxford: Clarendon, 1923), 243.

12. Mark Bence Jones, *Clive of India* (London: Constable, 1974), 225.

13. Some of the leading texts of the period are Alexander Dow, *The History of Hindostan*, 1770; Sir William Jones, *A Grammar of the Persian Language*, 1771; George Hadley, *The Practical and Vulgar Dialect of the Indostan Language Commonly Called Moors*, 1772; N. B. Halhed, *A Code of Gentoo Laws, or, Ordinations of the Pundits*, 1776, and *A Grammar of the Bengal Language*, 1778; John Richardson, *A Dictionary of English, Persian and Arabic*, 1780; William Davy, *Institutes Political and Military of Timour*, 1783; Francis Balfour, *The Forms of the Herkern*, 1781; Charles Wilkins, *The Bhagvet Geeta*, 1785; William Kirkpatrick, *A Vocabulary, Persian, Arabic and English, Containing such Words as Have Been Adopted from the Two Former Languages and Incorporated into the Hindvi*, 1785; Francis Gladwin, *Ayeen i Akberry or the Institutes of the Emperor Akbar*, 1783–86; and John A. Gilchrist, *A Dictionary English and Hindustanee*, part 1, 1787.

14. Great Britain, Parliament, *Third Report from the Committee appointed to Enquire into the Nature, State and Condition of the East India Company* (1773; London, 1803), 3:379.

15. Davy, *Institutes Political and Military*, li–liii.

16. Letter from William Davy to John Richardson, dated March 8, 1780, in Richardson, *Dictionary*, 2:xv.

17. Jones, *Grammar*, i, viii, ix, x.

18. Jones, *Grammar*, x.

19. K. D. Bhargava, ed., *Fort William–India House Correspondence* (Delhi: Manager of Publications, 1969), 6:110–11.

20. Garland Cannon, *Oriental Jones* (New York: Asia Publication House, 1964), 24; see also Garland Cannon, "Sir William Jones' Persian Linguistics," *Journal of the American Oriental Society* 78 (1958): 262–73.

21. Jones, *Grammar*, xiv–xv.

22. Jones, *Grammar*, xiv, xvi–xix.

23. Marshall, "Hastings as Scholar," p. 245.

24. W. H. Hutton, ed., "A Letter of Warren Hastings on the Civil Service of the East India Company," *English Historical Review* 44 (1929): 635.

25. Alexander Dow, "A Dissertation Concerning the Customs, Manners, Language, Religion and Philosophy of the Hindoos," in *The History of Hindostan*, 3rd ed. (London, 1792), l: xxvii; reprinted with a commentary in *The British Discovery of Hinduism in the Eighteenth Century*, ed. Peter Marshall (Cambridge: Cambridge University Press, 1970), 107–39.

26. In John Z. Howell, *Interesting Historical Events Relative to the Province of Bengal and the Empire of Indostan* (London, 1767).

27. Marshall, *British Discovery*, 46 nn. a and b.

28. John Z. Howell, *Interesting Historical Events Relative to the Province of Bengal and the Empire of Indostan*, in *The British Discovery of Hinduism in the Eighteenth Century*, ed. Peter Marshall (reprint; Cambridge: Cambridge University Press, 1970), 48–50.

29. Letter from the Governor General and Council to Court of Directors, Fort William, November 3, 1772, printed in Great Britain, House of Commons, *Reports from Committees of the House of Commons*, 4: *East Indies, 1772–3* (reprint; London, 1804), 345–46.

30. George R. Gleig, comp., *Memoirs of the Life of the Right Honourable Warren Hastings* (London, 1841), 1:400.

31. *Reports from Committees of the House of Commons . . . 1772–3*, 4:348–50.

32. *Reports from Committees of the House of Commons . . . 1772–3*, 4:348.

33. J. D. M. Derrett, "Sanskrit Legal Treatises Compiled at the Instance of the British," *Zeitschrift für Vergleichende Rechtswissenschaft* 63 (1961): 72–117; J. D. M. Derrett, "The Administration of Hindu Law by the British," *Comparative Studies in Society and History* 4 (1961): 10–52; J. D. M. Derrett, *Religion, Law and the State in India* (New York: Free Press, 1968); Marc Galanter, "The Displacement of Traditional Law in Modern India," *Journal of Social Issues* 24 (1968): 65–91; Lloyd and Susanne Rudolph, "Barristers and Brahmans in India: Legal Cultures and Social Change," *Comparative Studies in Society and History* 8 (1965): 24–49; Ludo Rocher, "Indian Reactions to Anglo-Indian Law," *Journal of the American Oriental Society* 92 (1972): 419–24.

34. Rosane Rocher, *Orientalism, Poetry, and the Millennium: The Checkered Life of Nathaniel Brassey Halhed, 1751–1830* (Delhi: Motilal Banarsiclass, 1983), 48–73.

35. N. B. Halhed, *A Code of Gentoo Laws; or, Ordinations of the Pundits* (London, 1776), x.

36. R. Rocher, *Orientalism*, 51.

37. Jones to Cornwallis, March 19, 1788, in *The Letters of Sir William Jones*, ed. Garland Cannon (Oxford: Clarendon Press, 1970), 797.

38. Jones to Wilkins, April 24, 1784, in Cannon, Letters, 646.

39. Sir William Jones, "'Preface,' Institutes of Hindu Law . . . ," in *The Works of Sir William Jones* (London, 1807), 7:37.

40. Jones to Pitt, February 5, 1785, in Cannon, *Letters,* 664.

41. Jones to Wilkins, March 1785, in Cannon, *Letters,* 666.

42. Jones to Russell, September 8, 1785, in Cannon, *Letters,* 680.

43. Jones to Macpherson, October 1785, in Cannon, *Letters,* 687.

44. Jones to Hastings, October 23, 1786, in Cannon, *Letters,* 718.

45. Murray B. Emmenau, "India and Linguistics," *Journal of the American Oriental Society* 75 (1955): 148.

46. Cannon, *Letters,* 643–44; Garland Cannon, "Sir William Jones and Edmund Burke," *Modern Philology* 54 (1956–57): 165–86; and see my "Law and the Colonial State in India," in Cohn, *Colonialism and Its Forms of Knowledge* (Princeton NJ: Princeton University Press, 1996).

47. Jones to Cornwallis, March 19, 1788, in Cannon, *Letters,* 795.

48. Jones to Chapman, September 28, 1785, in Cannon, *Letters,* 684.

49. Jones to Rouse, October 24, 1786, in Cannon, *Letters,* 721.

50. Jones to Cornwallis, March 19, 1788, in Cannon, *Letters,* 799.

51. George Lewis Smyth, *Monuments and Gennii of St. Paul's Cathedral and Westminster Abbey* (London, 1839), 2:631.

52. Nathaniel Halhed, *A Grammar of the Bengali Language* (1778; facsimile reprint, Menston, England: Scolar Press, 1969), i–ii.

53. H. P. Foster, *A Vocabulary in Two Parts, English Bongalee and Vice a Versa, Part I* (1799; Calcutta, 1830), iv.

54. Foster, *A Vocabulary,* i.

55. William Carey, *Dialogues Intended to Facilitate the Acquireing of the Bengali Language* (Serampur, 1801), v.

56. William Carey, *Grammar of the Bengali Language* (Serampur, 1805), iv.

57. Halhed, *Grammar,* xxi, xxii.

58. Halhed, *Grammar,* x–xi. See also Muhammad Abdul Qayyam, *A Critical Study of the Early Bengali Grammars: Halhed to Houghton* (Dhaka: Asiatic Society of Bangladesh, 1982), for a highly sophisticated analysis of the linguistic and historical context of Halhed's *Grammar.*

59. Halhed, *Grammar,* xii.

60. Halhed, *Grammar,* iii.

61. Halhed, *Grammar,* ix.

62. Halhed, *Grammar,* xi–xii.

63. For early British ideas about Indian languages, see John Fryer, *A New Account of East India and Persia* (London, 1909), 1:95, 2:41–42, 103; J. Ovington, *A Voyage to*

*Surat in the Year 1689* (London, 1929), 147; Thomas Bowrey, *A Geographical Account of the Countries around the Bay of Bengal* (Cambridge, 1903), 18:6; H. D. Love, *Vestiges of Old Madras* (London, 1913), 2:147, 3:128; Temple, *Diaries*, 2:192.

64. Edward Terry, *A Voyage to East India* (London, 1655), 232.

65. G. A. Grierson, "On the Early Study of Indian Vernaculars in Europe," *Journal of the Asiatic Society of Bengal* 62 (1893): 41–50; see also G. A. Grierson, "Bibliography of Western Hindi, Including Hindostani," *Indian Antiquary* (January 1903): 16–25; (February 1903): 59–76; (April 1903): 160–79.

66. George Hadley, *Grammatical Remarks on the Practical and Vulgar Dialect of the Indostan Language Commonly Called Moors* (London, 1772), vi, xii–xiii.

67. For Gilchrist's biography and selections from his works, see M. Atique Siddiqi, *Origins of Modern Hindustani Literature: Source Materials: Gilchrist Letters* (Aligarh, India: Naya Kitab Ghar, 1963), and Sadiq-ur-Rahman Kidwai, *Gilchrist and the "Language of Hindoostan"* (New Delhi: Rachna Prakashan, 1972).

68. Siddiqi, *Origins of Modern Hindustani*, 21.

69. John B. Gilchrist, preface to *A Dictionary English and Hindoostanee*, 2 parts (Calcutta, 1786, 1790). The preface was reprinted as an appendix to the *Grammar and Dictionary* (Calcutta, 1798). References here are to the 1790 edition.

70. Gilchrist, preface, vii, xiv.

71. Gilchrist, preface.

72. Gilchrist, preface, xxvi.

73. Gilchrist, preface, v.

74. Gilchrist, preface, xli.

75. Gilchrist, preface.

76. Gilchrist, preface, xix–xx.

77. Gilchrist, preface, xx.

78. Gilchrist, preface, iv.

79. Gilchrist, xxiii.

80. Gilchrist, preface, xxii.

81. Gilchrist, preface, xxii–xiv.

82. India Office Records and Library, Board's Collection, #1981, vol. 97.

83. For the history of the College of Fort William, see Sisir Kumar Das, *Sahibs and Munshis: An Account of the College of Fort William* (New Delhi: Orion Publications, 1978); David Kopf, *British Orientalism and the Bengal Renaissance* (Berkeley: University of California Press, 1969).

84. There is no agreement on the exact number of books published in Hindustani, Braj, and Urdu under the auspices of the college. Kidwai, *Gilchrist*, 25, lists sixty Urdu books published between 1800 and 1804; Das, *Sahibs and Munshis*, lists forty-four books in Hindustani produced at the college between 1802 and 1804. A. Locket, secretary of the college, listed twenty-eight works in Braj, Urdu, and

Hindustani published at the expense of the government between 1800 and 1812. India Office Library and Records, Board's Collection, #10708, vol. 446.

85. William Carey, *Dialogues*. For discussion of the significance and a partial linguistic analysis of these dialogues, see Sisir Kumar Das, *Early Bengali Prose: Carey to Vidyasagar* (Calcutta: Bookland, 1966), 68–75; Das, *Sahibs and Munshis*, 74–75.

86. Das, *Sahibs and Munshis*, 74.

87. John Borthwick Gilchrist, *Dialogues, English and Hindostanee: calculated to promote the Colloquial intercourse of Europeans in the most useful and familiar subjects, with Natives of India, Upon their arrival in That Country*, 2nd ed. (London 1809).

88. Quoted in Gilchrist's *Dialogues*, lxxx.

89. Gilchrist, *Dialogues*, lxxi.

90. J. B. Gilchrist, *The General East India Guide and Vade Mecum . . . Being a Digest of the work of the Late Cap' Williamson with Many Improvements and Additions* (London, 1825), 536–37.

91. John Briggs, *Letters Addressed to a Young Person in India* (London, 1828).

92. "Instructions by Major General Sir John Malcolm, To Officers Acting under His Orders in Central India, in 1821," in *The Political History of India, from 1784–1823*, by Sir John Malcolm (London, 1826), 2, appendix 7, cclxiii–cclxiv.

93. Briggs, *Letters*, 9, 50.

94. Gilchrist, *East India Guide*, 536–39; Gilchrist, *Dialogues*, 174–81.

95. Gilchrist, *East India Guide*, 546.

96. V. C. P Chaudhary, "Imperial Honeymoon with Indian Aristocracy," *Kashi Prasad Jayaswal Research Institute, Historical Research Series* (Poona), no. 18 (1980): appendix 13, 425–36.

97. Gilchrist, *East India Guide*, 551.

98. Gilchrist, *East India Guide*, 564–65.

99. Frederick John Shore, *Notes on Indian Affairs* (1837), 1:27.

100. Christopher King, "The Nagari Prachaini Sabha . . . ," PhD diss., University of Wisconsin, 1974; Rajendralal Mitra, "On the Origin of the Hindvi Language and Its Relation to the Urdu Dialect," *Journal of the Asiatic Society* 33 (1864): 489–515; John Beames, "Outline for the Plea for the Arabic Element in Official Hindustani," *Journal of the Asiatic Society* 35 (1866): 1–13; F. S. Growse, "Some Objections to the Modern Style of Hindustani," *Journal of the Asiatic Society* 35 (1866): 172–81.

101. W. C. Taylor, "On the Present State and Future Prospect of Oriental Literature Viewed in Connection with the Royal Asiatic Society," *Journal of the Royal Asiatic Society of Great Britain and Ireland* 2 (1835): 4, 9.

102. Letter printed as part of the introduction to Charles Wilkins, ed., *The Bhagvet-Geeta or Dialogues of Kreeshna and Arjoon* (London, 1785), 13.

103. Wilkins, *Bhagvet-Geeta*, 15.

104. Sir James Mackintosh, "A Discourse at the Opening of the Literary Society of Bombay, 26 November 1804," *Transactions of the Literary Society of Bombay* 1 (1819, reprinted 1877): xiv, xi.

105. H. T. Colebrooke, *Miscellaneous Essays*, ed. Sir T E. Colebrooke (London, 1873), 1:61, letter dated April 18, 1794.

106. "Minute by Governor General Warren Hastings, 17 April 1781," in *Selections from the Educational Records*, part 1: *1781–1839*, ed. H. Sharp (Calcutta, 1920), 8.

107. Ruth Gabriel, "Learned Communities and British Educational Experiments in North India: 1780–1830," PhD diss., University of Virginia, 1979, 109.

108. Gleig, *Memoirs of Warren Hastings*, 3:159.

109. Gabriel, "Learned Communities," 112–20.

110. Letter from Jonathan Duncan to Lord Cornwallis, January 1, 1792, in Sharp, *Selections*, 9–11.

111. Sharp, *Selections*, 33–36.

112. "Minute by Lord Minto, 6 March 1811," in Sharp, *Selections*, 19.

113. Lord Wellesley, "Notes with Respect to the Foundation of a College at Fort William," in *Despatches and Minutes . . . of the Marquis of Wellesley . . . In India*, ed. Montgomery Martin, (London, 1836), 2:329–30.

114. Das, *Sahibs and Munshis*, 7–21.

115. Bernard S. Cohn, "Recruitment and Training of British Civil Servants in India 1600–1800," in *Asian Bureaucratic Systems Emergent from the British Imperial Tradition*, ed. Ralph Braibanti (Durham NC: Duke University Press, 1966), 116–40.

116. India Office Library and Records, Board's Collection, vol. 465, #110708, for the list of books subsidized, and #11252 for the Court's remarks. For publications in the entire period of the College, see Das, *Sahibs and Munshis*, appendix E, 155–66.

117. Mathew Lumsden, *A Grammar of the Persian Language* (Calcutta, 1810), xxviii.

118. Das, *Sahibs and Munshis*, 107.

119. "Some Account of the Literary Life of Charles Philip Brown, Written by Himself," in C. P. Brown, *English–Telugu Dictionary*, 2nd ed. (1866; Madras, 1895), xiv.

120. Robert Caldwell, *A Comparative Grammar of South Indian Family of Languages*, 3rd ed. (1896; New Delhi: Oriental Books Reprint Corp., 1974), xii–xiii.

121. "Report of A. D. Campbell, 17 August 1823," in House of Commons, *Committee on the Affairs of the East India Company*, 1832–33, appendix, Public I.2, vol. 12, p. 353.

122. William Adam, *Reports on Vernacular Education in Bengal and Behar*, ed. J. Long (Calcutta, 1868), 20.

123. F. W. Ellis, "Note to the Introduction," in A. D. Campbell, *A Grammar of the Telagu Language* (Madras, 1820), 1–2. For a discussion of Ellis's work and significance, see Walter Eliot in *Indian Antiquary* 4 (July 1875): 219–21 and 7 (November 1878): 274–75; R. E. Asher, "Notes on F. W. Ellis and an Unpublished Fragment of His Commentary on the Tirukkural," *Proceedings of the First International Conference Seminar of Tamil Studies* (April 1966): 513–22.

124. India Office Library and Records, Board's Collection, vol. 12, #549, letter dated May 12, 1814, pp. 19, 47.

125. India Office Library and Records, letter dated May 12, 1814, pp. 47, 49–51.

126. Thomas R. Trautman, "The Study of Dravidian Kinship," in *Aryan and Non Aryan in India*, ed. Madhav M. Deshpande and Peter Edwin Hook, Michigan Papers on South and Southeast Asian Studies, no. 14 (Ann Arbor: Center for South and Southeast Asian Studies, University of Michigan, 1979), 153–54.

127. Caldwell, *Comparative Grammar*, xi–xii.

128. Brown, *Dictionary*, xv.

129. Kamil Zvelbil, "Tamil Literature," in *A History of Indian Literature*, ed. Jan Gonda (Wiesbaden: Harrassowitz, 1974), vol. 10, facsimile 1, p. 3.

130. Zvelbil, "Tamil Literature," 3–4.

# 3 | The Sociology of Islam

## The French Tradition

EDMUND BURKE III

### In Search of Islamic Sociology

Years ago, Clifford Geertz wrote a provocative article in the *New York Review of Books* in which he argued that the old explanations of North African society were no longer valid, if they ever had been.[1] Arriving in Morocco in 1965, with the classics of the French colonial tradition as his guide, Geertz looked immediately for the primordial groupings which he had been led to believe structured social relations at every level. He found instead that, on closer investigation, the concepts of tribe, saintly lineage, Sufi *tariqa*, and even the extended family tended to dissolve before his very eyes. The French literature seemed suddenly suspect; all now was dyadic ties. What had changed, of course, was not only North Africa. It was also the observer. As a consequence of the shifting patterns of world politics in the postwar era, as well as changes in intellectual fashions, Morocco was suddenly of interest to British and American social scientists. In these sea changes it was perhaps to be expected that the image of North African society went temporarily out of focus. But so too, in a way, did the French tradition of the sociology of Islam.[2] How and why it did so, and with what implications for present-day social scientists, is the subject of this essay.

The French tradition of the empirical study of Muslim societies began in 1798 with the Napoleonic expedition to Egypt. The central paradigms of the tradition were laid down in the volumes of the *Description de l'Égypte* and the work of the first generation of Frenchmen in Algeria.[3] The tradition developed over the next century and a half, largely within these early parameters. The major phases of its development correspond to the shifting patterns of French colonialism. By the outbreak of the Algerian War in 1954, it had become a mummified version of its former self, and in its evident inability to explain the outbreak of the war, or its raison d'être, collapsed of its own weight. Somehow a tradition that had begun with aspirations of bringing the fruits of the French Revolution to the lands of Islam had become an apologist for empire, a disseminator of racist stereotypes, and a producer of irrelevant folklore. It is no accident that the life span of this intellectual tradition may be demarcated by the beginnings of French imperialism in the Middle East, and its bloody and convulsive end.

But can there be said to be a French tradition of the sociology of Islam? The very terms of such a formulation are full of traps for the unwary. Indeed, at the risk of being perverse, I am tempted to observe that the sociology of Islam does not exist, and that it has until recently been preeminently a French tradition. Part of the problem, part of the misconceived *problematique* of the field is the assumption that Islam is an appropriate field for sociological inquiry.[4] The question of the relationship between the study of Muslim peoples and the discipline of orientalism, never an easy or straightforward one, is thereby posed. Then there is the fact that the bulk of the French sociology of Islam was produced by individuals who were not sociologists at all. Rather, they were colonial native affairs officers, civilian amateurs and orientalists. Academic sociologists did not interest themselves seriously in such questions until World War II. By this route we shall be led to consider the relationships between those whom we are here calling sociologists (using the word in its broad nineteenth-century sense), and intellectual circles in metropolitan France. A third objection can be raised to the title of this essay. It is the presumption that something called a *tradition* of the sociology of Islam exists. Such an intellectual exercise has implications of which we should be aware. What does it mean to speak of a tradition of the sociology of Islam? Before going on to discuss in greater detail the legacy of French sociology of Islamic societies (which, as we will see, is principally a sociology of North Africa), it is necessary to consider further these questions.

The study of Islamic subjects in France followed two paths.[5] One was the discipline of orientalism, a linguistically defined field based on the critical study of texts written in Oriental languages. The other was the less rigorous tradition of colonial studies of Muslim societies, which was the product of amateurs and enthusiasts, expatriate sojourners in an exotic world they sought to understand.

French orientalists dominated the study of Islamic subjects in the metropole. From the time of Silvestre de Sacy (1757–1838), who can in many ways be said to have single-handedly invented the field, orientalists conquered positions of institutional power within the Parisian academic establishment: the Department of Oriental Manuscripts of the Bibliothèque nationale, the École des Langues orientales, the Collège de France, and the Académie des Inscriptions et Belles Lettres of the Institut de France. Although their mastery of Islamic languages made them useful to the French government in its colonial ventures in North Africa (de Sacy, Berbrugger, and others served there), the fundamental impetus of the discipline moved in other directions. Resolutely hostile to the study of contemporary subjects and devoted to the formalist study of classical texts, orientalists looked with deep suspicion on colonial ethnographers. Engaged in a study that they regarded as the elaboration of "the historical science of the human spirit" (Renan), they refused to sully their intellectually noble calling with less worthy intellectual pursuits. Not until the end of the nineteenth century, with the introduction of comparative linguistics and a new concern with the spoken language, did the discipline undergo important changes that were eventually to lead to its renewal.[6]

What orientalism contributed to the study of Islamic societies was the concept of Islamic civilization. This had its advantages, as well as its liabilities. On the one hand, it compelled students of colonial North Africa to recognize the historical past of North African Muslims and their place in the wider world of Middle Eastern Islamic civilization. For a time, this inhibited the tendency to conceive of the Maghreb as an island cut off from its Mashriqi point of reference. On the other hand, by its method of civilizational studies, orientalism accredited essentialist notions about the nature of Islamic history, even while it systematically devalued the study of periods after the early Arab empire. For E. F. Gautier, the murky periods ("les siècles obscurs") included everything after the Arab conquest of North Africa.[7]

Nineteenth-century French orientalists also shared with the students of Islamic societies the romantic quest for the exotic, for *dépaysment*, perhaps ultimately for the self. Ethnographers, orientalists, painters and writers—people like Léon Roches, Daumas, Masqueray, Delacroix, Flaubert, and de Foucauld—were propelled from their secure moorings in metropolitan bourgeois society into an encounter with the other, the Arab, the Oriental. One of the most striking things about this imperialism of the spirit is the watchful impersonality that characterizes the closest personal encounters, a kind of voyeurism, an emotional ethnography of the other. Even in its most intimate and personal form, that of sexual relations, one finds this strange distanced watchfulness. The heroic couplings of Gide at Biskra, no less than Flaubert's affair with Kuchuk, or that of any number of French lieutenants of the Arab Bureau have this quality. Edward Said, who is our best guide to this encounter with the Orient, is therefore correct to insist on both its sexual nature and its paradoxical abstraction of the Other.[8] He is also right to point to the manner in which this encounter springs from a desire for power, for domination, which is the very opposite of mutuality. This romanticism was most potent in the first half of the century, but it continued to be an important current of thought and feeling until well into the twentieth century.[9] The psychosexual dynamics of the encounter with Oriental peoples are of central importance to any effort at understanding the complex origins and nature of French orientalism and colonial ethnography.

If the sociology of Islamic societies had an ambiguous relationship to French orientalism, it was frankly marginal to intellectual currents in France, an insignificant back eddy to the onrushing stream of French *science*. This is all the more true of its relationship to the discipline of sociology. The major figures of French sociology, from Comte and Le Play to Durkheim, Mauss, and Lévi-Strauss, were little interested in the Maghreb, or Islamic societies generally. Neither were their disciples. French ethnography of Islamic societies developed in a kind of intellectual ghetto, clearly subordinate to the metropolitan world, a little tradition against the greater French tradition. This explains why, despite what is a vast ethnological literature, no significant contribution to general sociological theory can be found in French studies on North Africa.[10]

Although it was marginal to metropolitan *science*, the sociology of North Africa was much closer to the French political arena. Often, indeed, it was dominated (to its detriment) by political questions. Thus the study of the nature of the system of landholding in rural Algeria was from the outset a highly charged political question for French settlers, and the literature on *arsh* land reflects this fact.[11] As a result of the interpenetration of the academy and politics in Algeria, and the leading role played by Algerian politicians in the *parti colonial* in the Chamber of Deputies like Eugène Etienne, the scholars of the École d'Alger could often display considerable political clout even in France itself. The bitter struggle between the École d'Alger and Alfred Le Chatelier for the control of research on Morocco at the beginning of the twentieth century is one reflection of this, as we shall see. All of this is to say that as a colonial social science, the sociology of North Africa was decisively shaped in important ways. This fact drastically informed its achievements from the beginning, skewing its central paradigms, suggesting false questions, and inhibiting the asking of important ones.

Already by the 1850s, the central assumptions of what I have elsewhere referred to as the colonial vulgate on the nature of North African society can be observed in the work of such writers as Eugène Daumas, Thomas Pein, Louis de Baudicour, and Charles Richard.[12] These assumptions included the anarchic state of precolonial society, the essentially negative and obscurantist role of Islam in North African society, the innate fanaticism of Islam, and the division of the society into dichotomous, mutually exclusive groupings: Arab and Berber, nomad and sedentary, rural and urban. From this it was but a step to conclude the congenital incapacity for independence of North Africans, and the legitimacy of French rule and of its civilizing mission. It is the platitudes of the colonial vulgate that provide the connecting thread between the liberal humanitarianism of the Saint-Simonians, the *vae victis* of the settlers, and the positivist social Darwinism of late nineteenth-century ethnologists. That such a set of assumptions had direct political relevance is evident. That it also helped to condition the questions that were asked and not asked, and the answers that were given, is no less true and demonstrable.

To speak of a tradition of French sociology of Islam involves an intellectual exercise the implications of which we should be aware. The result of such an effort at retrospective construction is to validate, to accord legitimacy, to assert the existence of such a tradition. A tradition in this sense, what Foucault calls a *discours*, is invested with a kind of *mana* that is ultimately highly interested.[13]

A tradition is ultimately a politically structured discourse, whose function is to dominate, control, and orient our understanding. As we are no longer contemporaries of the period in which this discourse flourished, there is no reason for us to accept its central assumptions. Because we are not innocent consumers of its product (colonial sociology), but are forced to have reference to it insofar as we are interested in North African society, it is crucially important that we situate its practitioners against the political and intellectual background in which they flourished, and their central assumptions about that society.

Finally, if we consider the characteristic emphasis of French *ethnologues* on certain topics (and not others), we may assert that we are indeed dealing with a tradition. The two topics that most interested the students of Algerian society were the forms and functions of the principal manifestations of Islam in the countryside (the *ulama*—Muslim religious scholars—and urban religious institutions more generally, were of little concern) and the structure and role of the tribes in Algerian society. A very substantial proportion of the ethnological literature on Algeria focuses on these topics, including much of the manners and customs (*moeurs et coutumes*) variety of reportage, but also a great many more ambitious treatises.[14] The Moroccan literature, the other important body of French sociological studies of Islam, developed only after the turn of the century. In addition to the two major themes of study contributed by the Algerian literature, it added two more: the study of cities, and the study of the relationship between the tribes and a central polity. This provided a central motif in Robert Montagne's work on the Berbers of the central High Atlas, of course.[15] But it also informs many lesser efforts. The French sociology of the Maghreb remained fixated on these questions until the eve of decolonization.

At the same time some important questions were never raised, and this helps almost as much to define the tradition. These included studies of contemporary social change (Montagne's work on the *bidonvilles* of Casablanca dates only from 1951) and the political economy of both the precolonial and colonial Maghreb. Other important absent concepts and themes were segmentary lineage structures (a British monopoly), the study of the ulama and Islamic legal system as it actually operated (what may be called *ulamology* is a postcolonial phenomenon), and the economic ties between city and country (French sociologists tended to presume economic autarchy). In a wider sense, as I have already mentioned, both the history of precolonial North Africa, and its manifold connections with other parts of the Islamic world were given little weight in the assessment of present circumstances.

### The French Tradition in Historical Perspective

The French tradition of the sociology of Islam had three major periods of efflorescence. These may be described as the Egyptian period (1798–1828), the Algerian period (1830–70), and the Moroccan period (1900–1930). Of the three, by far the most important was the Algerian period. Inevitably, just as the Indian colonial experience tended to shape the perceptions of British orientalists and anthropologists, so also the Algerian experience marked the French image of the world of Islam.[16] Most of the leading students of Islamic societies were formed in Algeria, and even those who were not tended to define themselves negatively with reference to the work of the French Algerian experts. One could do an interesting study, for example, of the efforts of French Africanists to free themselves from the influence of the Algerian paradigm. It was through an Algerian lens that the French viewed other Islamic societies.

Yet the Egyptian experience did not count for nothing. The twenty-three enormous volumes of the *Description de l'Égypte* provided a model of scientific completeness for the Algeria venture, and the volumes of the *Exploration scientifique de l'Algérie* (1844–67), edited by Pelissier de Reynaud, represent a conscious imitation of this early fruit of French colonial science.[17] Some of the scholars who had participated in the Egyptian effort later played a role in the first efforts to compile a thorough inventory of Algerian society. What is striking about both of these cases, and is also true of the work on Morocco that was to follow, is that within the span of a single generation the job was done. Successive generations confined themselves for the most part to further elaborations of the central themes laid down at this time.

Why was it that in each case, the generation of the conquest was invariably the most energetic and careful chronicler of the society? The further one gets from the blood and thunder of military conquest, so it seems, the less relevant and less reliable the ethnography. This perception, as we shall see, is not completely accurate. But there is considerable truth in it. The reasons why this should be so are not hard to discover. One is that the first generation had the advantage of being first, and of everything thus being new, fresh, and interesting. Insofar as many of the early observers were military men, or directly tied to the colonial enterprise, they had a vested interest in understanding the dense specificity of the society, and in being able to distinguish its chief components. Put simply, lives might depend on it. As the bureaucratic routine took over later on, officers had only to update the reports of their predecessors. At the same time, they were overwhelmed by increasing amounts of paperwork, and spent less time in the marketplace or on horseback frequenting their charges. For all of these reasons, therefore, the early periods were indeed formative.[18]

If we examine the French tradition of the sociology of Islam in historical perspective, it can be seen to consist of three broad strands, the complex patterning of whose interactions over a century and a half constituted the tradition: the Arab Bureaus, the civilian amateurs, and the academics. Inevitably, of course, there was considerable overlap between them. Attached to real social forces with real interests and perceptions of the society, these three groups are of primary importance in understanding not only the contributions to the intellectual tradition of colonial sociology, but also much of the dynamics of French colonial politics.

The most important of the three was the tradition of the Arab Bureaus. It began in 1844 with the appointment of Eugène Daumas (1802–71) by General Bugeaud as head of a Direction of Arab Affairs. From these "Robinson galonnés," as Jacques Berque has called them, came a major share of the most important works on Algerian society, customs, and religion.[19] Closely involved with the life of the tribes, the native affairs officers of the Arab Bureaus knew from direct observation and experience what the civilians and the academics seldom grasped: the attractiveness of Muslim society, its endless capacity for resistance, its subtleties as well as its vulnerabilities. From this alliance with the tribes sprang both the strengths and the weaknesses of the tradition of the Arab Bureaus. The model of tribal structure first worked out by Daumas, Pein, Richard, and Urbain and based on the patriarchal family continued to inspire work up to Montagne's 1930 thesis.[20] The culture of tribal society, no less than its "moral topography," was first outlined by the men of the Arab Bureaus. Techniques of oral investigation were developed that made possible Daumas's study of the Sahara and Carette's of Kabylia, on the basis of a careful cross-questioning of local informants.[21] The application of the same methods was later to produce such works as Émile Laoust's *Mots et choses berbères*, and August Mouliéras's study of the Rif.[22] Another early theme was the study of Sufi *turuq*, or brotherhoods. These were widely believed to be deeply involved in Algerian resistance to the French presence. Neveu's *Les Khouan* was the first of a series of inquiries based on the systematization of information on tariqa membership collected by means of an administrative questionnaire.[23] Together with Richard's *Étude sur l'insurrection du Dahra (1845–46)*, it represents a genre of studies of the popular religious roots of the Algerian resistance effort.

If we were to plot on a map the successive thrusts of French military advance in North Africa, we would find a close correspondence with the advance of knowledge about the society. By the end of the Second Empire the ethnographic inventory of Algeria was virtually completed; only the Sahara remained to be explored. For Tunisia, we have good ethnographies only for the southern regions, as only there was the system of military administration of the tribes on the Algerian model employed. The historical development of French knowledge about Morocco adhered to much the same outline: first the coastal districts and the central plain, then the cities of the interior, and only later on the tribes of the Rif, Middle and High Atlas, the Sous, and the Saharan steppe. In Morocco, however, the early studies were done primarily by French academics, and it was chiefly the Berber areas and the Saharan zones that were studied by the men of the Arab Bureaus. I will have more to say about the development of Moroccan colonial sociology further on.

The second major strand of French sociology of Algeria was the work of civilian amateurs and explorers, men like Camille Sabatier and Henri Duveyrier.[24] The civilians possessed neither the motivation nor the direct access to the Muslim populations. Their intellectual contribution to the field was therefore the weakest of the three. If that contribution is assessed in political terms, however, it emerges as fundamental. Even the few civilians who could speak with real authority on Algerian matters tended primarily to advance views of Muslim society that reflected the interests of French settlers. Indeed, it is this that gives them their importance. The bitter and unrelenting hostility of French settlers to the Arab Bureaus and their support of the great feudal Arab chiefs provided one of the leitmotifs of French settler politics, and seriously influenced the course of Algerian colonial history. For individuals like Dr. August Warnier, the men of the Bureaus were the real enemies of France in Algeria.[25] Lording it over the tribes, they lived the life of pashas; their corruption was legendary, and so was their duplicity. The aristocratic leanings and royalist sympathies of the officers were repugnant to the settlers, who loudly proclaimed their ardent republicanism. There can be no doubt that while the settlers greatly exaggerated, there was some substance to their charges. Many of the officers were of aristocratic origin; some were royalists. Others were Saint-Simonians and conducted social experiments on the tribes entrusted to their administration.[26] Many too were sympathetic with many features of Algerian society, and adopted a paternalistic attitude toward the Muslim populations. The main reason for the hostility of the settlers, however, was that as long as a region was under military government, settlers had a difficult time acquiring land there. The Arab Bureaus thus came to constitute the chief obstacle to the extension of colonization, civilian rule, and settler domination.

To be sure, there were instances of dialogue between the two strands of the French tradition. One such was the collaborative work of Hanoteau and Letourneux, *La Kabylie et les coutumes kabyles* (1872).[27] (Hanoteau was *chef de bureau* at Fort National, and Letourneux was an Algiers lawyer.) It was Letourneux who, with his barrister's eye for system and order, processed what had been the local oral customary practice (the *qanun-s*) into a kind of Berber administrative handbook, a useful instrument for combating the nefarious influence of the sharia. The influence of *La Kabylie et les coutumes kabyles* extended even to Morocco, where it helped to inspire the Berber policy of Lyautey and his successors.[28] The same *politique des races* was later applied in Syria and Lebanon with regard to the Druse and Alawi minorities during the mandate period, with equally unfortunate results.[29] In general it would seem that the chief result of efforts at collaboration between military men and civilians was to accentuate the tendency already inherent in the military tradition to turn local customary practices into fixed and rigid principles.

The intensification of the debate between settler interests and the chief protectors of the Muslim populations, the Arab Bureaus, led to the growing politicization of French ethnography. The issuance of the *sénatus-consulte* of 1863 (a misguided effort at halting speculation in tribal lands) provoked a new interest in Arab society for a time. The collapse of the regime in 1870 and suppression of the Moqrani rebellion opened the way to the triumph of settler interests, which inevitably took on a sharply antimilitary coloration. The ensuing settler backlash led to the dismantling of the Arab Bureaus (which were permitted to continue only in the Saharan region), and the enactment of a series of punitive regulations known collectively as the *code de l'indigénat*. The years that followed, 1870 to 1900, were disastrous ones for Algerian Muslims. But they were equally disastrous for the sociology of Algeria. From a quasi-autonomous intellectual by-product of the Arab Bureaus, the ethnography of Algeria became increasingly dominated by the discourse of French colonial politics.

Concretely this found expression in the full development of the stereotypes of the colonial vulgate. No longer a serious threat, Muslims did not have to be taken seriously. There was thus little incentive to study them. It is during this period that the Berberophilia of the Kabyle myth became fully elaborated.[30] The Kabyle were believed to be potentially assimilable into French civilization by virtue of the supposed democratic nature of their society, their superficial Islamicization, and the higher status of Kabyle women. For a time a policy of cultural assimilation of the Kabyles was attempted by the French government, but given the uneven results it was soon abandoned (though a few schools were permitted to continue). Elements of the Kabyle myth can of course be found in the writings of Abbé Raynal and precolonial French travelers. What is new about its post-1870 manifestations is the effort, no doubt influenced by the racialism of late nineteenth-century social theories, to erect these differences into a systematic policy. The Kabyle myth and other elements of the colonial vulgate exercised a particularly unfortunate impact on French writings on Algeria in the period up to the First World War.

French academics, the third strand in the tradition of the sociology of Islam, were involved in the study of Algeria from the time of the conquest. But it was not until after 1870 that academics emerged as a distinct group. The individual who more than any other endowed the academic study of Algerian society with prestige and legitimacy was Émile Masqueray. His *Formation des cités chez les populations sédentaires de l'Algérie* appeared in 1886.[31] As the secretary of Victor Cousin and a brilliant young graduate of the École Normale Supérieur, Masqueray was well connected in governmental circles and destined for an important career. His work shows the influences of the Berberophilia of the time—but also that of his training as a student of Roman history. (The influence of Fustel de Coulanges is particularly marked in his work.) Where his thesis differed sharply from the Algerian tradition is in its bold application of the comparative method and its rigorous attention to the verification of evidence and the testing of hypotheses. Masqueray was at the center of the intellectual currents of his time, rather than on its fringes, as were the other Algerian academics. It is this that enabled him to transcend, even if only partially, the crippling effects of the politicization of colonial sociology. It is no surprise that he had no imitators.

The emergence of a group of French academics interested in the study of Algerian society dates from the end of the nineteenth century. It was during this period in France that the modern system of higher education first took form. Under the impact of German thought and a repackaged Comtean positivism, new disciplines emerged (such as sociology), and older ones (such as history) were transformed into something like their modern shapes. In Paris, this was the age of the Nouvelle Sorbonne, of Durkheim and Lucien Herr, of Ernest Lavisse and Gaston Maspéro. Similar stirrings were evident in Algeria, in particular in the group that gathered at the École des Lettres around René Basset.[32] The École d'Alger group possessed considerable ambition, seeking for itself nothing less than the monopoly of scientific research on Algerian society. By 1902 it was beginning also to cast covetous eyes on Morocco. In Edmond Doutté they possessed an important intellectual leader, one who was in touch with the times. Doutté was the author of works on Algerian folk Islamic practices, and had accomplished several study missions to Morocco. His sociology was a curious amalgam of Frazer's *The Golden Bough* and the *Année Sociologique*. Essentially, the production of the École des Lettres group focused on the study of local dialects, folklore, and popular interest, and carefully avoided general syntheses. It was also highly politicized. This politicization was exacerbated by the fear of pan-Islamic uprisings and the general atmosphere of chauvinism that dominated the period leading up to the Morocco Crisis (1905).[33]

The period leading up to the First World War was one of crisis for the French tradition of the sociology of Islam. But instead of leading to the breaking of the paradigms of colonial social science and the emergence of alternative discourses, it ended in a reaffirmation of the central elements of the colonial vulgate and the professionalization of the field. The struggle between the École d'Alger and Alfred Le Chatelier for the control over research on Moroccan society was one aspect of this crisis.[34] The conflict between the academics and the officers of the newly reinvigorated tradition of the Arab Bureaus that lay behind the establishment of the Institut des Hautes Études Marocaines and the division of sociological labor arrived at under Lyautey is a second aspect. I do not have the space here to explain either of these in detail.

A third aspect of the crisis can be seen in the history of the *Revue du Monde Musulman*. In the history of the French sociology of Islam, the quixotic figure of Alfred Le Chatelier emerges as one of the most original.[35] Le Chatelier was a product of the tradition of the Arab Bureaus. (He was *chef de poste* at Ouargla from 1883 to 1886.) But he resigned his commission out of impatience with military routine and embarked on a series of studies of Islam in Egypt, the Hedjaz, West Africa, and Morocco. In 1903 he was named to the first chair of Muslim Sociology and Sociography at the Collège de France. As director of the Mission scientifique du Maroc, he played a major role in the compilation of the ethnographic inventory of Morocco. Both *Archives marocaines* and the *Villes et Tribus du Maroc* series were the result of his inspiration and supervision. Le Chatelier was also the editor of the *Re-*

*vue du Monde Musulman* (1906–26), and it is this aspect of his accomplishments that is of interest to us.

What was unusual about the *Revue du Monde Musulman* was, above all, its subject matter: contemporary Islamic societies from the Philippines to Morocco caught in the full rush of change, rather than learned disquisitions on minute points in obscure Islamic treatises, or the *fiches du tribus* of French military ethnographers. The composite portrait of Islamic society in the first quarter of the twentieth century that emerges from its pages was that of a living, vital community (indeed, a whole series of communities sharing the same "great tradition") caught in the rough hurly-burly of change—the very opposite of the colonial vulgate. Alone of the journals of the period, it showed an interest in attracting a Muslim readership, and opened up its pages to its readers, publishing translations of the Muslim press of the Caucuses, Central Asia, and India, as well as the Arab East, Turkey, and Persia. Muslims were for the first time the subjects as well as the objects of inquiry, and their societies were presented in all of their manifold differences and vitality. In important ways, the *Revue du Monde Musulman* broke sharply with the tradition of the sociology of Islam, but it did not lead to the shattering of the colonial paradigm, and the reasons for this are instructive.

A specter haunts the pages of the *Revue du Monde Musulman*. It is the specter of pan-Islam. Colonial officials everywhere at the beginning of the twentieth century were filled with apprehension at the thought of vast pan-Islamic conspiracies that threatened their ability to control their Muslim subjects. Le Chatelier was unconvinced of the reality of their fears. What he saw was that Muslims stood at a historic crossroads. If their realities, which could only be plural, could be made known to French readers, and if they could only be persuaded of French sympathy for their destinies, then that future need not result in strife and violence. Here we see the old paternalism of the Arab Bureaus, this time exalted to a world scale. Simultaneously, Le Chatelier sought to persuade French officials of the necessity of adopting an Islamic policy toward French Muslim subjects, but one grounded in empirical observation and not colonialist fantasy.[36] In this respect he anticipated the formation during World War I of an interministerial committee to plan policy toward its Muslim subjects. Thus, if there was something anachronistic about the *Revue du Monde Musulman*, in important ways it also anticipates the new age. There is much in the career of Le Chatelier that suggests that of Robert Montagne.

We may now return to a consideration of the first crisis of Islamology. In a number of ways the situation in the period 1890–1914 resembled the crisis of colonial sociology of the 1950s and 1960s. Important developments within the field were leading toward a change in self-definition and organization. Both the École d'Alger and the Mission scientifique groups self-consciously presented themselves as *sociologists*, and asserted their intellectual connections to the Durkheim school. Their research methods were resolutely modern: *travail en équipe*, problem orientation, and an early form of survey research techniques. Moreover, for a brief period (1900–1904) they seemed ready to renounce the convenient pieties of the colonial vulgate for a much more open, complex, and nuanced portrait of Moroccan society. The *Revue du Monde Musulman* was not alone, therefore, in its independent and maverick views.

In 1904, all this changed. Ethnologists who had earlier been asserting the inadequacy of the *makhzan/siba* (government/dissidence) model of presenting the political structure of Morocco for a more subtle and complex view now changed their tune. Where before there had been an open, experimental attitude, now there were the familiar dichotomies of the colonial vulgate. To understand what had changed, it is necessary to look briefly at the changes in the world of French politics. Until 1904, there was a sharp division of opinion within French political circles about an appropriate policy toward Morocco. The French colonial offensive, which began in earnest in 1900, sputtered incoherently for the next several years, while the proponents of alternative policies battled it out. In this period of indecision, the heavy dominance of North African sociology by colonial politics was temporarily alleviated. The signing of the entente cordiale in 1904 and the Franco-Moroccan loan agreement changed all this rather brusquely. The new policy called for the development of French interests in Morocco through the control of the makhzan. France now acquired a vested interest in a particular view of Moroccan society, and the stereotypes of the Moroccan vulgate fell rapidly into place. The political dominance of colonial sociology was strongly reasserted. The development of the sociology of Morocco was permanently affected.[37]

World War I and the subsequent emergence of nationalist movements ensured that there would be no possibility of reexamining these fundamental assumptions, until the cracking of the edifice of French colonial rule made possible the emergence of suppressed alternative views, and particularly the development of a nationalist counterdiscourse. But this is another story.

## On the Uses of Colonial Sociology

My interest in the French sociology of Islam does not spring from a desire to celebrate its accomplishments, or to denigrate them. They are what they are. As a historian of the modern history of the Maghreb, however, I cannot escape these individuals, or their writings. Much as I might be repelled by their blatant racism, their faith in the civilizing mission of France or in the idea of progress, they pursue me like an ineluctable fate. For the simple fact is that they bear witness, according to their individual talents and prejudices, to a society that is no more. They are a body of evidence that must be consulted if we are interested in the history of this society, just as surely as the account books of Fasi merchants, Berber qanun-s, or the *Miyar* of al-Wansharisi. Like all historical documents, they have their uses and their abuses. How, then, to utilize them?

It would be tempting to say that we can simply separate fact from theory in the work of French colonial sociologists: the facts are reliable, the theories, impregnated with a long-bypassed problematique, are suspect. Alas, if it were only as easy! We must recognize that the facts themselves derive from the theory, their very factness certified by it, giving substance and reality. To deconstruct even a single product of this tradition in the hope of arriving at the bedrock of solid fact beneath the tissue of ideology that surrounds it is to engage in a monumental self-deception. For no such bedrock exists, and if we pursue such a line of questioning, it is doubtful that a single fact will remain unscathed. Fundamental epistemological questions force us, then, to acknowledge that we must take these men and women and their work as they are: Colonel Daumas was an anti-Arab racist, *and* he was a sometimes shrewd observer of Algerian society.[38]

What separates us from the French sociologists of Islam is, in part, as Jacques Berque has argued, a *question d'époque*.[39] We live on the other side of that Copernican revolution that was the national liberation movements of the 1950s and 1960s. The very word "native" is one that we have learned to mistrust, to reject. But it is not simply that colonial sociology *accompanied* the forces of the industrial and democratic revolutions to the Third World, as Berque would have it. Colonial sociology was directly involved from the outset in the process of domination. What the men of the Arab Bureaus sought was finally not sociological understanding of these societies, but the key to their operation, the secret or secrets that, once known, would permit their domination. That is to say, from the beginning their quest was oriented by the very nature of their relationship to the tribes whose destinies they controlled. The men of the Arab Bureaus were of course not social scientists. It is thus anachronistic to tax them with not being what they could not have been. But what is true of the Arab Bureaus is also true of the École d'Alger, the Institut des Hautes Études marocaines, and the Institut français de Damas. The very existence of the relationship between colonizer and colonized, like the Heisenberg uncertainty principle, intervened to ensure that in the very act of observing, the phenomena being observed are modified.

What they observed, or what, more tellingly, they ignored, was a function of where and how they encountered it. That is to say, it derived from their relationship to the intellectual currents of their age, and to its political ideas and structures. It is only on this basis that a sociology of these sociologists, a sociology of knowledge of colonial sociology can be erected. What they saw was rooted in the dense specificity of the tribe, its way of life, beliefs and practices, relations with political authority, and its ties to the land. But it was the tribe viewed through the grid of the stereotypes of the colonial vulgate, that is to say, finally, an essentially unchanging tribe, one shorn moreover of its connections to a wider world and to the past. The transformations induced by the colonial presence, by the colonial observer, were largely ignored. Some few knew better, knew that the society was changing under their noses, that there were worlds that escaped them, and that what they were doing was increasingly anachronistic even in its own time. Even those observers whose ideological view threatens at times to distort totally were capable of insights that went beyond the paradigms of the tradition. All of them in the end were bound by the intellectual horizons and problematique of the colonial situation.

There is no substitute, accordingly, for placing these colonial sociologists in the multiple contexts, both political and intellectual, in which they existed. This means being sensitive to the points of conflict between the various strands of the French tradition of the sociology of Islam, as well as the points of agreement. It also means being alert to individual nuances in their expression. The writings of French sociologists of Islam can be utilized, on condition that they are treated as historical sources, in the full sense of that term. Provided they are treated with the proper precautions, they have a great deal of importance to contribute to an understanding of the recent past of some Islamic societies, especially the Maghreb. They are certainly not to be accepted uncritically, or rejected out of hand. To recognize a species of discourse is already to be vaccinated against it.

## Notes

1. Clifford Geertz, "In Search of North Africa," *New York Review of Books*, April 22, 1971, 20–24.
2. The term "sociology" is herein utilized in something like its broad nineteenth-century sense. It is not limited to, although it eventually includes, the academic discipline of sociology.
3. *Description de l'Égypte, ou recueil des observations et des recherches qui ont été faites en Égypte pendant l'expédition de l'armée française, publié par les ordres de sa majesté Napoléon le Grand*, 23 vols. (Paris: Imprimerie impériale, 1809–28).
4. On this point, see Roger Owen, "Studying Islamic History," *Journal of Interdisciplinary History* 4, no. 2 (1973): 287–90. See also Maxime Rodinson, "Situation, acquis, et problèmes d'orientalisme islamisant," in *Le Mal de voir. Ethnologie et orientalisme: politique et autocritique*, Cahiers Jussieu No. 2 (Paris: Editions Réunis 10/18, 1976), 242–57; and my "Islamic History as World History: Marshall Hodgson and *The Venture of Islam*," *International Journal of Middle East Studies* 10 (1979): 241–64.
5. Maxime Rodinson, "The Western Image and Western Studies of Islam," in *The Legacy of Islam*, ed. Joseph Schacht and C. E. Bosworth (London: Oxford University Press, 1974), 49–50.
6. *Cent-Cinquantenaire de l'École des Langues Orientales Vivantes* (Paris: Imprimerie nationale de France, 1948) especially Regis Blachère, "Arabe Littéral (1795)," 50.
7. E. F. Gautier, *Le Passé de l'Afrique du nord: Les siècles obscurs*, 2nd ed. (Paris: Flammarion, 1937), subsequently reprinted many times.
8. Edward W. Said, *Orientalism* (New York: Pantheon Books, 1978).
9. Jacques Berque, *Arabies* (Paris: Stock, 1978).
10. The judgment is that of Berque. See his "Cent-vingt-cinq ans de sociologie maghrebine," *Annales, E.S.C.* (1956): 320. On the general subject of the development of French colonial sociology, see Donald Ray Bender, "Early French Ethnography in Africa and the Development of Ethnology in France," PhD diss., Northwestern University, 1964.
11. Charles-Robert Ageron, *Les Algériens musulmans et la France (1871–1919)*, 2 vols. (Paris: P.U.F, 1968), 1:67–78.
12. Eugène Daumas, *Le Sahara algérien* (Paris, 1845), and *Le grand désert* (Paris, 1848). Also Daumas and Fabar, *La Grande kabylie études historiques* (Paris, 1847); Thomas Pein, *Lettres familières sur l'Algérie: Un petit royaume arabe* (Algiers,

1893); Louis de Baudicour, *La guerre et le gouvernement de l'Algérie* (Paris, 1853); Charles Richard, *Étude sur l'insurrection du Dahra (1845–46)* (Algiers, 1846).

13. Michel Foucault, *The Order of Things: An Archeology of the Human Sciences* (New York: Pantheon Books, 1970). See also Pierre Bourdieu, *Esquisse d'une théorie de la pratique* (Geneva: Droz, 1972), for whom the equivalent term is *doxa*.

14. Berque, "Cent-vingt-cinq ans." See also Philippe Lucas and Jean-Claude Vatin, *L'Algérie des anthropologues* (Paris: Maspéro, 1975).

15. Robert Montagne, *Les Berbères et le makhzen dans le sud du Maroc* (Paris, 1930).

16. On the British experience, see Roger Owen, "The Influence of Lord Cromer's Indian Experience on British Policy in Egypt, 1883–1907," in *St. Antony's Papers*, no. 17, ed. Albert Hourani (London: Oxford University Press, 1965), 109–39.

17. *Exploration scientifique de l'Algérie pendant les années 1840, 1841, 1842, publié par l'ordre du gouvernement*, 39 vols. (Paris: Imprimerie royale, 1844–67).

18. This was also the case for the ethnography of Morocco. See André Adam, *Bibliographie critique de sociologie, d'ethnologie et de géographie humaine du Maroc* (Algiers: n.p., 1972); *Mémoires du Centre de recherches anthropologiques, préhistoriques et ethnographiques*, vol. 20. (Algiers, CRAPE, 1972).

19. Jacques Berque, *Le Maghreb entre les deux guerres* (Paris: Seuil, 1962), 124. Many of the judgments in this paragraph are borrowed from Berque, "Cent-vingt-cinq ans."

20. Eugène Daumas, *Exposé de l'état actuel de la société arabe, du gouvernement, de la législation qui la régit* (Algiers: Imprimerie du gouvernement, 1844), and the same author's *Moeurs et coutumes de l'Algérie: Tell, Kabylie, Sahara* (Paris: Hachette, 1853). Also Pein, *Lettres familières sur l'Algérie*; Charles Richard, *Du gouvernement arabe et de l'institution qui doit l'exercer* (Algiers: Bastide, 1848); Thomas Ismail Urbain, "Algérie. Du gouvernement des tribus. Chrétiens et musulmans. Français et Algériens," *Revue de l'Orient et de l'Algérie* 2 (1847): 241–59. On Montagne, see n. 15 *supra*.

21. Eugène Daumas, *Le Sahara algérien: Études géographiques, statistiques et historiques sur la région au sud des Établissements français en Algérie* (Paris, 1845); E. Carette, *Études sur la Kabylie proprement dite* (1848), published as vols. 4–5 of *Exploration scientifique de l'Algérie*.

22. Émile Laoust, *Mots et choses berbères, notes de linguistique et d'ethnographie: Dialectes du Maroc* (Paris, 1920); Auguste Mouliéras, *Le Maroc inconnu*, 2 vols., vol. 1, *Exploration du Rif (Maroc septentrional)* (Paris, 1895).

23. E. de Neveu, *Les Khouan: Ordres religieux chez les musulmans de l'Algérie* (Paris, 1845).

24. Camille Sabatier, *Études sociologique sur les Kabyles* (Algiers, 1881); Henri Duveyrier, *Les Touaregs du nord* (Paris, 1864).

25. Dr. Auguste Warnier and Jules Duval, *Bureaux arabes et colons* (Paris, 1869). Also Auguste Warnier, *L'Algérie et les victimes de la guerre* (Paris, 1871).
26. Marcel Emerit, *Les Saint-Simoniens en Algérie* (Algiers: Les Belles Lettres, 1941).
27. Adolphe Hanoteau and A. Letourneux, *La Kabylie et les coutumes kabyles*, 3 vols. (Paris: Callamel, 1872–73). On the circumstances of the collaboration of the two authors, see Gen. Maurice Hanoteau, "Quelques souvenirs sur les collaborateurs de *La Kabylie et les coutumes Kabyles*," *Revue Africaine* 65, no. 314 (1923): 134–49.
28. Edmund Burke III, "The Image of the Moroccan State in French Ethnological Literature: A New Look at the Origin of Lyautey's Berber Policy," in *Arabs and Berbers*, ed. Ernest Gellner and Charles Micaud (London: Duckworth, 1973); Charles-Robert Ageron, *Politiques coloniales au Maghreb* (Paris: P.U.F., 1973), 109–48.
29. See my "A Comparative View of French Native Policies in Morocco and Syria," *Middle Eastern Studies* 9 (1973): 175–86.
30. Charles-Robert Ageron, "La France a-t-elle eu une politique kabyle?," *Revue Historique* 223 (1960): 311–52.
31. Émile Masqueray, *Formation des cités chez les populations sédentaires de l'Algérie* (*Kabyles du Djurdjura, Chaouia de l'Aurès, Beni-Mezab*) (Paris: Leroux, 1886). On Masqueray, see Fanny Colonna and Claude Haim Brahimi, "Du Bon Usage de la Science Coloniale," in *Le Mal de voir. Ethnologie et orientalisme: Politique et épistemologie, critique et autocritique*, ed. Henri Moniot, Cahiers Jussieu No. 2 (Paris: Editions Réunis 10/18, 1976), 221–41; Fanny Colonna, introduction to *Formation des cités chez les populations sédentaires de l'Algérie* by Émile Masqueray (1983; Aix-en-Provence: Edisud, 1986). See also Lucas and Vatin, *L'Algérie des anthropologues*, 27–28.
32. On the École d'Alger, see Henri Massé, "Les Études arabes en Algérie (1830–1930)," *Revue Africaine*, nos. 356–57 (1933). Also Jean Mélia, *L'Épopée intellectuelle de l'Algérie: Histoire de l'Université d'Alger* (Algiers: La Maison des Livres, 1950), and *Cinquantenaire de la Faculté des Lettres d'Alger (1891–1931)* (Algiers: Société historique algérienne, 1932).
33. On Doutté, see my "The First Crisis of Orientalism, 1890–1914," in *Connaissance du Maghreb*, ed. Jean-Claude Vatin (Paris: CNRS, 1984), 213–26. For a contrary view, see Lucette Valensi, "Le Maghreb vu du Centre," in the same volume.
34. On this, see my "La Mission scientifique au Maroc: Science sociale et politique dans l'âge de l'impérialisme," in *Actes de Durham Recherches Récentes sur le Maroc moderne*, special issue of *Bulletin économique et social du Maroc*, nos. 138–39 (1979): 37–56.

35. Raymond Messal, *La genèse de notre victoire marocain. Un précurseur. Alfred Le Chatelier* (Paris: Dunod, 1931). This is the official biography.

36. Alfred Le Chatelier, "Politique musulmane: Lettre à un Conseiller d'État," *Revue du Monde Musulman* 12, no. 9 (1910): 1–165.

37. See my "The First Crisis of Orientalism."

38. See Pierre Bourdieu, "Les conditions sociales de la production sociologique: Sociologie coloniale et décolonisation de la sociologie," in *Le Mal de voir*, 416–27. Also Fanny Colonna, this volume. Though differing with both Bourdieu and Colonna on points of analysis and interpretation, I wish to record here my debt to them both. The epistemological questions are fundamental in any reassessment of colonial sociology.

39. Berque, *Arabies*, 181, also 102–3.

# 4 | Scientific Production and Position in the Intellectual and Political Fields

*The Cases of Augustin Berque and Joseph Desparmet*

FANNY COLONNA

Translated by David Prochaska and Jane Kuntz

Using the cases of two well-known and often cited colonial authors, Augustin Berque and Joseph Desparmet, I address in this essay issues that all researchers on the Maghreb have tackled at one point or another with regard to the scholarly literature of the colonial period.[1] Clearly, we cannot ignore the existence of this literature nor do without it. Equally clear is the difficulty involved in using it in a way that is not spurious and tendentious, that is, lacking in rigor. What exactly are we doing when we use this scholarship? To what extent are the facts it reports reliable? What is there in the arguments put forward that expresses interests outside the intellectual field? There is a certain naïveté, I feel, in the position of those authors who strive to demonstrate that colonial science is colonialist, or that its knowledge is a reflection of the power field in which it was produced.[2] A moment's reflection leads us rapidly to the conclusion that the opposite would in fact be more surprising. Wouldn't the truly naïve position consist in believing that there could ever exist a knowledge without power, or a science without interests? Or more precisely, in thinking that the knowledge each of us produces or attempts to produce escapes these conditioning factors that we perceive so easily in the knowledge of others, especially when it belongs to other intellectual fields, to other times or places.

I hope to demonstrate with regard to Berque and Desparmet—though I could very well have chosen almost any other author—that objective knowledge is not necessarily a product of "goodwill." Rather, certain social groups or isolated individuals might have an interest at a given moment in time in producing *genuine knowledge*, given both their relation to the object of

174

study and their position within the field of intellectual production to which they belong but that exists outside of them. I am thinking here, apart from my two examples, of the officers of the Arab Bureaus of colonial Algeria (Bureaux arabes)[3] and of Émile Masqueray.[4] Conversely, we might ask what we would know today about Algerian society if we had only the accounts written by so-called pro-Algerian authors (*indigénophiles*) like Jean Mélia or Albert Truphémus, whose texts are in other respects fascinating and well intentioned.[5]

Finally, a couple of remarks to justify my choice of these two authors. First, why two rather than just one? Because we always have a favorite author that we secretly feel to be less colonialist than the others.[6] To think through two cases demonstrates that we can think through all of them when attempting to build up the whole set of relations between personal position and intellectual discourse. Second, why these authors? Joseph Desparmet and Augustin Berque are widely read authors whose work is often drawn on either directly or indirectly. Their works are in a sense required reading for knowledge of Algerian society between the French invasion in 1830 and the Second World War. Yet they were tightly linked to colonization, very much part of it in their lives as much as in their ideologies. Berque never made any secret of what he wanted to know, namely, how to rule better. In his texts Desparmet is often racist in trivial ways, but it is exactly this type of case that I must think through in order to be convincing, rather than ambiguous cases like that of Masqueray. In this essay I consider the "lessons" of Desparmet and Berque, that is, what they teach us about Algerian society in the colonial period, before inquiring into the basis of their knowledge.

### The Lessons of Berque and Desparmet

How can authors such as Berque and Desparmet have any relevance for us today? One thing they share in common is that they both raised issues generally left untreated by the scholarly literature of the period in which they lived, but that were at the very center of colonial practice. In other words, they formally posed in intellectual terms (or para-intellectual, it matters little since this is not my point here) vitally important political issues not dealt with by scholars during this period: for Desparmet, that of *cultural resistance,* and for Berque, that of *relations among social groups and classes within the colonized society.*

Desparmet's importance resides in the fact that he constituted as an object of intellectual inquiry a number of practices and productions that were not explicitly connected and that moreover appeared at different points in time: popular poetry, the oral, less learned tradition, on the one hand, and the discourse of the reformist *ulama* on the other.[7] In other words, faced with a religious movement that appeared at the very end of his intellectual career,[8] Desparmet immediately understood what it was all about and, more specifically, how it was connected to what he had written about previously. What I mean is this: one need not have been a genius to see that both movements had something to do with the Arabic language, and as such both cases therefore involved resistance to the symbolic domination of French, although we might wonder to what extent this parallel was recognized by contemporaries.[9] But then Desparmet was always one for making seemingly incongruous connections. In this particular case, however, he did not settle for merely drawing a parallel, but described a field in which *a struggle* was taking place:

> We should not believe that in effect . . . the battle over language in Algeria comes down to a duel between Arabic and French. Let us imagine a philological map of languages in Algeria, and we shall see that the "Maghrebi genius" [*génie maghrébin*] has barricaded itself behind a triple linguistic wall. The first and oldest line of defense is formed by the Berber dialects, which function like so many fortresses that in the past defended the spiritual autonomy of the indigenous peoples against Muslim culture. These idioms have been slowly crumbling, and numerous breaches are now visible. They can be compared to a stronghold now in ruins but which continues to resist the invaders. The second protective wall is colloquial Arabic [*l'arabe barbaresque ou usuel*], which also has served the cause of independence against foreign usurpers in the past and could hardly be considered devoid of defensive value. Yet the strategists of Maghrebi Islam [*l'Islam maghrébin*] doubt its sturdiness, for it is not in step with more recent attitudes. So without downgrading it entirely, it has been relegated to the background. On the frontline face to face with the enemy, the thinkers from among the people and their advisors are at present feverishly building up a defensive and offensive system of classical Arabic [*l'arabe coranique*]. . . . In our study we will put to one side the various Berber patois, which make up

the rearguard, and will focus our attention on *the reciprocal situation and the conflict between the three competing languages, namely, colloquial Arabic, classical Arabic and French.* We will be making an on the spot appraisal of the fundamental fact of the century: the systematic "koranization" of the masses. In the process we will be watching as Islam offers up its sacred reserves [*réserves sacrées*] and substitutes the Arabic of the Holy Book for colloquial Arabic as the language of struggle against the language of the invader and against the danger of Frenchification [emphasis F.C.].[10]

One has to be careful with the terms "the reciprocal situation" and "the conflict between the three competing languages." We should also note the *elimination of Berber* from this problematic, an elimination that undoubtedly constitutes a simplification but that in fact is necessary in order not to get diverted by issues of particularism (the reactivation of primary solidarities in the manner of Geertz) or of populism, which would obscure the fact that linguistic Berberism was in the colonial period above all a grievance of marginalized elites.

Moreover, Desparmet goes beyond simply situating the three languages in relation to each other to sketch out the idea that what is involved here is in fact the relationships between the social groups:

These studies encompass two very different generations and fall naturally into two parts: in the first, the documents are drawn entirely from *popular literature*. At first *the outward manifestations were an instinctive racial reflex, spontaneous, disorderly and mystical in nature.* The country's defense had to be improvised with *traditional resources.* In the second part, the defense was organized with the inspiration of the *intellectual elite.* Polemics at the time developed with all the refinements of an age-old culture in the political language of pan-Islam. Where the popular poetry of the first generation did little more than console the people over their colonial subjection, the newspapers and magazines of the second period preached hope and paved the way for regeneration [emphasis F.C.].[11]

Of course, Desparmet identifies these types more in terms of *generations* than of *opposing social groups*, in other words, in an evolutionist manner and not in terms of synchronic struggles. He also fails to properly identify the social groups that make up his first generation, the proponents of *beurbri* and of popular poetry.[12] But then the problem is not a simple one, and we would be wrong to fill in the blank he has left with the word "peasantry." If the adherents of classical Arabic were at that time (and only at that time) easier to identify as the urban bourgeoisie now reappearing (or appearing), the beurbri speakers were clearly more varied, a mixture of city folk and country folk, but also including the landed aristocracy, what remained of the religious aristocracy, the noble warrior class (*l'aristocratie d'épée*), and so on.

To be sure, a theory of cultural resistance has yet to be developed, or at least completed. But all the elements are there in Desparmet to demonstrate that we are in the presence of a complex phenomenon that, while it obviously constitutes an *external reaction* to colonization, is also an *internal struggle* among social groups interested in the defense of different forms of linguistic competence. In other words, this internal struggle occurs in fact between the "traditional" urban bourgeoisie, on the one hand, and on the other hand with social groups that previously possessed cultural and religious legitimacy, namely, the religious or maraboutic aristocracy,[13] and the Sufi brotherhoods (Ar. pl. *turuq*; sing. *tariqa*).

A body of work such as that of Desparmet is somewhat disconcerting because of the gap between the accumulation of facts and the rather loose and undisciplined theory. This theory is more a matter of having a feel or sense of Algerian society than of scholarly knowledge (*savoir*) about it. And yet to have this feel or sense of Algerian society, this intuitive, practical knowledge (*savoir pratique*) is what is most important to Desparmet, as well as to Berque, for that matter. We would be wrong to underestimate this kind of approach, even though it is to the theory of domination what categories of indigenous thought are to the theory of primitive societies.

To take into account this intuitive knowledge (*savoir intuitif*) raises the issue of the respective status of the data and theoretical propositions in colonial historiography.[14] There is an approach that is more or less explicit, more or less conscious, and that consists of acting as if the facts in this literature were reliable in a thoroughgoing way while the conclusions drawn from them are to be rejected because they are colonialist.[15] Without going into the question here of the relationship between the arrangement of the facts and the theory that justifies it, it must be pointed out that when faced with this literature, we are in a situation of having to take *all or nothing*. If we want to disregard Desparmet's theses, which are implicit most of the time, we also have to throw into doubt even his translations of poetry and newspaper articles, which would result in the disappearance of his entire oeuvre. Clearly, the issue of how to use colonial scholarship (*science coloniale*) needs to be raised about this type of author, since such authors preclude the application of any double standard on our part. Because such authors do not apply a double standard, they prevent us in effect from resorting to dissociation, either/or choices, and censorship. We will see that the problem is quite similar in the case of Berque.

### Augustin Berque and the Relationships between Social Groups in Precolonial and Postconquest Society

Before addressing the case of Berque, I would like to say a word about the issue his work raises, namely, the relationships between social groups in Algeria, since its importance is less obvious than that of cultural resistance. It would be impossible to understand, on the one hand, the Islamic reform movement, whose importance in the later colonial period extended far beyond that of the narrowly nationalist movements since it was primarily a linguistic and religious movement and only secondarily a political movement.[16] On the other hand, it would be impossible to understand the absence of a national bourgeoisie espousing a nationalist strategy, which was the central parameter in determining the nature of power in the later colonial period, if, first, we fail to *reconstitute the structure of precolonial society*; that is, we must identify the social groups in place, and in particular their relative weight and their relationships. Second, and more important, we must provide an account of the behavior and the different evolutions of each of these groups as a result of the shock of the French conquest. To be sure, we can observe the facts, the trends—for example, the absence of an urban bourgeoisie, the resurgence of the Islamic brotherhoods—but these facts themselves can be interpreted in different ways depending on our idea concerning the *relations between groups* within colonial Algerian society in the first half of the twentieth century. For example, what does the phrase "the expansion of the brotherhoods" mean if we know nothing of the situation at the beginning of the eighteenth century?

The work of Augustin Berque, or more specifically, the three articles on which I base my arguments here,[17] does not answer these questions definitively, at the level of proof. Only work in social history, particularly economic history, could accomplish that. But these articles suggest at least two general directions for future research that I feel to be absolutely crucial. In the first place, Berque sees the relationships among social groups in *tribal society* in terms of opposing pairs:

ı A first opposition occurs between the rural aristocracy (which he refers to as the *juwad*) and the *mrabtin* (or marabouts), that is, between the warrior nobility and the religious nobility.[18]

ı A second opposition is that between the marabouts and the Sufi brotherhoods, that is, between a religious group based on birth and another based on voluntary membership.[19]

ı A third opposition occurs between tribes and brotherhoods, or in other words, between the principle of fragmentation and that of centralization.[20]

For Berque, the law (*sénatus-consulte*) of 1863,[21] by breaking up both the institution of the tribe and the juwad lineages,[22] initially engendered the rise of the religious aristocracy. But once this aristocracy was swept up in its turn in the larger disintegration of tribal structure, an unprecedented expansion of the religious brotherhoods occurred. Thus, a balance of power was followed by a definite disequilibrium which tilted in the direction of centralization.

With regard to *urban society*—and this is the second area for further research—Berque believed that there was never an urban bourgeoisie in sociological terms in Algeria, both because Algeria in 1830 was little urbanized and relatively decentralized, and because of the nature of Turkish rule, the second point being perhaps a consequence of the first.[23] Berque also thought that for perhaps the first time a kind of middle class began to take shape from around 1860, "which far from being an Islamic phenomenon, remains an economic phenomenon linked exclusively to our civilization."[24] We can obviously deplore the *absence of a theory of the relationships between urban society and tribal society* in this schema. But having said this, the combination of Berque's three sets of observations on the religious brotherhoods, the bourgeoisie, and the juwad make it possible to understand both the absence of a national bourgeoisie (such as the Old Destour Party in Tunisia) within the nationalist debate in Algeria,[25] and the sociological basis of the Islamic reform movement, which reflects not the reappearance of a bourgeoisie but the appearance of a traditional bourgeoisie, that is, a rising yet anachronistic bourgeoisie. This in turn would explain the Algerian bourgeoisie's lack of political assurance and its weak economic base, the two features being tied to each other as well as to its absence of tradition and historic roots. As a result, the role of the Islamic brotherhoods takes a different historical direction, namely, as transitional institutions at a crucial moment of social change, institutions that can be located somewhere between a segmentary type of social organization and a centralized kind of social organization such as the Islamic reform movement.[26] This makes it possible to understand a number of seemingly contradictory phenomena. For what is at issue here is the relative weight and the relationships of different kinds of groups, for example, bourgeoisie and brotherhood. Although no real theory is advanced, it is nonetheless certain that this way of looking at things provides food for thought. Here again the hypotheses are as important as the facts (which indeed are most often secondhand facts).

### The Men behind the Work

What I have just outlined is what I consider to be the entirely original contributions of these two authors. Two questions remain to be answered regarding these theoretical propositions and the data on which they are based. First, how do they relate to social reality? Second, why did these authors come up with these theories and documentation but not others?

The first question can be quickly eliminated because it poses a false issue. What matters in the theoretical propositions of Desparmet or Berque is not whether they are completely or partly right, or whether their theses are totally true or not.[27] What matters is that they offer *an interpretation* (*une lecture*), *a paradigm* that we most likely would not have thought of otherwise. Of course, these theoretical propositions are, strictly speaking, hypotheses; it remains for us to confirm them. But I want to repeat the argument I made earlier, namely, that these theses of colonial scholarship are as important as, and in fact more important than the facts of colonial scholarship, which, moreover, would not exist without them.

The second question is why do we find these stimulating and innovative readings of social reality in these authors but not others? Perhaps the answer lies in the distinctive characteristics of our two authors. The first thing that is striking about them is that they both were marginal with respect to the intellectual field of colonial Algeria in their period, in spite of how they may appear at first. Thus, Berque is a doer, a *practitioner*, initially an administrator of the mixed communes (*communes mixtes*) and later an official in the Native Affairs administration (*chargé de mission aux Affaires indigènes*).[28] Although fluent in Arabic, he was not an orientalist either by education or by occupation. Moreover, within his peer group, the administrators of mixed communes, he was considered a "parvenu" who had climbed up through the ranks rather than graduating from the École coloniale. (For example, we know that his father was an army veterinarian who died when Berque was in his teens, and that he was something of an autodidact.) It was his 1919 article on the Sufi brotherhoods that brought him to the attention of J.-D. Luciani, then director of Native Affairs for the Algerian Gouvernement Général.[29] In short, Berque was a practitioner, not an academic, as well as being an autodidact who did not make his way up via the established career path.

Desparmet was not a university academic either. As a secondary school teacher (*professeur de lycée*), he always taught in the provinces, "in the interior," as it was said in the Maghreb at the time, in Philippeville (today Skikda) and Blida, except from 1921 to 1928, the latter being the year of his retirement.[30] With a doctoral degree in Arabic (*agrégé d'arabe*), Desparmet specialized in spoken Arabic, the teaching of which was soon to be replaced in secondary schools by classical Arabic. His rare teaching stints at the university level were as a part-time substitute. In the last analysis and despite the importance of his published work, Desparmet was viewed at the time as a folklorist, a sort of provincial notable who prided himself on being an intellectual. As for the articles that concern us here, they went virtually unnoticed.

### Fields and Subfields

To understand how both these men succeeded in *raising the key questions about Algerian society*, the questions that confronted this society in concrete, brutal ways, namely, language and the relationships between internal forces, one would have to do a much more complete analysis than I can sketch out here. I will limit myself to simply limning the broad outlines, in the process suggesting two or three directions for future work.

### The Intellectual Field of the Period

We have seen that Berque and Desparmet were marginal with respect to the intellectual field in colonial Algeria. Does this mean that truth is always produced outside the reigning paradigm? Indeed, did a single paradigm exist in the colonial intellectual field at that period? This is not at all certain. For historical reasons, *this particular intellectual field*, that of the University of Algiers from 1900 to 1950, *was sterile* when it came to the kinds of questions it could raise about the conquered society. In the first place, it was completely dominated by the political field, the concerns of which were not directed at that time toward learning more about the colonized society but rather in reducing it further.[31] People learned less Arabic generally, including those in the colonial administration; thus the collaboration between Luciani, who was no doubt a fine Arabist, and Berque.

Neither Berque nor Desparmet were very representative of the political field at the time, because it was highly structured and tightly sealed off from outside influences, totally cut off from the metropolitan French intellectual field and the international intellectual community, as even a cursory analysis of the reviews in the *Revue africaine* would demonstrate.[32] Individual dynasties (Marçais, Basset) and personal cliques, for example, that of former *medersa* professors, defined the rules of the game.[33] This is a historically specific case of a highly structured intellectual field with strict playing rules, whose degree of autonomy with regard to power and to the dominant colonial ideology was practically nil. In short, it was an intellectual ghetto.

### Intellectual Field and Subfields

In this intellectual field, there were a number of subfields. Desparmet defined himself in opposition to the subgroup of orientalists. He was a *transgressive orientalist*, because he was interested in dialectal Arabic and not classical Arabic, and in oral culture rather than Islamology. By way of comparison, a much more lackluster author such as Alfred Bel produced a few articles on local customs, while his most lucid work dealt with issues of Islamology.[34] Desparmet was also a transgressive orientalist because he was more interested in the social functions of language and of poetry than in language and poetry in and of themselves. In other words, he was an antiformalist, whereas the orientalists of the time were formalists.

Berque for his part was a product of the Arab Bureaus whose origins lay in the army rather than the civil administration, that is, the French colonial administration run by civilians. More precisely, he was among the few administrators who continued the defunct Arab Bureaus' tradition of inquiry into Algerian colonial society up to the Second World War. This tradition produced a massive body of literature. Indeed, everything we know today about nineteenth-century Algeria comes from this source. Its character seems to bear little relationship to the type of conquest or "pacification" that these officials otherwise practiced on the Algerians—but in fact it does. For the Arab Bureau officers got to know the tribes they defeated and then administered, precisely because such knowledge was of vital importance to them. By the twentieth century, day-to-day administration was no longer a life-or-death matter, which makes the intellectual curiosity and vision of Berque seem, therefore, anachronistic. For instance, we might well ask why he wrote his two major articles on the Sufi brotherhoods, the marabouts, and the tribes in 1919 at a time when the problem of the Islamic brotherhoods was completely outdated (as, moreover, he himself acknowledged).[35]

In the final analysis, Berque prolonged the life of a bygone tradition of inquiry, that of the Arab Bureaus, which no longer had its earlier political raison d'être. Similarly, Desparmet defined himself in negative terms relative to what ought have been his peer group of orientalists. Yet it is precisely their marginal positions (relative to the colonial political and intellectual fields) that enabled Berque and Desparmet to see what others had not seen, since their interests in these fields were not the ones that constituted the basis on which competition occurred within them.

## Conclusion

On the basis of these cases we can conclude that there is a tight relationship between the quality of the issues raised and the position of those who produce knowledge (*producteurs scientifiques*). In the first place, this is the case with regard to the object of study. We would need to know, for example, why Desparmet is a populist, why he identifies with the Arabic folk poets and despises the Islamic reformists,[36] something that enabled him to see a side of the reformists that escaped Marçais or even Berque, whose articles on the Algerian ulama are very disappointing.

Second, it is important to note that marginality is not a virtue in itself within the field of intellectual production. Outsider status vis-à-vis the intellectual field is a valid explanation for these two authors. But another explanation would have to be sought for Masqueray, for example, who articulated what was in fact a powerful intellectual current in the 1880s also found in Jules Ferry, Albin Rozet, and later Emile Combes.[37]

What I have just said does not come down to supporting the view that there is a relationship between an individual's position in a series of fields and the knowledge that the person produces. Such a position would be simplistic and therefore useless. Rather, I am arguing that *there are positions that, whatever the relationship to power, have an interest in truth.* In other words, it is not a matter of one camp being right and the other wrong. That would be an oversimplification. This argument logically has a number of consequences. First, we need only reverse the reasoning to see that there is no such thing as a disinterested position, and therefore no pure scholarship (*science*) either. In particular, there is no scholarship absolved of sin by decolonization, nor, with certain exceptions, of links to the ideological and practical objects of such scholarship, and that goes for national (that is, Algerian) scholars as well as for others. In particular, there is no reconquest of self-knowledge by postcolonial society; there are *still* groups who have an interest in certain truths and not in others.

There is always a risk in choosing a theoretical proposition from the colonial stock, of adopting even as a hypothesis a reading deriving from such a specific social condition. If we admit that all readings involve interests — including our own, of course — we see that the risk is not new. Every thesis runs the danger of turning out to be untrue, as well as the much more serious one of being distorted and used for evil social or political purposes. "Decolonized knowledge" is no exception. At the same time, producers of knowledge who are tightly linked to power could — can — have an interest in truth, because it is in the interest of power.

### Notes

This essay originally appeared as "Production scientifique et position dans le champ intellectuel et politique. Deux cas: Augustin Berque et Joseph Desparmet," pp. 397–415 in ed. Jacques Moniot, *Le Mal de voir. Ethnologie et orientalisme: Politique et épistemologie, critique et autocritique*, Cahiers Jussieu no. 2, Université de Paris VII (Paris: Collection 10/18, 1976), and was reprinted in Fanny Colonna, *Savants paysans: Éléments d'histoire sociale sur l'Algérie rurale* (Algiers: Office des Publications Universitaires, 1987), 121–31, with minor changes. Original note citations by Professor Colonna (nos. 8–11, 15, 18–20, 22, 24, 31) were augmented and completed by David Prochaska. Professor Colonna has graciously permitted us to reprint it here, although she wishes to state that were she to write it today, it would no doubt take a somewhat different shape.

1. Augustin Berque (1884–1946) was head of the Native Affairs section of the Algerian Gouvernement Général. See the posthumous collection of his writings, edited by his son: Jacques Berque and Jean-Claude Vatin, *Écrits sur l'Algérie*

(Aix-en-Provence: Edisud, 1986). Joseph Desparmet was a lycée professor in Algiers. In addition to the articles discussed here, he published "L'oeuvre de la France jugée par les indigènes," *Bulletin de la Société de Géographie d'Alger* (1910): 167–86, 417–36, and "L'entrée des Français à Alger par le cheikh Abdelkader," *Revue africaine* (1930): 225–56. His published articles and books total over two thousand pages. Due to the remarkable relevance of his work to the study of popular language and culture in contemporary Algeria, I [F.C.] am presently (1999) preparing for publication his published and unpublished works in six volumes. — Trans.

2.  In French *science* is used to describe both natural science and social science and the humanities, where the term *sciences humaines* (human sciences) is often utilized. Here *science* and *scientifique* have generally been translated as "scholarly" or "intellectual." — Trans.

3.  The Arab Bureaus were a corps of French military administrators charged with the administration of Muslims in Algeria who had not been placed under French direct rule. Between the early 1840s and the 1870s (later in the Algerian Sahara) they functioned as the chief intermediary between the French colonial administration and the Algerians, sometimes siding with the Algerians in disputes with the *colons*, or European settlers. See Kenneth J. Perkins, *Qaids, Captains and Colons* (New York: Africana Publishing, 1981). — Trans.

4.  Émile Masqueray (1843–1894) was appointed professor of history at the Lycée Arabe-français in Algiers in 1872 after receiving his *agrégation d'histoire* in France. In addition to history, he was interested in archaeology, Arabic, and Berber, both of which languages he learned. In 1880 he moved to the École des Lettres in Algiers as chair of the Department of African History and Antiquities. In 1886 he published his doctoral thesis, *Formation des cités chez les populations sédentaires de l'Algérie (Kabyles du Djurdjura, Chaouia de l'Aurès, Beni-Mezab)* (Paris: Leroux, 1886), republished with an introduction by Fanny Colonna (Aix-en-Provence: Édisud, 1983). See Fanny Colonna and Claude Haim Brahimi, "Du bon usage de la science coloniale," in *Le Mal de voir*, 221–41. See also the judgment of Charles-Robert Ageron, *Les algériens musulmans et la France (1870–1919)*, 2 vols. (Paris: P.U.F., 1968), 1:422: "Treated as an amateur by the Arabists and archeologists of his time, detested in Algeria where he was never forgiven for respecting and defending the Muslims, Émile Masqueray remained unknown, and still today is considered a second-rank publicist, whereas as a poet, writer, journalist and scholar he was one of those who contributed the most to making known Algeria and the Algerians." See also Masqueray's superb, recently republished *Souvenirs et visions d'Afrique* (1894; Paris: Boîte à documents, 1997). — Trans.

5.  Jean Mélia (1871–195?) was president of the French League in Favor of the Muslim Natives of Algeria (la Ligue française en faveur des indigènes musulmans d'Algérie), and author of *L'Algérie et la guerre (1914–1918)* (Paris: Plon, 1918) and *La France et l'Algérie* (Paris: Plon, 1919). Albert Truphémus (1873–1948) was a French political figure, member of the Socialist Party, and inspector of native education in Algeria (1909–1924), best known as the author of the novel *Ferhat, Instituteur indigène*, a defense of the Algerian Muslim population against the settlers.—Trans.

6.  This is, of course, precisely the claim made by Edward Said with regard to Jacques Berque, Clifford Geertz, Louis Massignon, and others in *Orientalism* (New York: Pantheon, 1978).—Trans.

7.  The ulama (Ar. sing. *alim*) are the scholars or learned men of Islam. The Salafiyya, or the movement of Islamic reform, began in the Arab East. Its spread to Algeria is often said to date from the visit of the Egyptian Muhammad Abduh in 1903. From this time reformism won an increasing number of adherents and, more important, developed a distinctive Algerian strain identified especially with Abd al-Hamid Ben Badis in the 1920s and 1930s. On the reformist ulama, see, among others, Ali Merad, *Le réformisme musulman en Algérie de 1925 à 1940: Essai d'histoire religieuse et sociale* (Paris: Mouton, 1967).—Trans.

8.  In 1931, the date when his article on "the linguistic reaction" was published, he was nearly seventy. See Desparmet, "La réaction linguistique en Algérie," *Bulletin de la Société Géographique d'Alger* 36 (1931): 1–33.

9.  In his obituary on Desparmet in the *Revue africaine* Henri Pérès wrote condescendingly of his two articles on vernacular Arabic language: "Having lost daily contact with the native population, Desparmet, in the latter part of his life, proved to be *nothing more* than a memorialist whose work future historians will turn to their advantage. This aspect of his oeuvre, *although lacking the solidity of his ethnographic and folkloric studies*, is nevertheless far from being negligible" (emphasis F.C.). See *Revue africaine* 86 (1942): 258. The two articles in question are "La réaction linguistique en Algérie" and "Les réactions nationalitaires en Algérie," *Bulletin de la Société Géographique d'Alger* 37 (1932): 173–84.

10. Desparmet, "La réaction linguistique en Algérie," 2–3; emphasis added.

11. Desparmet, "Les réactions nationalitaires en Algérie," 183–84.

12. According to Desparmet, *beurbri* was the vernacular term used in the nineteenth century to designate dialectal Algerian Arabic.—Trans.

13. A marabout was the head of a local saintly lineage, often popularly believed to possess special charisma, including the ability to heal.—Trans.

14. Colonna distinguishes between *théorie* (theory), a fully worked out theoretical statement or paradigm, and *thèses* (theoretical propositions, theses), which are informed by or have theoretical import but are not presented as or claim the sta-

tus of abstract theory. Thus, the work of Berque and Desparmet, though not, strictly speaking, theoretical, arrive at numerous theses.—Trans.

15. This is the only excuse made for using Desparmet's work, for example, in certain recent studies.

16. Such "narrowly nationalist movements" included the successive political organizations founded by Messali Hadj, the Étoile Nord Africaine (ENA), Parti Populaire Algérien (PPA), and the Mouvement pour le Triomphe des Libertés Démographiques (MTLD).—Trans.

17. The three articles are "Essai d'une bibliographie critique des confréries musulmanes algériennes," *Bulletin de la Société d'Archéologie et de Géographie d'Oran* 39 (1919): 135–74, 193–233; "Esquisse d'une histoire de la seigneurie algérienne," *Revue de la Méditerranée*, nos. 29 and 30 (1949): 18–34, 168–80; and "La bourgeoisie algérienne ou la recherche de César Birotteau," *Hesperis* 35 (1948): 1–29. All are re printed in Augustin Berque, *Écrits sur l'Algérie.*—Trans.

18. According to Berque:

> The invasion of confraternity-style maraboutism, since the French conquest [in 1830 and] in particular between 1866 and 1900, can be explained especially by the decrease in opposing forces that had until then contained it. This triumph of the shaykh and the ikhwan, who by the close of the 19th century had reached their peak, is the final phase of a struggle whose origin dates back to the Muslim Middle Ages. Freed from secular antagonisms, whose decline we most probably hastened with our superior motive of civilizing action, zaouias increased their intense influence ten-fold. They remain the only force of attraction in Arab-controlled lands; and a fresh polarisation of influence is taking place to their advantage, something that for centuries had been neutralized toward the Muslim masses." ("Essai d'une bibliographie critique," 158)

Also: "Between the nobleman of military stock and the nobleman of marabout stock, there is a rivalry not about to disarm" ("Esquisse d'une histoire," 19–20).

19. Berque, "Essai d'une bibliographie critique," 199.

20. Berque, "Essai d'une bibliographie critique," 158.

21. The *sénatus-consulte* of 1863 was one of the four main land reforms carried out by the French in the nineteenth century and the centerpiece of Napoleon III's policy that Algeria was an "Arab kingdom" under imperial protection. It was intended to defend local Muslim property from settler greed, but ironically hastened Muslims' dispossession. See John Ruedy, *Modern Algeria* (Bloomington: Indiana University Press, 1992).—Trans.

22. Berque, "Essai d'une bibliographie critique," 202.

23. The period of Turkish rule in Algeria (1525–1830) can be described as "semi-colonial" rather than (fully) colonial both because Turks and Algerians shared

a common religion in Islam, and because Turkish power did not extend as far or as deep as French power later did. See Ruedy, *Modern Algeria.*—Trans.

24. Berque, "La bourgeoisie algérienne," 24.

25. The Destour Party was based in the old urban bourgeoisie of Tunis. It was also referred to as the Old Destour Party, in contrast to its successor, the Neo-Destour Party, which was founded in 1934 by Habib Bourguiba and which led Tunisia to political independence in 1956. See Dwight L. Ling, *Tunisia: From Protectorate to Republic* (Bloomington: University of Indiana Press, 1967).—Trans.

26. The identification of segmentary lineages as the basic building block of Maghrebi social organization has a long and contested history. See, for example, Dale Eickelman, *The Middle East: An Anthropological Approach* (Englewood Cliffs NJ: Prentice-Hall, 1981); E. E. Evans-Pritchard, *The Sanusi of Cyrenaica* (Oxford: Clarendon Press, 1949); Jean-Claude Vatin, ed., *Connaissances du Maghreb* (Paris: Centre national de la recherche scientifique, 1984); David Prochaska, *Making Algeria French: Colonialism in Bone, 1870–1920* (1990; New York: Cambridge University Press, 2004), 55, 275.—Trans.

27. For example, the thesis of the disappearance of the landed aristocracy from the local political scene, which is at the heart of Berque's article on the seigneury, has been challenged by Peter von Sivers on *juwad* families up to the First World War. See his "Les plaisirs du collectioneur: Capitalisme fiscal et chefs indigènes en Algérie (1840–1860)," *Annales ESC* 35, nos. 3–4 (1980): 679–99. Also "Insurrection and Accommodation: Indigenous Leadership in Eastern Algeria, 1840–1900," *International Journal of Middle East Studies*, 6 (1975): 259–75, and "Algerian Landownership and Rural Leadership, 1860–1914: An Authoritative Approach," *Maghreb Review* 4 (1979): 58–62.

28. The main administrative divisions in colonial Algeria were *communes mixtes, communes de pleine exercice,* and *communes indigènes.* See the glossary in Prochaska, *Making Algeria French.*—Trans.

29. J.-D. Luciani was a leading French Algerian official in charge of native policy. Among other works, he published "Chansons kabyles de Smâil Azikkiou, texte et traduction," *Revue africaine* 43 (1899): 17–33, 142–71, and 44 (1900): 44–59.—Trans.

30. Philippeville was a small port in eastern Algeria, and Blida was a small town located south of Constantine also in eastern Algeria.—Trans.

31. Paradoxically, one witnesses around this date a renewed interest in native cultures—and no longer in structures—in folklorist terms. But this is not contradictory.

32. The *Revue africaine*, the leading scholarly journal in colonial Algeria, was published from 1856 to 1961 by the Société historique algérienne. As the eminent historian Charles-André Julien gently put it, the *Revue*'s "contributors were inclined

to judge colonial policy if not always favorably, at least and often (times) with indulgence." See Julien, *Histoire de l'Algérie contemporaine: La conquête et les débuts de la colonisation (1827–1871)* (Paris: Presses Universitaires de France, 1964), 511.—Trans.

33. Georges Marçais is the author of *Le costume musulman d'Alger* (Paris: Plon, 1930). René Basset wrote, among other works, *L'insurrection algérienne de 1871 dans les chansons populaires kabyles* (Louvain: Istras, 1892). A *medersa* (*madrassa*) was a Muslim institution of higher education, especially for law and theology.—Trans.

34. Alfred Bel is the author of the classic of late colonial ethnography, *La religion musulmane en Berbérie: Esquisse d'histoire et de sociologie religeuses* (Paris: Geuthner, 1938). Note also his influence on Clifford Geertz in the latter's *Islam Observed: Religious Development in Morocco and Indonesia* (New Haven CT: Yale University Press, 1968).—Trans.

35. The 1919 article was published in two lengthy parts. See note 17 supra.—Trans.

36. This is ultimately a biographical and even psychological question.—Trans.

37. Jules Ferry was a republican senator and prime minister in Third Republic governments in the 1880s, and the author of an 1892 report, *Le gouvernement de l'Algérie*, which proposed a series of wide-ranging reforms affecting the Muslim populations of Algeria. Albin Rozet was a moderate republican deputy in various French governments in the 1890s, close to the *indigénophile* group in Algeria. Émile Combes was a prominent republican politician in several early Third Republic governments, a proponent of French education for Kabyles, and a militant anticlerical. See Ageron, *Les algériens musulmans et la France, 1871–1919.*—Trans.

# 2 | CULTURE

# 5 | The "Passionate Nomad" Reconsidered

## A European Woman in l'Algérie française
## (Isabelle Eberhardt, 1877–1904)

JULIA CLANCY-SMITH

As a nomad who has no country beside Islam
and neither family nor close friends,
I shall wend my way through life until it is time
for that everlasting sleep inside the grave.[1]

In the spring of 1897 a young Russian woman and her mother arrived for the first time in Bône (Annaba), a thoroughly Europeanized port on the Mediterranean coast of Algeria, which by then had been uneasily under French rule for nearly seventy years. The two women had gone to North Africa seeking refuge from personal tragedy and domestic unhappiness. There they offended the smug sensibilities of Bône's European residents by spurning the city's modern French neighborhoods for a modest house in the older Arab quarter. Before the year was out, Isabelle Eberhardt (1877–1904) buried her mother, Madame de Moerder, in the Muslim cemetery located outside Bône's northeast gates, since both women claimed to have converted to Islam.[2] For the next seven years, Eberhardt regarded North Africa, particularly Algeria, as her true homeland, much to the dismay of the civilian settlers. Forced on several occasions back into "exile" in Europe by hostile colonial authorities and poverty, Eberhardt's sensational death during a desert flash flood in 1904 finally allowed her to remain permanently in her country of adoption.

Algerian historiography of the past 132 years appears as the "imperial man's world" par excellence.[3] The history of L'Algérie française even today is peopled almost exclusively by men, whether French military "heroes" like General Bugeaud, celebrated in colonial hagiography, or Muslim resistance figures such as Amir Abd al-Qadir, venerated as an early nationalist leader by the Algerians. One of the few exceptions in the fin de siècle period is the enigmatic Isabelle Eberhardt; no other individual from Algeria's hybrid European society has been the object of so much passionate attention. Immediately after her death, a number of works devoted to Eberhardt were published, along with some of her own writings; soon thereafter, the author of *The Oblivion Seekers* fell into literary and historical oblivion.[4] The past decades have witnessed a revival of interest in the "passionate nomad," who has become somewhat of a cult figure. The growing body of literature on Isabelle Eberhardt demands critical analysis, as does the life of this flamboyant woman.[5]

Many of the recent works fall into three different, although related categories: the history-cum-nostalgia for the colonial past in which biographies of heroic white women constitute a subgenre; second, studies that portray Eberhardt as a proto-nationalist and even as a proto-feminist; and, last, works written by the formerly colonized, particularly Algerians attracted by Eberhardt's sympathy for Islam and Arab North African civilization.[6] Few, if any, recent studies examine her squarely within the proper historical perspectives—European orientalism of the late nineteenth century, on the one hand, and on the other the peculiar colonialism of Algerian pied-noir society which, as Eberhardt arrived on the shores of Africa, was just reaching maturity.[7] By placing this woman within these two mutually reinforcing systems of domination, she becomes less of an anomaly or a social aberration. If she became a cause célèbre in French Algeria it was not—as both her detractors and admirers claim—because she truly was "an enemy of France," nor was she, as others have asserted, "profoundly Algerianized."[8] I will argue instead that Eberhardt was a collaborator in the construction of French Algeria. Moreover, her ambiguous niche in the imperial social order reveals in unambiguous ways how gender, class, and race fused to produce the half-breed of colonization. Thus, a European woman labeled by officials as disorderly, undesirable, and marginal was in fact central to—even emblematic of—the colonial encounter.

### A Life of Her Own: Geneva, 1877–1897

Most biographers divide Eberhardt's life into two neat segments, which wrongly suggests that there was little political connection—beyond youthful, romantic yearnings for the exotic—between the young woman of stifling

Geneva and the Isabelle Eberhardt of the Sahara.[9] Nevertheless, she (and many like her, both male and female) was a cultural exile long before leaving the European continent. More importantly, Eberhardt was a participant of sorts in imperial ventures before setting foot in North Africa at the close of the century. Conversion to Islam, membership in an Algerian Sufi (mystical) order, and marriage to an Arab Muslim only heightened her personal involvement in the French colonial enterprise.

By the early nineteenth century, Paris and other European cities were already deeply influenced by orientalism, defined by Edward Said as a field of study, a mode of thought and discourse, and as a "Western style for dominating, restructuring, and having authority over the Orient."[10] As Eberhardt was growing to troubled adolescence in the 1880s, many peoples of Asia and Africa were either already under various forms of colonial control or soon to be; most of northern Africa bordering the Mediterranean represented an imperial backyard for France and Great Britain.[11] Travelers and officials who had spent time in the "Orient" returned from Egypt, Tunisia, or Algeria laden with Eastern curios and cultural artifacts. These added panache to world's fairs held in London and Paris and furnished European drawing rooms—paradoxically the matrix of the cult of bourgeois domesticity—with the bric-a-brac of subjugated non-Western societies.[12] Colonial exhibitions and drawing room exoticism both advertised Western global hegemony and provided a powerful stimulus for many bored Europeans to travel to the East.

The illegitimate offspring of an Armenian Orthodox ex-pope turned anarchist, Alexandre Trophimovsky, and an aristocratic German woman, Isabelle Eberhardt was raised in a wildly eccentric household located in one of Geneva's sedate suburbs. Tutored at home by the nihilist Trophimovsky, who within the family was as much an autocrat as the Russian tsars he conspired against, Eberhardt and her hapless siblings were raised to despise middle-class and Christian morals. She received an extensive education at the hands of her oppressive father—classical and European languages as well as Arabic, history, geography, and philosophy—which provided the only relief in childhood from the morbid atmosphere of the family compound. From an early age, she wore only male clothes and was taught to ride a horse as vigorously as any man, two formative influences that served her well later in North Africa but also may have contributed to the "fluidity" of her own gender identification.[13]

As a girl she dressed up in the romanticized costume of a *spahi* or a Bedouin, read Pierre Loti's *Aziyade* (published in 1879), as well as colonial novelists, and later, while still in Switzerland, corresponded regularly with a French lieutenant stationed at an Arab Bureau in the Algerian Sahara.[14] She also took as one of her many lovers a youthful diplomat assigned to the Turkish consulate in Geneva. A dark, Levantine Armenian converted to Islam, Rehid Bey fed her fantasies, sexual and otherwise, about the "mysterious Orient."[15] At the age of eighteen, two years before her initial trip to Africa in 1897, she donned the Arab garb of a "dashing desert cavalier" for a photograph in one of Geneva's studios where Europeans could indulge in the fiction of an Eastern voyage without leaving home.[16] The next year she fashioned a "Muslim" identity for herself by employing the pseudonym "Mahmoud Saadi" in her letters written in Arabic to an Egyptian litterateur living in political disgrace in Paris. Isabelle Eberhardt was an orientalist writer, actress, and playwright in-the-making. The costumes and part of the script had been constructed in Europe; what was lacking was an adequate mise-en-scène.

Her first journey to Algeria in 1897 at the age of twenty was motivated by emotional distress as well as ambition. Unlike many other European women of her class and generation, she was never involved in any social campaigns or political causes on the Continent before setting out for the colonies.[17] However, one (and perhaps two) of her unstable brothers dabbled briefly in the subversive politics—and drug dealings—of the expatriate Russian anarchist community in Geneva; already in her teens she may have acquired a fondness for opiates from her brother Augustin.[18] She always claimed to eschew politics, although this was more out of political naïveté than an ideologically motivated rejection.

While she was beginning to publish articles, using male and female noms de plume, in avant-garde Parisian literary magazines, she felt the urge to travel—at last—to the long dreamed of Dar al-Islam.[19] There she would establish her credentials as a writer and secure some measure of financial security. At the same time, she and her mother could flee the enervating melancholia of their home in Geneva, dominated by the abusive Trophimovsky, and hopefully build a new life in colonial Algeria. In one sense, Eberhardt's motives for going to North Africa did not differ from those of other European immigrants, particularly those from the poorer, overpopulated southern Mediterranean countries. However, unlike the lower-class Maltese and

Corsicans, who outnumbered the French in Algeria by the turn of the century, she also embarked on a voyage of self-discovery as much as self-promotion.[20] And her journey can be seen as a contrived pilgrimage to achieve the sort of liminal states conferred by cultural *dépaysement*, normally only the privilege of the privileged. (And Eberhardt was, in many respects, very much the aristocrat, despite her vagabond ways.)

Thus, as was true for a whole host of disaffected, peripatetic Europeans, the invented "East" represented an antidote to mental anguish, social malaise, or personal angst, a haven whose façade of social liberation was underwritten by colonial subjugation. Eberhardt's trips to Algeria were preceded by nearly half a century of French military "pacification" in North Africa, which had rendered travel to and within the region a relatively safe matter.[21] Paradoxically her self-discovery through travel to foreign places would only be partially, if ever, realized. She landed in the bigoted, self-righteous community of Bône, whose inhabitants suffered from acute "status anxiety," as did most other members of colonial society.[22]

### L'Algérie française: "Ici, c'est la France"

By the end of the century, Algeria had become as vital to France's imperial self-confidence as India was to Great Britain's sense of global superiority; still, the country presented myriad unresolved contradictions. As David Prochaska nicely put it, "Algeria was a French colony—the colonizers maintained hegemony over the colonized, and at the same time Algeria was not a French colony—it was an integral part of France. In short, Algeria had been incorporated but not integrated into France in 1870, ingested but not digested."[23] And the obstacles to full digestion were not only the Muslim Algerians but also the large numbers of non-French Europeans living there, people such as Isabelle Eberhardt and her mother. In effect, a "secondary colonization" existed in which the French-born lorded it over the southern Mediterranean groups (or the *petits blancs*, as they were disparagingly called); all Europeans, no matter of what origins, despised the Algerian Muslims. Like other colonial societies, class, race, and ethnicity together formed the infrastructure of social stratification. Nevertheless, "the Algerian melting pot did not dissolve individual European ethnic differences, but instead created a heady new Mediterranean stew—what later came to be known as the pied-noir community."[24] Thus, Algeria was very much an "imagined community" whose heterogeneous, and potentially antagonistic, components were kept in unsteady equilibrium by the creation of the Algerian Muslim Other. In the eyes of the *colons*, Isabelle Eberhardt compromised that equilibrium by fraternizing, both culturally and sexually, with those relegated to the "other side of the tracks," and in so doing, she threatened to expose the phantasms of the invented community.[25]

Soon after her arrival in Bône, the young Russian woman provided idle tongues with ample ammunition for malicious gossip. Dressed in Arab male garb—fez, turban, and so on—Mahmoud Saadi, as she called herself, wandered through the streets and markets at all hours of the night, at times unaccompanied, at others, with Algerian male companions.[26] Already quite conversant in classical Arabic, she perfected her spoken Arabic by hanging out in the quintessential space for Mediterranean men, irrespective of religion or culture—the popular café; there she may also have indulged in what was later to become an addiction—her passion for hashish. Avoiding the company of the European settlers, whom she found insufferable, Eberhardt prayed at the city's mosques—dressed as a man—and sought to deepen her knowledge of Islam by studying with local Muslim scholars. In cultivating friendships within Bône's Muslim community, she not only ignored gender boundaries but class divisions as well, frequenting all manner of people, the great and the humble. And on the few occasions when she dressed as an Algerian woman, several young Arab men sought her hand in marriage.[27]

All of this naturally shocked and horrified the European community, which was as conservative in defining gender roles as traditional Muslim society was.[28] Civilian pied-noir opprobrium, however, was replaced by growing official consternation over Eberhardt's public and private behavior. She may have participated—inadvertently—in a popular Muslim riot against the abuses of the colonial regime in the months following her mother's death. Fearing reprisals and fleeing her creditors, she took off to the Sahara, where she fell in love with "that mysterious void known as the great Sahara," the nomadic way of life, and perhaps with a few of the desert's male denizens.[29] A noble at heart and in matters of finance (she borrowed money shamelessly, mainly from her Muslim friends), Eberhardt retreated back to Geneva in 1898 when her funds gave out and news of Trophimovsky's deteriorating health reached her.[30] Her father's death and the prospect of married life with an Oriental in a non-Oriental setting—Rehid Bey, by then posted to Holland, had proposed to her—impelled her back to North Africa in the summer of 1899. In Tunis, she further scandalized both the Europeans and the Tunisians, who had been placed under a French protectorate in 1881.[31]

## Fin de siècle Decadence and Colonial Control

Drugs, alcohol, sexual digressions, and other kinds of amusement were cultivated as an art form in fin de siècle Paris and other European capitals, at least among certain classes. And transvestism, whether employed to circumvent social strictures upon ordinary females or indulged in as a tantalizing pastime by urban demimondaines, was not frowned upon in some social milieux.[32] Wearing disguises—often costumes appropriated from other cultures—was a passion; Pierre Loti, whom Eberhardt admired fiercely, frequently donned Turkish or Berber clothing to escape from himself and make his mark on Parisian society.[33] Isabelle Eberhardt, who visited Paris on several occasions in 1900, would not have been terribly out of place in the metropole's sophisticated capital. Yet in French Algeria, prim and parochial, such comportment could not be condoned, at least not in public and thus within view of the Muslims, whose domination was justified by the principle of innate European moral and cultural superiority.[34]

Moreover, the premise of Western superiority undergirded another operative myth in the period—that of "assimilation." Manipulated by colonial administrators to soothe liberal consciences in the metropole and to dampen political activism by the few Muslim *évolués* (evolved), assimilation held that some Algerians would someday enjoy the same privileged civil status already conferred upon the colons.[35] But first they had to become culturally like Frenchmen. Isabelle Eberhardt's extravagant attempts to "go native" threw assimilationist theory into disarray by suggesting that indigenous culture had its own intrinsic merits. The fact that Eberhardt, who at least by birth came from the upper ranks of European society, had crossed class and racial lines to mix freely with those at the very bottom of the colonial hierarchy could not be tolerated.

Most writers opine that Algerian Muslim society was more tolerant of Eberhardt because she had ostensibly embraced Islam, joined a Sufi order, and dressed like an upper-class Arab man, which gave her access to male public and, particularly, religious spaces.[36] Nevertheless, it must be emphasized that Eberhardt had the weight of the French imperial system behind her—however reluctantly—when she entered sacred spaces normally off limits to Europeans of whatever gender and to Algerian Muslim women. While she did establish true friendships with the colonized, the Arab Muslims were relatively powerless and had no choice but to tolerate whatever she chose to do. Moreover, her claims to being a fervent Muslim—while buttressed by Eberhardt's apparently scrupulous observance of the daily prayers and ritual fasting—were compromised by her growing penchant for alcohol, drugs, and illicit sexual unions, all absolutely forbidden by Islamic law. Thus, she flouted the norms of both societies; more serious still to the colonizers, she mocked the European myth of moral ascendancy over the Muslims.

During her first journey to the Sahara in 1899, Eberhardt had discovered the desolate beauty of the oasis of El Oued, the "town with a thousand white domes." Perhaps the Sahara would prove less socially confining than the settler towns of the north. El Oued was part of the Algerian desert that was then under military administration; the coastal regions had passed under civilian rule after 1870. The officers responsible for the region's security were suspicious of this European woman dressed in Arab garb. Some suspected her of involvement with Methodist missionary efforts, others of being an English spy. While she cast herself in the role of a nomad, riding wildly over the dunes with Bedouins, Foreign Legion types, and the riff-raff of caravans, and reveling in her apparent total freedom, the military bureaucracy was tracking her movements. She had to obtain a permit from the Arab Bureau to travel into the deep south—there were administrative limits to exoticism as lived.[37] If their European counterparts in Algerian cities were beset by status anxiety, military officials were obsessed by fears of insurrection; this led them to assign more political importance to this disorderly Western woman (or man?) than she deserved. While Eberhardt professed to dislike the French military—for nonpolitical reasons—she was quite comfortable in the company of officers, and later agreed to aid them in the takeover of southeastern Morocco.

Chased for a second time from North Africa by poverty and ill health at the end of 1899, Eberhardt returned the next summer intent upon settling permanently in El Oued, although she was still a Russian citizen. In the oasis she first encountered the man who eventually became her husband. Slimene Ehnni was a junior officer in the spahis, a Muslim, and, significantly, a French citizen, one of a handful of Algerians to enjoy this status. Eberhardt followed him from posting to posting with his military contingent until her official expulsion from the country in 1901 as an "undesirable." It was also at this time that she began keeping a journal of her wanderings and musings. In her diary, she often excised the European presence in its cultural and, above all, political manifestations, just as the colonial literary and pseudoscientific production on Algeria's history banished the Algerian and the Islamic from its pages.[38] Yet what Eberhardt reinserted in her works as genuinely North African, Arab, and Muslim was only partially true, if that. As stated earlier, she arrived in the country already imbued with the orientalist fable as told in Europe. What she saw and how she perceived it had already been filtered—indeed, veiled—by earlier orientalist writers, like Loti, whom Eberhardt may consciously or unconsciously have emulated.[39]

### The Diary: Writing as Expatriation

As exposed in the diary, Eberhardt's views of Africa, the North Africans, and Islam are generally—though not always—informed by the same kinds of sentimental stereotypes and racist caricatures employed by other, less unconventional writers of the period.[40] Rather than a subversive text—that is, one that offered a counterreading of indigenous society and culture—her writings may have confirmed the worst European biases regarding the Muslims' innate inferiority and thus their unworthiness for political equality. "The beloved fateful land of Barbary"—Mediterranean Africa—was, for Eberhardt, intoxicating, heady, pungent; her descriptions of Algeria's coast are reminiscent of the pied-noir maxim that "L'Algérie monte à la tête" (Algeria goes to your head).[41] In contrast, the Sahara is "mysterious" and a "bewitching and magnificent expanse" where indigenous life is "slow and dreamy." The desert's inhabitants are described—using staged, photographic-like clichés—as "primitive men," "biblical," and belonging to "primitive humanity." As for Islam, the religion is "mysterious and dreamlike," brings "ecstasy," and, of course, demands fatalism and total resignation before God, the latter representing the single most pervasive (and inane) stereotype of Islam among Westerners then, as even today.[42]

Algerian men fare scarcely better in the diary. They "all resemble one another" physically, their collective Arab persona is one of "harshness and violence," attributes that did not discourage Eberhardt from initiating countless sexual liaisons with indigenous men. Even the beloved Slimene, whom she married in a civil ceremony in Marseilles in October of 1901, is described as childlike and in need of tutoring to instruct him in "all the things he does not know [i.e., Western civilization], which is a tall order."[43] Thus, the paternalism of the colonial order was re-created in Eberhardt's sexual relationships. Ironically, marriage with Slimene conferred French nationality upon her and the right to return to Algeria later that year, despite the expulsion decree and official opposition. This was the ultimate challenge to the colonial order of things. Isabelle Eberhardt, a Russian and thus a part of the "foreign peril," became a citizen of France by virtue of marriage to an Arab Muslim. (Marriages between Muslims and Europeans were exceedingly rare in this period.)[44] Cultural expatriation had its rewards.

But what of her views of women, both European and colonized? Eberhardt's diary says little about females, for whom she betrayed scant empathy or even interest. In general, the female character provides a negative foil to the male personality: "Invincible will and integrity [are] two traits that are so hard to find in women." Aside from her own mother, for whom she displayed sincere affection, Eberhardt judged harshly the few European women that she wrote about: "a horrible revolting creature" was how she described one unfortunate French lady.[45] These sentiments are probably representative of her attitudes toward Western women as a social category. While Eberhardt's own gender conflict (and the snubs she encountered from straitlaced European women) may have fueled her distrust of and distaste for females, there was another dimension to this.

In a settler colonial society, such as Algeria, where racism was rooted in the notion of cultural superiority, European women were the vanguard of the *mission civilisatrice*, the divinely ordained civilizing mission of France. "White" women defined social distance from, and political control over, the Muslims; Islam was intrinsically inferior to Western civilization precisely because of female status in the Other's holy law and culture. Thus, women were the measure of all things, particularly in the last decade of the century, when a new sociocultural synthesis had finally emerged, that of the pied-noir community. Moreover, the civilizing mission had as one of its goals the deorientalization of the Oriental, who was to be assimilated culturally to the West, forcibly or otherwise, at least in theory. By "making Algeria French," the colonial agenda, in Eberhardt's mind, threatened to remove the exotic backdrop so necessary for her own cherished expatriation.[46]

While Arab women are dealt with a bit more sympathetically in the diary, they are usually portrayed as passive and resigned, more like strange, decorative objects, exiles in their own land.[47] The one exception is an Algerian female saint and mystic, Lalla Zaynab (1850–1904), who befriended Eberhardt in 1902. Due to her piety, advanced Islamic learning, and ability to work miracles, Lalla Zaynab was immensely powerful within her own Arabo-Berber society; she was also an ascetic and had taken a vow of celibacy. Overlooking the European woman's dissolute ways, Zaynab welcomed Eberhardt to the family Sufi *zawiya* (lodge or monastery) in the Sahara, consenting to be her spiritual mentor and confidant. This relationship between a colonized woman, whose life was wholly devoted to self-abnegation, and a Western woman, whose manic personality impelled her to sensual excess, is remarkable in the annals of North African history.[48] Eberhardt's profession of Islam and her membership in a Sufi order probably gave her an entree into Zaynab's circle, as did the Arab custom of hospitality and courtesy toward guests.[49] Yet as important was the fact that their friendship developed in the Sahara—away from the centers of European implantation with their increasingly rigid lines of social demarcation. In the desert, which was overwhelmingly inhabited by indigenous Algerians, there was no need to maintain the fiction of assimilation.

Despite the innocuous nature of the friendship, the colonial police closely surveyed Eberhardt's visits to Zaynab, seeking to discover the subject of their conversations.[50] In part, this was related to concerns about assuring the Sahara's political calm on the eve of a planned military sweep into neighboring Morocco. In addition, army officials held the mistaken belief that the European woman exerted influence over the North Africans because of her command of Arabic, conversion to Islam, and her involvement with a Sufi brotherhood. This might be turned to France's advantage.

### A Colonial Accomplice in Spite of Herself?

By 1902 colonial authorities regarded Eberhardt as more than a debauched eccentric; a bitter debate over her conduct was waged in the colonial press. When she and her Arab husband, Slimene, settled in Tenès, an ultraconservative and politically divided pied-noir town, a press campaign was launched against the couple, with Eberhardt as the principal target of vituperation. Observing her preference for the company of the Muslims or—worse still—for a few resident French "Arabophiles," the town's administrators accused her of spreading hostile propaganda among the Algerians; others charged that she was setting herself up "as some kind of prophetess."[51] By then she enjoyed the support of a small cohort of liberal French journalists, among them the well-known writer Victor Barrucand. Barrucand defended her in the newspapers and offered her the position of special correspondent with the newly created daily, *El Akhbar*, in 1903. Mounting hostility toward Eberhardt among settlers in northern Algeria probably convinced Barrucand to send her to the desert that year to cover General Lyautey's "absorption" of southeastern Morocco.

By 1903 the only obstacle to a vast French empire stretching from southern Tunisia to West Africa was Morocco. A proponent of yet another colonial myth, that of *pénétration pacifique*, Lyautey's aim was to weaken the Moroccan sultan's authority over the truculent tribes of the ill-defined border regions between the two countries. This policy of "colonialism on the cheap" sought to avoid costly, protracted warfare in gaining new territories; it also demanded winning local indigenous allies who would not resist the French army's "gentle pushes" onto Moroccan soil. From the oasis of Ain Sefra, Eberhardt, dressed in male garb and using her assumed name of Mahmoud Saadi, sent back accounts of French military activities to Barrucand in Algiers—in addition to spending much time with Foreign Legion soldiers in cafés. Eventually introduced to the commanding general, she agreed to perform some reconnaissance missions to advance Lyautey's "peaceful penetration." In effect, she became a paid, although unofficial, agent of the Deuxième Bureau, which conferred upon her a horse, complete liberty of movement, and enough money to subsist on. This was the lifestyle she had long craved but that had been denied her by the European settlers in northern Algeria out of fear of her cross-cultural fraternizing and cross-gender behavior. Ironically, Eberhardt may also have struck the bargain with Lyautey to redeem her tarnished reputation as anti-French.[52]

In General Lyautey she found a kindred spirit. The general genuinely admired her precisely because she was a "réfractaire" (rebel) and scorned the hypocrisy of pied-noir bourgeois society. And being a career officer, Lyautey shared the military's latent hostility to the civilian colonial administration.[53] Moreover, Lyautey, like Eberhardt, desired that the "Orient" remain orientalized and not be "degraded" by debasing mixtures of European modernity. By 1904 Eberhardt's dispatches to *El Akhbar* began to betray the general's influence, particularly her op-ed pieces on proper tactics for winning new lands and peoples for France. "It would not be impossible for us to gain some profit from our conquest and to organize it without disturbing Morocco's illusion that it possessed these regions."[54]

Eberhardt's affiliation with the Qadiriyya Sufi order convinced the general that she alone could perform a delicate diplomatic mission in 1904.[55] Seeking to neutralize potential political opposition in the contested Algerian-Moroccan areas, Lyautey commissioned her to visit the Sufi shaykhs of the regionally powerful Qnadsa (or Kenadsa) brotherhood and prepare the way for the French advance. Posing as a young Muslim male scholar in search of mystical learning at the Qnadsa zawiya, Eberhardt was warmly received by the head shaykh, Sidi Brahim, who was aware of her identity and intentions. Given an austere cell in which to live, pray, and meditate, she soon grew weary of her guise as an aspiring mystic since she was deprived of alcohol, drugs, and sex and kept more or less in isolation. Some sources credit her with a pivotal role in convincing Sidi Brahim to accept France's "protection" and thereby renounce allegiance to the Moroccan sultan.[56] It seems more likely that Eberhardt, less and less enthused by the rigors of true monastic life, was able—at best—to furnish information on the Qnadsa to the French command back in Ain Sefra. In effect, Sidi Brahim had outmanipulated her, and indirectly Lyautey, by forcing the European woman to play fully, for the first time, the role in which she had long cast herself: an expatriate seeker of mystical truth.

Suffering from bouts of malaria and probably syphilis in its advanced stages, Eberhardt refused Sidi Brahim's offer of escorts so that she could push further west into Moroccan territory. Instead she returned in October of 1904 to Ain Sefra, where an autumn flash flood engulfed the hut she was residing in; her body was discovered in the attire of an Arab cavalryman surrounded by the muddied pages of her writings. She had drowned in the desert.[57]

Grief-stricken, Lyautey arranged a Muslim burial for Eberhardt in the cemetery at Ain Sefra. Yet the general refused the deceased one final honor. Her tombstone was not inscribed with the preferred masculine name of Mahmoud Saadi; rather, the feminine "Lalla Mahmoud" was employed.[58] Lyautey had the scattered remnants of Eberhardt's manuscript sent to Victor Barrucand, who already possessed some of her earlier, unpublished works. In 1905, Barrucand published selections from her writings (to which he added his own sensational prose) under the melodramatic title *Dans l'ombre chaude de l'Islam*. The book was a best-seller for the period, going into three editions and selling thirteen thousand copies. In addition to listing himself as coauthor (and cashing in on the royalties), Barrucand exoticized Eberhardt's life even further, inserting suggestive material that bordered on the pornographic.[59]

Nevertheless, if Eberhardt had become a sort of colonial apologist in her press articles—once again due to her political immaturity—a profound transformation can be detected in the many stories and literary sketches she wrote in the period just before her death. No longer the dreamy, cliché-ridden orientalist prose, her fiction presents painfully realistic, almost ethnographic, accounts of indigenous life in its confrontation with a conquering, alien civilization.[60] Paradoxically, by shedding one set of assumptions—that of orientalism—about the Arab-Islamic world, she was seduced by another—Lyautey's heterodox notions of pacification through peaceful co-optation underscored by the threat of superior military might.

Eberhardt had desperately sought not only to adopt another culture, but also to construct another gender identity through writing and living as a passionate nomad. Yet her story was appropriated—and exploited—by one of her dearest male associates, Barrucand. Likewise, her other close male companion, Lyautey, imposed a female (and false) identity upon Eberhardt in the grave. She was, thus, confined to a European literary harem in colonial North Africa, a victim of her own thirst for exoticism, which, like orientalism and imperialism, was a male-dominated endeavor.

### From Europe to Africa and Back Again

Part of Europe's flotsam and jetsam thrown up on the French-ruled shores of Africa, Isabelle Eberhardt resembled T. E. Lawrence in her frantic, relentless search for the glamour of strangeness. Algeria was her private theater; French colonialism provided the staging, the North Africans offered backdrop color. Eberhardt not only dabbled in that archetypal colonial genre—the European travel account—but also embodied the genre itself; she was the most outré expression of travel as expatriation. In a diary entry of 1901 she stated: "There are women who will do anything for beautiful clothes, while there are others who grow old and grey poring over books to earn degrees and status. As for myself, all I want is a good horse as a mute and loyal companion, a handful of servants hardly more complex than my mount, and a life as far away as possible from the hustle and bustle I happen to find so sterile in the civilized world where I feel so deeply out of place."[61]

But political expatriation is very often an act of cultural appropriation. Like Loti, André Gide, and many others, Isabelle Eberhardt attempted to appropriate another culture and its ways; her principal tactic was that of gender manipulation, which was partially the product of her own deeply felt gender conflict. Gender transvestism permitted her to engage in cultural transvestism, which ultimately rendered her marginal to both cultures—the hybrid European community of French Algeria and Muslim North African society. Isabelle Eberhardt was an extreme example of cultural hyphenation. Yet it can be argued that she was representative—indeed totemic—of the entire colonial enterprise in L'Algérie française, which today lives on in the collective memories of pied-noir communities, forcibly repatriated after 1962 on the northern shores of the Mediterranean.[62]

## Notes

1. Isabelle Eberhardt, *The Passionate Nomad: The Diary of Isabelle Eberhardt*, trans. Nina de Voogd, introduction and notes by Rana Kabbani (Boston: Beacon Press, 1987), 2; hereafter cited as *Diary*.

2. David Prochaska's *Making Algeria French: Colonialism in Bône, 1870–1920* (New York: Cambridge University Press, 1990) is a first-rate study of French colonialism. Prochaska contrasts British India, where the attraction of the summer hill stations was precisely the absence of large numbers of Indians, to French Algeria: "Were not the European settlers, the *pieds-noirs*, so firmly ensconced in Bône that there was little need to get away—at least from the Algerians?" (208). Whether North African or Indian, the carefully nurtured myth of Western superiority dictated that Europeans observe special behavioral norms in front of the natives.

3. Women, whether European or indigenous, are notably absent in the two standard historical studies of Algeria, Charles-André Julien, *Histoire de l'Algérie contemporaine (1827–1871)*, vol. 1 (Paris: Presses Universitaires de France, 1964), and Charles-Robert Ageron, *Histoire de l'Algérie contemporaine (1871–1954)*, vol. 2 (Paris: Presses Universitaires de France, 1979). The Algerian war of national liberation, 1954–62, produced a number of heroines, such as Jamila Boupasha, whose story is told by Simone de Beauvoir and Gisèle Halimi, *Djamila Boupacha: The Story of the Torture of a Young Algerian Girl Which Shocked Liberal French Opinion* (New York: Macmillan, 1962).

4. Isabelle Eberhardt, *The Oblivion Seekers and Other Writings*, trans. Paul Bowles (San Francisco: City Lights, 1975). The title for this collection of stories and sketches was inspired by one of Eberhardt's pieces written in 1904, immediately

before her death. Paul Bowles, himself a cultural exile living in Morocco for decades, might be considered as a sort of latter-day American version of Eberhardt in his capacity as a writer and professional expatriate.

For a critical analysis of the work on Eberhardt from 1904 until 1982, see Simone Rezzoug, "État présent des travaux sur Isabelle Eberhardt," *Annuaire de l'Afrique du Nord* 21 (1982): 841–47; Rezzoug rightly characterizes these works as "numerous but of poor quality" (841). In addition, Eberhardt's biography inspired at least two plays: *L'Esclave errante (The Wandering Slave)*, which opened at the Théatre de Pans in 1924, and *Isabelle d'Afrique* (1939). In 1987 a surrealistic film was made on her life with the unfortunate title *There Was an Unseen Cloud Moving*.

5.  In his *Femmes d'Algérie: Légendes, traditions, histoire, littérature* (Paris: La Boîte à Documents, 1987), Jean Déjeux devotes a chapter to Isabelle Eberhardt, his only chapter entirely devoted to a European woman in Algeria (207–56). His bibliography (337–41) lists at least sixty works on her.

6.  The question of why Eberhardt's story, once forgotten, is now remembered needs to be raised. In addition to recent biographies, Eberhardt's own writings, including her diaries, are being republished both in French and in English translation. The answer lies in the nature of late twentieth-century sensibilities. Nevertheless, the current rage for colonial backdrops in literature and cinema—romantic cross-cultural escapism—has an invidious side. In this global village we call our own, the colonial moment conjures up false images of a past stability and order when Africans and Asians "knew their place" and had not yet emerged as both a challenge and threat to the West. The republication of the writings of female travelers, for example the travel account of Edith Durham (1863–1944), first published in 1909 and republished as *High Albania*, introduction by John Hodgson (Boston: Beacon Press, 1985), is evidence of this nostalgia. An analysis of present-day interest in Eberhardt among Algerians is found in Déjeux, *Femmes*, 239–56.

7.  The origins of the term *pied-noir* are still disputed in the literature on French Algeria. Here the term is employed to designate the European settlers—at first mainly French in nationality but later from all over southern Europe—who arrived in Algeria as colonists soon after the initial French invasion of 1830. Originally intended to settle land expropriated from the indigenous Muslim Algerians, the *colons* eventually clustered in cities and towns. By the end of the nineteenth century, the pied-noir community had evolved into a culturally hybrid society that was, in many respects, distinct from France and from the French of the metropole.

8.  The colonial newspaper *Petite Gironde* described her as an "enemy of France," and Eberhardt, significantly, felt compelled to refute this accusation in her letter

of April 27, 1903, cited in Déjeux, *Femmes*, 253. Paul Catrice in his "Femmes écrivains d'Afrique du nord et du proche orient," *L'Afrique et l'Asie* 59, no. 3 (Paris, 1962): 23–44, published the year of Algerian independence, characterized Eberhardt as being of "Russian origins but profoundly algerianized" (24).

9. Edmonde Charles-Roux in his *Un Désir d'Orient: Jeunesse d'Isabelle Eberhardt, 1877–1899* (Paris: Bernard Grasset, 1988) entitles chapter 5, which deals with Isabelle's departure for North Africa, "Ruptures."

10. Edward W. Said, *Orientalism* (New York: Pantheon Books, 1978), 3.

11. For the intellectual antecedents of nineteenth-century orientalism and imperialism, see Ann Thomson's *Barbary and Enlightenment: European Attitudes towards the Maghreb in the Eighteenth Century* (Leiden: E. J. Brill, 1987).

12. There were a number of Expositions universelles held in Paris during the nineteenth century, for example in 1867 and in 1889; on the world exhibition as part of the colonial encounter, see Timothy Mitchell, "The World as Exhibition," *Comparative Studies in Society and History* 31, no. 2 (1989): 217–36; and Çelik and Kinney, this volume.

13. The toll that Trophimovsky's nihilist philosophy exacted from the five children in his care was high (only Isabelle was certainly his own child; Augustin's paternity remains doubtful; the rest were from Madame de Moerder's marriage to a Russian officer in the tsar's army). Two of Eberhardt's brothers and a niece committed suicide; several fled the family when the opportunity for freedom arose. On Isabelle Eberhardt's early life, see Cecily Mackworth, *The Destiny of Isabelle Eberhardt* (London: Quartet Books, 1977); and Annette Kobak, *Isabelle: The Life of Isabelle Eberhardt* (New York: Knopf, 1989). Her sexual identity is a complex affair; she may have been in love with her brother Augustin for a while, according to Kobak, *Isabelle*, 31–37.

14. Mackworth, *The Destiny*, 20–25. The *spahis* were Algerian Muslim troops in the service of the French colonial army.

15. Mackworth, *The Destiny*, 24–25.

16. Kobak, *Isabelle*, 33. Popular orientalism reached its height in the late nineteenth century, as seen in the European fad for chinoisérie and Ottoman furnishings and dress. World's fairs and colonial exhibitions not only displayed expropriated Oriental cultural artifacts but also the colonized peoples themselves to gawking European audiences; this represented cultural imperialism-cum-voyeurism at its worst. The photographer's appropriation of other cultures and civilizations was not limited to European studios. For a fine discussion of the colonial postcard and colonized women, see Malek Alloula's *The Colonial Harem*, trans. Myrna Godzich and Wlad Godzich (Manchester, England: Manchester University Press, 1987); the title of the French edition, *Le Harem colonial: Images d'un sous-érotisme* (Geneva: Editions Slatkine, 1986), is more accurate.

17. Eberhardt's attraction to French Algeria contrasts sharply with the pull-push factors that brought British women to India.

18. Mackworth, *The Destiny*, 26–36.

19. Kobak, *Isabelle*, 38–47. A tendency toward necromancy is already manifest in her early writings; this later developed into a fascination with graveyards and an obsession with death, as seen in her diaries.

20. In some respects, Eberhardt resembled other women travelers of the period who sought social mobility, self-assertion, and liberation through treks in foreign yet conquered lands. Like Mary Kingsley, she was clearly a "tortured soul"; see Helen Callaway's review of Katherine Frank's *A Voyager Out: The Life of Mary Kingsley* and of Dea Birkett's *Spinsters Abroad: Victorian Lady Explorers* in *Women's Studies International Forum* 13, no. 4 (1990): 405. In large measure, the relative ease of travel was due to refinements in the "tools of empire"—tremendous changes in communications technology made it feasible to reach Asia or Africa rapidly. Eberhardt noted in her journal (*Diary*, 17–18) that the sea crossing from Marseilles to Algiers in 1900 took roughly twenty-four hours, which is still true today. Thus the social phenomenon of women travelers at the turn of the century was the product of three interrelated forces: transformations in European female status that made it acceptable for women, even unaccompanied by men, to journey alone; the "New Imperialism," which made northern Africa into Europe's southern frontier; and significant advances in travel technology.

21. The progressive "pacification" of places like Algeria is reflected in the changing titles of European travel literature during the course of the nineteenth century. From the "expeditions" of the early conquest period (1830–ca. 1850) to later travel accounts entitled, significantly, "scenes from the sunny south," the forced domestication and appropriation of the Algerians' culture and land is clear.

22. Prochaska, *Making Algeria French*, 204.

23. Prochaska, *Making Algeria French*, 137.

24. Prochaska, *Making Algeria French*, 155.

25. The notion of imagined communities is taken from Benedict Anderson's provocative work, *Imagined Communities: Reflections on the Origin and Spread of Nationalism* (London: Verso, 1983). While Anderson's main focus is the "invention" of the nation-state and nationalism, one could argue that this invention went hand-in-hand with imperialism and colonialism. Of course, all communities, whether national or not, are imagined and invented to a certain degree.

In French Algeria, the pied-noir community, despite—or perhaps because of—its diverse ethnic and linguistic components, came close to embodying an invented or imagined subnational political and ideological entity. By the turn of the twentieth century, this entity had its own peculiar spoken patois or dialect, a distinct political culture and literature, and thus a collective awareness of its own subjective existence. (On the emergence of pied-noir culture, see Prochaska, *Making Algeria French*, 206–29.) Nevertheless, it was a highly volatile community since class lines did not always, in reality, match racial-ethnic divisions between white Europeans and Muslim Algerians. Moreover, the Europeans were highly stratified socially, and deeply rooted antagonisms existed between the metropole and the settlers. Therefore, these potentially disruptive social (and political) fault lines among the Europeans were kept in a steady state by *colon* fears or phantasms of indigenous insurrection, violence, and sexuality.

26. As Mackworth, *The Destiny*, 39, correctly points out, cross-gender dressing (i.e., women clothed as men) was acceptable for some strata of Algerian Muslim society in certain situations, although it was certainly not the norm. Eberhardt's preference for male disguises undoubtedly scandalized the Europeans of Bône more than its indigenous inhabitants. As a recent biographer of Gertrude Bell (another well-known female traveler in the Middle East during exactly the same period) observed, the wearing of trousers by European women was "an almost unheard of sartorial departure for a woman." H. V. F. Winstone, *Gertrude Bell* (New York: Quartet Books, 1978), 58.

Eberhardt's ability to pose as a man was aided by her physical appearance; a French woman who had known her in Tunis described her in the following way: "She lived like a man—or a boy, because she was far more like one, physically. She had a hermaphrodite quality—she was passionate, sensual, but not in a woman's way. And she was completely flat chested . . . her beautiful hands were tinted with henna, her burnous was always immaculate." Lesley Blanch, *The Wilder Shores of Love* (New York: Schuster, 1954), 293.

27. Mackworth, *The Destiny*, 37–45; Kobak, *Isabelle*, 50–57; Charles-Roux, *Un Désir*, 329–42.

28. In "Rethinking Colonial Categories: European Communities and the Boundaries of Rule," *Comparative Studies in Society and History* 31, no. 1 (1989): 134–61, Ann Laura Stoler observes that European women were the "custodians of morality," and that colonial (white) prestige and female honor were closely linked.

29. Despite the mass of publications devoted to her, the chronology of Eberhardt's life in North Africa is far from certain. Some works claim that she returned at the end of 1897—after her mother's death—to Geneva; see, for example, Marie-Odile Delacour and Jean-René Huleau in the annotated edition of Isabelle Eberhardt, *Oeuvres complètes: Écrits sur le sable* (Paris: Bernard Grasset, 1988), 1:23. Another work states that she took off briefly for the Sahara: L. Blanch, *The Wilder Shores*, 295. Still another claims that she took part in the revolt of March 1899 in Bône: Kobak, *Isabelle*, 62–65. The quote is from the *Diary*, 10–11.

30. Eberhardt's indolent lifestyle was often financed by the Algerians whom she importuned to lend her money; *Diary*, 24, 25, 45.

31. Kobak, *Isabelle*, 81–86; Mackworth, *The Destiny*, 46–49.

32. Eugen Weber, *France, Fin de Siècle* (Cambridge MA: Harvard University Press, 1986), 27–50.

33. Lesley Blanch, *Pierre Loti: Portrait of an Escapist* (London: Collins, 1983), 146.

34. The view that most Europeans held of the indigenous Algerians was expressed by Hubertine Auclert in *Les Femmes arabes en Algérie* (Paris: Editions Littéraires, 1900), 3: "In Algeria, there is only a very small elite minority of Frenchmen who would place the Arab race in the category of humanity."

35. On the myth of assimilation, see Martin D. Lewis, "One Hundred Million Frenchmen: The 'Assimilation' Theory in French Colonial Policy," *Comparative Studies in Society and History* 4, no. 2 (1962): 129–53.

36. For example, Mackworth, *Destiny*, 39.

37. Mackworth, *Destiny*, 56–63; *Diary*, 56–58.

38. Eberhardt often sublimated the worst abuses of the colonial regime in its treatment of the indigenous population. When she does describe the workings of European imperialism, it is usually to lament the fact that modernity was eroding the aesthetic appeal of the picturesque, quaint, and "traditional" in North African life. For example, in the *Diary*, 32, she states that "Arab society as one finds it in the big cities, unhinged and vitiated as it is by its contact with a foreign world, does not exist down here [in the Sahara]."

39. For example, in the *Diary*, 31, she quotes a passage from Loti's *Aziyade* in which he depicts a moonlit graveyard in Istanbul; she then compares Loti's fantastic landscape to her own landscape artfully composed of a cemetery in the Sahara under moonlight.

40. Alain Calmes, *Le Roman colonial en Algérie avant 1914* (Paris: Harmattan, 1984); Albert Memmi, ed., *Anthologie des écrivains français du Maghreb* (Paris: Présence Africaine, 1969). For critical assessments of French colonial perceptions of the colonized Other, see the collected works contained in Jean-Robert Henry, ed., *Le Maghreb dans l'imaginaire français: La colonie, le désert, l'éxil* (Aix-en-Provence: Edisud, 1985), and Julia Clancy-Smith, "In the Eye of the Beholder: Sufi and Saint in North Africa and the Colonial Production of Knowledge, 1830–1900," *Africana Journal* 15 (1990): 220–57.

41. Eberhardt's descriptive writings bear an uncanny resemblance to those of Albert Camus; there is, however, another, more important parallelism in their works. While she often makes only oblique references to the political underpinnings of the colonial system of domination, Camus in his two most celebrated novels, *L'Étranger* (1942) and *La Peste* (1957), deliberately omits, for the most part, the Algerian Muslims, who by then outnumbered the Europeans by at least eight to one.

42. *Diary*, 7, 10, 41, 23, 28, 79, 20, 68.

43. *Diary*, 20, 79, 88.
44. Prochaska, *Making Algeria French*, 207.
45. *Diary*, 4, 21.
46. In the *Diary*, 91, she states that "Despite the riff-raff French civilisation has brought over here, whore and whoremaster that it [France] is, Algiers is still a place full of grace and charm."
47. *Diary*, 4, 25, 35.
48. I have deliberately employed the term "manic" in a clinical sense to imply that Eberhardt may have suffered from acute manic depression. Some writers, notably Rana Kabbani in her introduction to *The Passionate Nomad*, v, suggest that she was afflicted by anorexia nervosa. I would argue instead that her somatic or physical conditions (amenorrhea, lack of breasts, lanugo, etc.) were a function of drug and alcohol addiction, which were in turn manifestations of manic-depressive psychosis; see Rudolph M. Bell, *Holy Anorexia* (Chicago: University of Chicago Press, 1985).
49. Eberhardt's first visit to Zaynab in 1902 is described in Eglal Errera, ed., *Sept années dans la vie d'une femme: Isabelle Eberhardt, lettres et journaliers* (Arles: Actes Sud 1987), 188–90; on Lalla Zaynab and the Sufi *zawiya* of al-Hamil, see Julia Clancy-Smith, "The Shaykh and His Daughter: Coping in Colonial Algeria, 1830—1904," in *Struggle and Survival in the Modern Middle East, 1850–1950,* ed. Edmund Burke III (London: I. B. Tauris, 1992); and on the friendship between Lalla Zaynab and Isabelle Eberhardt, see Julia Clancy-Smith, "The House of Zaynab: Female Authority and Saintly Succession in Colonial Algeria, 1850–1904," in *Shifting Boundaries: Women and Gender in Middle Eastern History*, ed. Nikki Keddie and Beth Baron (New Haven CT: Yale University Press, 1992), 254–73.
50. Kobak, *Isabelle*, 191.
51. Kobak, *Isabelle*, 204. Opposition to Eberhardt may have taken more violent forms than mere character assassinations in the colonial press. In 1901, she was attacked by a knife-wielding Algerian male in the Sahara and narrowly escaped death. The authorities "solved" the affair by attributing it to Muslim hostility toward Christians. However, some journalists at the time suspected that the colonial regime had paid her assailant to do away with a disorderly and embarrassing foreign woman; see Robert Randau, *Isabelle Eberhardt: Notes et souvenirs* (Paris: La Boîte à Documents, 1989).
52. Kobak, *Isabelle*, 207–19; Ursula K. Hart, *Two Ladies of Colonial Algeria: The Lives and Times of Aurélie Picard and Isabelle Eberhardt* (Athens: Ohio University Center for International Studies, 1987), 98–100. The Deuxième Bureau was a French intelligence service that normally relied upon indigenous (paid) informers; see also Mackworth, *The Destiny*, 192.

53. General Catroux, *Lyautey, le Marocain* (Paris: Hachette, 1952), 86–88.

54. A quote from one of Eberhardt's reports cited by Kobak, *Isabelle*, 215.

55. Eberhardt had joined the Qadiriyya Sufi order sometime in 1901 disguised as an Arab male (although Algerian females were also members of the order) and befriended the brotherhood's local elites in the Algerian Sahara. There are suggestions, however, that the Sufi notables admitted her into their inner circle for political reasons—they believed she was secretly allied with French authorities, and thus sought to make use of the European woman. See Kabbani's notes to the *Diary*, 111, nn. 25, 27.

56. Hart, *Two Ladies*, 100–101, states, "Sidi Brahim had become a major lever in French penetration and there seems little doubt that Isabelle had had a hand in making it so." However, once again, this attributes to Eberhardt more political clout than she really had.

57. Accounts of her death are found in Kobak, *Isabelle*, 231–38; Mackworth, *The Destiny*, 219–23. Blanch in *The Wilder Shores*, 285, appears to have been the first to point out the irony of her drowning in the desert.

58. Hart, *Two Ladies*, 109.

59. Isabelle Eberhardt, *Dans l'ombre chaude de l'Islam, ed.* Victor Barrucand, with a biographical essay on her life (Paris: Librarie Charpentier et Fasquelle, 1906). Kobak, *Isabelle*, 241, offers a fine analysis of why the book was so appealing to European audiences.

60. Kobak, *Isabelle*, 217. An example of the transformation in her writing is seen in the short story entitled "Outside" published in *The Oblivion Seekers*, 19–22.

61. *Diary*, 59.

62. Nostalgia for the colonial past has produced a number of sentimentalized works devoted to the *pied-noir* community in Algeria, for example, Marie Cardinal's *Les Pieds-Noirs* (Tours: Belfond, 1988).

# 6 | The Unspeakable Limits of Rape

## Colonial Violence and Counterinsurgency

JENNY SHARPE

E. M. Forster's *A Passage to India* reenacts in the drama surrounding a rape
the fears and fantasies of an imperial nation over the intermingling of two
races, the colonizer and the colonized.[1] Adela Quested, who is English, ac-
cuses the educated Muslim, Dr. Aziz, of sexually assaulting her in one of the
Marabar Caves. By reading Aziz's "crime" as "the unspeakable limit of cynicism, untouched since 1857" (*PI* 7), the English residents of Chandrapore
place the alleged rape within the racial memory of the Mutiny, also known
as the Sepoy Rebellion.[2] Eighteen fifty-seven has entered the colonial records
as nothing less than the barbaric attack of mutinous Sepoys on innocent
women and children. Yet, as one of the largest anti-British uprisings, 1857 is
also known to Indian nationalists as the First War of Independence. During
the 1920s, when Forster was finishing his novel, Vinayak Savarkar's *Indian
War of Independence of 1857*—a highly polemical book written to rouse Indians into armed struggle against the British—was widely circulated despite
its proscription.[3] The memory of 1857 was thus a site of historical contention during those volatile years of early decolonization. I take from Forster's
presentation of Adela's attack within the frame of 1857 the license to read his
novel as a narrative that reveals the limits of an official discourse on native
insurgency. It is a discourse that racializes colonial relations by implicating
rebellion in the violence of rape.[4]

*A Passage to India* holds up for public scrutiny the racialization of imperial
discourse by generating its narrative desire through the indeterminate status of the rape. Since the reader is not privy to what happened in the caves,
she or he is faced with the contradictory evidence of Adela's accusation and
Aziz's denial. The accuracy of Adela's judgment is undermined during the

215

trial when, upon interrogation, she suddenly withdraws the charge. Forster's staging of the court scene around the reversal of a rape charge disrupts the taken-for-grantedness of the racially motivated assumption that "the darker races are physically attracted by the fairer, but not *vice versa*" (PI 218–19). The roles of assailant and victim are now dramatically reversed as the novel reveals the "real crime" of imperialism to be an abuse of power that can only lead to its demise. Yet we are never told whether the attempted rape was real or imagined, and the question of what happened in the Marabar Caves continues to intrigue readers of the novel. Whereas early inquiries investigated the mystery for what it revealed about Forster's narrative technique or Indian metaphysics, recent criticism has shifted the terms of the debate toward issues of race and gender.

I situate my own reading of the rape in *A Passage to India* within the current effort of feminist theory to account for the heterogeneous text of women's history. As we attempt to pry apart the singularity of a female tradition, we often presume race to be a unified and homogeneous field of otherness. By treating race as a transhistorical category, we thus fail to dislodge the dominant discourses that wrench racial (and sexual) constructions out of history and present them as essentializing categories of difference. The demand on contemporary feminism, then, is to disrupt the taken-for-grantedness of such categories through an excavation of the histories that produce racial and sexual difference. In response to this demand, I trace the signification of rape in Forster's novel to the historical production of a colonial discourse on the native assault of English women in India. Upon making this move, however, I do not wish to suggest that literature and history are repetitions of each other. While the historical records produce a racial memory that is silently constitutive of Anglo-Indian fiction, the familiar plots of such fictions render India "imaginable" for historical narration. In this regard, my interest in *A Passage to India* lies in the particularly strategic role it has played in establishing the terrain for recent revisions of the Raj.

A replaying of the last days of the Raj in the ongoing drama of movies like *Gandhi* and *A Passage to India* and the series *The Jewel in the Crown* exhibits a nostalgia for empire even as it masquerades as self-criticism. Forster's critical look at imperialism presents a problem that is particularly vexing for feminists. Upon questioning whether the real crime is Adela's accusation or Aziz's assault, *A Passage to India* sets up an opposition between "the English woman" and "the Indian man." If one decides, in keeping with the novel's anti-imperialist theme, that the crime lies in a system capable of reducing an Indian man to his pathological lust for white women, then even the slightest hint of an actual rape cannot be entertained. Conversely, a defense of Adela's fear of assault brings with it a condemnation of the Indian patriarchy and Aziz's objectification of women as sex objects. The ambiguities surrounding the alleged rape thus force the critic to defend either the native man or the white woman against his or her opponent. It is this either/or decision (but never both) that has divided an anticolonial criticism of A Passage to India along gender lines.

Critical opinion tends to favor Adela's hallucination as the most likely explanation for what happened in the caves. Offering her sexual repression as evidence, such accounts discredit Adela's charge against Aziz as not only mistaken but also misguided. Even those readings that critically engage the problems of colonial representation treat Adela's cry of rape as an expression of her desire.[5] Although A Passage to India does suggest the imaginary nature of the attack, it does not provide sufficient evidence for presupposing that Adela's musings on Aziz's handsome appearance should translate into a sexual fantasy of rape. In his screen adaptation of the novel, David Lean legitimates this common reading by adding a scene which eliminates any doubt that, on at least one other occasion, the unattractive Adela suffered a bout of sexual hysteria. The scene shows Adela leaving the safety of the European compound to venture out on bicycle alone. She chances upon an ancient Hindu temple, whose sexually explicit carvings arouse her curiosity and interest. The threatening aspect of her sexual arousal is figuratively represented in the aggressive monkeys that swarm over the statues and scare her away. Adela returns to Chandrapore breathless, pale, and sweating. Having just broken off her engagement to Ronny Heaslop, she now says she will marry him. His query—"What happened?"—and her response—"Nothing"—are emblematic of the film's message regarding the cave scene. In a flashback of Adela staring fixedly at Aziz's silhouetted shape looming in the cave's entrance, Lean repeats the image of her pale and frightened face after her encounter with the monkeys. The conclusion to be drawn is so obvious that the film does not find it necessary to provide further elaboration.

A masculinist reading of the mystery in the cave (such as Lean's) is based on the "common knowledge" that frigid women suffer from sexual hysteria and that unattractive women desire to be raped. This interpretation works backward from the imaginary rape, positing the effect of an effect as its cause. The argument consequently produces its own tautology: Adela hallucinated the rape because she was sexually repressed, the proof of which lies in her hallucination. Feminist criticism of *A Passage to India* has dismantled this tautology by revealing the "making into meaning" of its assumptions. Rather than discounting the imaginary nature of the attack, feminists respond to the critical verdict against Adela by retracing her hallucination to a first cause of patriarchal authority rather than sexual hysteria. Elaine Showalter, for instance, reads the hallucination in terms of Adela's apprehensions about committing herself to a loveless marriage that is nothing short of "legalized rape."[6] In "Periphrasis, Power, and Rape in *A Passage to India*," Brenda Silver also links the imaginary rape to the gender roles suggested by marriage. Since Adela enters the cave disturbed about her forthcoming marriage to Ronny Heaslop, argues Silver, she is forced to acknowledge her social status as a sex object and thus to confront "the material and psychological reality of what it means to be rapable."[7]

Although they are correct to situate the alleged rape within the larger frame of women's oppression, Showalter and Silver fail to address the historical production of the category of rape within a system of *colonial* relations. Feminist criticism has thus replaced the masculinist tautology with another one. The feminist tautology goes something like this: Adela experiences the conditions of rape because she is objectified as a woman, the proof of which lies in her experience of rape. What does it mean for an English woman's experience of her oppression to be staged as a scenario in which she is the potential object of a native attack? In other words, how does the feminist critic negotiate the either/or opposition between the colonial female and the colonized male that the novel sets up? I would begin by insisting that Adela's confrontation of "what it means to be rapable" is framed by racial tensions that cannot be understood as simply another form of patriarchal violence.

What is immediately noticeable about the representation of gender roles in *A Passage to India* is the fracture between Adela's social positioning and that of Anglo-Indian women.[8] From the early pages of the novel there are suggestions that colonial women are protectively cloistered behind an anachronistic code of chivalry and honor. "Windows were barred lest the servants should see their memsahibs acting," the narrator informs us, "and the heat was consequently immense" (*PI* 24). Fielding's refusal to behave chivalrously toward English women "would have passed without comment in feminist England" (*PI* 62), we are told, but not in Anglo-India. Unfamiliar with their customs, Adela is surprised that club members have chosen to perform *Cousin Kate*, a play that Showalter reminds us is "a mildly anti-feminist comedy."⁹ Thus establishing an opposition between the emancipated women of England and the stalled liberation of the memsahibs, *A Passage to India* plots Adela's movement from one side of the East-West divide to the other.

It is not just that Adela enters the cave contemplating a marriage that will subsume her identity into that of her husband. More importantly, she recognizes the danger of assuming the Anglo-Indians' racist assumptions about India and its inhabitants. "Well, by marrying Mr. Heaslop, I shall become what is known as an Anglo-Indian," she says to Aziz as they make their way toward the caves:

> He held up his hand in protest. "Impossible. Take back such a terrible remark."
>
> "But I shall! it's inevitable. I can't avoid the label. What I do hope to avoid is the mentality. Women like—" She stopped, not quite liking to mention names; she would boldly have said "Mrs. Turton and Mrs. Callendar" a fortnight ago. (*PI* 145)

Adela's inability to identify Mrs. Turton and Mrs. Callendar as the insensitive imperialists that they are demonstrates her newfound loyalty to Anglo-Indian women. Her transformation into a memsahib was already under way the moment she agreed to marry Heaslop. "She was labeled now" (*PI* 94), *she* thought to herself at the time. If the label is inevitable, the mentality is inescapable. A disregard for Indians to the degree of rendering them invisible is an offense that Anglo-Indian women repeatedly commit.¹⁰ By the time Adela enters the cave, her self-consciousness about what it means to be an Anglo-Indian is forgotten. After presuming that Aziz has more than one wife by virtue of being a Muslim, Adela is oblivious to having offended him and, being so wrapped up in her own thoughts, she is not even aware of his presence. "Quite unconscious that she had said the wrong thing, and not seeing him, she also went into the cave, thinking with half her mind 'sight-seeing bores me,' and wondering with the other half about marriage" (*PI* 153). Only half of Adela's mind is on thoughts of marriage; the other expresses a boredom with Aziz's elaborate efforts to show her "the real India." Her divided mind reveals a tension between the Anglo-Indian woman's double positioning in colonial discourse—as the inferior sex but superior race. It is a contradiction that must be addressed in any discussion of the sexual assault.

When Adela emerges from the cave accusing Aziz of rape, she consolidates the identity she would rather deny. That is to say, she reconfirms the colonizer's racist assumption that, given the slightest opportunity, the native will revert to his barbaric ways. In her haste to escape she flees through cacti, lodging thousands of minuscule spines into her flesh. Her mutilated condition confirms the violence of the attack, but it also reduces her sensibility to her tortured body. "Everything now was transferred to the surface of her body, which began to avenge itself, and feed unhealthily" (*PI* 193). Her fellow expatriates react to the news of the assault from within their code of honor and chivalry: they treat Adela as a mere cipher for a battle between men. "Miss Quested was only a victim, but young Heaslop was a martyr; he was the recipient of all the evil intended against them by the country they had tried to serve; he was bearing the sahib's cross" (*PI* 185). The age-old equation of female chastity with male honor is reinscribed within the language of the colonial civilizing mission. By virtue of that mission, the white man reenacts a Christian allegory of self-sacrifice so that the weaker races might be raised into humanity.[11] The objectification of Adela into a passive victim denies her an entry into the grand narrative of the white man's burden even as that victimage reaffirms the self-sacrifice of the men who serve the colonial mission. *She* cannot save the natives from their depravity, but neither can she save herself. Adela, the memsahib, the Anglo-Indian woman, has strayed far from the borders of "feminist England." She may have entered the caves with some semblance of her former identity, but she emerges as a violated body bearing the visible signs of the natives' ingratitude.

*A Passage to India* consciously invokes, in its animation of a sexual assault that transforms Adela into a sign for the victimage of imperialism, a nineteenth-century colonial discourse of counterinsurgency. During the 1857 uprisings, a crisis in colonial authority was managed through the circulation of "the English Lady" as a sign for the moral influence of colonialism. A colonial discourse on rebellious Sepoys raping, torturing, and mutilating English women inscribed the native's savagery onto the objectified body of English women, even as it screened the colonizer's brutal suppression of the uprisings. When the Anglo-Indians of Chandrapore read "rape" as "the unspeakable limit of cynicism, untouched since 1857," they are not only associating the attack in the cave with the racial memory of those earlier "unspeakable" acts, but also reproducing its effects.

Feminist explications of *A Passage to India*, however, tend to ignore the racial memory that forms the historical frame to its theme of interracial rape. Silver, for instance, does not allude to a colonial past, but rather a history that demystifies the myth of the black rapist in the American South. Her discussion of "the Negro" in the place of "the Indian" suggests a continuity between the divergent histories of slavery and imperialism.[12] To read racial stereotypes in terms of the discontinuous histories of colonial conquest, slavery, and imperialism is to see that the selection of certain attributes for exaggeration has to do with the ideological sanction they provide. In her careful documentation of lynching, Ida B. Wells reveals that the fearful stereotype of "the Negro rapist" sanctioned the upsurge in violence against black men, women, and children that was aimed at reversing their political and economic gains.[13] Her evidence is reinforced in Eugene Genovese's observation that "the violence-provoking theory of the superpotency of that black superpenis, while whispered about for several centuries, did not become an obsession in the South until after emancipation, when it preserved the purposes of racial segregationists."[14] The myth of the black rapist presupposes even as it reproduces the Negro's lustful bestiality. The Oriental male, by contrast, is constructed as licentious, not lustful, duplicitous rather than bestial.

In the absence of its colonial constructions, Silver discusses racial codes on a level of generality that reduces geopolitical differences. It is an absence that permits her to write the condition of both the black rapist and the colonized under the name of "woman." By understanding rape to be a discourse of power that objectifies colonial women and colonized men alike, she suggests that Aziz is figuratively raped by the accusation of rape. "When spoken of as Indian within the discourse of English and Indian, sahib and native," she writes, "he himself [Aziz] is objectified; he enters the 'category' of woman and becomes rapable."[15] Although Silver expresses that she is "aware of 'feeling privileged as a woman' to speak to and for third-world women (and in this case third-world men as well),"[16] it is her problematical reading of Third World men as occupying the space of First World women that permits the latter to serve as a model for all oppressed peoples. Since she *is* attentive to the dangers of substituting gender for race, I do not dismiss her essay as misinformed. Rather, I regard her informed reading as symptomatic of the persistent difficulty Anglo-American feminism has with dislodging the (white) woman as a privileged signifier for "otherness." It is a privilege that can be unlearned, but only through an attention to the historical production of our categories for class, race, and gender relations. If feminism has anything to teach us, it is that an official history has produced a category of "woman" that keeps women, to invoke Sheila Rowbotham, hidden from history. By deploying "rape" as a master trope for the objectification of English women and natives alike, Silver produces a category of "Other" that keeps the colonized hidden from history.

I submit reports on the 1857 uprisings as the beginning of a racial discourse on brown-skinned men sexually assaulting white women in India. Since, as Edward Said reminds us, beginnings are always strategically posited to enable a critical enterprise,[17] I initiate my discussion of the rape in *A Passage to India* with 1857 so as to demonstrate that "what it means to be rapable" does have a history. When viewed historically, the category of rape can be seen to be so invested with the value of the "English Lady" that its metaphoric extension to Indian men is foreclosed in literature written prior to decolonization. By reconstructing the historical production of a colonial discourse of rape, I hope to show that Aziz cannot enter the category of woman and become rapable.

### The "Reality Effect" of Historical Fictions

Give full stretch to your imagination — think of everything that is cruel, inhuman, infernal, and you cannot then conceive anything so diabolical as what these demons in human form have perpetrated.
— *Lahore Chronicle Extra*, June 17, 1857

Manufacturers of gup [gossip], as it was termed, had a lively time, and imagination was freely called into play; yet imagination and fiction, with every advantage, were beaten by the truth, for I remember no story, however horrible, that equaled the realities of Cawnpore.
MRS. MUTER, *Travels and Adventures*

May 10, 1857, has been set down in colonial records as the most infamous day in Anglo-Indian history. For the first time in their hundred-year stay in India, the British faced rebellions on a scale that threw the authority of their rule into crisis. A strange and horrifying tale took hold of the colonial imagination, spreading throughout Anglo-India and all the way back to England. Mutineers, the story went, are subjecting "our countrywomen" to unspeakable torments. Natives, the story continued, are systematically raping English women and then dismembering their ravished bodies. Long before the British army regained control over its Indian territories, the tales of terror were discredited as having little or no historical basis. "Fortunately the actual occurrence of these horrors was seldom proved," reports Pat Barr in her apologia for Anglo-Indian women, "but they served to inflame public opinion in England and Anglo-India—particularly because the principal victims were said to have been women. The press in both countries waxed hysterical [*sic*] in demands for more severe punitive measures to be taken, and the rituals of revenge-killing were enacted even in the nurseries and schoolrooms of the homeland."[18] Thus was the British reading public invited to share the terror of the white settlers, and their revenge, as letters, stories, and eyewitness reports slowly made their way back from India.

Our perception of 1857 has been colored by the years of myth making that have gone into popularized narrations of the revolt. The accounts of white settlers in a state of exhaustion, terror, and confusion have since been sealed with the stamp of authenticity that guarantees all eyewitness reports. The rebellion was not quite the military insurrection that its designated name of "Mutiny" suggests. Although initiated by Sepoy mutineers at Meerut, the uprisings included a heterogeneous cross-section of the North Indian population that extended far beyond the military ranks.[19] Nor was it simply a case of Sepoys suddenly turning against their colonial masters and slaughtering British officers and their families. The battles were far more protracted, involving maneuvers and countermaneuvers between the British and relatively autonomous native factions for control of disparate regions. Rebels (sometimes armed with heavy artillery) lay siege to colonial towns, while loyal soldiers were marched from one part of the country to another to reclaim fallen territories. Anglo-Indian communities trapped within towns were often cut off from food, water, medicine, and other necessary supplies. The East India Company, then entrusted with colonial administration, was unable to restore law and order for the good part of two years. Most Europeans, including women and children, suffered the "mutilation" of bullet wounds or else "fell victim" to diseases contracted during the long sieges. They did not, as was commonly believed, die at the sadistic hands of roving bands of *bad-mashes*. This latter belief, however, was reiterated and reproduced in literature, paintings, and lithographs depicting leering Sepoys with their swords raised over the heads of kneeling women and children. The primary referent for the popular image of the Sepoy was the Cawnpore massacre.

Upon retreating from Cawnpore before an approaching British army, the Hindu rebel leader Nana Sahib ordered that his two hundred hostages, all of them women and children, be executed. The British army subsequently preserved Bibighar (the house in which the women were killed) with its dried blood and rotting remains as a kind of museum for passing troops to visit. Locks of hair from the dead women's heads were carried off as mementos and passed from hand to hand as the fetish objects of an erotic nightmare. Thus began the mythic invention of the dying women's torments, as soldiers covered the walls with bloody inscriptions in the hands of the "ladies," directing their men to avenge their horrible deaths.[20] Nana Sahib has since been vilified in colonial historiography for having committed the unforgivable crime of desecrating English womanhood. Barr exhibits a predictable understanding of the Cawnpore massacre when she writes that there, "one of the most revered of Victorian institutions, the English Lady, was slaughtered, defiled and brought low."[21] The occurrence of even one massacre such as Cawnpore endowed all the tales of terror with their reality effect. British magistrates who were entrusted with investigating the stories, however, could find no evidence of systematic mutilation, rape, and torture at Cawnpore or anyplace else.

Anglo-Indian descriptions of the tortures drew on a stockpile of horrors culled from the great works of Western civilization. The Bible, Homer, Virgil, Dante, and Shakespeare all provided the Mutiny narratives with their charged plots of martyrdom, heroism, and revenge. The familiar and easily recognizable plots thus enabled the British to make sense of what was an incomprehensible event—impossible to comprehend because anticolonial insurgency had previously been unthinkable. Yet, it is the details concerning the crimes against English women that gave the familiar plots their historical efficacy. Although the British and Anglo-Indian presses claimed the stories to be "too foul for publication,"[22] they disclosed fragments of information in hints and innuendoes that prompted their readers to search their imagination for the awful deaths. The following editorial, which appeared in a London newspaper during the early stages of the Mutiny, establishes the "fact" that women and children were killed by first declaring little knowledge of events, then appealing to the imagination as a privileged source of information, before finally reporting what has only been heard: "Others, and amongst them a large number of women and children, fell into the hands of the infuriate crew, thirsting for the blood of the infidel, and frenzied with *bhang*. We know little of the exact scenes which transpired, and imagination hesitates to lift the veil from them. We hear, however, that about 50 helpless women and children who had hid themselves in the palace on the outbreak were subsequently discovered, and the whole murdered in cold blood."[23] As the mystery that imagination will reveal from behind the veil of ignorance, rumor has already been declared a truth.

The press tended to rely on the personal testimonies of people, many of whom were not present at the scenes they described. Attempts to establish the sources of stories proved that, as is the case with rumor, their origins were unknown.[24] Upon further questioning, so-called eyewitnesses admitted that what they "saw" did not happen in their town but elsewhere, in the next town perhaps.[25] Some English readers did question the validity of the reports, while others, more sympathetic to the plight of the rebels, protested the brutal methods used for quelling the uprisings.[26] The general tenor of the editorials and letters, however, exhibits a desire to transform rumor and hearsay into fact and information. The invented stories could be explained—and Barr does explain them—as a terror-induced response to the discovery that rebels did not spare the lives of European women. Yet, the Victorian male's horror over anticolonial insurrection invading the sanctity of his home does not sufficiently account for the sexualization of the women's deaths.

The sensationalist accounts, which are to be found in private letters, news reports, and published narratives, all circulate around a single, unrepresentable center: the rape of English women. Upon declaring the crime "unspeakable," the reports offer a range of signification that has the same effect as the missing details. In other words, they "speak" a discourse of rape. After sorting through innumerable colonial reports, I was struck by a common narrative structure many of them shared. A particularly notorious version of this plot appears in a letter from a clergyman that was first published in the London *Times*. It tells of forty-eight "delicately nurtured ladies," most of them girls, who were "violated" and kept for "base purposes" for a week. The letter goes on to describe the women being paraded naked through the streets of Delhi, publicly raped by "the lowest of the people," before being submitted to a slow death by dismemberment.[27] Karl Marx, reporting on India for the New York *Daily Tribune*, points out that the story came from "a cowardly parson residing at Bangalore, Mysore, more than a thousand miles, as the bird flies, distant from the scene of the action."[28] The clergyman's letter was also identified as fictitious in an 1858 publication representing the attempt of one Edward Lecky to provide a "credible history" to the rebellions.[29] Variations on the basic structure of, in this case, an invented story—the humiliation, sexual assault, torture, and death of English women—recur again and again in Mutiny accounts. Its plotting belongs to a discourse of rape, a specifically sexual form of violence that has as its aim an appropriation of women as "the sex."[30] This appropriation takes place through the objectification of women as sexualized, eroticized, and ravaged bodies.

The narratives that stage the deaths of English women as a public spectacle constitute a violent appropriation of their bodies. As the following words of Sir Colin Campbell demonstrate, these stories bypass the mutilation of men to give a step-by-step account of the crimes perpetrated against women. What is noteworthy about this particular account is that the agent of torture is missing; it could be any native or every one. We will later see why no Indian—male, female, young, or old—escapes suspicion. The details concerning the disfiguration of English women have the effect of reducing them to their mutilated bodies. A construction of the women as "the sex" is visible in the necessity to subject both their primary and secondary sexual organs to attack. In this narrator's hierarchy of tortures, the "most horrible" mutilation is the loss of identity through an effacement of the facial features. By the time Campbell has finished with his account, there is nothing left to the English woman but her brutalized body:

> Tortures the most refined, outrages the most vile, were perpetrated upon men, women and children alike. Men were hacked to pieces in the presence of their wives and children. Wives were stripped in the presence of their husband's eyes, flogged naked through the city, violated there in the public streets, and then murdered. To cut off the breasts of the women was a favourite mode of dismissing them to death; and, most horrible, they were sometimes scalped—the skin being separated round the neck, and then drawn over the head of the poor creatures, who were then, blinded with blood, driven out into the blazing streets. To cut off the nose, ears and lips of these unhappy women (in addition, of course, to the brutal usage to which they were almost invariably submitted), was merciful.[31]

The scene is staged in a manner that forces us to view the women's rape and mutilation through the "husband's eyes." We do not know what it means for the women to see their husbands killed, even though men are included among the victims. We are here reminded of the line from *A Passage to India* that depicts an Anglo-Indian response to news of Adela's assault: "[The wife] was only a victim, but [the husband] was a martyr; he was the recipient of all the evil intended against them by the country they had tried to serve" (*PI* 185). Forster's words can be read as an indictment of narratives like Campbell's that formulate the assault of English women as an indirect attack on colonial men. The mutilations described, then, reenact a sexual nightmare that fixates on the bodies of not just women, but *women who belong to English men.*

The unacknowledged terror of the rape and mutilation stories is to be found in the element of doubt the uprisings introduced to the language of racial superiority. This terror can be read in the absence of narratives that objectify English men through descriptions of their mutilated bodies. The reports hold no elaborate details concerning the torture of men and certainly no mention of the male sexual organ being removed. Such a fragmentation of the male body would allocate English men to the objectified space of "the class of women,"[32] a status denying British power at the precise moment that it needed reinforcing. Once an English man has been struck down, then anything is possible; in death his mortality is revealed and sovereign status brought low. A focus on the slaughter of defenseless women and children displaces attention away from the image of English men dying at the hands of native insurgents. Through an animation of "women and children," the fiction of racial superiority could be upheld even as the seriousness of the revolt was recognized.

The Mutiny reports transform Anglo-Indian women into an institution, the "English Lady," by selectively drawing on the Victorian ideal of womanhood. This transformation permits a slippage between the violation of English women as the object of rape and the violation of colonialism as the object of rebellion. The value of the "English Lady"—her self-sacrifice, moral influence, and innocence—is thus extended to the social mission of colonialism. Because of its close association with her moral worth, the category of rape is reserved for English women alone. The rape of Indian women is not directly revealed in the information of the reports. It is revealed, however, in their repeated disavowals that, unlike the treacherous Sepoys, English soldiers did not rape enemy women. In even the most telling accounts, which are to be found in private correspondences rather than published narratives, the rape of Indian women remains unacknowledged: "We advanced to the village and the general gave it up to the tender mercies of the 84th, as he said, to do as they liked with. They did clear it with a vengeance, for in 5 minutes there was not one *live* nigger in the village."[33] What happens to Indian women when subjected to the "tender mercies" of British soldiers is predictably missing from this report. In the place of that absent narrative, we have representations of Indian women inciting the mutineers to rape and torture.

Contrary to stereotypical colonial constructions of Indian women as passive, the Mutiny narratives explicitly describe them as "active instigators of the Sepoys in their worst atrocities."[34] A particularly notorious actor in these crimes is the woman warrior: characterized as a hag or a she-fiend, she is nearly always dreadful in appearance. The most famous of these women warriors, the Rani of Jhansi (whom the British called "the Jezebel of India"), is uncharacteristically noted for her handsome looks but then also her lasciviousness.[35] The British officer responsible for her death said of her: "The Indian Mutiny has produced but one man, and that man was a woman."[36] In the following account, which appeared in the *Bombay Times*, the Rani is positioned in a decidedly masculine role. As the one who orders her men to rape, humiliate, and torture their female victims, she exercises a power of speech that is capable of violating English womanhood:

> Shortly after, the whole of the European community, men, women, and children, were forcibly brought out of their homes; and, in the presence of the Ranee, stripped naked. Then commenced a scene unparalleled in historical annals. She, who styles herself "Ranee," ordered, as a preliminary step, the blackening of their faces with a composition of suet and oil, then their being tied to trees at a certain distance from each other and having directed the innocent little children to be hacked to pieces before the eyes of their agonized parents, she gave the women into the hands of the rebel sepoys, to be dishonoured first by them, and then handed over to the rabble. The maltreatment these poor creatures had received was enough to kill them, and several died ere the whole of the brutal scene had transpired; but those who still lingered were put to death with the greatest cruelty, being severed limb from limb. The death the men were subject to was by no means so intensely cruel as that which our countrywomen received at the hands of their ravishers.[37]

The difficulty of representing a stereotypically passive Indian woman as an active agent is overcome by the double move of racially positioning her victims as lowly natives and sexually positioning the Rani as the one who directs the rape and torture. Before the Rani can exercise her will over the lives (and deaths) of the Europeans in this narration, she must first break their code of racial superiority. The English are consequently transformed into natives through a darkening of their faces. Yet even in an instance of gender role reversal such as this, the report saves English men from objectification through mutilation. But more importantly, this account banishes into the realm of impossibility the rape of Indian women captured by an avenging army.

It would be difficult for a British reading public to envision the rape of native women after being presented with the image of the Rani directing the sexual brutalization of English women (an action that semantically positions the Sepoys in a passive role). According to the Mutiny reports, the native woman is not rapable. The closest the official discourse comes to depicting such rape is in the description of *English* women with their blackened faces. In this masquerade of race and gender roles, we are presented with the fantastic image of the Rani as the native woman who is behind the rape of other "native" women. What we see in the making is a more explicitly race-oriented idiom that is being put into place through a semiosis of "woman."

Since it articulates the contradictions of gender and race *within the signifying system of colonialism*, the sexual discourse of rape is overdetermined by colonial relations of force and exploitation.[38] It is helpful, when unpacking a colonial economy of signs, to consider Elizabeth Cowie's important insight into the cultural production of women as not only exchange objects but also as signs.[39] According to Cowie, the exchange of women that reproduces their social roles of wife, mother, and so on constitutes a transaction that also produces value for a particular signifying system. In the case of the Mutiny reports, I would argue that the display of the violated bodies of English women produces the "English Lady" as a sign for a colonial moral influence under threat of native violation. The signifier may be "woman," but its signified is the value of colonialism that she represents. This might explain why, despite the narrative energy going into a discourse on the English woman, stories of the women themselves escape the narrations. Since the signifying function of woman-as-victim in the Mutiny reports depends on her social role of wife and her restriction to the "innocent" space of the domestic sphere, the English woman's access to colonial power is denied. There exists, as a consequence, a fracture between the colonial woman's positioning within the Mutiny reports as passive victim or violated body and her own sense of "self."

What is striking about the English women who narrate their Mutiny experiences is their reliance upon a language of colonial authority.[40] As they express their horror and fears in personal diaries, journals, and letters they do not always respond to the threat of rape and torture from within their socially constructed gender role. In other words, they do not necessarily turn to their husbands for protection. There are, of course, the Harriet Tytlers who write of keeping poison nearby and instructing their husbands to avenge their deaths.[41] But there are also the wives of officers and civil servants who claim to have scared off hostile villagers by speaking to them authoritatively. These women were not always successful, and some of them were killed for attempting to intimidate the rebels with commanding voices. By appealing to their own sense of authority under conditions that did not always guarantee its success, however, these women demonstrate a modicum of faith in their ability to command the natives. An official history negates the Anglo-Indian woman's access to colonial power, for her value to colonialism resides in her status of "defenseless victim" alone. In this regard, as feminists, we should not similarly efface European women's agency by constructing them as the victims of colonial relations that are patriarchal alone.[42]

We see, in the invented stories of rape and mutilation, colonial power relations being written on the bodies of women. Their savaged remains display a fantasy of the native's savagery that screens the "barbarism" of colonialism. Presupposing their women to inhabit a domestic sphere that was safe from colonial conflict, Anglo-Indian men responded as good soldiers, fathers, and husbands to the stories of rebels executing their women and children. They reasserted claims over what was rightfully theirs by protecting the victims and punishing the offenders. And the honor of the victim was often defended by making the punishment fit or (as was more often the case) exceed the crime. After the British regained control over Cawnpore, they forced captured rebels to lick floors clean of dried blood before hanging them. It was also common practice to tie mutineers to the front of cannons and explode their bodies into minuscule pieces. The roads down which an avenging army marched were lined with the dead bodies of Indian men, women, and children dangling from the trees as a message to the populace about the consequences of rebellion. Upon recapturing Delhi, the British army was reported to have massacred anywhere from twenty-five thousand to thirty thousand of its inhabitants. The response of revenge for the dishonor of English women thus not only reestablished a claim of lawful (sexual) ownership but also enforced violent strategies of counterinsurgency.

Mutiny historiography understands the brutality with which the uprisings were suppressed as the uncontrollable rage of Victorian men responding to the desecration of their women. When posited as a cause, the rape and mutilation of English women explains British reprisals as the aberrant response of otherwise civilized men driven mad at the thought of their tormented women. Thus adhering to the logic of colonialism as a civilizing influence, this explanation reconfirms the morality of the civilizers. By reading the sexualization of insurgency in the reports as the *effect of a violence already sanctioned by the structures of colonialism*, we see that the discourse of rape in fact normalizes repressive measures against anticolonial insurgency. Almost immediately after the outbreak of the Mutiny in May, an act giving summary powers to officers was passed. It was superseded by a more extreme act of June 6. "Under that last Act," records Sir George Campbell in his memoirs, "such powers were given wholesale to all and sundry, and barbarities were committed with a flimsy pretext of legality."[43] The campaign of terror was thus already under way long before the news of Cawnpore (the massacre occurred on July 15) reached the ears of British soldiers.[44] What confirmed the atrocities against English women were the punishments that supposedly reflected them. Conducted as highly ritualized and publicized spectacles designed to maximize native terror, British retribution against rebels served as its own model for the torture and mutilation the army was ordered to quell.[45] "My object," Brigadier General Neill, one of the more infamous avenging officers, admits, "is to inflict a fearful punishment for a revolting, cowardly, barbarous deed, and to strike terror into these rebels."[46] The narratives of sexual violence cleared a space for what Neill, alluding to the punishment he administered, calls a "strange law."[47] His words reveal a discourse of power that violently enforced colonial law in the name of English women. What I am suggesting is that the sexual signification of the Mutiny reports sanctioned the use of colonial force and violence *in the name of* moral influence. During the course of the nineteenth century, the "English Lady" came to be invested increasingly with the self-sacrifice of colonialism, its ideological mission that was silently underpinned by apparatuses of force.

The sexual nightmare of rape and mutilation remained fixed within the British imagination throughout the nineteenth century, forming a historical memory of 1857 as the savage attack of brown-skinned fiends on defenseless women and children. It was possible, by the end of the nineteenth century, to relive the "heroic myth" of British martyrdom by making a pilgrimage to all the major sites where Europeans had been killed.[48] One place of particular mythic proportion was Cawnpore, where a plaque was placed on the well into which Nana Sahib threw the dead bodies of his hostages. Its inscription appropriately captures the racial memory produced about the Mutiny: "Sacred to the perpetual memory of a great company of Christian people, chiefly women and children."[49] This inscription, like the imaginary ones on the English women's bodies, was a spectacular sign of Indian savagery to be read by future generations. The tales of sexual violence consequently screened the even more savage methods used to ensure that natives knew their proper place *as well as* the vulnerability of colonial authority. It is here, in the memory of 1857 as the violent attack of natives on English women, that we are to find a historical explanation for the plotting of rape in *A Passage to India*.

### The "Ideological Effect" of Literary Plots

The Mutiny—that nightmare of innumerable savage hands suddenly upraised to kill helpless women and children—... has been responsible for deeds that would have been impossible to Englishmen in their right frame of mind.

EDWARD THOMPSON, *The Other Side of the Medal* (1925)

They had started speaking of "women and children"—that phrase that exempts the male from sanity when it has been repeated a few times.

E. M. FORSTER, *A Passage to India*

Due to the highly charged nature of its "atrocities," the Mutiny not only haunts Anglo-Indian novels as a terrifying memory but is also silently constitutive of their stories. Anglo-Indian fiction finds its mythic brown-skinned rapist in the violence of 1857–58, which it repeats and embellishes into a pornographic fantasy of rape.[50]

There exists no other stereotype produced on the scale of the "Sepoy fiend" that expresses an aggressive Indian male sexuality. In keeping with the

perceived decadence of the Mogul Empire that sanctioned a British colonization of India, the sexuality of the "Oriental type" was typically decadent—the
licentious sensuality of an Aziz who visits prostitutes in Calcutta and offers
to arrange "a lady with breasts like mangoes" (*PI* 120) for his friend Fielding.
Standard colonial stereotypes of the "Hindoo" depict him as licentious but
effeminate, cruel yet physically weak, duplicitous rather than savage. His racial type of passivity explained the long history of India as a conquered nation even as it permitted the British to cast themselves as mere players in a
prewritten script. According to this script, the European civilizers were sav-
ing the natives from Eastern despotism until a future time of self-govern-
ment. When the violent rebellions of 1857 erupted upon the colonial scene,
the British found themselves without a script on which they could rely. The
popular basis to the uprisings was read as an attempt to restore the aging
mogul king of Delhi as sovereign over India. In the absence of a stereotype
for the "savage Hindoo," the "blood-thirsty Musselman" was often identified
as the instigator and perpetrator of its worst crimes. Like the men identified
as the most savage mutineers, the man who stands accused of rape in *A Passage to India* is a Muslim, and one that indulges in orientalist fantasies about
his Mogul ancestors at that.

When he began writing *A Passage to India* after a visit to India in 1913, Forster conceived of its plot as an illicit romance between an Indian man and an
English woman.[51] By the time he completed the novel after a second trip in
1921, the story of an interracial love mired in cultural differences was out of
step with the events of history. The story of an interracial rape, more volatile by far, plays out the tensions between a dissenting native population and
a defensive European minority. The India of the 1920s, with its demonstrations, general strikes, and civil disturbances, reminded the ruling white minority of those earlier crisis-ridden years of 1857–58. One event that especially
revived the Mutiny memory was the 1919 massacre at Amritsar, where General Dyer ordered his men to fire on unarmed protesters attending a banned
meeting. Approximately five hundred Indian men, women, and children were
killed and fifteen hundred wounded. The name of "Amritsar" was for Indians
synonymous with massacre much in the same way that "Cawnpore" reso-
nated with the murder of innocents within the Anglo-Indian community.[52]
Although *A Passage to India* makes no explicit reference to the scandal of
Amritsar, the shadowy presence of the massacre—and the martial law that
sanctioned it—haunts the novel.[53] The major's uncontrollable outburst for

the Chandrapore community to "call in the troops and clear the bazaars" (*PI* 187) is reminiscent of Dyer's directive at Amritsar. Mrs. Turton's command that every Indian who dare look at an English woman should crawl from Chandrapore to the Marabar Caves echoes the law Dyer passed six days after the massacre, which forced Indians to crawl on all fours through the street on which an English woman had been attacked. In turn, General Dyer's "crawling order" repeats Colonel Neill's "strange law" of 1857.

The Amritsar massacre, which spoke of British soldiers firing mercilessly on defenseless Indian women and children, transformed the colonizers into the object of their own emblem of barbarism. As a consequence, the two discrete historical moments of 1857 and 1919 were read as continuous. On the one hand, there were the supporters of British imperialism who defended the events at Amritsar as a necessary measure against a bloodbath on the order of 1857. At an inquiry into the massacre eight months later, Dyer claimed that he had averted a second mutiny.[54] Several of the leading Anglo-Indian newspapers defended his actions by confirming that he did indeed face a situation as serious as the early stages of the Mutiny.[55] Critics, however, held the Mutiny memory itself responsible for the massacre. "What is immediately relevant," writes historian Edward Thompson in *The Other Side of the Medal* (1925), "is for us to note that at Jallianwalla [the Amritsar public square] and during the outcry which our people made afterwards we see the workings of imperfectly informed minds obsessed with the thought of Cawnpore and of merciless, unreasoning 'devils' butchering our women."[56] In *A Passage to India*, Forster is also critical of a community obsessed with the racial memory of 1857.

The Anglo-Indians of Chandrapore turn to the Mutiny as a convenient proper name for characterizing the events surrounding Adela's accusation of rape and Aziz's subsequent arrest. The district superintendent of police, Mr. McBryde, advises Fielding to "read any of the Mutiny records" (*PI* 169) for understanding the psychology of the Indian criminal mind. As the court case draws nearer, the explosive atmosphere of 1857 is recreated in the club members, who debate what they should do about the hostile Indian mobs demanding that Aziz be released. Their discussion centers on defending their "women and children," a particularly charged phrase for eliciting cries of revenge. One young, golden-haired woman whose husband is away is afraid to go home "in case the 'niggers attacked'" (*PI* 181). Her fellow Anglo-Indians invest the image of "her abundant figure and masses of corn-gold hair" with the full value of colonialism; for them, "she symbolized all that is worth fighting and dying for" (PI 181). Parodies of this sort can be read as sobering reminders of colonial retributions against a rebellious Indian population committed in the name of English women.

A Passage to India recreates in the drama surrounding Aziz's arrest the precariousness of the imperialist mission under threat of insurrection. It is a vulnerability that necessitates the positing of a native desire for white women as the "chief cause" for interracial conflict. In all those scenes that allude to Dyer's command at Amritsar and the racial memory of the Mutiny, the novel also shows the fear of a native assault on English women to be a screen for imperialist strategies of counterinsurgency. In other words, it draws attention to a discourse of rape deployed in the management of anticolonial rebellion. Such stagings, however, do not disrupt the dominant Mutiny narrative but simply question its premises. What does reveal the fictionality of colonial truth-claims is the element of doubt Adela introduces into the certainty of a crime confirming the native's depravity.

During the trial, Adela delivers a verdict that throws the place of imperial law into chaos. "Dr. Aziz never followed me into the cave," she declares, "I withdraw everything" (PI 229). When situated within the racial memory of the Mutiny, her extension and withdrawal of her charge drives a wedge of doubt between a colonial discourse of rape and its object. In other words, Adela's declaration of Aziz's innocence undermines the racist assumptions underpinning an official discourse that represents anticolonial insurgency as the savage attack of barbarians on innocent women and children. Yet Forster does not replace the certainty of an attack with its negation but rather with a narrative suspension that opens up the space for a mystery.[57] After the trial, Fielding explores with Adela four possible explanations for what happened: either Aziz did molest her; she claimed he did out of malice; she hallucinated the attack; or someone else followed her into the cave (the guide and a Pathan are offered as two likely assailants). Although Fielding rules out the first two possibilities, Adela gives no indication to him (or the reader, for that matter) whether she reacted to a real or imaginary assault. She finally admits that the only one who knows for sure is Mrs. Moore, whom she claims to have acquired her knowledge through a telepathic communication. As he keeps forcing Adela to return to the question of what happened in the caves, Fielding soon realizes that the very multiplicity of explanations offers no easy resolution to the mystery: "Telepathy? What an explanation! Better withdraw it, and Adela did so. . . . Were there worlds beyond which they could never touch, or did all that is possible enter their consciousness? They could not tell. . . . Perhaps life is a mystery, not a muddle; they could not tell" (*PI* 263). As readers, we are perhaps less satisfied than Fielding with the "life is a mystery" response, for critics have, and still do, search their imaginations for an explanation. Forster himself imagined at least one possibility in a scene that does not appear in the published version of his novel.

The deleted scene contains such a detailed description of the assault in the cave that it would be practically impossible to read what transpired there as Adela's hallucination. Here we have no helpless woman seeking the protection of others, but one who calculates the right moment to make her move and manages to fight off her attacker:

> At first she thought that <she was being robbed,> he was <holding> \taking/ her hand as before/ to help <out>, then she realised, and shrieked at the top of her voice. "Boum" <went> \shrieked[?]/ the echo. She struck out and he got hold of her other hand and forced her against the wall, he got both her hands in one of his, and then felt at her <dress> \breasts/. "Mrs. Moore" she yelled. "Ronny—don't let him, save me." The strap of her Field Glasses, tugged suddenly, was drawn across her throat. She understood—it was to be passed once around her neck, <it was to> she was to be throttled as far as necessary and then. . . . [Forster's suspension points] Silent, though the echo still raged up and down, she waited and when the breath was on her wrenched a hand free, got hold of the glasses and pushed them at \into/ her assailant's mouth. She could not push hard, but it was enough to <free her> hurt him. He let go, and then with both hands on her weapon/ she smashed <him to pieces> \at him again/. She was strong and had horrible joy in revenge. "Not this time," she cried, and he answered—or <perhaps it was> the cave \did/.[58]

Like the Anglo-Indian women who survived the 1857 attacks, Adela's act of self-defense is at odds with a dominant discourse that constructs the "English Lady" as a passive victim. As a consequence, one cannot help but notice a resemblance between the absent text of her struggle and an official discourse that erases colonial women's agency. In fact, feminist critics have submitted Forster's deletion of this scene as the sign of a more pervasive silencing of women or the repression of a misogyny that returns in subtler forms throughout the novel.[59] What these readings cannot account for, however, is that the "passive victim" is recorded in the deleted script as "feminist England," but only at the risk of confirming the attempted rape. A clearing up of the mystery in favor of Adela's guilt or innocence consequently adheres to the terms of a discourse that displaces racial signification away from colonial relations onto narratives of sexual violence. We see that a restoration of the silenced stories of English women alone cannot disrupt a colonial plotting on interracial rape.

The racial and sexual significance of rape in *A Passage to India* does not issue from Adela's experience in the cave; the answer is not to be found there. To clear up the mystery of what happened in the caves by searching our imagination for the missing details involves reading Forster's novel according to the narrative demands of the Mutiny reports. To read the mystery itself as an effect *of* that colonial history, however, is to see in its indeterminacies the imprint of a racial memory and "to trace the path which leads from the haunted work to that which haunts it."[60] In the place of "What happened in the caves?" I offer a different kind of question, one suggested by Adela's cry in the deleted assault scene. Managing to free herself from the grip of her attacker, Adela screams—"Not this time." What are the other times, the other assaults to which her triumphant cry alludes? I think that I have already answered that question.

If we are to study literature for its disruption of an ideological production that prevents social change, we can no longer afford to restrict our readings to the limits of the literary text. Rather, we should regard the literature as working within, and sometimes against, the historical limits of representation. *A Passage to India* contends with a discourse of power capable of reducing anticolonial struggle to the pathological lust of dark-skinned men for white women. Adela serves the narrative function of undermining such racial assumptions, but then, having served her purpose, she is no longer of interest to the concerns of the novel. The "girl's sacrifice" (*PI* 245) remains just that, a sacrifice for advancing a plot centered on the impossibility of a friendship between men across the colonial divide. As feminists, we should not reverse the terms of the "sacrifice," but rather negotiate between the sexual and racial constructions of the colonial female and native male without reducing one to the other. Like Fielding and Adela, who confront the mystery in the multiplicity of explanations, we should recognize that there are no easy resolutions.

# Notes

This essay is the product of discussions with friends and colleagues at various stages of its development. I would like to take this opportunity to thank Lata Mani, Jeff Decker, Robin Lydenberg, and Sandra Joshel for their interest in my work and the insights that helped develop these thoughts.

1. E. M. Forster, *A Passage to India* (New York: Harcourt, Brace and Jovanovich, 1952). All further references to this work, abbreviated *PI*, are included in the text.

2. Sepoys were the native soldiers in the British army. As an outcome of the 1857–58 rebellions, the East India Company was abolished and its administrative duties transferred to the British Crown. Since India was not consolidated as the Indian Empire until after the Revolt, I use the term colonialism for discussing Indo-British relations prior to 1858 and imperialism for the post-1858 era.

3. Ainslie Embree, *1857 in India: Mutiny or War of Independence?* (Boston: D. C. Heath, 1963), 39.

4. I read the racialization of colonial discourse as primarily a defensive strategy emerging in response to attacks on the moral and ethical grounds of colonialism.

5. The following select list offers some indication of the range of criticism that presumes Adela's accusation of rape to be a sign of her sexual desire and/or repression: Lionel Trilling, *E. M. Forster* (New York: New Directions, 1943), 144–49; Wilfred Stone, *The Cave and the Mountain: A Study of E. M. Forster* (London: Oxford University Press, 1966), 335; Louise Dauner, "What Happened in the Cave? Reflections on *A Passage to India*," in *Perspectives on E. M Forster's "A Passage to India*," ed. V. A. Shahane (New York: Barnes, 1968), 51–64; Benita Parry, *Delusions and Discoveries: Studies on India in the British Imagination* (London: Allen Lane, 1972), 294–95; Barbara Rosencrance, *Forster's Narrative Vision* (Ithaca NY: Cornell University Press, 1982), 207; Abdul P. JanMohamed, "The Economy of Manichean Allegory: The Function of Racial Difference in Colonialist Literature," in *"Race," Writing and Difference*, ed. Henry Louis Gates Jr. (Chicago: University of Chicago Press, 1986), 94–95; David Rubin, *After the Raj: British Novels of India Since 1947* (Hanover NH: University Press of New England, 1986), 66; Sara Suleri, "The Geography of *A Passage to India*," in *E. M. Forster's A Passage to India*, ed. Harold Bloom (New York: Chelsea House, 1987), 109–10.

6. Elaine Showalter, "*A Passage to India* as 'Marriage Fiction': Forster's Sexual Politics," *Women & Literature* 5, no. 2 (1977): 3–16.

7. Brenda R. Silver, "Periphrasis, Power, and Rape in *A Passage to India*," *Novel* 22 (fall 1988): 100, reprinted in Lynn Higgins and Brenda R. Silver, *Rape and Representation* (New York: Columbia University Press, 1991).

8. Anglo-Indians, more commonly referred to as English or Europeans, were the British residents of India.

9. Showalter, "*A Passage to India* as 'Marriage Fiction,'" 6.

10. Mrs. Turton addresses Indian women in the third person, as if they do not exist, and Mrs. Callendar stares right through Aziz when she takes his carriage. Forster has justifiably been taken to task for situating the evils of imperialism in the attitudes of Anglo-Indian women. What I am attempting to do here, however, is to read the strategic deployment of "the memsahib" in colonial discourse, one that demands her scapegoating in an anti-imperialist statement like *A Passage to India.*

11. The heroic image of colonial martyrdom is splendidly captured by Charlotte Brontë in the eulogy of St. John Rivers with which *Jane Eyre* (New York: Norton, 1971), 398, ends: "As to St. John Rivers, he left England: he went to India. . . . A more resolute, indefatigable pioneer never wrought amidst rocks and dangers. Firm, faithful, and devoted; full of energy, and zeal, and truth, he labours for his race: he clears their painful way to improvement: he hews down like a giant the prejudices of creed and caste that encumber it . . . and the toil draws near its close: his glorious sun hastens to its setting."

12. The following statement, for instance, alludes to Aziz as a black man: "However powerful the representation of the black man as penis, illustrated by Fanon, may appear to the English, it functions as well to reduce Aziz to a physicality that can then be subordinated to the authority vested in the greater power of the (phallic) legal system and the symbolic order that engenders and supports it." Silver, "Periphrasis, Power, and Rape," 98.

13. Ida B. Wells-Barnett, *On Lynchings: Southern Horrors, A Red Record, Mob Rule in New Orleans* (reprint ed.; Salem NH: Ayer, 1987).

14. Eugene Genovese, *Roll, Jordan, Roll: The World the Slaves Made* (New York: Vintage, 1976), 462.

15. Silver, "Periphrasis, Power, and Rape," 97.

16. Silver, "Periphrasis, Power, and Rape," 88.

17. Edward Said, *Beginnings: Intention and Method* (New York: Columbia University Press, 1985).

18. Pat Barr, *The Memsahibs: The Women of Victorian India* (London: Secker & Warburg, 1976), 143.

19. In *Theories of the Indian Mutiny (1857–59)* (Calcutta: World Press, 1965), 1, Sashi Bhusan Chaudhuri aptly captures the heterogeneity of the rebellion in his opening description of its popular base:

    The villagers impeded the march of the British avenging army by withholding supplies and information which they freely gave to the rebel forces: wage earners vented their rage on the system of foreign exploitation by a wholesale destruction of the British-owned factories; the social destitutes to whom borrowing was the only means of livelihood turned against the bankers, *mahajans* (capitalists) and usurers, the class protected by the British courts; the priests and prophets preached *jehad* against the *feringhis*; and other elements of society, not always amenable to law and order, broke out into uncontrollable fury, attacked police and revenue establishments, destroyed government records and court-buildings and telegraph poles, in fact everything which could remind them of the English.

20. Sir John Kaye, *Kaye's and Malleson's History of the Indian Mutiny of 1857–8* (London: Longmans, Green, 1898), 2:299.

21. Barr, *The Memsahibs*, 113.

22. *Times* (London), August 6, 1857.

23. *News of the World*, July 19, 1857.

24. The source of a news story was never identified as rumor. Rather, the term was reserved for the stories circulating among the Indian populace, which predicted the end of British rule. As Ranajit Guha points out, the systematic dismissal of word-of-mouth transmissions as rumor and superstition negates the mobilizing power of oral reports in preliterate societies. See his *Elementary Aspects of Peasant Insurgency in Colonial India* (Delhi: Oxford University Press, 1983), 220–77.

25. Sir George Campbell, *Memoirs of My Indian Career*, ed. Sir Charles E. Bernard (London: Macmillan, 1893), 1:400; Christopher Hibbert, *The Great Mutiny, India 1857* (London: Penguin, 1980), 213.

26. It is perhaps worth noting that the Irish supported the Sepoys and criticized the British army for its attacks on the Indian peasantry. The London *Times*, November 8, 1857, makes a point of expressing its disapproval of the "foolish fanatics in Ireland who write Sepoy sentences, and paste Sepoy placards on walls and gate-posts, calling upon Ireland to awake, and rise up, and 'give 3 cheers for old Ireland, and 3 more for the Sepoys.'"

27. Letter from a clergyman dated July 4 and published in the *Times* (London), August 25, 1857.

28. Karl Marx, *Colonialism and Modernization*, ed. Shlomo Avineri (Garden City NY: Anchor, 1969), 226.

29. Edward Lecky, *Fictions Connected with the Outbreak of 1857 Exposed* (Bombay: Chesson & Woodhall, 1858).

30. My discussion of rape as a violence that reproduces the gender roles of women is indebted to Monique Plaza's "Our Damages and Their Compensation, Rape: The Will Not to Know of Michel Foucault," *Feminist Issues* 1 (summer 1981): 25–35.

31. Sir Colin Campbell, *Narrative of the Indian Revolt from Its Outbreak to the Capture of Lucknow* (London: George Victers, 1858), 20.

32. This is the term that Plaza used for the sexual positioning of the rape victim, which can include men.

33. Letter dated August 4, 1857, in the letters of Col. Hugh Pearce Pearson, MSS Eur C231, India Office Library, London.

34. *News of the World*, November 22, 1857. The term "atrocity," which is so common in British accounts of 1857, condemns anticolonial insurgency to the morally reprehensible annals of the "great crimes." "Atrocity," observes Michel Foucault, "is a characteristic of some of the great crimes: it refers to the number of natural or positive, divine or human laws that they attack, to the scandalous openness or, on the contrary, to the secret cunning with which they have been committed, to the rank and status of those who are their authors and victims, to the disorder that they presuppose or bring with them, to the horror they arouse." *Discipline and Punish: The Birth of the Prison*, trans. Alan Sheridan (New York: Vintage, 1979), 56.

35. Hibbert, *The Great Mutiny*, 377–78; 385. For a study of the Rani as a heroic figure in Indian literature, see Joyce Lebra-Chapman, *The Rani of Jhansi: A Study in Female Heroism in India* (Honolulu: University of Hawaii Press, 1986).

36. (London) *Times*, October 16, 1885, quoted in *India, Before and After the Mutiny*, by an Indian Student (Edinburgh: E. S. Livingstone, 1886), 40.

37. *Bombay Times*, March 31, 1858, cited by Lecky, *Fictions*, 171–72.

38. Stuart Hall explains overdetermined instances as "the product of an articulation of contradictions, not directly reduced to one another." "Race, Articulation and Societies Structured in Dominance," *Sociological Theories: Race and Colonialism* (Paris: UNESCO Press, 1980], 326.

39. Elizabeth Cowie, "Woman as Sign," *m/f* 1 (1978): 49–63.

40. My observations are based on readings of journals, memoirs, and diaries, primarily written by officers' wives. In keeping with their claims to be representing the viewpoints of "a lady," they largely discuss domestic concerns such as the hardship of maintaining a civilized decorum in the absence of servants, most of whom ran away. The authority with which these women speak reflects their class standing as much as a racial superiority. I recognize, as a limitation to my reading, the class bias built into a reliance on written records. Despite the absence of working-class women's writings, it is possible to account for their subject positionings by reading the official discourse symptomatically. I include such readings in the longer study to which this essay belongs.

41. *An Englishwoman in India: The Memoirs of Harriet Tytler, 1828–1858*, ed. Anthony Sattin (Oxford: Oxford University Press, 1986), 160. This is one of the few women's diaries to have been recently reprinted.

42. An exception is Margaret Strobel's "Gender and Race in the Nineteenth-and Twentieth-Century British Empire," in *Becoming Visible: Women in European History*, ed. Renate Bridenthal, Claudia Koonz, and Susan Stuard, 2d ed. (Boston: Houghton Mifflin, 1987), 375–96, which is attentive to the contradictions of the European woman's privileged yet subordinate role in colonial society.

43. Campbell, *Memoirs*, 231.

44. Sashi Bhusan Chaudhuri has chronicled instances in which the British reprisals identified as acts of revenge in Kaye's and Malleson's *History of the Indian Mutiny* often took place before the massacres to which Kaye alludes. See his *English Historical Writings on the Indian Mutiny, 1857–1859* (Calcutta: World Press, 1979), 106–7.

45. In *Shamanism, Colonialism, and the Wild Man* (Chicago: University of Chicago Press, 1987), 134, Michael Taussig explains reversals of this kind as "a colonial mirroring of otherness that reflects back onto the colonists the barbarity of their own social relations, but as imputed to the savagery they yearn to colonize."

46. Cited by Francis Cornwallis Maude and John Walter Sherer, *Memoirs of the Mutiny* (London: Remington & Company, 1894), 1:71. Maude, a British officer who served during the Mutiny, writes, "I believe our feeling was not so much of revenge as a desire to strike terror into the hearts of those natives who were in any way either sympathizing with or had been aiding and abetting in these horrors" (1:70).

47. Cited by Kaye, *English Historical Writings*, 2:300. Tactics similar to the ones the British used against the Sepoys were deployed against Sikh rebels in 1872 and during the Second Afghan War of 1879. See Edward Thompson, *The Other Side of the Medal* (London: Hogarth, 1925), 87–94. Edward Thompson, whose writings include novels and histories on India, served as an educational missionary in Bengal. He resigned from the ministry upon his return to England in 1923 and for the next ten years taught Bengali at Oxford. He was the father of the British cultural Marxist and pacifist E. P Thompson.

48. Bernard Cohn, "Representing Authority in Victorian England," in *The Invention of Tradition*, ed. Eric Hobsbawm and Terence Ranger (Cambridge, England: Cambridge University Press, 1984), 179.

49. Inscription on the well at Cawnpore, cited by Vincent Smith, *The Oxford History of India*, 2nd ed. (Oxford: Clarendon Press, 1923), 719. The plaque was removed along with other colonial historical markers after Independence.

50. The Mutiny is one of the most popular themes in Anglo-Indian fiction. For a nineteenth-century review of Mutiny literature, see "The Indian Mutiny in Fiction," *Blackwood's Edinburgh Magazine* (February 1897): 218–31. For a more updated bibliographical study, see Sailendra Dhari Singh, *Novels on the Indian Mutiny* (Delhi: Arnold-Heinemann, 1980). Patrick Brantlinger ends with a dis-

cussion of *A Passage to India* in his chapter, "The Well at Cawnpore: Literary Representations of the Indian Mutiny of 1857," in *Rule of Darkness: British Literature and Imperialism, 1830–1914* (Ithaca NY: Cornell University Press, 1988), 199–224.

51. Forster's outline for the 1912–13 manuscript reads:

     Aziz & Janet [Adela's name in the early manuscript] drift into one another's arms—then apart. \marriage impossible./ She—theoretically—immoral: he practically, but believes it impossible with an Englishwoman. \she is ugly./ Discovers she loves him—less offensive \than Englishmen/. . . .

     A's Horror of falling in love with Englishwomen—not due to natural reverence but since they could be only obtained on terms of marriage which is impossible & since of purity of blood.

     Oliver Stallybrass, *The Manuscripts of A Passage to India* (New York: Holmes & Meier, 1978), 580.

52. The effects of the Amritsar massacre were not felt in England until several years later. In 1919, the events at Amritsar received little attention in the British press and were largely ignored by the intelligentsia. Upon examining the "charges that have been brought against the English as a nation," however, Forster does refer to the massacre as one of those indefensible "examples of public infamy." "Notes on the English Character," 1920, in *Abinger Harvest* (London: Edward Arnold, 1936), 13.

53. For a mapping of the historical events surrounding the 1919 Amritsar massacre onto the narrative of the novel, see G. K. Das, *E. M. Forster's India* (London: Methuen, 1977), 46–54. Other studies that read *A Passage to India* as a comment on the political instability of the 1920s include Jeffrey Meyers, *Fiction and the Colonial Experience* (Totowa NJ: Rowman & Littlefield, 1973), 29–53; Molly Mahood, *The Colonial Encounter: A Reading of Six Novels* (London: Rex Collings, 1977), 65–91; Hunt Hawkins, "Forster's Critique of Imperialism in *A Passage to India*," *South Atlantic Review* 48, no. 1 (1983): 54–65; Frances B. Singh, "*A Passage to India*, the National Movement, and Independence," *Twentieth Century Literature* 35, nos. 2/3 (summer/fall 1985): 265–78.

54. *Times* (London), December 15, 1919.

55. Reported in *News of the World*, December 31, 1919.

56. Thompson, *The Other Side of the Medal*, 95.

57. Although it is possible to read such indecisiveness as an expression of Forster's liberalism, one must remember that he was writing out of a disillusionment with the failure of liberalism to bring about social change.

58. Stallybrass, *The Manuscripts of A Passage to India*, 242–43.

59. Silver, "Periphrasis, Power, and Rape," 86; Frances Restuccia, "'A Cave of My Own': The Sexual Politics of Indeterminacy," *Raritan* 9, no. 2 (fall 1989): 110–28.

For other citations of the deleted scene, see June Perry Levine, "An Analysis of the Manuscripts of *A Passage to India*," *PMLA* 85 (March 1970): 287–88; Jo Ann Hoeppner Moran, "E. M. Forster's *A Passage to India*: What Really Happened in the Caves," *Modern Fiction Studies* 34 (winter 1988): 596–97.

60. Pierre Macherey, *The Theory of Literary Production*, trans. Geoffrey Wall (London: Routledge & Kegan Paul, 1978), 94.

# 7 | Telling Photos

DAVID PROCHASKA

One day we set out into the Rajasthani desert rather than sticking more or less to the road. The *gram sevak* (village-level worker) and I were making a "tour" to check how the crops were doing. Actually, he wanted to see a *sarpanch* (village headman), and I wanted to take some pictures. After walking for a good while, more than long enough to leave any village behind and to notice how quiet it was, we arrived at a dry creek bed. On the rise behind it, a several-centuries-old Rajput stone house sat, lording it over the scene. Square, two-storied, it was rather decrepit now. Most of the plaster had flaked away, taking with it the original as well as the retouched paintings and drawings that had once adorned it. At each corner the second story extended out over the first just enough to enable the inhabitants to use the hole placed there to good effect. Over the years—decades? centuries?—the excrement had formed a rock-hard stalagmite of dung three to six feet high. Inside, many rooms were closed off, the bottom floor was given over to sheltering animals and storing goods, with the living quarters located upstairs; these rooms ringed a central, uncovered courtyard.

Luckily for us, the sarpanch was home, and we spent the next several hours talking, telling jokes, swapping stories, eating, and listening to Rajasthani folk music, which consisted of a slightly demented youngster singing in an excellent voice and plucking a simple stringed instrument. During all this time we wandered back and forth between the open central courtyard and the adjoining rooms, now leaning against the walls, now lounging on old tattered solid-color rugs, now sitting on rope beds (*charpoys*).

The sarpanch lived up to the village-level worker's favorable advance billing and more. Elderly but not old, with a twinkle in his eye and an easy smile, he radiated a quiet dignity. His movements, his gestures were not so much slow as they were deliberate; he never raised his voice, but then he didn't have to—it was clear who was in charge here. I have no idea what it was like to work for him, say, as a sharecropper or agricultural laborer—he was a relatively wealthy man—or what it was like to be a member of the extended family, but to while away the better part of a day in his company, eating snacks and listening to folk music, made me feel at the time as though I had stepped into some kind of time warp and come out in the middle of a Mughal miniature—exoticism, primitivism come alive.

Prior to leaving I took out my camera. I had it in mind to take some *desi* (down-home) photographs, candid snapshots, Indian-style: the sarpanch at home surrounded by his subjects and hangers-on plus pieces of material culture. It took me a minute, therefore, to correct my mind-set when they began to compose their own portrait photograph. In place of the day's leisurely pace they started moving like crazy. First, they settled on a relatively unweathered wall outside rather than the inside room covered with soot from the *chula* (cooking stove). Then, from some inner sanctum, they conjured up wooden chairs that I had not seen before. Now they were set: the sarpanch sitting in a chair flanked by the village-level worker on one side and a family member on the other. But just as I was ready to click the shutter they interrupted the proceedings: something was not right, something was missing. Finally, an illustrated Hindi wall calendar was brought out from its previously hidden place in the interior of the house and hung on the wall behind the trio. At last they were ready to have their picture taken [Figure 7.1].

I   I   I

The Algerian family used to live in the house at the corner. That was their first stop after they left the *vieille ville*, the old, predominantly Muslim section of Bône-become-Annaba. Once the French left after the Algerian Revolution in 1962, they promptly moved from the corner house and into the villa next door—a 1950s-style suburban French villa of the sort often seen in southern France, set back from the road and surrounded by a fence. I was told that the villa had been the home of the Bône leader of the extremist Organisation Armée Secrète (OAS), but I have not been able to verify this. For their part, the Algerian family had resided in one part or another of Annaba for three centuries. The current head of the family was the di-

7.1. Indian acquaintances, Rajasthan, ca. 1969. Photograph by the author.

rector of the municipal bus system and had been elected to the Assemblée Nationale in Algiers. The living room upstairs was European in furnishings, but guests were served the customary mint tea or Turkish-style coffee. Prominently displayed on one wall was a large, framed photograph of a brother-in-law killed during the Revolution. The photograph was a blowup of a police-style mug shot: scruffy prison garb, barbed wire in the background, an expression part vacant, part sullen.

|   |   |   |

It has taken me a long time to be able to tell something about these two photos. First, it has taken time to understand some things about India and Algeria, and my experience in India and Algeria. Second, it takes time to learn what a photo does not say as well as what it does say. I first began this essay with the idea of trying to summarize some of what we know about photos taken in the former colonial world. About how the history of photography is an intellectually "hot" subject today in art history and visual culture—think of common issues of appropriation, representation, instrumentality—but somewhat less so in colonial and postcolonial studies. About how photographic theory has developed primarily in the context of and applies disproportionately to Western as opposed to non-Western photography: Barthes on photographic culture, Benjamin on aura, Foucault on archive, Rosalind Krauss on index, Susan Stewart on collecting, Jonathan Crary on vision and modernity, Martin Jay on ocularcentrism, Abigail Solomon-Godeau on gendered photographic representation, Allan Sekula on body and archive, Geoffrey Batchen on the tactility of photos, Olu Oguibe on the surface of images.[1] About how the discourse of non-Western photography encompasses far fewer theoretically informed analyses and far more straightforward descriptive studies, many of which take the form of out-and-out colonial nostalgia.[2] My initial intention, therefore, was to bring to bear on photos of the former colonial world a semiotic interpretation of photographic history with intellectual filiations to poststructuralism over and against the received view, which tends to aestheticize photography.[3] A historicized photographic history that looks at photographs through the eyes of nineteenth- and early twentieth-century viewers and sees artisans instead of artists, documents instead of art objects, views instead of landscapes, generic types instead of individual portraits. A postcolonial photographic history that moves beyond simplistic dichotomies of colonizer and colonized, and documents the trafficking back and forth of photographers and photographs on both sides of the colonial divide.

But the more I read about photography and the more photographs I looked at, the less certain I became about how much any one photo said or what could be said about it. The more I looked, the more multivalent the photos appeared. So I resolved to write an essay brushing photographic history against the grain to see how far such an approach would take us, an essay about two photos where I could bring to bear the contexts of these images on the interpretation of the photos themselves.[4] My question became, therefore, not What can we say about colonial photography? but What can I tell about these two photos, drawing on India and Algeria, plus photographic theory?

Telling photos. What struck me most about the photograph from India was the contrast between the picture I took and the picture they had me take. With my 35mm. handheld camera, I was culturally predisposed to take a snapshot, a candid photo "capturing" the way they "really" are, their "nature," their "essence." At the same time I wanted my photo to be set in and to set off the "picturesque" exoticism of their surroundings, chiefly the old Rajasthani stone house.[5] What do I mean here by "picturesque"? By capital P Picturesque, we generally refer to the eighteenth-century aesthetic that originated in England, was transplanted to colonial India, and was embodied in the production of such photographic firms as Bourne and Shepherd.[6] But by small p picturesque, I have in mind a more generic picturesque, a sort of *National Geographic* picturesque, a usage that allows me to talk about photographs like those of Rajasthan that Raghubir Singh published in 1980.[7]

"I was born a Rajput. Rajasthan was our home." Raghubir Singh's native land is a land of fortresses, cities (mostly old), and peasant villagers. I was going to reproduce here Singh's color photo of the mid-fifteenth-century Jodhpur Fort, located west of Jaipur deep in the desert, taken late in the day, the deep blue sky contrasting sharply with the reddish browns of the fort's stone, the camera tilted upward to take in the soaring battlements, and a flag waving at the very top.

> "The stories my mother and father told provided us with a treasure around which we built our childhood games. In our fantasies we believed ourselves to be part of a fairy-tale world of fearless warriors on galloping horses and battling elephants. When we played with toy cars and airplanes, the passengers were always princes, especially the Maharaja of Jaipur who led his team to victory on the polo fields of France and England."[8]

The "polo fields of France and England"—that's a nice touch.[9]

Singh's mother, born in Chittor in southern Rajasthan, traces her family history back before the arrival of the Mughals in India, before the rivalry between Rajputs and Mughals. Here was to go Singh's photo of a traditional, "picturesque" Gujar villager at Pushkar, famous for its camel market, his head wrapped in a voluminous deep red turban, smoking a *bidi*, a *desi* cigarette, and wearing a wrist watch—a nice juxtaposition.

> One of its [Chittor's] memorable highlights is about the "lotus-fair" Padmini. According to legend, she aroused the desire of Ala-ud-din Khilji, the Afghan, when he heard tales of her exquisite beauty. In 1303 he besieged Chittor. The Rana was held captive in the Sultan's camp. The defenders, led by Gora and the twelve-year-old Badal, rescued the Rana but could not resist the invader's organized strength. They chose death over dishonor. What followed is described by James Tod [the best-known early British traveler and ethnographer of Rajasthan]: "The funeral pyre was lighted within the great subterranean retreat . . . and the defenders of Cheetore beheld in the procession of the queens, their wives and daughters, to the number of several thousands. The fair Padmini closed the throng . . . and the opening closed upon them, leaving them to find security from dishonor in the devouring element."[10]

> Since India became independent in 1947, there have been more than forty reported cases of widow burning in Rajasthan.[11]

The caption to another of Raghubir Singh's photographs that I wanted to reproduce reads, "A priest performs *puja* [worship]; handprints symbolize women who immolated themselves to become *sati*, Bikaner Fort."[12] The left half of the photo is a pink wall with twenty-two handprints originally imprinted in wet plaster and now streaked with paint; only the caption makes clear what the handprints on the wall signify. When his father died in 1957, Singh writes, "my mother retired into the life of an orthodox Hindu widow . . . everyday . . . my mother prays and lights an oil lamp. For Rajput women, the modest flame of an oil lamp, or the flames in which the women of Chittor flung themselves to save their honor when their men galloped in vain against the Moguls, both symbolize courage and devotion."[13]

> On September 4, 1987, 18-year-old Roop Kanwar, married only seven months, died on her husband's funeral pyre in Deorala village, about 2 hours from Jaipur, the capital of Rajasthan. The event was reportedly witnessed by hundreds of people.[14]

There is a difference between *sati*, self-sacrifice of a widow on her husband's funeral pyre, and *jauhar*, mass suicide of women by fire to avoid capture. There is a difference between sati in Bengal in the east and Rajasthan in the west. But go tell the women involved.

In 1957 Raghubir Singh's father died, and the extended family in which he had been raised in Jaipur split up. "I went to live in Paris with my French wife."[15] Singh knew modern Rajasthan, but in his photographs he chose to emphasize Rajput fortresses and the Jaipur built by Maharaja Sawai Jai Singh II in the early eighteenth century. Here I was going to reproduce Singh's photo of Jantar Mantar, the astronomical observatory Jai Singh had built 1727–33, with six women in peasant dress carrying cloth bundles. Jantar Mantar appears in all the tourist guidebooks as a Jaipur "must-see," as if to say "See how advanced they were back then," a point underscored by the peasant women, although the site is located in downtown Jaipur. Singh knew the poverty of village India but chose to focus on peasant culture, the culture that outsiders dub "folklorique," "picturesque."

> Conjuring up images of a desert state, it [Rajasthan] is a place no one would think of . . . producing crowds of brightly turbaned men with proud moustaches and women whose beauty is lethal, though, alas, veiled. But that is exactly what the desert state of Rajasthan is.[16]

Singh's Rajasthan is all color photographs, shot at dusk or early morning, when the colors are most vivid and the shadows longest. "The magic hours of two hours after dawn and before sunset are the best period for photographs."[17]

"My" Rajasthan is colorful, too, but not so much so: on days when the sand is blowing the sky takes on a brownish cast, erasing the horizon and reducing the colors to a monochrome. "I find it futile to add to the volumes written on the poor of India," Singh writes. "But it is important to point out that in spite of this poverty, the peasants of Rajasthan have spun out a wealth in folk culture."[18] These are the very peasant *loog* (folks) I was hanging out with in the desert.

I had selected the four photos described above to illustrate the points I have just made regarding Singh's photos of his native Rajasthan. Raghubir Singh died in 1999; when I recently contacted the family in order to reproduce them here, I was denied permission by his daughter.

Dear Prof. David Prochaska,

I am very sorry but I'm not sure how his work would fit into a book on Orientalism.... In the last twenty years his work has very much become part of contemporary photography.
    With best regards,
    Devika Singh[19]

His wife and daughter today live in Paris (I called the night before his widow flew to New York on a visit). I phoned to follow up on the daughter's categorical denial of my request.

Dear Prof. Prochaska,

I'm sorry I missed your call. Thank you for sending an excerpt of your text [the text above in which I discuss Singh's photos].
    I am very sorry but as I explained in my first email I do not wish photographs by my father Raghubir Singh to be reproduced in a publication on Orientalism.
    With best regards,
    Devika Singh[20]

In a way, she was right. I am arguing, although I have not come right out and said it, that Singh's Rajasthan photos are orientalist, which is the specific form exoticism (what I have been calling the "picturesque") takes in the Indian case.[21] Ms. Singh wants to aestheticize her father's oeuvre as "contemporary photography," and (in the process) decontextualize it from its time and place; I want to situate and historicize it. Uncomfortable thought: Indians manifest orientalist attitudes, too. The irony is that Singh's daughter wanted to depoliticize her father's photos by aestheticizing them, yet in fact she was politicizing them, making a political point in her reaction to the term "orientalism," but without even considering my approach to the subject: namely that I, too, am critical of orientalism. She thought that by denying me permission to reprint the photos here that I would not write about them—or her.

To return now to my friends' photo, I would say that what struck me most was the active way they constructed it: getting chairs out, hanging up a picture calendar, the way they grouped themselves around the sarpanch, he sitting. It was definitely a production, a break from the rest of the day. It was as if they were arranging themselves for a studio photographer, except that the photographer had come to them. So far, so straightforward. Yet the result to my mind was a "picturesque" photo: a little bit quaint, old-fashioned, one they had not gotten quite right. To me the key question has always been Where did they get the idea of how they wanted themselves photographed? Somewhere, somehow they were drawing on knowledge of studio photography, of fairly standard European conventions of photographic portraiture, conventions providing for the "ceremonial presentation of the bourgeois self" now extended down the social scale and out to the colonies.[22]

We need to constantly remind ourselves how quickly photographic technology arrived in India, just six months after Daguerre's invention in 1839. Photographic societies formed in Bombay in 1854, in Calcutta and Madras in 1856. A technology introduced by the colonial British, practiced in large measure by the British, photography nonetheless quickly caught on and spread among Indians.[23] We need to constantly remind ourselves, moreover, how many Indians obtained equipment, learned techniques, took their own pictures, and launched their own businesses. At least 150 Indian photographers active in the nineteenth and early twentieth centuries have been identified, working in thirty-one different locales. It has been estimated that there were 30 Bengali and 70 European photographers working in Calcutta in 1857, 130 Bengali and 200 European photographers in 1860.[24] Thus, we need to speak of a tradition of Indian photography from the nineteenth century—a relatively rare phenomenon in the former colonial world.

The pictures Indians took have been viewed most often in one of two ways. Most of the work on colonial photography still in fact concerns British colonial photography: British photographers photographing British subjects, subjects both in the sense of people and topics. Unsurprisingly, therefore, the much smaller body of work on Indian photographs made by Indian photographers has tended to subsume photographers and photographs alike under British and Western—read colonial—aesthetic categories: art and documentary, artist and oeuvre, the picturesque.[25] Another view of Indian photographs that stresses difference rather than similarity sometimes goes so far as to claim that there exists an Indian way of looking at the world, an Indian vision, an Indian gaze.[26] "Indian photographers used the camera to reflect and extend an Indian conception of reality," writes Judith Mara Gutman. "Physical reality was unimportant. A person was often depicted with gestures and symbols that connected him to ideas, his particular mortal presence much less important than the conceptualized idea he personified." Many photos were painted over, often heavily, to create such effects, the painterly reinforcing the photographic, and vice versa. Discussing a painted photograph with Hamchandra, a painter, Gutman asked, "'Who is he?'... 'The priest,' [her interlocutor] answered. 'Did he look like that?' I asked. 'Oh no,' he said. 'He's a priest.' I waited a minute, then asked, 'Is he perfect?' 'Oh, yes,' was the instant answer."[27]

Such an "Indian vision" wreaks havoc on all our pat ideas about formal criteria such as depth of field, flatness, point of view. It would seem that an argument alleging a peculiarly Indian gaze has to be considered seriously. Unfortunately, it is a tricky argument to demonstrate convincingly, compounded by the fact that the photography historian in question is not a specialist on India.[28] "Gutman has made extravagant claims for the 'Indianness' of locally produced photographs," her verdict "too determined by a hyperbolic essentialization of an Indian alterity," Christopher Pinney argues.[29] The problem seems to be that "Gutman's observations contain insights but are too broadly stated," that what is necessary is "a more sensitive reading of ... local practice" and "an account of the historically complex construction of local portrait aesthetics."[30] Fair enough. Yet when Pinney takes a stab at the same problem, he appears to categorize Western photos as indexes and Indian ones as icons:

> From the point of view of Peircean semiotics, the occlusion of the photograph with a non-indexical veil of paint is surprising, for one might anticipate that in the attempt to recover the individual as a permanent visual trace one would relinquish indexical traces last of all. Seen as the technological apotheosis of perspectival picturing, photography is—within Peircean theory and Western folk ontology—privileged over its earlier painterly antecedents grounded only in mere resemblance. The historical narratives which mark this invention record the supersession of the handwrought icon by the machine-made index. Indian practice inverts this archeology.... Photography ... is not lexically or semiotically marked in local discourse as indexical, and in most cases is not differentiated from other techniques of iconic representation.[31]

Sounds pretty essentialist to me.

Rather than becoming hopelessly entangled myself in this dichotomous debate, however, I want to suggest another possible perspective. In the past several years, there has been a good deal of work in what some refer to as colonial studies. One aim has been to revise an earlier, dichotomous colonizer versus colonized binary view—often pinned on Edward Said's *Orientalism*—and soften it with a more nuanced, interactive, to-ing and fro-ing back and forth between colonizers and colonized.[32] Most, if not all, of these latter approaches share in common a sympathy for and interest in hybridity, a sort of mingling, if not commingling, of colonizers and colonized, what some term a "Third Space," or "contact zone."[33] One of the key texts in this literature is Homi Bhabha's essay in which he looks at colonial discourse in terms of mimicry:

> Mimicry is . . . the sign of a double articulation . . . which "appropriates" the Other as it visualizes power . . . from this area between mimicry and mockery, where the reforming, civilizing mission is threatened by the disciplinary gaze of its disciplinary double . . . a discursive process by which the excess or slippage produced by the *ambivalence* of mimicry (almost the same, *but not quite*) does not merely "rupture" the discourse, but becomes transformed into an uncertainty which fixes the colonial subject as a "partial" presence. By "partial" I mean both "incomplete" and "virtual." It is as if the very emergence of the "colonial" is dependent for its representation upon some strategic limitation or prohibition *within* the authoritative discourse itself.[34]

The notion of mimicry gives rise to mimic men, in T. B. Macaulay's words, "a class of interpreters between us and the millions whom we govern—a class of persons Indian in blood and colour, but English in tastes, in opinions, in morals and in intellect."[35] The mimic man "can be traced through the works of Kipling, Forster, Orwell, Naipaul."[36]

Bhabha couches his discussion of mimicry in terms of British texts, texts of colonial Indian discourse. But why can it not be applied to Indians, and to visual materials?[37]

To anyone accustomed to the exotic dress and indolent poses of the people shown in many commercial photographs of the Middle East, the portrait of the Acar family [figure 7.2] may seen startling, not least because in its

7.2. The Acar family. Photograph by Derounian Brothers, Aleppo, Syria, ca. 1906. From Sarah Graham-Brown, *Images of Women: The Portrayal of Women in Photography of the Middle East, 1860–1950* (London: Quartet Books, 1988) Engin Gargar, Istanbul, private collection.

style and presentation of the 'family group' it so closely resembles Western family portraiture of the same era. . . . The question arises—why do these portraits commissioned by Middle Eastern families appear so similar to those taken in Europe at around the same time?[38]

The answer, I would suggest, has to do with mimicry.

If we now view the sarpanch and his friends through the filter of mimicry, we can say that my friends' photo constitutes their mimicking the imaginary studio photographer, with the result that they have gotten it almost but not quite right. They have taken the studio idea and plunked it down in the Rajasthani desert, and it is the gap produced thereby, the displacement, that makes the photo seem, for me, a little bit quaint, a bit old-fashioned.

You may or may not like my looking at my acquaintances through the lens of mimicry, but the notion of hybridity considered more generally I think certainly helps make sense of someone like Raja Deen Dayal, the foremost Indian photographer of the late nineteenth and early twentieth century (figure 7.3). According to the received view, Dayal is considered a "genius," "unique," "the Master." It has been said that he "detailed . . . every aspect of Anglo-Indian life during the last quarter of the nineteenth century." What this commentator presents us with is a portrait of the photographer as an artist: "The significance of Dayal's oeuvre lies in the aesthetic elegance of his images, all of which were carefully planned and composed."[39] "The Master," "every aspect of Anglo-Indian life"—this is all a bit much. Hyperbole aside, it is also a good example of the tendency of twentieth-century commentators to aestheticize nineteenth-century photographic practices that, more often than not, were not considered as such by people at the time.

Note first of all that Dayal enjoyed "a comfortable intimacy with Indian princes and British civil servants."[40] In fact, he originally learned photography from the British:

> In 1874 I began to study photography as an amateur and was greatly encouraged in my efforts by Sir Henry Daly, K.C.B., C.I.E., C.C.O, who was ever ready to patronize and help me as far as possible; through him I was able to secure a group of Lord Northbrook [the viceroy] and friends during his visit to Indore and also a group of H.R.H. the Prince of Wales (and the Royal party in 1875–6). . . . Having found that the public greatly appreciated my views and a consequent demand for them having arisen, I took

7.3. Indian boy, 1902. Photograph by Lala Deen Dayal. From Clark Worswick, *Princely India: Photographs by Raja Deen Dayal, 1884–1910* (New York: Knopf, 1980).

[a] furlough for two years in order to complete my series. Whilst at Simla I again secured two groups from H.E. the Viceroy (Lord Dufferin)—a family group and a "Legislative Council" group, in addition to a group of Sir Frederick Roberts, V.C. [being nominated for photographer to H.E. the Commander in Chief in India]. . . . In 1884 H.R.H. the Duke of Connaught visited [the] Mhow Camp Exercises and I was appointed photographer to H.R.H.[41]

As the court photographer to the Nizam of Hyderabad, Dayal photographed the Nizam's three-times-weekly *durbars*, or meetings; as the photographer who accompanied Viceroy Curzon on his annual fall tour of the native states, he photographed the 1903 British durbar in Delhi. Dayal's work

7.4. Rajput prince, 1890s. Photograph by Lala Deen Dayal.
From Clark Worswick, *Princely India: Photographs by Raja
Deen Dayal, 1884–1910* (New York: Knopf, 1980).

7.5. Studio portrait, Bombay, 1890s. Photograph by Lala Deen Dayal.
From Clark Worswick, *Princely India: Photographs by Raja
Deen Dayal, 1884–1910* (New York: Knopf, 1980).

appeared as illustrations in several books written by British authors.[42] He operated commercial studios at one time in three central Indian cities: Bombay, Secunderabad, and Indore. These studios specialized in portraits (figure 7.4)—"governors, generals, native princes, touring statesmen, and local business, artistic, and scientific personages all trooped to Dayal's Bombay studio to be 'done'"[43]—of both British and Indians, women as well as men, as the following makes clear (figure 7.5):

> Mr. Lala Deen Dyal announces the opening of a *zenana* photographic studio he has fitted up in Hyderabad. He has placed an English lady of high photographic attainments and well-known there, in charge. As this studio is for photographing native ladies only, special arrangements had to be made to protect them from the gaze of the profane and the stern. So the place is surrounded by high walls, and all day long within this charmed enclosure Mrs. Kenny-Levick, aided by native female assistants, takes the photographs of the high-born native ladies of the Deccan [central India]. How lovely! One revels in the thought of the Arabian Nights.[44]

There are no women in my friends' photo. In fact, I cannot recall seeing any women of the household the entire day except to serve food and quickly disappear, no doubt to work while their menfolk played.

What Dayal did was to tack back and forth between the Indian and colonial British communities, working within photographic genres recognized at the time. By the late 1880s, his stock included "photographs of archaeological sites and of places of historical importance.... Other sets of photographs ... Dayal's own firm offered for sale ... included railways, ... army maneuvers, native types, trades and castes, industries, and ... personages of importance, military groups" (figure 7.6).[45] In the passage quoted above concerning his training, for example, Dayal refers to the commercial success he enjoyed with his "views" photographs.

Albums Available from Raja Lala Deen Dayal & Sons ca. 1895 ...
    2. *Views of Rajputana*: 100 photos, Dilwara Temples (Mt. Abu), Jeypore, Ajmere, etc. R[upee]s 175.
    3. *Views of Mewar*: 30 photos. Rs. 30. ...
    5. *Views of Central India*: 80 photos, Indore, Mhow, Bhopal, Mandi, Sanchi, Rutlam, etc. Rs. 150.

7.6. Native lancer and equipment, Secunderabad, 1905. Photograph by Lala Deen Dayal. From Clark Worswick, *Princely India: Photographs by Raja Deen Dayal, 1884–1910* (New York: Knopf, 1980).

6. *Views of Important and Historical Palaces in His Highness the Nizam's Dominions*: 100 best views in this superior album. Rs. 200.[46]

Art historian Rosalind Krauss contrasts "landscape" and "view" by linking the former to an aesthetic discourse and a "space of exhibition," most often a museum wall, and the latter to a scientific, topographical discourse and what she terms the "space of the stereoscope," the apparatus in which the stereograph view was viewed.[47] Thus, views is one example of a genre recognized at the time Dayal was working.

Another genre, related to views, was architectural and archaeological photography. For example, during his career Dayal sold more than 250 photos of historical monuments to the colonial Archaeological Survey of India (figure 7.7).[48]

In 1851 in France the Commission des Monuments Historiques hired Edouard Baldus, Henri Le Secq, Gustave Le Gray, Hippolyte Bayard, and other photographers to carry out the "Mission héliographique" to photograph France's architectural patrimony. In a kind of metropolitan salvage operation, the Mission photographers documented more than 120 sites in forty-seven French *départements*. As early photography critic Ernest Lacan put it, "Time, revolutions and natural upheavals may destroy them [architectural monuments] down to the last stone, but henceforth they will live on in our photograph albums."[49]

A third genre Dayal practiced was native "types" (figure 7.8).[50] Photography of native types drew on nineteenth-century anthropological notions of race and human evolution. "Races were seen as forming a natural but static chain of excellence in human kind, representing differing stages in the evolution of species, of which the northern Caucasian was the highest and the Negro the lowest. . . . Within the evolutionary structure the fixity of races had particular importance in the establishment of the notion of 'types' which were the essence of classificatory method."[51] In colonial India different castes practicing different occupations were depicted in types photographs in which "the photographed subjects are usually isolated from their work environments."[52] Decontextualization is a prime pictorial strategy used in types photography precisely because it conduces to a view of people as generic types instead of as portraits of individuals:

7.7. View of the interior of a Jain temple, Mt. Abu, Rajputana, 1880s.
Photograph by Lala Deen Dayal. From Clark Worswick, *Princely India:
Photographs by Raja Deen Dayal, 1884–1910* (New York: Knopf, 1980).

To reflect upon the Indian people is to behold a variegated multitude,
brown, black or yellow, sinewy and lean, square and stocky, or softly
rounded with good living and heredity, whom nothing could bind but
the claim that they are, they truly are, the Indian people.[53]

Now, in the case of my photo—I mean *their* photo—we have a photograph that looks more British and Western than Indian and non-Western.
Yet I have stressed that it is *their* photo, that I recorded them the way they
wanted. Does this mean, then, that they have *taken on*, internalized, as if by
osmosis, a foreign, Western notion of a photographic portrait? And to pitch
the argument in the starkest possible terms, that they are still bound by orientalism, that they cannot escape the constraints of a visual field ultimately
defined in Western terms, that we have here a residue of symbolic domination, of the "colonization of consciousness"?[54] Whatever the precise mixture of influences here, I want to conclude by underscoring the constructed
nature of my friends' photo, which is evident from such framing devices as
the Hindi wall calendar they insisted on hanging as a backdrop. The slogan
on the calendar, "Congress Zindabad" (Victory to Congress), plus the large

7.8. Man with *Bora* headdress, 1890s. Photograph by Lala Deen Dayal. From Clark Worswick, *Princely India: Photographs by Raja Deen Dayal, 1884–1910* (New York: Knopf, 1980).

photo of Nehru, explicitly ties it to the Congress Party. The sarpanch was a member of the Congress Party, represented Congress in his village hamlet, and was connected to larger regional Congress Party elites. At the time, Congress's continuous rule since Independence in 1947, the party of Gandhi and Nehru, had not yet been broken, and was being carried on, albeit shakily, by Indira Gandhi, who was already outfoxing male Congress bigwigs who had installed her in power originally as a pushover they could control. The Rajput gram sevak with whom I was on tour took care to toe the political line, was almost certainly a Congress Party member, as was the MA-in-English BDO (block development officer), who was his supervisor. In short, what this photo presents is in particular the public political persona the sarpanch, ranged by his hangers-on, wanted to communicate.

In India, I was struck by the active way my acquaintances constructed the photo they had me take. In Algeria, I was struck at seeing a police mug shot of a dead relative in the family sitting room.

On one level, the explanation of this photo-as-mug shot is straightforward enough. The Revolution, the Algerian Revolution fought by the Alge-

7.9. Algerian woman. Photograph by Marc Garanger. From his *Femmes algériennes 1960* (Paris: Contrejour, 1982).

rians against the French eight long years, 1954–62. The Revolution, and its terrible cost; in Arabic, the "Revolution of a Million Martyrs." The movie *The Battle of Algiers* (1966) distorts the Revolution in the sense that it took place primarily in the countryside and not the cities, that it involved peasants more than urban guerrillas. Yet the film does capture the sense in which it was a war against the whole population, in which civilians suffered disproportionately, because it was virtually impossible to distinguish combatants and noncombatants, Front de Libération Nationale (FLN) members and FLN sympathizers.

7.10. Algerian woman. Photograph by Marc Garanger. From
his *Femmes algériennes 1960* (Paris: Contrejour, 1982).

*The Battle of Algiers* also plainly portrays the active role played by women.
Unveiled, wearing Western clothes, they take the war to the European quarters, carrying dynamite in their handbags, which detonates in Le Milk Bar.
Scholars have underscored the active role of women depicted in *The Battle
of Algiers*, documented their widespread participation during the Revolution, and the post-Independence restrictions, limitations and obstacles for
women, two steps forward, one step backward.[55] Director Gille Pontecorvo,
following Frantz Fanon, most likely overemphasizes the active role played by
women during the Revolution, but certainly independent Algeria has failed
to deliver on the Revolution's implicit promise that their lot would improve
more than it has. In any case, some of the hardest photos to look at from the
Revolution are by Marc Garanger (figure 7.9).

In 1960 I did my military service in Algeria. The French army had decided that the natives had to have a French identity card to better monitor their movements. So I photographed nearly 2,000 people, largely women, at the rate of two hundred per day [figure 7.10]. In every village the inhabitants were called together by the local commandant. What affected me most was the gaze of the women. They had no choice. They had to unveil themselves and let themselves be photographed. They looked at me pointblank—the first indication of their silent, violent protest. I want to bear testimony to them [figure 7.11].[56]

And he continues to do so. His *Femmes algériennes* photos are, if anything, more widely known today than when first published; individual photos are not only reproduced, but they also appear on book covers.[57] When I contacted him to request permission to reproduce the three here and described my essay, he graciously sent copies and waived all fees, "Je vous fais un cadeau!" (I'll give them to you as a present!).

In Annaba in eastern Algeria, the war came home, sporadically, in outbursts, generally of gunfire. There was blood enough and more, but it was not as bad in Annaba as in the other main coastal port cities, Algiers and Oran. A bomb blew the roof off the *mairie* (city hall), but in Oran I saw a square city block still in rubble after fifteen years. Just outside Annaba, in the direction of the ruins of Augustine's Hippo, huge concentration-like camps had been erected. Perhaps it was here that the family member was detained, photographed, interrogated, disposed of. I don't know.

Between 1954 and 1962 the Annabis, and the rest of their Algerian confrères, were turning the historical tables, reversing the course French colonialism had taken since 1830, from the particularly harsh form of colonialism, settler colonialism, which the French had practiced on the Algerians.[58] In 1830 Annaba was only the second city—Algiers was the first—to be invaded by the French.

In India at the time, Col. James Tod was compiling his *Annals and Antiquities of Rajast'han.*[59]

In 1856–57 F.-J. Moulin went to Algeria under the auspices of the French minister of war. He was the first photographer to produce an important

7.11. Algerian woman. Photograph by Marc Garanger. From his *Femmes algériennes 1960* (Paris: Contrejour, 1982).

body of work on Algeria. More than three hundred photographs of Algerian inhabitants, French military men, and archaeological monuments fill six volumes (figure 7.12). It is not I but another historian of photography who argues that far from being "objective," Moulin's "portraits of French military figures and of Algerians friendly to France are clearly distinguishable from those depicting adversaries of the Emperor's [Napoleon III] policies. In these Moulin deploys a kind of formal deprecatory rhetoric, emphasizing reclining postures, the absence of vertical lines, low levels and areas that are blurred and indistinct. In other words, the colonialist ideology is expressed in Moulin's photographs not so much through the subject chosen, rather through their figurative modalities and their composition."[60]

7.12. The ex-Khalifat of Constantine, ca. 1850. Photograph by F. J. Moulin.
From Collection of the Service Historique de la Marine, Fort de Vincennes.

The Salon of 1845 was the Salon immediately following the crucial Battle of Isly—the climax of French action against the Algerian rebel forces led by Abd-el-Kader. . . . Abd-el-Kader was chased from his country and took refuge in Morocco. There he gained the support of the Sultan Abd-el-Rahman—the very sultan that Delacroix had sketched and whose reception he had so minutely described when he had visited Meknès with the Comte de Mornay on a friendly diplomatic mission more than ten years earlier.

Delacroix had originally planned to commemorate the principal event of Mornay's mission by including, in a prominent position, members of the Sultan's delegation at the Sultan's reception. . . . When the defeated Abd-el-Kader sought refuge with the Sultan . . . Moroccan affairs abruptly took a turn for the worse. . . . Abd-el-Rahman was forced to eject the Algerian leader from his country. . . . Delacroix took up the subject . . . in 1845, but in a new form with different implications, based on a new political reality. In the final version . . . it is a vanquished opponent who is represented. He is dignified, surrounded by his entourage, but an entourage that includes the defeated leaders of the fight against the French and as such constitutes a reminder of French prowess. In Delacroix's *Moulay-Abd-el-Rahman, Sultan of Morocco* . . . , there is no longer any question of mingling the French presence with the Moroccan one.[61]

Moulin was not the only one to practice "a kind of formal deprecatory rhetoric."

Moulin also made erotic photographs, or pornographic ones, if you prefer (figure 7.13). In fact, he and two others were fined and sentenced to prison in 1851. A contemporary describes how "prints seized from their homes were considered to be so obscene that to repeat the titles of the material which occasioned their warrant would be an outrageous offense against public morality; thus, the reading of this document and the discussion of the court case was held *in camera*."[62] In short, "Moulin seems never to have stopped producing pornographic images."[63]

It is a long way from Moulin to the mug shot on the mantel. Or is it? Both the mug shot and Garanger's photos of Algerian women are police photos; they are used to keep track of people, to apprehend people. In this regard, they are the ultimate photographic document, wholly instrumental, the apotheosis of the photo-with-a-purpose.

7.13. S. D., ca. 1852. Photograph by F. J. Moulin.
From Collection Serge Nazarieff, Geneva.

When I was looking for historical archives in Oran, the city of Albert Camus's *La Peste* (*The Plague*), I was asked, "How will your study profit Algeria?"

We tend to forget how many photographs are primarily instrumental, documentary in purpose. Allan Sekula has not forgotten. For years he has been making connections between the police and other institutions, and photography, between the police and social documentary photography, peeking behind the "liberal humanist myth of the wholly benign origins of so-

7.14. Alphonse Bertillon, ca. 1891. From Paris Préfecture
de Police, Direction de la Police Judiciaire.

cially concerned photography," to see how beginning in the nineteenth century people such as André Bertillon and Francis Galton sought to regulate
social deviance by means of photography (figure 7.14). "These pioneers of
scientific policing [Bertillon] and eugenics [Galton] mapped out general parameters for the bureaucratic handling of visual documents." Sekula finds it
"quite extraordinary that histories of photography have been written thus
far with little more than passing reference to their work. . . . It is even more
extraordinary that histories of social documentary photography have been
written without taking the police into account."[64]

One reason the instrumental uses of photography have tended to be occluded in the history of photography has to do with the way discourse on
photography has evolved from viewing photos as documents to seeing them

as art, and from classifying them as indexes to some combination of both icons and indexes (to employ the philosopher Charles Peirce's semiological categories).[65] In the 1980s Rosalind Krauss articulated the photos-are-indexes argument most strongly:

> Photography is an imprint or transfer of the real; it is a photochemically processed trace causally connected to that thing in the world to which it refers in a way parallel to that of fingerprints or footprints or the rings of water that cold glasses leave on tables. The photograph is thus genetically distinct from painting or sculpture or drawing. On the family tree of images it is closer to palm prints, death masks, cast shadows, the Shroud of Turin, or the tracks of gulls on beaches. Technically and semiologically speaking, drawings and paintings are icons, while photographs are indexes.[66]

Index cards are organized in card files. To view photos as indexes implies putting them in catalogues, archives. Archives imply in turn a system of organization, of classification with the result that "the camera is integrated into a larger ensemble: a bureaucratic-clerical-statistical system of 'intelligence.' This system can be described as a sophisticated form of the archive. The central artifact of this system is not the camera but the filing cabinet."[67]

> The photographic genres Lala Deen Dayal practiced—portraiture, views, types, architectural and archaeological photography—all constitute files in the archive of nineteenth century photography.

So far I have been talking about my landlord's photo mug shot in terms of the Algerian Revolution, the police, instrumentality, index, archive. But, of course, it is not filed away in some official's drawer, but hanging on the family mantel. Audience, reception is everything (well, almost). The photo may have been taken originally by the French army for identification, surveillance, but it is not looked at in the same way by my Algerian landlord and his family. Instead, the context of the photo is the family sitting room. And this context of the photo—the frame it is in, its size, the place it is hung—everything about the photo except the photo per se, the photo-as-mug shot, codes it as a family photo. Rather than an index, therefore, the Algerian family has reversed the French appellation of "mug shot," instead coding it "family portrait," and in the process has imbued it with the aura of an icon.

Roland Barthes's argument that two messages coexist in a photograph is helpful here. The denoted message is that scene which the photograph records, it is "absolutely analogical." Given a photograph's status as an index, the denoted message is, in semiotic terms, without a code, a noncode. On the other hand, the connoted message consists of a cultural construction based on a culturally determined semiotic code; it "is the manner in which the society to a certain extent communicates what it thinks of it." This leads to Barthes's notion of "the photographic paradox," which consists of "the coexistence of two messages, the one without a code, . . . the other with a code."[68] Are we back to photos as both indexes and icons? In any case, Barthes's point here is that while we can separate the denoted from the connoted message for purposes of analysis—in a manner "analogous to that which allows the distinction in the linguistic sign of a signifier and a signified (even though in reality no one is able to separate the 'word' from its meaning . . .)"—in practice "the viewer of the image receives *at one and the same time* the perceptual [denoted] message and the cultural [connoted] message."[69] This is because "the image—grasped immediately by an inner metalanguage, language itself—in actual fact has no denoted state, is immersed for its very existence in at least an initial layer of connotation, that of the categories of language."[70] In the case of the photo mug shot, it appears to consist of a denoted message only, to be "absolutely analogical," but it consists of a connoted message as well, because even such apparently "objective" photographs have their own history and utilize specific photographic conventions that make them look like what our culture terms "mug shots." Q.E.D.

What, then, of the context in which the mug shot is placed: the sitting room? In what relation does it stand to the photo? Let us turn again to Allan Sekula, who analyzes photographs in a way that is relevant here. In one essay he looks at two photographs, Alfred Stieglitz's *The Steerage* (1907) and Lewis Hine's *Immigrants going down gangplank, New York* (1905).[71] A "traditional" history of photography analysis would approach the Stieglitz photograph in terms of art and the Hine in terms of documentary. Instead, Sekula's strategy is to shift the perspective and ask What is the context, the discourse, the viewpoint of the publication in which these photos first appeared? Stieglitz's photograph first appeared in his art-oriented *Camera Work*, and Hine's in a social work journal originally entitled *Charities and Commons* and later *Survey*. Sekula then delineates the political and aesthetic contexts, discourses of these photographs, demonstrating that "the Hine discourse displays a manifest politics [liberal-reformist] and only an implicit esthetics [realist mysticism in the tradition of Millet and Tolstoy], while the Stieglitz discourse displays a manifest esthetics [high-art photography grounded in romanticism and symbolism] and only an implicit politics [the category 'photographer-as-genius' is possible only when the photographer and the social context of the image are dissociated]."[72] And the Algerian photo? The photograph is a French army mug shot, but by its context, by featuring it prominently in the family sitting room, my landlord's family has coded it a family photo, has placed it within a discourse about family.

In this family discourse surrounding the photo-in-the-sitting-room there is, however, a glaring absence, namely, women. My landlord's wife, a teacher with a full-time job, the lady of the house, served us coffee and sweets at the beginning of my visit, but then she absented herself. Women participated in the Revolution, frequently putting their lives on the line, but there are no photos of female family members in this room. Women may be occluded, but they are not absent. Professor Aida Bamia, a colleague at the University of Florida, was born in Palestine and raised in Egypt, and lived and worked as a faculty member at the Université de Annaba for eleven years. She knows women in Annaba well; in her writings and in her photographs she shows us an entire dimension of Annabi society that I, a male living in Annaba, never saw. Although I do not have an image to reproduce here, one of her photos depicts a group of Algerian women at leisure in a women-only interior scene, unveiled, wearing inexpensive flowery print dresses. "After generations of repression, women had finally escaped [during the Algerian Revolution] the constant surveillance and control of the male members of their families," she writes. "They were determined to work with men side by side in building an independent new Algeria. As a result, women's conduct became amazingly daring and quite shocking to traditional Algerian society." Professor Bamia describes the mixture of defiance and compromise characteristic of many Algerian women. One acquaintance, Saida, told Bamia, "'I refused to prepare a traditional trousseau . . . because I did not want to submit to my family for whom traditions count very much,'" yet "Saida explained how she gradually discovered the importance of diplomacy and how to attain her goals through indirect means."[73]

There is still more about the family photo and its context, for the family stakes a claim through the photo's discursive context for the family's legitimacy in postrevolutionary Algeria. What the family says in effect through the photo-in-the-room is, We occupy a privileged position in Annaba today, but we deserve it, because we have contributed a martyr to the Revolution. This constitutes the family's raison d'être for their high socioeconomic and political position in Annaba today. But this family myth is just that: a story they tell others about themselves. As a story, it presents family history in black-and-white, us-versus-them, French-versus-Algerian terms. But it oversimplifies what surely is a more complex history, as family stories always do. I was told that they also owned a house in Seraidi, the hill station–like settlement twenty miles away in the nearby three-thousand-foot-high foot-hills, a place where they spent a good deal of time during the Revolution. What were they doing up there? And when they were in town why did they live one house away from the local leader of the terrorist OAS? Of all families in the neighborhood, why were they the ones in a position to expro-priate the villa after 1962? I raise these questions not to challenge the revo-lutionary credentials of a family that was always friendly to me (especially when I paid my rent on time), but simply to point out that their relationship with the French surely was more entangled than their family-photo-in-the-family-room story would have it.

Mohammed Boudiaf. Born 1919 M'Sila. Died 1992 Annaba. One of "*neufs historiques*," the nine leaders who formed in 1954 the Comité Révolution-naire d'Unité et d'Action (CRUA) to launch the Algerian Revolution. Orga-nized outbreak of Revolution November 1, 1954, in wilaya 2, eastern Algeria, including Annaba. Left Algeria October 25 to organize resistance outside. October 24, 1954, six CRUA leaders still in Algeria "went into a Bab-el-Oued photographer, each emerging with a still moist print of a group photo in his pocket. It was an uncharacteristic breach of their previously impeccable security, as well as being perhaps a strange display of vanity. . . . Inept and under-exposed as it is, the photograph is a historic document. With their ill-fitting clothes and awkward poses the six . . . look somehow more like the over-earnest members of a local darts team . . . than hardened revolu-tionaries."[74] Arrested October 22, 1956, along with FLN leaders Ben Bella, Khider, Ait Ahmed when their plane flying from Morocco to Tunisia hi-jacked and forced to land in Algiers by French army. Held in France with Ben Bella and others until 1962, in time to negotiate agreement ending war in 1962. Fell out with Ben Bella after release. "Ben Bella and Boudiaf, after spending five years in jail together, couldn't stand each other. They would argue over anything—whether the tea should be served hot or cold, how much sugar should be in it. It was just like a scene out of Sartre's *No*

*Exit.*[75] Founded opposition group 1962. Arrested by Ben Bella 1963, later released. Supported 1964 insurrection against Ben Bella. Went into exile in Morocco in 1964 for twenty-eight years. In 1988 in Algiers FLN used tanks to repress demonstrations by Muslim fundamentalists, Front Islamique du Salut (FIS). The FIS then won parliamentary elections; FLN annulled elections, banned FIS, removed President Benjedid Chedli. Boudiaf returned from exile at request of FLN to become president, early 1992.[76]

On June 29, 1992, President Mohammed Boudiaf was assassinated in Annaba by one of his bodyguards as he delivered a speech. During the summer of 1992 on French TV an Algerian TV clip of Boudiaf's death was played over and over. From my Annaba family's mug-shot-on-the-mantel to the 1992 film clip of Boudiaf's death in Annaba, Annaba and Algeria had traveled far.

There was more to come. Driven underground, the Islamists splintered into nonviolent and violent opposition groups. The militant Islamist organization Groupes Islamiques Armé (GIA) mounted guerrilla attacks, and virtual civil war broke out in Algeria. Over the decade of the 1990s more than 100,000, perhaps 150,000 people were killed on both sides, but no one knows for sure. As with unyielding, fiercely repressive governments elsewhere, the only perceived recourse has been violence, especially terrorism. In the first years of the ongoing fighting the atrocities committed on both sides bore an uncanny, too-close-to-home resemblance to terrorist actions, including stomach-churning body mutilations, practiced by both sides during the Algerian Revolution.

One reason there have been relatively few pictures of the violence in Algeria during the past fifteen years or so is that Islamists have targeted foreigners and Algerian intellectuals, killing more than sixty journalists and photographers.[77] Michael von Graffenried has compiled the most extensive photographic record of contemporary Algeria, taking photos surreptitiously on numerous visits.

When I lived in Annaba I, too, took photographs on the sly, to avoid both crowds and comments. I went with a friend who distracted passersby by engaging them in conversation in Arabic while I photographed streets and buildings. My rules of thumb were (1) not to take people's portraits and (2) not to photograph anything made of metal: no buses, no cranes at the port—"national security" tended to be interpreted very broadly.

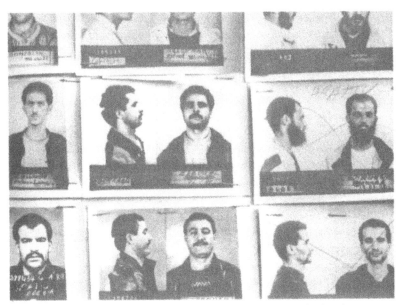

7.15. In a police station, portraits of wanted Islamists are displayed.
Detail of photograph by Michael von Graffenried. From his
*Inside Algeria* (New York: Aperture, 1998).

Von Graffenried argues that "a profound anti-photography culture exists in Algeria" which he claims is rooted in Islamic aniconism plus recent
political history. He recalls the French army practice of photographers like
Garanger making photo identification cards of unveiled Muslim women.
"Having to face the camera unveiled like this was a gross violation, almost
a form of rape."[78] Today the Algerian government uses the same stock, mug
shot format described by Bertillon, employed by Garanger and by his French
army comrades-in-arms who photographed the Algerian family member. In
a police station photos of wanted Islamists are posted; police and security
forces cross out those killed; the one on the middle right (figure 7.15) has
been crossed out and on it is written *abattu* (killed; literally, slaughtered).

## Notes

1. Roland Barthes, "The Photographic Message" and "Rhetoric of the Image," in
   *Image-Music-Text* (New York: Farrar, Straus and Giroux, 1977), 15–31 and 32–51;
   Walter Benjamin, "The Work of Art in the Age of Mechanical Reproduction," in

*Illuminations* (New York: Schocken Books, 1969); Rosalind Krauss, *The Originality of the Avant-Garde and Other Modernist Myths* (Cambridge MA: MIT Press, 1985); Susan Stewart, *On Longing* (Baltimore: Johns Hopkins University Press, 1984); Martin Jay, *Downcast Eyes: The Denigration of Vision in Twentieth-Century French Thought* (Berkeley: University of California Press, 1993); Jonathan Crary, *Techniques of the Observer* (Cambridge MA: MIT Press, 1990); Abigail Solomon-Godeau, *Photography at the Dock* (Minneapolis: University of Minnesota Press, 1991); Allan Sekula, "The Body and the Archive," *October*, no. 39 (1986): 3–64; Geoffrey Batchen, "Vernacular Photographies," in *Each Wild Idea: Writing, Photography, History* (Cambridge MA: MIT Press, 2001), 56–80; Geoffrey Batchen, *Forget Me Not: Photography and Remembrance* (New York: Princeton Architectural Press, 2004); Olu Oguibe, "Photography and the Substance of the Image," in *In/sight: African Photographers, 1940 to the Present*, ed. Clare Bell, Okwui Enwezor, Danielle Tilkin, and Octavio Zaya, (New York: Guggenheim Museum, 1996), 321–50.

2. Renato Rosaldo, "Imperialist Nostalgia," *Representations*, no. 26 (1989): 107–22.

3. Charles S. Peirce, "Logic as Semiotic: The Theory of Signs," in *The Philosophy of Peirce: Selected Writings*, ed. Justus Buchler (New York: Harcourt, Brace, 1950), 98–119; Krauss, "Photography's Discursive Spaces," in *Originality of the Avant-Garde*, 131–50.

4. I had always been intrigued with Erving Goffmann's not-often-enough-referred-to *Gender Advertisements*, in which he looked not at what the ads explicitly said about gender relations, but what they implicitly said through relative size, function ranking, ritualization of subordination, and licensed withdrawal. Likewise, I was struck by Allan Sekula's reading of one photo by Alfred Stieglitz and one by Lewis Hine in which he interpreted the publications in which they originally appeared rather than the photos themselves. See Erving Goffman, *Gender Advertisements* (New York: Harper, 1979). On Sekula, see below.

5. G. H. R. Tillotson, *The Rajput Palaces: The Development of an Architectural Style, 1450–1750* (New Haven CT: Yale University Press, 1987).

6. Bernard Cohn, "The Past in the Present: India as Museum of Mankind," unpublished manuscript, 1984.

7. Raghubir Singh, *Rajasthan: India's Enchanted Land* (New York: Thames and Hudson, 1981).

8. Singh, *Rajasthan*, 10.

9. In his foreword to Singh's book of photographs, Satyajit Ray, the great Bengali filmmaker who died in 1992, invokes the picturesque quality of Rajasthan even more explicitly than Singh does:

   When we were very young, a Bengali book we were much taken with was called *Rajkahini*, or Princely Tales. The tales were about real kings and real princes; but so filled were they with the stuff of romance and chivalry that they didn't seem real. We read of a land of desert and forest and mountain fastnesses; of marble palaces rising out of lakes like gem-studded lotuses; of brave Hindu warriors on faithful, fearless steeds charging into battle against invaders; and of their womenfolk who threw themselves into the flames rather than be snatched away as prizes by alien conquerors. Rajasthan, whence these tales emerged, . . . seemed magically to evoke a faraway, fairy-tale land. (Singh, *Rajasthan*, 7)

10. Singh, *Rajasthan*, 19–20. Singh continues, "This extraordinary courage and chivalry have made Chittor a place of pilgrimage for all Indians. I have visited it four times." Col. James Tod's major work is *Annals and Antiquities of Rajast'han, Or, The Central and Western Rajput States of India*, 2 vols. (London, 1829–32).

11. Lata Mani, "Cultural Theory, Colonial Texts: Reading Eyewitness Accounts of Widow Burning," in *Cultural Studies*, ed. Larry Grossberg, Cary Nelson, and Paula Treichler (New York: Routledge, 1992), 406.

12. Singh, *Rajasthan*, plate 40.

13. Singh, *Rajasthan*, 12.

14. Rajeswari Sunder Rajan, "The Subject of *Sati*: Pain and Death in the Contemporary Discourse on *Sati*," *Yale Journal of Criticism* 3 (1990): 2.

15. Singh, *Rajasthan*, 17.

16. Samuel Israel and Bikram Grewal, eds., *Insight Guides: India* (Singapore: Apa Publications, 1989), 135.

17. Israel and Grewal, *India*, 347.

18. Singh, *Rajasthan*, 24.

19. Email communication, February 28, 2007.

20. E-mail communication, March 5, 2007.

21. Frederick Bohrer, *Orientalism and Visual Culture* (New York: Cambridge University Press, 2003), chap. 1: "Exoticism as System."

22. Allan Sekula, "The Body and the Archive," *October*, no. 39 (1986): 6.

23. Ray Desmond, "Photography in India During the Nineteenth Century," *India Office Library and Records: Report for the year 1974* (London: Her Majesty's Stationery Office, 1976), 5–38; Ray Desmond, *Victorian India in Focus* (London: Her Majesty's Stationery Office, 1982); Ray Desmond, "Photography in Victorian India," *Journal of the Royal Society of Arts* 84 (1985): 48–61; John Falconer, "Photography in Nineteenth-Century India," in *The Raj: India and the British, 1600–1947*, ed. C. A. Bayly (London: National Portrait Gallery, 1990), 264–77; *India Magazine* (New Delhi) 10 (December 1989), special issue, "Images in Time: 150 Years"; James Ryan, *Picturing Empire: Photography and the Visualization of the British Empire* (Chicago: University of Chicago Press, 1998).

24. Judith Mara Gutman, *Through Indian Eyes: 19th and Early 20th Century Photography from India* (New York: Oxford University Press, 1982), xi–xii, 99.

25. The two chief exceptions here are Gutman, *Through Indian Eyes*; and Christopher Pinney, *Camera Indica: The Social Life of Indian Photographs* (Chicago: University of Chicago Press, 1997).

26. In *Through Indian Eyes* Gutman repeats the phrase "Indian vision" three times on pp. 94–95, and states, for example, on p. 8, that "the compelling frontal fields with multiple pockets of interest activating the picture plane were Indian, a hallmark of an Indian vision."

27. Gutman, *Through Indian Eyes*, 5, 47.

28. Earlier she had published *Lewis W. Hine, and the American Social Conscience* (New York: Walker, 1967). Cf. Desmond, *Victorian India*, 38.

29. Pinney, *Camera Indica*, 93, 95.

30. Pinney, *Camera Indica*, 95, 223–24, n. 47.

31. Pinney, *Camera Indica*, 138, 131. I discuss icon and index further below.

32. Frederick Cooper and Ann Laura Stoler, eds., *Tensions of Empire* (Berkeley: University of California Press, 1997).

33. Homi Bhabha, *The Location of Culture* (New York: Routledge, 1994); Mary Louise Pratt, *Imperial Eyes: Travel Writing and Transculturation* (New York: Routledge, 1992).

34. "Of Mimicry and Man: The Ambivalence of Colonial Discourse," in *The Location of Culture* (New York: Routledge, 1994), 86. Emphasis in the original.

35. T. B. Macaulay, "Minute on Education," in *Sources of Indian Tradition*, vol. 2, ed. William Theodore de Bary (New York: Columbia University Press, 1958), 49, quoted in Bhabha, "Mimicry," 87.

36. Bhabha, "Mimicry," 87.

37. In fact, it is rather interesting, if not downright odd, that Bhabha's essay is confined solely to texts when its context and intellectual pedigree is taken into account. It appeared first in *October*, coedited by Rosalind Krauss, and was reprinted in a collection of articles from *October* along with a translation of Roger Caillois's "Mimicry and Legendary Psychasthenia." (Bhabha's article appears on pp. 317–25 and Caillois's article on pp. 58–74 of Annette Michelson, Rosalind Krauss, Douglas Crimp, and Joan Copjec, eds., *October: The First Decade, 1976–1986* [Cambridge MA: MIT Press, 1987]). The latter appeared originally in 1935 in *Minotaure*, the surrealist journal associated with Georges Bataille and André Breton. Furthermore, Krauss herself discusses Caillois's article in one of her essays on surrealist photography, where she argues that it constitutes one of three "linked concepts that . . . combine to redefine the visual: Bataille's *informe*, Caillois's mimicry, Lacan's 'picture.'" Rosalind Krauss, "Corpus Delicti," in Rosalind Krauss and Jane Livingston, *L'Amour fou: Photography and Surrealism* (New York: Abbeville, 1985), 82. (By "the visual" Krauss is referring here to surrealist photography in the early 1930s. Cf. pp. 70, 74, 78.) Aside from two refer-

ences to Jacques Lacan in his essay, however, Bhabha says nothing that serves to situate his essay in its intellectual or political context. Similarly, while Bhabha draws repeatedly on psychoanalysis, he shuttles back and forth between Freud and Lacan but without positioning himself vis-à-vis these different thinkers. In short, "it is curious that he [Bhabha] is himself silent about the historical conditions and provenance of the concept[s] he uses." Robert Young, *White Mythologies* (New York: Routledge, 1990), 144. (Young is referring here to Bhabha's use of the term "fetish," but what he says applies equally to other concepts Bhabha employs.) This is an important issue for someone working in the field of colonial discourse, because it raises one of the larger issues "posed by Bhabha's work, namely his employment of the transcendental categories of psychoanalysis for the analysis of the historical phenomenon of colonialism" (Young, *White Mythologies*, 144).

38. Sarah Graham-Brown, *Images of Women: The Portrayal of Women in Photography of the Middle East, 1860–1950* (London: Quartet Books, 1988), 92–93.

39. Clark Worswick, *Princely India: Photographs by Raja Deen Dayal, 1884–1910* (New York: Knopf, 1980), 7, 20, 18, 22. The quote from p. 7 is in the foreword, written by John Kenneth Galbraith. I thank Clark Worswick for his alacrity and willingness to grant me permission to reproduce whichever of Dayal's photos I wanted.

40. Worswick, *Princely India*, 21.

41. Deen Dayal quoted in Worswick, *Princely India*, 19.

42. The first book with his photographs was George Aberigh-Mackay, *The Chiefs of Central India* (Calcutta: Thacker, Spink, 1879). Lepel Griffin, *Famous Monuments of Central India* (London, 1886) included eighty-nine photographs; Henry Hardy Cole, *Preservation of National Monuments in India* (Calcutta, 1884–85) included eleven; and twenty-four photographs appeared in *Photographs of Places of Interest in India*. Cf. Worswick, *Princely India*, 149; Desmond, "Photography in India," 31; Pinney, *Camera Indica*, 78, 82–85.

43. Worswick, *Princely India*, 20.

44. *Journal of the Photographic Society of India* (January 1892): 10, quoted in Worswick, *Princely India*, 149. Pinney, *Camera Indica*, figure 42, reproduces the obverse of a Lala Deen Dayal cabinet card from the late 1870s–80s.

45. Worswick, *Princely India*, 149.

46. Extract from the firm's catalogue, quoted in Worswick, *Princely India*, 150.

47. Rosalind Krauss, "Photography's Discursive Spaces," in *The Originality of the Avant-Garde and Other Modernist Myths* (Cambridge MA: MIT Press, 1985), 131–50.

48. Worswick, *Princely India*, 149; Desmond, "Photography in India," 31.

49. Quoted in Jean-Claude Lemagny and André Rouillé, eds., *A History of Photography* (New York: Cambridge University Press, 1987), 56.

50. Cohn, "The Past in the Present"; David Prochaska, "The Archive of *Algérie imaginaire*," *History and Anthropology* 4 (1990): 373–420.
51. Elizabeth Edwards, "Photographic 'Types': The Pursuit of Method," *Visual Anthropology* 3 (1990): 236.
52. Christopher Pinney, "Classification and Fantasy in the Photographic Construction of Caste and Tribe," *Visual Anthropology* 3 (1990): 269–70.
53. Israel and Grewal, *India*, 65.
54. The reference is to a phrase from Jean and John Comaroff, *Of Revelation and Revolution: Christianity, Colonialism, and Consciousness in South Africa* (Chicago: University of Chicago Press, 1991).
55. Nora Benallegue, "Algerian Women in the Struggle for Independence and Reconstruction," *International Social Science Journal* 35 (1983): 703–17; Marie-Aimée Helie-Lucas, "Women, Nationalism, and Religion in the Algerian Struggle," in *Opening the Gates*, ed. Margot Badran and Miriam Cook (Bloomington: Indiana University Press, 1990), 104–14; Juliette Minces, "Women in Algeria," in *Women in the Muslim World*, ed. Lois Beck and Nikki Keddie (Cambridge MA: Harvard University Press, 1978), 159–70; Fadela M'rabet, "Les Algériennes," in *Middle Eastern Women Speak*, ed. Elizabeth Warnock Fernea and Basima Qattan Bezirgan (Austin: University of Texas Press, 1977), 319–58. One of the most accessible and moving accounts of active female participation during the Revolution is part 3, "Voices from the Past," of Assia Djebar's acclaimed novel, *Fantasia: An Algerian Cavalcade*, trans. Dorothy S. Blair (1985; Portsmouth NH: Heinemann, 1993).
56. Marc Garanger, *Femmes algériennes 1960* (Paris: Contrejour, 1982), p. 7. See also Benjamin Stora, *Photographier la guerre d'Algérie* (Paris; Marval, 2004).
57. See, for example, David A. Bailey and Gail Tawadros, eds., *Veil: Veiling, Representation, and Contemporary Art* (Cambridge MA: MIT Press, 2003); Mary B. Vogl, *Picturing the Maghreb: Literature, Photography, (Re)Presentation* (Lanham MD: Rowman & Littlefield, 2003).
58. See my *Making Algeria French: Colonialism in Bône, 1870–1920* (1990; New York: Cambridge University Press, 2004).
59. Tod, *Annals and Antiquities of Rajast'han.*
60. Rouillé in Lemagny and Rouillé, *History of Photography*, 58. Rouillé's specialty is Second Empire (1851–71) photography.
61. Linda Nochlin, "The Imaginary Orient," in *Politics of Vision* (San Francisco: HarperCollins, 1989), 54–55.
62. *Annals de l'imprimerie*, no. 6 (1851), quoted in André Rouillé and Bernard Marbot, *Le Corps et son image: Photographies du dix-neuvième siècle* (Paris: Contrejour, 1986), 126.
63. Serge Nazarieff, *The Stereoscopic Nude, 1850–1930* (Berlin: Benedikt Taschen Verlag, 1990), 158.

64. Sekula, "Body and the Archive," 56. But see, for example, Sandra S. Phillips, Mark Haworth-Booth, and Carol Squiers, *Police Pictures: The Photograph as Evidence* (San Francisco: San Francisco Museum of Art and Chronicle Books, 1997).

65. Peirce, "Logic as Semiotic."

66. Rosalind Krauss, "The Photographic Conditions of Surrealism," in Rosalind Krauss and Jane Livingston, *L'Amour fou: Photography and Surrealism* (New York: Abbeville, 1985), 31.

67. Sekula, "Body and Archive," 16.

68. Barthes, "The Photographic Message," 20, 17, 19.

69. Barthes, "Rhetoric of the Image," 37, 36; emphasis in original.

70. Barthes, "The Photographic Message," 28–29. Barthes ties up his argument when he states, "We know that every language takes up a position with regard to things, that it connotes reality . . . the connotations of the photograph would thus coincide, *grosso modo*, with the overall connotative planes of language" (29).

71. Sekula, "Photographic Meaning," 3–21.

72. Sekula, "Photographic Meaning," 17.

73. Aida Bamia, "Refusing to Melt in Their World," *The World & I*, February 1988, 499, 501, 506,.

74. Alistair Horne, *A Savage War of Peace: Algeria, 1954–1962* (New York: Viking, 1978), 87.

75. Mabrouk Belhocine, quoted in Horne, *Savage War of Peace*, 536.

76. On Boudiaf, see, in addition to Horne, *Savage War of Peace*, Henri Alleg, ed., *La Guerre d'Algérie*, 3 vols. (Paris: Temps Actuels, 1981); Benjamin Stora, *Dictionnaire biographique de militants nationalistes algériens* (Paris: L'Harmattan, 1985). Cf. David Prochaska, "The Return of the Repressed: War, Trauma, Memory in Algeria and Beyond," in *Algeria and France 1800–2000: Identity, Memory, Nostalgia*, ed. Patricia M. E. Lorcin (Syracuse NY: Syracuse University Press, 2006), 257–76.

77. The murder of the Berber writer Tahar Djaout in 1993 has occasioned an especially large number of responses, in English as well as in French. A recent English-language meditation, for example, is Julija Šukys, *Silence Is Death: The Life and Work of Tahar Djaout* (Lincoln: University of Nebraska Press, 2007).

78. Michael von Graffenried, *Inside Algeria* (New York: Aperture, 1998), 15. As a commercial photojournalist, von Graffenried's photos command steep prices, so I thank him all the more for enabling me to reproduce one of his photos here.

# 8 | Ethnography and Exhibitionism at the Expositions Universelles

ZEYNEP ÇELIK AND LEILA KINNEY

The Parisian *expositions universelles* were elaborate mechanisms of cultural production, systems of representation on a grand scale. Among their novel technologies was the creation of ersatz habitats; these scenarios of a reductive presentation of different cultures generated easily apprehended, symbolic imagery. In such an environment the stereotype acquires authenticity; it gathers strength for a seemingly inexhaustible cycle of repetition and regeneration. One of the stereotypes that gained currency at the world's fairs, and remains viable today, is the *danse du ventre*.[1]

An enactment of the eroticized mystique of the Orient, the belly dance could be described as a pivotal element in what Barthes has designated "a second order semiological system," a myth of Islamic culture.[2] The account that follows is less concerned with a technical description of that system than with its "motivation" and "waves of implantation"—a plot of interlocking sectors leading from the fairs to their periphery, to Montmartre and beyond. What is significant about the phenomenon is not simply its spectacular geography, the unlikely cast of characters, or even the range of visual practices involved. In this deceptively simple by-product of the nineteenth-century fairs, one finds a manifestation of the interacting structures of patriarchy and orientalism. Yet for all the evidence of this interaction, its precise nature remains in question.

The postulate that patriarchy operated similarly in diverse circumstances has forged an uneasy alliance between the feminist and postcolonial critiques of European cultural authority.[3] The uneasiness has arisen, in part, because the alliance was not formed strategically; rather, it emerged from a convergence on a common set of theoretical principles: the inert and timeless status

286

of the dominated entity, the controlling nature of the empowered observer, and the tendency to speak for the silenced group—in short, the exercises of power associated with the categories of the Other, the Gaze, and the Voice. If less connected to each other than to a similar lexicon, which itself was used strategically, the feminist and postcolonial affiliation can best be observed when both speak from the position of the Other. This term marks the cognitive territory where the procedures of each discourse coincide and conflict between them emerges.

Devising analytic procedures to explain the operations of power in realms as diverse as political, economic, or gender relations without first assuming the outcome—a similar pattern of patriarchal oppression—remains especially challenging. Our attempt to do so begins with (or, to be more precise, *began* with)[4] a recognition of the inadequacy of dualism and demystification to the task.[5] As the circuit of representation followed by the belly dance in Paris will suggest, the dynamic of cultural contact was the occasion for unpredictable interactions, which continually reformulated cultural identities and destabilized the binary system on which otherness is based. By holding in place the problem of the Other without expecting to find in it a tailor-made resolution, we hope to address a number of still fundamental questions: Is cultural authenticity a demand as well as an illusion in the age of mass communication? Is the feminization of the Orient—most notoriously expressed in fantasies of the harem—integral to its subjugation? Are the binary oppositions inherent in the construction of the Other disrupted when differences of gender and culture coincide? Does exoticism—and its projection of a pseudo-distance—collapse when obsessively repeated and reenacted?

The universal expositions of the nineteenth century were intended as microcosms that would summarize the entire human experience, past and present, with projections into the future. In their carefully articulated order, they also signified the dominant relations of power. Ordering and categorization ranked, rationalized, and objectified different societies. The resulting hierarchy portrayed a world where races, sexes, and nations occupied fixed places assigned to them by the exposition committees of host countries. The forms through which non-Western cultures were represented at the fairs were predicated on the social arrangements already established in the "host" culture, France; thus it is important to describe the parameters established by the exhibition committees, for they set the patterns of national representation and provided the channels of cultural expression through which the knowledge produced by the expositions would be fashioned.

The site plans of the expositions, for example, signify power relations graphically.[6] Beginning with the 1867 universal exposition in Paris, a dual system was established: a Beaux-Arts plan, highlighted by imposing structures for the main displays of industrial and artistic artifacts, and a picturesque array of buildings interspersed in the parks and gardens of the exhibition grounds (figure 8.1). A major component of the non-Western exhibits almost always was situated in the picturesque sections, where technological novelties, entertainment, and commercial attractions were located.[7] This spatial division—between inside and outside, center and periphery—was reinforced by the architecture of the exhibition pavilions, as described, for example, by Hippolyte Gautier in 1867. The center of the exposition, he noted, was occupied by a large circular building representing the globe, which recalled a Roman circus, where the marvels of industry, science, and art were conglomerated. Outside the external walls of this "circus," he continued, was a crowd of "bizarre constructions . . . a strange city, composed of specimens from all kinds of architecture." Walking through this section was similar to embarking on a world tour. It was no longer necessary to take a boat to the Orient from Marseilles, for the expositions created a prefabricated and idealized tourism *en place*.[8]

This distinction between the didactic and the picturesque zones, where entertainment and exotica commingled, remained a feature of the design of later fairs, even as the site plans varied. Frequent references by official guides and visitors to this basic division of space suggest that it was deliberately imbued with significance, yet designed to be apprehended casually, as an effect of the imaginary "voyage autour du monde." Since this topographical system coincided with other kinds of information about the relative status and nature of foreign cultures, the fairgrounds constructed social relations on multiple levels. They significantly expanded the persuasive mechanisms of previously established accounts of other cultures; the expositions were more powerful than pictorial, literary, or journalistic descriptions because they presented simultaneously a physical, visual, and educational discursive field, organizing a range of perceptual responses to a global hierarchy of nations and races.

Alterations in the site plans indicate successive attempts to stage and visualize these affiliations effectively. In 1878 the exhibition hall for France's most

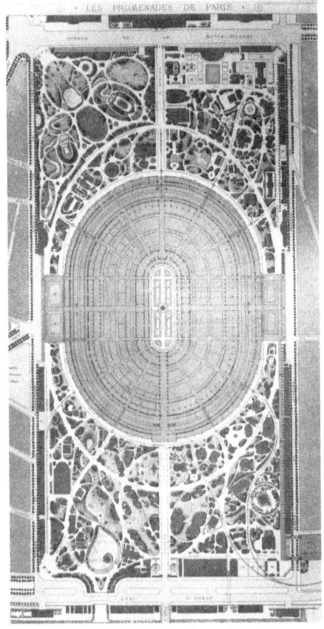

8.1. Site plan of Exposition Universelle, 1867. From Alphonse
Alphand, *Les Promenades de Paris* (Paris, 1867–73).

important and turbulent colony, Algeria, was placed in front of the Trocadero Palace. The palace's eclectic style referred to the Islamic architecture of the colonies, but its siting, size, and form as a whole created an image of France as a protective father/master with his arms encircling the colonial village. In 1889, however, the French colonies were given a separate location on the Esplanade, occupying a huge area between the Quai d'Orsay and the rue de Grenelle; the modification was made in order "to convey a real idea of the economic state of [France's] diverse possessions overseas."[9]

Another adjustment occurred in 1900, when the pavilions of the two most prominent colonies, Algeria and Tunisia, were placed in the Trocadero Park, on the main avenue that bisected it and the Champs de Mars and connected the Trocadero Palace to the Eiffel Tower via the Iena Bridge. Viewed from the bridge, looking toward the palace, the Algerian and Tunisian pavilions defined the axis and stylistically complemented the Trocadero's Islamic references. When seen from the palace looking toward the Eiffel Tower, the white stucco architecture of the pavilions, abstracted from various precolonial monuments, contrasted with the engineering aesthetics of the tower (figure 8.2). The industrial progress of the empire, therefore, was juxtaposed with the preindustrial forms of its colonies. This arrangement symbolically replicated the tactics of assimilation and contrast that dominated French colonial policy.

The transformations in the planning principles for each exposition thus articulated power relations and revealed a desire to enhance supremacy through representation.[10] In addition, the cross-cultural character of the international exhibitions produced a formalized comparative apparatus; although its conceptual model was industrial competition, its form of enunciation often was aesthetic and cultural. France's colonial possessions had a dual role to play in this context. Their very existence demonstrated French material power. Yet not only their economies, but also their indigenous cultures were extensively displayed at the expositions. They, too, glorified French industrialization, but in an antithetical sense. Since indigenous cultures were offered as evidence of local conditions and contemporary reality, their present state seemed to recall that of the industrialized nations' past and therefore provided a measure of their relative advancement and superiority.[11]

The elaborate forms of presenting people at the exhibitions contributed to this politicized chronology. The human displays were organized into na-

8.2. View toward Eiffel Tower from the Trocodero Park, with the
Tunisian Palace to the left and the Algerian Palace to the right, 1900.
From *Figaro illustreé* 124 (July 1900); from Département des Imprimés,
Bibliothèque Nationale de France, Paris, fol. Lc13 9ter, 13, 1900.

tional and racial hierarchies in accordance with the norms of the emerging
discipline of anthropology.[12] A "science of other men in another Time," as
Johannes Fabian describes it, anthropology tends to assume a "petrified relation" between the observer and other societies, whose history is perceived
to be fixed and unchanging.[13] Indeed, spatial and temporal distance determined the display format of other people in the world's fairs. Architecture
provided an "authentic" setting and a visual summary of the represented
culture. In the Islamic exhibits from 1867 on, mosques, baths, caravanserais,
houses, and rows of shops were built, drawing on examples well known from
architectural surveys and expeditionary literature. "Natives" were placed in
this scenery, dressed in regional costumes and performing artisanal tasks that
seemed to belong to another age (figure 8.3). Such architectural villages were
considered to be one of the most scientific aspects of the fairs, because they
claimed authentically to reconstruct other cultures.[14] In effect, however, these
societies were assimilated into the conceptual order of the exhibitions, reinforcing a perception of their apparently underdeveloped status. The fabri-

cated streets, shops, artisans, and merchants created a visible difference from the industrialized nations within a framework of familiar categories.

Ultimately, however, the success of the ethnographic displays rested on their theatrical presentation, in which documentation intermingled with certain kinds of entertainment deemed culturally authentic. This component of the indigenous exhibits received greater emphasis over the decades during which the expositions evolved. For example, while the Islamic quarters in the 1867 exposition were presented with minimal human animation of their architecture, in 1878, theaters were introduced; thereafter, they became indispensable to every Muslim display. In these theaters, music accompanied tableaux vivants from local daily life, in which weddings or shopping at a bazaar, for example, were enacted. In spite of the variety of activities presented, belly dances formed the core attraction from the beginning, to judge by the coverage they received in official and unofficial accounts of the exhibits and their increasingly elaborate choreography in successive fairs. In 1889 the number of spectators who came to watch the Egyptian belly dancers averaged two thousand per day.[15] As Gautier had remarked in 1867, the universal expositions brought the Orient to Paris; Europeans unable to travel to the Near East could now flock to the exhibition's Islamic theaters and there catch a glimpse of the lasciviousness attributed to the sultans. How did the belly dance become the representative Islamic art form at the universal expositions?

In Egypt, a semiautonomous governate of the Ottoman Empire in the nineteenth century until it came under British sovereignty in 1882, belly dancing had never been such a spectacle. The dance went back to the ancient kingdoms; it was also widespread in the early Roman period; thus it predated Islam. The *ghawazi*, the dancing women of Egypt, performed unveiled in the streets to small audiences. On special occasions, such as a marriage or the birth of a child, they would dance in the courtyard of a house or in front of its entrance, for both men and women. They would not be allowed inside a harem (the women's quarters of a household), but it was not uncommon for the ghawazi to entertain a private party of men in the men's quarters. In 1834, however, the street performances of the ghawazi were prohibited, and the dance was restricted to private quarters alone.[16] In other words, just as Egyptians attempted to remove belly dancing from public view, orientalist painting and travel literature were reversing this phenomenon by presenting belly dancing to Parisian audiences as an Islamic theatrical performance.

8.3. "Cordonniers Algériens," 1889. From Département des Estampes et de la Photographie, Bibliothèque Nationale de France, Paris, H52145.

A similar custom existed in Istanbul, where dancers called *çengis* could be hired for special events in both the male and female quarters of Muslim houses. Although the performance corresponded to the definition of the belly dance in other cultures—feet stable on the ground while other parts of the body moved—these dances were not characterized in Ottoman accounts by the accentuated eroticism of the belly dance in the exhibition settings. Furthermore, at precisely the moment that belly dancing was being presented in Paris as a reflection of Ottoman culture, it was disappearing from upper-class households in Istanbul. There, as part of the Ottoman Empire's modernization, the importation of European social and cultural models changed patterns of entertainment in both public and private settings. European-style ballet was substituted for belly dancing, even in the harems.[17]

Colonial Algeria presented a different pattern. Here the dancers, young Ouled-Nail girls, came from the poorest desert tribes. The commercialization of the dance of the Ouled-Nails was closely associated with the growth of prostitution under French rule; it also provided a means of accumulating a dowry.[18] In Algeria, the dance became increasingly erotic as it changed locales from the desert between Bou-Saada and Laghouat to urban centers and, eventually, to the stages of the Parisian universal expositions. The French feminist Hubertine Auclert recognized this transformation at the time. The belly dances she saw at the Paris fairs, she concluded, were a "grotesque spectacle . . . nothing but a horrible imitation," compared to the dances in the Algerian countryside. The Ouled-Nails in the desert, whom Auclert called "charming," provoked the erotic imagination of spectators without being vulgar; the dances symbolized lovemaking without literally representing it: in her words, "l'amour sans l'amour."[19] Auclert's attempt to recover the innocence of the belly dance by (re)situating it in a more pristine place of "origin," free of the contamination of recent history and commercialized sexuality, could be characterized as an example of "the salvage paradigm."[20]

These three cases demonstrate variable forms of negotiating the control of belly dancing. In Egypt the government tried to counteract the promotion of the belly dance in French painting and travel literature; in Istanbul the tables were turned, as the elite imported French dances; and in Algeria, where French colonizers encouraged the belly dance, this exploitation was in some measure exploited in turn by the Ouled-Nail dancers, who used it to enhance their marriageability. It was, therefore, an anything but pure belly dance that was presented as an Islamic ethnic form at the universal expositions, where, moreover, its performative aspects were refashioned for the benefit of Parisian audiences.

The belly dances reenacted in flesh and blood one of the aspects of Muslim life most intriguing to Europeans, which had been disseminated by orientalist painters and writers in the generic mode of "manners-and-customs" for at least seventy-five years.[21] It is important to realize that protests of the rampant typification of the Orient, and of the sexualized representation of Oriental women in particular, surfaced as early as the formulations themselves, although they are rarely mentioned in standard histories. The Ottoman writer Ahmed Mithad Efendi, for example, described the typical odalisque of European fantasy in his 1889 *Avrupa'da Bir Cevelan* (A Tour in Europe):

> [This] loveable person lies negligently on a sofa. One of her slippers, embroidered with pearls, is on the floor, while the other is on the tip of her toes. Since her garments are intended to ornament rather than to conceal [her body], her legs dangling from sofa are half naked and her belly and breasts are covered by fabrics as thin and transparent as a dream. Her disheveled hair over her nude shoulders falls down in waves. . . . In her mouth is the black end of the pipe of a *narghile*, curving like a snake. . . . The ornament in the room consists of an inlaid cupboard, chair, book stand, and chandeliers. . . . A black servant fans her.[22]

In capturing the Ingresque formula, Mithad Efendi indicates the epistemological status that such representations had achieved. The belly dances, in other words, depended for effect on a deliberate redundancy of representation. They amplified the calculated eroticism in countless orientalist paintings of women by making it more accessible; if anything, they heightened the "reality effect" of a body of orientalist imagery already legitimized by travelogues and paintings.

This passage also exemplifies, in a highly condensed form, the dilemmas that will characterize tactics of demystification. Laced with sarcasm, Mithad Efendi's hypothetical description acquires a critical edge that, at first, only insinuates the distortion inherent in such imagery. He then goes on to decry it as a "misconception," one that contradicts reality:

This is the Eastern woman Europe depicted until now. While such an image consists of beautiful things that please the eye, it is not reality, but only a dream, a poem. It is such a dream that the opinion and the belief it generates also become unreal. It is assumed that this body is not the mistress of her house, the wife of her husband, and the mother of her children, but only a servant to the pleasures of the man who owns the house. What a misconception![23]

Having relegated the image to an aesthetic, if not fully psychic, imaginary, Mithad Efendi pronounces it exaggerated, illusory, partial—a falsification, in a word. At a crucial juncture, a moment of reckoning that can be found in most critiques, an impulse "to correct" emerges. In general, it can be elaborated as follows: If representation can establish social fact, then countering its claims would appear to be strategically effective; if the problem is ignorance, misrepresentation, or bad faith, an adequate solution can be found in knowledge, re-presentation, and good faith.

The limitations of this type of response have been widely rehearsed. One lies in its static nature; ultimately, it regenerates the struggle for power, with its drive to substitute one truth or representation for another, to reclaim the hierarchy by inverting it. Another is an inability to account for the resilience of fantasy and its purchase on opinion and belief. The problem remains: How is the persistence, the appeal of a particular distortion sustained? The duplicity of myth demands, to recall Barthes, a different kind of consumption: "The reader lives the myth as a story at once true and unreal."[24]

The axiomatic element in this instance is not difficult to locate: the self-evident assumption that the "Eastern woman" be circumscribed by juridical, if not exclusively sexual, relations to "the man who owns the house." The supposition that the women in question (the ones represented and the ones not) are an expression of "The Rights of Man" propels gender into an ambiguous role. When men speak both of and through the intermediary category of women, the narrative of power relations can be described as a form of free indirect discourse in which the masculine position, exploiting the advantages of mobility, remains neither completely absorbed by nor entirely severed from the values that the feminine position entails.

Certainly, then, distortion and ignorance of indigenous societies can be demonstrated; the belly dance is a fabricated, simulated difference. Yet to situate it only in relation to what it was not—an authentic representation—

assumes that something of the sort is possible.[25] In addition, it reinforces the dubious claim to authenticity that the representational system of the expositions made in the first place. It is more useful to trace the pattern of distortion itself, which reveals the highly selective nature of cultural importation. Cultural information, that is, must be packaged in ways that are physically and economically profitable, capable of a kind of reproduction that reinvents the form while eliciting a willing investment in its structure of belief and opinion. The ethnographic displays at the exhibitions recontextualized an erotic fascination with Muslim women in a spectacle that linked imperial power, legitimate edification, and libidinal motivation.

There was more to these tableaux, however, than an expansive repetition of the *déjà-lu* and *déjà-vu*. Indeed, tautology is one of the signal attributes of myth. Yet the belly dance became part of an unforeseeable synthesis. Although culled from the orientalist stock of imagery, its entry onto the Parisian cultural scene required an interplay with specific local institutions and social practices; if the imagery provided the belly dance's condition of appearance, the interplay dictated the terms of its survival. In addition to the painting gallery, the model for display of foreign people at the universal expositions is to be found in the Parisian entertainment industry, in the cabarets, café-concerts, *jardins d'hiver*, and *bals publics* abundant and flourishing in Paris during the second half of the nineteenth century. With their capricious nomenclature—the Eldorado, New Athens, Madrid, Japanese Divan—and geographically diverse style and decor, the Parisian establishments provided the rationale for the entertainment districts in the indigenous quarters of the exhibitions, which otherwise would have appeared strikingly uncharacteristic and illogical.[26]

The *brasseries à femmes* are one crossroads of the ethnographic project of the fairs and the Parisian economy of leisure. Although not unknown before the 1867 exhibition, they acquired a distinctive identity there. Designed as sample rooms for beverages and comestibles, their regionally attired waitresses at the same time purported to stage national forms of sociability, all the while turning a profit. Detached from this environment and established in the Parisian economy by the end of the following decade, they acquired new functions, notably as hospitable milieux for unlicensed but informally organized prostitution and for other attractions as well.[27] To mention one well-known example, Agostina Segatori's café Le Tambourin, where Van Gogh and Toulouse-Lautrec exhibited paintings in 1886–87, was populated by waitresses in Italian costume to accompany the decor of tambourines illustrated with dancing women.[28] While shedding the context of ethnographic demonstration, the brasseries à femmes retained some significance on this level, if only as trademark. The prefabricated, ornamental quality of cultural difference in these establishments perhaps renounced any pretense to effective representation of it. But what is abandoned on one level may return to advantage on another. The sheer number of ethnic and racial types gathered into the peripheral regions of the fairs may have camouflaged the placement of cultural difference in categories structurally similar to, if not identical with, class stratifications. The migration of the brasseries à femmes from the fairs into the Parisian economy thus provides a jolt of recognition, in which the latent concatenation of cultural and social hierarchies is realized.

With generic odalisques or peasant, Andalusian, and Irish women on offer, it would seem that any old difference could find favor, as long as the rule of exoticism was obeyed. Should the belly dance be measured against this kind of equivalence, in which all concoctions of difference merge into an indifferent similarity? As one unit in the overall pattern of exoticism, perhaps; but as a discrete activity, it remained distinctive. Exoticism is dependent on trade and transportation.[29] In practice, it requires a transplantation of some sort, one that can simultaneously preserve the peculiarity of the foreign object and insert it into a new environment. The belly dance survived on different soil by aligning with a part of the entertainment industry that capitalized on and domesticated eccentricity. Introduced, we recall, in 1878, in what could be designated a second wave of theatricalization in the ethnographic displays, the belly dance was situated within the orbit of popular dancing, and its organization and personnel came to resemble that of the entrepreneurial sector of dance in Paris. The emergence of "stars" of the belly dance is one indication of its incorporation into this aesthetic economy.

The ascendance of the eroticized female performer in nineteenth-century Parisian culture is most often situated within the sexual politics of the ballet, whose history is institutionalized and whose carnally motivated male patrons—the Jockey Club—are readily identifiable.[30]

A somewhat different chronology and set of issues figures in a history of popular dance, but a similar feminization of performance and orchestration of titillation can be found there. And the production of the "star" is even more conspicuous in this less formalized domain. The bals publics that became prominent in Paris during the July Monarchy were characterized by unrehearsed routines interspersed with virtuoso displays of technique more or less improvised, depending on the locale.[31] Toward the middle of the century, female exhibitionism increasingly replaced the earlier emphasis on male agility. So-called choreographic celebrities appeared as early as the "polkamania" craze of the 1840s, and the notoriety of these women began to change the dynamics of the dance hall. The substitution of spectatorship for participation in Parisian dance halls over a period of thirty to forty years is an even more graphic indication of the sexualized appropriation of working-class female bodies than the traditional rituals of entertainment at the Opéra or drama theaters.

Celebrity, of course, cannot stand alone. The least autonomous of phenomena, it requires the support of word and image in their most institutionalized forms. And the apparatus of publishing and publicity that surrounded Parisian entertainment readily encompassed one type of dance and another. The roster of "choreographic celebrities" emerged complete with ghostwritten memoirs (notably those of Céleste Mogador and the infamous Rigolboche), detailing stories of immigrant struggle in the streets of Paris, discovery in predictable locales, and overnight rises to fame.[32] A journalist described this pattern, evidently well established by 1865, in an account of a certain "Fille de l'Air," a dancer at Mabille:

> Within two weeks, she will become a European celebrity, within six months, she will write her memoirs, and within one year, she will make a fortune in Berlin, [just] like Rigolboche and Finette, two ex-stars of the Parisian balls, who still pass abroad as the latest novelty. Then, within two years, nobody will be talking about her at all, because in Paris, everything is forgotten.[33]

Compare the story of Rachel Bent-Eny, who was known as "La Belle Fathma," after the Prophet Mohammed's daughter, even though she was of Algerian Jewish origin (figure 8.4). She had come to Paris not from Algeria but from Tunisia, along with her father, who was a member of the orchestra recruited for the colony's display at the 1878 exhibition. "The Giant of Susa," as he was known, made little Fathma, so the legend goes, dance in front of a crowd. About seven or eight years old at the time, she immediately became a big success and performed her variation of the belly dance several times a day. After the exposition closed, Fathma's family stayed in Paris for economic reasons, like many other immigrants. She grew up and "blossomed" in the streets of Paris, established her reputation in the commercial fairgrounds on the outskirts of the city, and eventually performed on her own stage within the grounds of the Concert de Paris on the Champs Elysées, where she "triumphed." After first appearing at the Grand Theater and in the rue du Caire at the 1889 exhibition, she moved to her own *boîte*, the Concert Tunisien, a hall with a capacity of one hundred spectators (figure 8.5).[34] Thus Fathma already was a star attraction by the time she performed at the 1889 exhibition, presumably as evidence of the indigenous culture of Tunisia, rather than of Paris, as she had become.

The minor media explosions that accompanied each universal exposition helped to promote this burgeoning literature, as Paris turned itself inside out for foreign and touristic consumption. Packaged and promoted above all were the sexualized attractions of Parisian entertainment. The perceived licentiousness of popular dancing had attracted official surveillance and intervention from the beginning. Without the *Gazette des Tribunaux*'s depositions of revelers hauled in by the vice squads, the practice of the cancan and chahut—reputed to be indecent deformations of the quadrille—would not be datable to the 1830s, but rather to the 1880s, the period of their standardization in dance hall routines and representation in modern life painting.[35] Bureaucratic wisdom apparently feared just what the literati and journalists relished: that energetic bodily movement verged on sexual pantomime and that moral defiance schooled political resistance.[36] The boulevard press, anecdotal literature, and naturalist novels of the period vied in their attempt to catalogue the vice and pleasure of the city, and popular dance figured prominently in their descriptive inventories. It is difficult to say whether these accounts thrived more on the attraction or the revulsion provoked by popular dancing, but they elaborated and promoted fantasies about working-class women, gradually producing a response instinctively applicable to the belly dance as well.

Joris-Karl Huysmans's account of Raffaëlli's *The Quadrille at the Ambassadeurs* includes a particularly trenchant example of the exaggerated carnality found in this genre of writing. The so-called naturalist quadrille retained the chahut's suggestive acrobatics and the cancan's frothy titillation, while intensifying the precision movements.[37] Yet the visual properties of the watercolor in question are barely adequate to the atmosphere Huysmans evokes: "You have to see the carnivorous smiles of those mouths, the dance of these little cattle, the cancan of the eyes on these three-franc 'lays,' which light up

8.4. "La Belle Fathma," wood engraving, from the cover of *La Seine*, October 10, 1886. From Département des Estampes et de la Photographie, Bibliothèque Nationale de France, Paris, D285.

8.5. "L'Exposition Universelle—Au champs de Mars—Le Concert Tunisien de la rue de Caire," wood engraving after E. Dousdébès, 1889. From Département des Estampes et de la Photographie, Bibliothèque Nationale de France, Paris, H56917.

the depths of corridors or lure, for a quick piece of work, in the wasteland of the night."[38] The cluster of bestial and predatory figures in Huysmans's characterization of the dancers, which continues throughout the passage, subsumes into his description the erotic degradation that popular dancing was called on to enact in an increasingly professionalized manner. Huysmans did not invent these terms; they were typical of nineteenth-century discourse on sexuality. But he did fashion them into a stylish amalgam of working-class slang and polished crudity, which is more pronounced than any effort to record or classify. *Who* is seen in this image, finally, is less important than the incitement *to* see it ("il faut le voir") and, by extension, the locales that offer such sensational provocation.

Secondary or tertiary descriptions of popular dance presume a viewer concordant with the setting. Seurat's *Le Chahut* (1889–90; figure 8.6) pictures this "archetypal" viewer, at least according to the painting's owner, the poet and critic Gustave Kahn:

> As a synthetic image of the public, observe the pig's snout of the spectator, archetype of the fat reveler, placed up close to and below the female dancer, vulgarly enjoying the moment of pleasure that has been prepared for him, with no thought for anything but a laugh and a lewd desire.[39]

In the "diagram of ideas" that, Kahn argues, the painting aspires to be is registered a conscription of sexuality for the purposes of commercial diversion. The linear armature and shimmering surface manage to hold in contact a peculiar combination of rigidity and evanescence, an alloy of degradation and pleasure that reveals to Kahn the psychosocial dynamic of the dance hall. In his "demonstration of the subject," the transaction of looking is structured by the animal nature of the spectator, not of the dancers, and the pyramid of gender and class on which the act is built flickers through its rhythmic figuration.

At what juncture do these habits of looking and association overlap with those elicited by the "indigenous" dancers at the expositions? Two further examples may help to locate this imbrication.

Edmond de Goncourt's memoirs treat the rue du Caire constructed for the 1889 fair virtually as a red-light district. After dining in the Eiffel Tower with the Zolas, Daudets, and Charpentiers, Goncourt and his party descend to the street lined with monuments, houses, and shops composed of frag-

8.6. Georges Seurat, *Le Chahut*, 1889–90, oil on canvas, 171.5 x 140.5 cm.
Otterlo, Rijksmuseum Kröller-Müller.

8.7. Rue de Caire. Photograph from Delort de Gléon, *La rue du Caire à l'Exposition Universelle de 1889* (Paris, 1889).

8.8. Photograph of La Goulue (Louise Weber), 1886. From Département
des Estampes et de la Photographie, Bibliothèque Nationale
de France, Paris, B109855.

ments salvaged from buildings demolished in Cairo (figure 8.7).[40] He characterizes it as a magnet for "libertine curiosity in Paris" (including, apparently, his own), filled with what he calls a "population in heat reminiscent of cats spraying on the coals."[41] Not to be outdone by his colleague Flaubert, presumably, Goncourt's description of the danse du ventre is filled with sexual fantasies: "For me, it would have been interesting danced by a nude woman," he begins. He then surveys the dancer's body, especially the "dislocation" of the "belly" and "ass." He associates her gyrations with sexual movements and provides a taxonomy of the differing "pitch and roll" characteristic of fornication with Moorish as opposed to European women.[42] From the author of a bal public scene (in the novel Germinie Lacerteux) threatened with censorship when it was staged in 1888, we might expect such connoisseurship of the carnal. And we can safely assume that the imagery providing momentum for this transformation of the belly dance into a striptease is the corpus of nude, semipornographic photographs of dancers in wide circulation (figure 8.8).[43] Although commercial studios duly expanded this genre to encompass Oriental dancing, some photographs of Muslim dancers published concurrently with the expositions retain a documentary aura, captured in imperfectly posed figures and uncertain gazes (figure 8.9).[44] If Goncourt's response is in any way exemplary, it is because it demonstrates the possibility of merging different kinds of appropriation, one psychic and sexual, another ethnographic and detached, a potential that anchors colonial power at the individual level. These models of possession, though divergent in inception and focus, collaborate in the constitution of a colonized female body.

Descriptions of the performances intended for a wider readership are more circumspect, but still loaded with fantasy and condescension; an excerpt from a long article written for the Figaro Illustré on the Egyptian dancers in 1900 is representative:

> As though pinched by a needle, the dancer started moving with the hideous contortions that all the Fathmas and Féridjées have saturated us with. With the vibrations of her hips and torso, she gives the illusion of a sea that calms down and where the long and slow waves die on the sand, like wings that rise and palpitate.[45]

The lyrical transport to distant shores is embedded in a topography of the dancer's body generated by that familiar equation of woman and nature.

8.9. Egyptian dancers on rue de Caire, 1889. Photograph from Delort de Gléon, *La rue du Caire à l'Exposition Universelle de 1889* (Paris, 1889).

8.10. "Pays des Fées," program, ca. 1889. From Département des Estampes et de la Photographie, Bibliothèque Nationale de France, Paris, H58473.

Whatever embodiment of imperial power the entertainment districts realized depended on the invitation to make such projections.

The composition of an intelligible Oriental subject required an assimilation of fragments of knowledge, experience, and imagery that no single rule of demonstration or mode of representation can reveal. Because the ritual of appropriation remained approximate, contingent, and variable, it seemed to require interminable repetition. If a saturation point was reached by the turn of the century, it was only after the belly dance infiltrated Parisian entertainment even further.

In addition to the expanded use of entertainment in ethnographic displays, the appearance of enterprises designed explicitly to capitalize on the crowds of visitors attracted by the fairs characterized the 1889 exhibition. The Pays de Fées, an amusement park built on the Avenue du Rapp outside the principal entrance to the fair on the Champs de Mars, demarcates the economic and cultural orbit that eventually extended from the ethnographic exhibits to the dance halls of Montmartre (figure 8.10). This prototype of Disneyland and countless later theme parks was promoted as an incarnation of both the *Contes de Perrault* and the *One Thousand and One Nights*. The youthful blond parisienne of Jules Chéret's invention never had a more appropriate milieu to announce, appearing in a poster for the establishment as the primordial Tinkerbell (figure 8.11). Alongside sets based on various European fairy tales was Ali-Baba's cave and a blue elephant whose belly housed a platform for a dancer known as "La Belle Féridjée" (figure 8.12). Implied in these juxtapositions is a notion of the Orient as the childhood of European civilization; the admixture of innocence and fantasy purifies the precept and enables its dissemination across generations. After this temporary establishment closed, its elephant was removed to the outdoor garden of the Moulin Rouge, the dance hall in Montmartre that opened just after the close of the exhibition (figure 8.13).[46] Apparently the vice squad took up residence in the elephant, but, according to contemporary accounts, "La Belle Zhora" performed Ouled-Nail belly dances nearby.[47]

The Moulin Rouge is more identified than any other establishment with the transformation of the bal public from an arena of relatively unregulated sociability into one of lucrative exhibitionism; in this process, the cult of celebrity dancing was pivotal. Thanks to the Moulin Rouge's mobilization of nearly all the available forms of publicity—memoirs, interviews, gossip columns, guidebooks, celebrity cartes-de-visite, posters, and postcards—most elements of the economic, commercial, and artistic network through which it functioned can be identified. We know the dancers' outrageous and poignant stage names: "La Sauterelle" (The Grasshopper), "Nini Pattes en l'Air" (Nini, Paws in the Air), "La Goulue" (The Glutton), "Môme Fromage" (Kid or Mistress Cheese), "Grille d'Égout" (Sewer Grate), and "Valentin-le-Désossé" (Valentin-the-Double-jointed). We know their employer, Joseph Oller; their impresario, Charles Zidler; their salaries, three hundred francs a month; where to find their public relations, *Paris illustré, Le Courrier français*.[48] And, finally, we know a great deal about their image maker, Henri de Toulouse-Lautrec.

As the premier poster artist in Paris, Chéret was engaged to advertise the opening of the Moulin Rouge. By commissioning Lautrec to design the poster for the following season (winter 1890–91), Zidler launched the young artist's career. He proved, in turn, to be a master of publicity. Featuring the Moulin Rouge's star dancers, La Goulue and Valentin-le-Désossé, instead of the generic *chérette* on his poster, Lautrec inaugurated a new dimension of their celebrity; the glamorous feudalism of a "star system" attached to a particular commercial establishment was born. And the system served the artist as well, who wrote proudly to his mother, "They're being very nice to me in the newspapers since my poster."[49]

8.11. Jules Chéret, *Exposition universelle de 1889, Le Pays de Fées, jardin enchanté, 31 Avenue de Rapp*, poster, ca. 1889, 74 x 55 cm. Musée de l'Affiche.

8.12. "La Belle Féridjée," photograph, ca. 1889. From Département des Estampes et de la Photographie, Bibliothèque Nationale de France, Paris, P86594.

8.13. "Une Répétition au Moulin Rouge." Color photograph from *Figaro illustré*, June 3, 1896, from Département des Imprimés, Bibliothèque Nationale de France, Paris, fol. Lc13 9ter, 7, 1896.

One measure of the success of Lautrec's publicity can be found in La Goulue's private venture four years later, which also discloses, in one ensemble, the metamorphosis gradually undergone by the belly dance over the previous two decades. Although retrospectively described as the beginning of her inevitable decline into poverty and obscurity, it is more likely that La Goulue risked an entrepreneurial endeavor on her own at the height of her acclaim. Not that the predictable accounts of her life would grant such savvy to a child of the streets. Née Louise Weber, La Goulue had come to Paris from Alsace-Lorraine and reportedly worked as a flower vendor, then as a laundress, before being noticed for her exuberant dancing at Montmartre bals publics. She progressed from the Boule Noire, or some said the Médrano, to the Moulin de la Galette, the Elysée Montmartre, where she achieved notoriety, and finally to the Jardin de Paris, before being recruited by Oller for the Moulin Rouge, reportedly for twice the usual salary.[50] Lautrec first caught up with her in 1887, when she appeared in a small composition on

8.14. "La Baraque de la Goulue à la foire de Neuilly [sic]." Photograph from *Figaro illustré* 145 (April 1902), photograph. From Département des Imprimés, Bibliothèque Nationale de France, Paris, fol. Lc13 9ter, 13, 1902.

cardboard with Valentin, already her partner—or was she his protégée?[51] In any case, in 1895 she erected a booth at the Foire aux Pains d'Épices on the Place du Trône (thus also known as the Foire du Trône), where she starred in a so-called Moorish dance.

The booth was situated on the *place* itself, which was divided into ten sectors, all dedicated to popular attractions, including a huge cyclorama of Tunisia and Algeria, a children's playground, animal acts, and games (figure 8.14). In a prominent position at the entrance to the Avenue du Trône, the theater district, La Goulue occupied the borderline between sensational and dramatic entertainment. The booth itself, with its onion dome and crescent-and-star insignia marking the entrance, retained a few impoverished features of the Islamic pavilions at the world's fairs, enough to signify in the manner dubbed "basquity" in Barthes's exemplary analysis.[52]

For this occasion, La Goulue engaged Lautrec to paint the booth's two façade panels. One portrayed La Goulue's familiar role with Valentin on

8.15. Henri de Toulouse-Lautrec, *The Dance at the Moulin Rouge* (panel for the booth of La Goulue at the Foire du Trône), 1895, oil on canvas, 298 x 316 cm. Musée d'Orsay. Photograph by Giraudon.

the floorboards of the Moulin Rouge (figure 8.15), the other her solo performance of the "Moorish" dance on an elevated platform (figure 8.16).[53] "They're gigantic jokes," *La Vie Parisienne* clued in its readers, "it's the cha-hut in fresco, the enormous swaying hips of a symbolic *bal public*."[54] It is also a virtual diagram of the mechanisms and motivation of integrating the belly dance into Parisian entertainment. Eventually cut into fragments of portraiture by a dealer and now reassembled, the panels in their present condition exaggerate the ghostly effect of Lautrec's mordant line and spare pigment, his "language of silhouette for conversing with the public," in Arsène Alexandre's phrase.[55]

The Moulin Rouge panel recombines elements of Lautrec's previous depictions of La Goulue and Valentin. The other panel is more novel, but only

8.16. Henri de Toulouse-Lautrec, *The Moorish Dance* (panel for the booth of La Goulue at the Foire du Trône), 1895, oil on canvas, 285 x 307.5 cm. Musée d'Orsay. Photograph by Giraudon.

insofar as it traces with great clarity the component parts of the hybrid that Islamic dancing in Paris had always been. If in the exposition environment the cabaret settings and the half-familiar movements were a mnemonic screen against which the belly dance could be registered, here figure and spectator come forward simultaneously. The crescent motif from the exterior façade is repeated on the flat that serves as backdrop to La Goulue's dance of the *almée*, a dance that seems to contain the characteristic can-can kick. In the foreground, a crowd of observers from Montmartre and abroad (Jane Avril of the Moulin Rouge, amid Oscar Wilde, Félix Fénéon, and the champagne vendor, photographer, and amateur Maurice Guibert) is arranged so that they present a "celebrity endorsement." The scenery on the right recalls descriptions of Fathma's boîte at the 1889 exhibition, which had included a stage covered with carpets and an elevated seat in front of a large mirror, used for musical performances. The seated *fathma* in Lautrec's panel and her turbaned male partner, who serve as percussionists, are placed in the position usually occupied by the *corbeille* of women in a café-concert setting. The entire scenario—booth, decoration, music, and the dance itself—was meant to resonate with the Islamic entertainment districts devised for the world's fairs.[56]

Meanwhile, another hybrid was being produced in the belly dances performed at the universal expositions. In 1889 the dancers were limited to swords and mirrors, signaling the long-established European association of Islam with violence and its women with mystique. The dances in 1900, however, used more elaborate devices and added to the repertoire of "typical" Islamic accoutrements—such as the narghile—objects that obviously were industrial and Parisian (figure 8.17).[57] The dance of the chair (figure 8.18), performed with a chair balanced in the mouth, was reminiscent of the notorious quadrille of the Louis XIII chair, which in 1886 had become the "signature dance" of Aristide Bruant's Le Mirliton, as rendered in Lautrec's illustration published on the cover of the cabaret's journal.[58]

During the same period that the belly dance was imported to Paris, Parisian dancing was being exported abroad. As early as the 1860s, the stars produced by the bals publics were seen in Berlin and London. By the 1880s, this network had extended to Istanbul. Official modernization programs begun by the Ottoman government at first adopted military technology, and thereafter, French social and cultural norms. Eventually, Parisian entertainment became fashionable among the Ottoman court and upper classes.[59] Nightclubs with names referring to Parisian sites (Montmartre, Parisiana, and Concordia) or evoking Parisian images (Flamme and Café Crystal) or even deriving from Islamic legends created by the Parisian entertainment industry (Alhambra and Alcazar) became commonplace.[60] The place occupied by belly dancing in Paris, in other words, was filled in Istanbul by Parisian dancing. In time, the belly dance would be reformulated in many Islamic countries along lines similar to those we have described: as a commercial concoction for tourists presented in the guise of an indigenous art form.

Given the migrations of the belly dance and the ensuing inversions of its cultural meaning, perhaps our essay can best be described as an attempt to present a counterdiagram of the site plans, which instead maps the circulation of colonized women's bodies. Several principles of its construction will bear reiterating. The imperial power relationship is not simply a process of

8.17. "La danse du narghilé [*sic*]," 1900. From *Figaro illustreé* 124 (July 1900).

8.18. Dancer with chair. From *Figaro illustreé* 124 (July 1900).

cultural exchange or appropriation; rather, it operates through a continuous circulation of imagery and redefinition of meaning. It cannot be grasped by squaring two pairs of oppositions, between man and woman and colonizer and colonized. Who is the Other when La Goulue interprets the dance of La Belle Féridjée? And who is in which position when Suzanne performs for an audience in Istanbul, in a place called Le Café du Luxembourg?[61] La Belle Fathma, La Goulue temporarily vacate one form of identity only to be caught failing to achieve another. It is the density of cultural interchange in specific historical situations that made us question the most frequently used concept in postcolonial and feminist discourse—the Other. And it may be useful, in conclusion, to recall briefly the circumstances in which the Other became the name for a solution to a common problem; this will amount to treating the concept as a device, not as a law.

The aggression accentuated in Jean-Paul Sartre's reworking of the Hegelian problematic of the Other in *Being and Nothingness* (1943) was released, in the postwar period, exactly in the realms where it most mattered. In his *Anti-Semite and Jew* (1946), Simone de Beauvoir's *The Second Sex* (1949), and Frantz Fanon's *Black Skins, White Masks* (1952) the concept acquired a performative, protopolitical function.[62] For example, Beauvoir's consideration of how this "fundamental category of human thought" became attached to the division of the sexes was premised on a universal explanation of patterns of oppression:

> Whether it is a race, a caste, a class, or a sex that is reduced to a position of inferiority, the methods of justification are the same. "The eternal feminine" corresponds to "the black soul" and to "the Jewish character."[63]

As astonishingly undifferentiated as these equations may now appear to be, the detection of a rule of judgment applicable in such diverse circumstances provided enormous momentum for cultural critique. At the same time, the concept operated at the level of individual agency; the unavoidable repression of the Other in human existence was held to account. Notwithstanding the aspects of her existential philosophy no longer considered viable, it is still possible to extrapolate from Beauvoir's argument how gender functions as an exercise of power, even where sexuality itself is not at stake. Although she devoted her entire book to dismantling the "natural" link between sexual difference and the hierarchy inherent in the Self/Other dyad, the duality of sexes continues to be constructed ("perceived," she would have said) as primordial and thus is used to stipulate multiple relations of domination and submission. The existentialist stress on the individual burden of choice, even within the inevitable alterity of human relations, enabled Fanon, during the same years, to propose a rehabilitation of the colonial subject in terms of the concept of the Other. In his psychoanalytic modification of the ontology of othering, native difference would serve as a corrective to the divided self, and his revolutionary subject could achieve a unified and politically conscious identity, which would facilitate decolonization.[64]

Written between 1954 and 1956, Barthes's *Mythologies* also was marked by gestures to Sartre, one of the chosen masters of experimental, artificial myth.[65] With an exemplary Negro soldier saluting the Empire and a petit-bourgeois turning to exoticism for emergency relief from the Other, "Myth Today" appeared ideally situated to steer analysis from the problem of representing identity to the process of identification inherent in cultural coding through signification. Semiology, with its momentum of displacement and differentiation, appeared to break open the binary logic of the Other, to reverse its stasis and entropy. Yet it, too, ran aground, as Barthes himself noted in 1971. Not that mythmaking had ceased. Nor was the problem really that the chorus of denunciation had yet to "change the object itself." But demystification had proven embarrassingly prey to mythification itself.[66] Barthes's suspicion that the science of the signifier would need to be revamped culminated in an ambivalent prescription, pointing to the Lacanian imaginary as an answer.

A series of contexts that reinforced the instrumentality of the Other was succeeded by its dispersal, in the academic vernacular, into a nebulous, free-floating force signifying its own autonomy and deconstructive or psychoanalytic authority. The protest in the past two decades against feminism's complacent use of woman as subject nevertheless has suggested that dualism lingers; often expressed in postcolonial rhetoric, the challenges to feminism frequently indict a form of Cartesian cogito that had claimed to be living a Lacanian existence.[67] The shift from an objectifying, substantive, distancing Other to one of deferral and desire is a subject in itself, much too complicated to explore here.[68] Finally, the concept is an expression of a cultural condition as much as an analysis of it.

Suffice it to say that feminist and postcolonial critics should question bipolar logic. The concept remains useful, provided it is not allowed to descend into essential antitheses or multiple mirrorings of prejudice. It reminds us to evaluate not simply the validity of constructions of the Other, but also to see in them the motives, desires, and fears of the image makers. In addition, it enables the isolation of similar patterns of domination in circumstances as different as those structuring the representation of Islamic culture at the world's fairs and working-class women in the dance halls of Montmartre.

Regressive theories of representation would suggest that the belly dance be read symptomatically, as the token or alienation of an already-given doctrine: colonial discourse, the denigration of feminine lack. Often, however, this procedure settles accounts by trivializing the contents of difference while leaving the framework of power intact. For the moment we have preferred to write a skeptical ethnography of one aspect of Parisian culture, greatly doubting, to put a final spin on Barthes's words, that yesterday's truths will be the exact match of today's laws.[69]

## Notes

1. To wit, Malcolm Forbes's Moroccan birthday bash in August 1989, with its hundreds of belly dancers and charging cavalry. The extensive press coverage lambasted its conspicuous consumption but never questioned its reinvigoration of the same old stereotypes of Islamic culture.

2. Roland Barthes, "Myth Today" [1957], in *Mythologies*, selected and translated by Annette Lavers (New York: Hill and Wang, 1972), 128.

3. One indication of this conjunction of interests may be found in Said's observation, six years after the publication of *Orientalism*, the founding text for postcolonial criticism: "Thus, for example, we can now see that *Orientalism* is a praxis of the same sort, albeit in different territories, as male gender dominance, or patriarchy, in metropolitan societies: the Orient was routinely described as feminine, its riches as fertile, its main symbols the sensual woman, the harem, and the despotic—but curiously attractive—ruler." Edward Said, "Orientalism Reconsidered," *Cultural Critique* 1 (fall 1985): 103.

4. Our collaboration developed from joint sessions of courses held in the History, Theory, and Criticism and Aga Khan programs at MIT during the academic year 1988–89; we considered the issues surrounding orientalism, postcolonial and feminist theory.

5. Of course, demystification is thoroughly appropriate, not to mention enjoyable, in many circumstances. In the case of Gauguin, for example, see Abigail Solomon-Godeau, "Going Native," *Art in America* 77, no. 7 (July 1989): 118–28, 161.

6. For a more extensive discussion of the architectural representation of Islamic

cultures at the nineteenth-century world's fairs, see Zeynep Çelik, *Displaying the Orient* (Berkeley: University of California Press, 1991).

7. In 1867, for example, two electrically lit towers or "lighthouses" were erected by France and England in the park surrounding the main exhibition building. See Patricia Mainardi, "The Eiffel Tower and the English Lighthouse," *Art Magazine* 54 (March 1980): 141–44; Patricia Mainardi, *Art and Politics of the Second Empire: The Universal Expositions of 1855 and 1867* (New Haven CT: Yale University Press, 1987), 146–47.

8. Hippolyte Gautier, *Les Curiosités de l'exposition universelle de 1867* (Paris, 1867), 2:85–86.

9. G. de Wailly, *À travers l'exposition de 1900* (Paris, 1900), 8:6.

10. Timothy Mitchell has argued, in fact, that the "process of exhibiting" epitomized the expositions as well as the Western "experience of order and truth." See Timothy Mitchell, "The World as Exhibition," *Comparative Studies in Society and History* 31, no. 2 (April 1989): 217–36; the article is based on the first chapter of his book *Colonizing Egypt* (Cambridge, England: Cambridge University Press, 1988), 1–33.

11. James Clifford, Virginia Dominguez, and Trinh T. Minh-ha address such temporal and social hierarchies in "Of Other Peoples: Beyond the 'Salvage' Paradigm," in *Discussions in Contemporary Culture* 1, ed. Hal Foster (Seattle: Bay Press, 1987), 121–30, 131–37, 138–41, respectively, and 142–50 for a discussion.

12. Burton Benedict, "The Anthropology of World's Fairs," in *The Anthropology of World Fairs*, ed. Burton Benedict (Berkeley: Scholar Press, 1983), 2. Ralph Greenhalgh points out that the rise of anthropology as a discipline occurred between 1878 and 1889 in Paris. See his *Ephemeral Vistas, the Expositions Universelles, Great Exhibitions, and World's Fair, 1851–1939* (Manchester, England: Manchester University Press, 1988), 86. Anthropology was largely influenced by Arthur de Gobineau's *Essai sur 'inégalité des races humaines* (Paris, 1853). Hannah Arendt suggests that by 1900 Gobineau's text had become "a king of standard work for race theories in history." See Hannah Arendt, *Imperialism* (1951; New York: Harcourt, Brace, Jovanovich, 1968), 50–51.

13. Johannes Fabian, *Time and the Other: How Anthropology Makes Its Object* (New York: Columbia University Press, 1983), 143.

14. See Edward Kaufman, "The Architectural Museum from the World's Fair to Restoration Village," *Assemblage* 9 (1989): 21–39; Debora L. Silverman, "The 1889 Exhibition: The Crisis of Bourgeois Individualism," *Oppositions* 8 (spring 1977): 70–91.

15. Anouar Louca, *Voyageurs et écrivains égyptiens en France aux XIXe siècle* (Paris: Didier, 1970), 193–94.

16. See Edward William Lane, *An Account of the Manners and Customs of the Modern*

*Egyptians, Written in Egypt During the Years 1833–1835* (London: Dover, 1978), 373–75; Sarah Graham-Brown, *Images of Women: The Portrayal of Women in Photography of the Middle East 1860–1950* (London: Quartet Books, 1988). Other accounts of the belly dance, which uncritically present it as an Islamic art from, can be found in Morroe Burger, "The Arab *danse du ventre*," *Dance Perspectives* 10 (spring 1969): 4–41; Wendy Buonaventura, *Serpent of the Nile: Women and Dance in the Arab World* (New York: Interlink Publishers, 1989).

17. See, for example, Ahmed Mithad, *Jön Türk* (The Young Turk) (Istanbul, 1910), cited and discussed in Orhan Okay, *Bati Mediniyeti Karsisinda Ahmed Mithad Efendi* (Ahmed Mithad Efendi vis-à-vis Western Civilization) (Ankara: n.p., 1975), 99–100; Fanny Davis, *The Ottoman Lady: A Social History from 1718 to 1918* (New York: Greenwood Press, 1986), 162.

18. The Algerian commander Abd al-Qadir, who had led the first uprising against the French between 1832 and 1841, attempted unsuccessfully to ban the Ouled-Nail girls from traveling to different parts of Algeria to dance and to practice prostitution. See Hubertine Auclert, *Les Femmes arabes en Algérie* (Paris, 1900), 116. Algerian-born women remained a small percentage of *registered* prostitutes in France during the second half of the nineteenth century, according to records compiled by Corbin. For the period 1880–86, only 4.74 percent of *filles soumises* in Paris were foreigners. In the port town of Marseilles, not surprisingly, a greater percentage were foreign-born (the largest number were Italians, followed by Spaniards, Swiss, and Germans); exact figures are not given for Algerian women, but they look from his graph to be roughly 4.6 percent of the foreign-born women and 1.3 percent of the total number of 3,584 tallied. See Alain Corbin, *Les Filles de noce: Misère sexuelle et prostitution, 19e et 20e siècles* (Paris: Aubier Montaigne, 1978), 75; see 97 for map.

19. Auclert, *Les Femmes arabes*, 114.

20. See Clifford et al., "Of Other Peoples."

21. See Edward W. Said, *Orientalism* (New York: Vintage Books, 1979), and, for the first article to grasp its significance for the interpretation of nineteenth-century painting, see Linda Nochlin, "The Imaginary Orient," *Art in America* 71, no. 5 (May 1983): 118–31, 187–91.

22. Ahmed Mithad, *Avrupa'da Bir Cevelan* (Istanbul, 1890), 164–65.

23. Mithad, *Avrupa'da Bir Cevelan*, 164–65. In a scene from Mohammad al-Muway-lini's novel *Ar-Rihla Ath-thaniye*, which takes place at the 1900 exposition, the main character Isa is distressed and embarrassed by the performance of belly dancers in the Egyptian theater and argues that the dance does not represent his country. See Louca, *Voyageurs et écrivains égyptiens*, 232.

24. Barthes, "Myth Today," 128.

25. In spite of Said's repeated attempts to dissociate himself from a search for "au-

thentic" representation, many studies published in the wake of *Orientalism* seemed to take its central argument as an injunction to do just that. See "Orientalism Reconsidered," and, especially, *Orientalism*, 273–74, where he refers to Barthes on the issue of representation as deformation.

26. In fact, Oriental decor was featured in Parisian establishments from the late 1830s on; for example, a Moroccan tent covered the dance floor at La Grande Chartreuse (founded 1838). See Edmond Texier, *Tableau de Paris*, 2 vols. (Paris, 1850), 1:173–75. Its successor, the Closerie de Lilas, was decorated with "gawdy Oriental paintings that some joker dubbed the Alhambra genre." Alexandre Privat d'Anglemont, *La Closerie de lilas: Quadrille en prose* (Paris, 1848), 19. On parallels between the Islamic districts and the café-concert noted by commentators in 1889, see Sylvianne Leprun, *Le Théâtre des colonies: Scénographie, acteurs et discours de l'imaginaire dans les expositions 1855–1937* (Paris: Editions L'Harmattan, 1986), 72–78.

27. See Corbin, *Les Filles de noce*, 250–54. Further information on the brasseries à femmes, unfortunately simplistically applied to the paintings of Manet and Degas, can be found in Theresa A. Gronberg, "Femmes de Brasserie," *Art History* 7, no. 3 (September 1984): 329–43.

28. Mariel Oberthur, *Cafés and Cabarets of Montmartre* (Salt Lake City UT: Gibbs M. Smith, 1984), 55–57.

29. In fact, in the early modern period the word was used primarily for plants and merchandise. See Vincenette Maigne, "Exotisme: Evolution en diachronie du mot et de son champ sémantique," in *Exotisme et création*, Actes du Colloque international, Lyons, 1983 (Lyons: L'Hermès, 1985), 9–16 ; Jacques Huré, "Exotisme et rencontre des cultures: La Route de la soie," in *Exotisme et création*, Actes du Colloque international, Lyons, 1983 (Lyons: L'Hermès, 1985), 217–27.

30. The most pointed of a number of discussions of this issue is Abigail Solomon-Godeau, "The Legs of the Countess," *October 39* (winter 1986): 65–108.

31. The standard, thoroughly documented source on popular dancing is François Gasnault, *Guinguettes et lorettes: Bals publics et danse sociale à Paris entre 1830 et 1870* (Paris: Aubier, 1986). For later periods, the primary source is the Rondel Collection of the Bibliothèque de l'Arsenal, which has informed the literature on Toulouse-Lautrec. Other useful discussions can be found in Alex Potts, "Dance, Politics and Sculpture: *Jean-Baptiste Carpeaux* by A. M. Wagner," *Art History* 10, no. 1 (March 1987): 91–109; Gale B. Murray, "The Theme of the Naturalist Quadrille in the Art of Toulouse-Lautrec: Its Origins, Meaning, Evolution, and Relationship to Later Realism," *Arts Magazine* 55, no. 4 (December 1980): 68–75; Jean-Claude Lebensztein, *Chahut: Seurat revisité* (Paris: Hazan, 1989).

32. *Adieux au monde* sold six thousand copies of an edition of ten thousand before

being seized in 1854. See Gasnault, *Guinguettes et lorettes*, 237–40 ; [Ernest Blum], *Mémoires de Rigolboche* (Paris, 1860).

33. Gérôme, unidentified clipping, 1865, Dossier Ro. 12910, Bibliothèque de l'Arsenal, Paris.

34. See *La Seine*, October 10, 1886; Arthur Pougin, *Le Théâtre à l'exposition de 1889* (Paris, 1890), 120–21; Julien Tiersot, *Musiques pittoresques, promenades musicales, l'exposition de 1889* (Paris, 1889), 82–83.

35. Gasnault, *Guinguettes et lorettes*, 47–56.

36. Gasnault, *Guinguettes et lorettes*, chaps. 2–3. Official policy, of course, varied with administrations; there was also an opinion that entertainment served to distract the populace from conspiracy and therefore should be surveilled but not condemned or restricted (see p. 82).

37. *Paris Cythère* (Paris, 1894), cited in Philippe Huisman and M. G. Dortu, *Lautrec by Lautrec*, trans. Corinne Bellow (New York: Charwell Books, 1964), 78, and in Murray, "The Theme of the Naturalist Quadrille."

38. Joris-Karl Huysmans, "Bartholomé—Raffaëlli—Stevens—Tissot—Wagner—Cézanne—Forain," in *Certains* (1889; reprint, Paris: n.p., 1975), 302; translation altered from Murray, "The Theme of the Naturalist Quadrille," 72.

39. Gustave Kahn, "Seurat," *L'Art moderne* 11 (April 5, 1891), cited in *Seurat in Perspective*, ed. Norma Broude (Englewood Cliffs NJ: Prentice-Hall, 1978), 24–25.

40. For documentation of this street, see Delort de Gléon, *La rue du Caire à l'Exposition Universelle de 1889* (Paris, 1889).

41. Edmond de Goncourt, *Journal: Mémoires de la vie littéraire* (Monaco: Les Éditions de l'Imprimerie Nationale de Monaco, 1956), July 2, 1889, 16:100.

42. Goncourt, *Journal*, 16:101.

43. On the origins of pornographic and erotic photographs of dancers, laundresses, and artists' models in the 1860s, see Elizabeth Anne McCauley, *A. A. E. Disdéri and the Carte de Visite Portrait Photograph* (New Haven CT: Yale University Press, 1985); Solomon-Godeau, "The Legs of the Countess." The demand for small, portable depictions of women's bodies evolved into a burgeoning market in postcards of colonial women; see Malek Alloula, *The Colonial Harem*, trans. Myrna Goldzich and Wlad Goldzich (Minneapolis: University of Minnesota Press, 1987); Graham-Brown, *Images of Women;* David Prochaska, "L'Algérie imaginaire: Jalons pour une histoire de l'iconographie coloniale," *Gradhiva* 7 (winter 1989): 29–38.

44. For photographs of Oriental dancers, see Graham-Brown, *Images of Women*, 170–81.

45. René Maizeroy, "Les Théâtres ephémères à l'exposition, le théâtre égyptien," *Figaro Illustré* 124 (July 1900): 142–43.

46. See Charles Rearick, *Pleasures of the Belle Epoque: Entertainment and Festivity*

in *Turn of the Century France* (New Haven CT: Yale University Press, 1985), 121; *Fêtes de l'Exposition: Programme offert par Le Rappel*, May 6, 1889, Séries "Actualités," Bibliothèque Historique de la Ville de Paris.

47. Marcel de Bare, "Les Mémoires du Moulin Rouge: Anecdotes et souvenirs inédits sur le bal célèbre," *Oeuvres libres* 48, June 1925, Dossier Ro. 12965, Bibliothèque de l'Arsenal, Paris.

48. On Oller, see Rearick, *Pleasures of the Belle Epoque*; Ferran Canyameres, *L'Homme de la Belle Epoque* (Paris: Les Editions Universelles, 1946). On the Moulin Rouge, see especially "Moulin Rouge," Dossier Ro. 12967, Bibliothèque de l'Arsenal, Paris; Georges Montorgueil, *Paris dansant* (Paris: Théophile Bélin, 1898); Götz Andriani, *Toulouse-Lautrec* (London: Thames and Hudson, 1987); Jean Sagnes, *Toulouse-Lautrec* (Paris: Fayard, 1988), 221–53.

49. Letter 133 to his mother, January 25, [1892], in *Unpublished Correspondence of Henri de Toulouse-Lautrec*, ed. Lucien Goldschmidt and Herbert Schimmel, trans. Edward B. Garside (London: Phaidon, 1969), 139.

50. Sagnes, *Toulouse-Lautrec*, 232, puts her salary at eight hundred francs a month. See also Dossiers Ro. 12912 "La Goulue," Ro. 12913 "Grille d'Égout," and Ro. 12923 "Nini Patte-en-l'air," Bibliothèque de l'Arsenal, Paris; *Grille d'Égout et la Goulue: Histoire réaliste* (Paris, 1885); Montorgueil, *Paris dansant*, 170–79.

51. *At the Moulin de la Galette, La Goulue and Valentin le Désossé*, oil on cardboard, 52 x 39.2 cm, Musée Toulouse-Lautrec, Albi, Dortu II, p. 282; see Adriani, *Toulouse-Lautrec*, 65–66, fig. 23.

52. Barthes, "Myth Today," 125, 127.

53. Dossier RF 2826, Musée d'Orsay, Paris; Luce Abèlés, *Toulouse-Lautrec: La Baraque de la Goulue*, exhibition catalogue, Cahiers Musée d'Art et d'Essai, Palais de Tokyo, no. 14 (Paris: Éditions de la Réunion des Musées Nationaux, 1984).

54. *La Vie Parisienne*, July 6, 1895, 392.

55. Arsène Alexandre, "Toulouse-Lautrec," *Figaro Illustré* (April 1902): 13.

56. Abèlés, *Toulouse-Lautrec*, 8, suggests that La Goulue was inspired by the popularity of the belly dance at the 1889 fair, which was taken for granted in earlier literature. André Warnod even claims that La Belle Fathma is shown with La Goulue: "Que vont devenir les Toulouse-Lautrec peints pour la Goulue?" unidentified clipping, October 2, 1929, Ro. 12909, Bibliothèque de l'Arsenal, Paris. In 1900 the American dancer Loïe Fuller commissioned Henri Sauvage to build a pavilion for the exposition, where she performed a dance of the veils, another variation on "Islamic" dancing. For a discussion of Fuller's dance in the context of art nouveau, see Debora L. Silverman, *Art Nouveau in Fin-de-Siècle France: Politics, Psychology, and Style* (Berkeley: University of California Press, 1989), 299–300.

57. Maizeroy, "Les Théâtres ephémères," 144.

58. "Quadrille de la Chaise Louis XIII à L'Elysée-Montmartre," *Le Mirliton*, December 29, 1886. The drawing is in the Musée Toulouse-Lautrec, Albi, Dortu V, D. 2973.

59. For a discussion of this phenomenon, see Serif Mardin, "Super Westernization in Urban Life in the Ottoman Empire in the Last Quarter of the Nineteenth Century," in *Turkey: Geographic and Social Perspectives*, ed. Peter Benedict, Erol Tümertekin, and Fatma Mansur (Leiden: Brill, 1974), 403–46.

60. See Okay, *Ahmed Mithad Efendi*, 101–7; Said Naum-Duhani, *Vieilles gens, vieilles demeures, topographie sociale de Beyoglu au XIXème siècle* (Istanbul: n.p., 1947), 70–71.

61. Naum-Duhani, *Vieilles Gens*, 100.

62. See Jean-Paul Sartre, *Being and Nothingness: An Essay on Phenomenological Ontology*, trans. Hazel E. Barnes (New York: Philosophical Library, 1956); Jean-Paul Sartre, *Anti-Semite and Jew*, trans. George J. Becker (New York: Schocken Books, 1948); Simone de Beauvoir, *The Second Sex*, trans. H. M. Parshley (New York: Vintage Books, 1974); Frantz Fanon, *Black Skins, White Masks*, trans. Charles Lam Markmann (New York: Grove Press, 1967).

63. Beauvoir, *The Second Sex*, xxvii.

64. Fanon's later books are *A Dying Colonialism (L'An V de la révolution algérienne)*, trans. Haakon Chevalier (New York: Grove Press, 1965), whose chapter on Algeria's European minority first appeared in *Les Temps modernes* 159–60 (May–June 1959), and *The Wretched of the Earth*, preface by Jean-Paul Sartre, trans. Constance Farrington (New York: Grove Press, 1968), whose chapter on violence first appeared in *Les Temps modernes* 181 (May 1961).

65. Barthes, "Myth Today," 126 n. 7, 133 n. 11, 136, 152.

66. Roland Barthes, "Change the Object Itself: Mythology Today" [1971], in *Image—Music—Text*, trans. Stephen Heath (New York: Hill and Wang, 1977), 165–69.

67. "Dr. Lacan" had appeared in the footnotes of *The Second Sex* as well as in those of *Black Skins, White Masks*. In her discussion of childhood, Beauvoir notes the significance of "the mirror stage" for the ego, which "retains the ambiguous aspect of a spectacle" (303). Fanon asserts that Lacan's concept establishes that "the real Other for the white man is and will continue to be the black man" (*Black Skin, White Masks*, 114). Here is a glimpse of the conflict between feminism and postcolonialism that will emerge, as well as of the leading role that psychoanalysis will assume in defining the Other. Sartre and Beauvoir first met Fanon in Rome in 1961, the year of his death, although *Les Temps modernes* had previously published his work. See Simone de Beauvoir, *The Force of Circumstance*, trans. Richard Howard (New York: G. P. Putnam's Sons, 1964), 583, 595–97, 606–7;

Annie Cohen-Solal, *Sartre: A Life*, trans. Anna Cancogni, ed. Norman Macafee (New York: Pantheon Books, 1987), 404, 431–35.

68. The phenomenological Other is radically incompatible with the proposition of split subjectivity and linguistic drift. This incompatibility is implied in all of Homi K. Bhabha's references to Fanon and in his attempt to reorient the latter's existential Other in a Lacanian framework. See especially "The Other Question: The Stereotype and Colonial Discourse," *Screen* 24, no. 6 (November–December 1983): 18–36. For reservations about this use of Fanon's writing, see Benita Parry, "Problems in Current Theories of Colonial Discourse," *Oxford Literary Review* 9, nos. 1–2 (1987): 27–58.

69. "Utopia is an impossible luxury for [the mythologist]: he greatly doubts that tomorrow's truths will be the exact reverse of today's lies." Barthes, "Myth Today," 157.

# 3 | POWER

# 9 | Orientalist Counterpoints and Postcolonial Politics

*Caste, Community, and Culture in Tamil India*

NICHOLAS B. DIRKS

If under colonialism caste became the foundational basis of Indian society, it became so in part as a form of civil society that could be used both to explain how Indian civilization survived its history of despotisms and political failures and to justify British colonial rule. Even as caste became the central trope for India, it was made into a unitary social form that could be recognized as fundamentally religious rather than political, as not only autonomous from but opposed to the "state."[1] When H. H. Risley—writing in 1909 just after the *swadeshi* movement had introduced the possibility of mass agitational politics as well as the specter of communal violence in Bengal—contemplated the political implications of the caste system, he was clear that caste opposed nationality and would hinder the growth of nationalist politics.[2]

Now that colonial history has metamorphosed into postcolonial politics, caste has become central to new forms of contradiction, reworking colonial legacies with new difficulties and dangers. Caste continues to be seen as one of the major impediments to modernity even as it is thought by many to survive as the sedimented marker of traditional forms of privilege, oppression, and exclusion. The debate over the report of the Mandal Commission, which recommended a dramatic increase in quotas for government employment and university admission to backward castes, and its intended uses by V. P. Singh highlighted some of the contradictions in the contemporary politics of caste, creating conditions that made it possible for proponents of Hindutva to assert that a newly defined notion of Hinduism might be less divisive than caste as a focus for national politics. Some have accordingly tried to turn caste into a symbol of traditional decadence, to be replaced by other forms of tradition—chief among which seem now to be the equation of Hindu-ness with Indian nationality and the celebration of Hinduism's extraordinary history of tolerance and incorporation—that will counter the contestatory use of caste by new political parties and movements seeking to redress the traditional domination of upper-caste groups.[3]

If contemporary political discourse seems at times to echo many of the key features of colonial sociology and history, it is important to recognize that any attempt today to simply wish caste away inevitably finds itself in possible ideological alliance with forces of communalism that appear to make the myriad problems of caste a political ruse. Similarly, attempts to argue that caste, when harnessed to the discursive power of affirmative action policies, will become simultaneously stronger and more "colonial" often end up working against a variety of progressive impulses toward social legislation, even if those impulses on some occasions become affiliated to populist politics of uncertain political pedigree. Through the maze of these now highly politicized debates, anthropology, and the allied study of the history of colonial sociology and social transformation, is now cast well outside the academy, for it must address the politics of the study of caste, even as it attempts to evaluate the history and politics of caste itself.

When turning our attention to the cultural politics of southern India, the possible alliance of discourses about caste with the terrifying proliferation of communalist sentiment, politics, and violence may seem less immediately dangerous than it does in most other parts of India. However, even as communal political sentiment becomes increasingly prevalent in southern India, there are evident dangers when the voices of progressive politics seem—to many observers from outside the specific world of Tamil political discourse—to be preoccupied with caste alone. Can a colonial and postcolonial preoccupation with caste provide adequate grounds for an emancipatory politics not just in southern India, but in the larger and more complex Indian nation today (and conversely, does not the preoccupation with caste end up playing right into the hands of the Hindu Right)?

The problematic relationship between postcolonial politics and orientalist forms of knowledge also raises another set of questions about the political uses of history. For it is now widely accepted that the general conviction underlying much Dravidian radicalism—that the subjection of non-Brahman Dravidian peoples and cultures was based in the Aryan conquest of the

Dravidian south—was in large part an invention of evangelical Christian missionaries, in particular Robert Caldwell.[4] Caldwell, who labored for fifty years in the Tinnevelly Mission, struggled against the hold of Brahmanic orthodoxy and caste consciousness, and like most other missionaries who had to justify the fact that they could report conversions of only the very lowest caste groups, was especially resentful of the role of Brahmans in frustrating his efforts to proselytize.[5] Caldwell developed a theory of cultural hegemony that was predicated on the ascription of foreignness, difference, and domination onto Brahmans, who were affiliated with Aryan languages rather than Dravidian, northern India rather than southern, Brahmanic preoccupations with caste purity and ritual process rather than Dravidian receptiveness to devotional religion, and ultimately with racial attributions that, for the late nineteenth century, made the ultimate argument about difference. Much current scholarship—from nationalist history to general anthropology—continues to accept Caldwell's philological sociology of southern India, asserting that Brahmans and non-Brahmans occupied fundamentally different cultural spheres, and that the roots of the anti-Brahman movement can be found in the social facts of south Indian adherence, in the absence of extensive Islamic influence, to primordial forms of Hindu hierarchy and social structure.

In the context of our own interrogation of the history of orientalism, as well as our attempt to rethink the possibilities for history writing and ethnographic representation in a scholarly world that has been transformed by the critiques of and repercussions around Edward Said's work, we face other perplexing questions. We are now clear that orientalism did the work of colonial power in constituting a world of colonizers and colonized, conquerors and conquered, and civilizations ascendant and civilizations lost, and in naturalizing the terms, categories, and assumptions of colonial rule. We are also now more aware than ever of the implication not only of our own scholarship, but of the brute realities we take as the objects of our knowledge in the world colonialism has made. We acknowledge that colonialism has bequeathed legacies as diverse as the domestic English novel and the disarticulated organization of the international garment industry. But so deep is this history of implication, so pervasive its effects, that we still struggle when we attempt to break down the monolith of colonial power, even as we are unsure how to voice the myriad ambivalences in colonial discourse that render the politics of critique both highly specific and historically problematic. In this essay, I explore a rupture in the history of colonialism around the serious tensions between official colonial and missionary discourses and interventions; I follow these tensions through what becomes a troubling postcolonial question: How does a postcolonial critic respond when a colonial tradition of learning and critique has been appropriated and celebrated within the only slightly modified terms of a colonized discourse?

There is an attendant tension in tracing the genealogies of Tamil social discourses to Caldwell in particular and missionary interventions in southern India more generally. Caldwell's antipathy to Brahmans, both to their social domination and their cultural hegemony, has secured a hallowed place in the citational structures and justificatory rhetorics of anti-Brahmanism up to the present day. At least two conspicuous features of Caldwell's discourse, however, have been dropped. First, Caldwell's dislike of Brahmans was directly connected to his concern that Brahmans not only resisted conversion to Christianity but exerted their considerable influence to prevent lower social strata from doing so as well; Brahmans, in other words, were the principal enemy of the Church in India. Second, raising a different kind of concern, Caldwell's rhetorical condemnation of Brahmans was part of a larger critique of caste altogether. Caldwell, and indeed the entire missionary movement in southern India in the mid- to late nineteenth century, wrote against the iniquity of caste, frequently charging that until caste was abolished there would be no hope for either Christian conversion or social progress. While this condemnation of caste was in large part a condemnation of Indian society that participated in more general orientalist critiques of Indian society (though many other orientalists, particularly in the late eighteenth and early nineteenth centuries, applauded caste as a wonderful invention for social order and organic solidarity), it frequently anticipated the kinds of radical critiques of caste that have been aligned to the most progressive movements in south Indian politics. As we shall survey in this essay, one of the major breaks in the Dravidian movement surrounded E. V. Ramaswamy Naicker's concern to obliterate caste altogether, encouraging his followers, as a century before European missionaries had encouraged theirs, to engage in intercaste marriages and eschew all reference to caste in their everyday dealings with issues of ritual, devotion, marriage, commensality, and residence.

One more worry at the outset. The conviction of primordiality, the sense that there are some fundamental institutions and beliefs that are simultaneously (as it were) premodern and transcendent of historical process and origins, is perhaps one of the most basic signs of modernity. But the kind of historical unmasking we engage in to justify our new historicist critiques of colonialism rarely works to reshape political and phenomenological commitments. Indeed, historical critique is often taken to undermine the use of historical charters and justifications for progressive political movements. Even more troubling, perhaps, is the recognition that one form of unmasking can be seen in other contexts as simply a different form of masking. What I seek to understand in this essay, in part through tracing historical genealogies, in part by excavating contemporary cultural politics and discursive formations, is the way in which caste has been strengthened and reshaped in southern India. In particular, caste now refers to macro-categories of social classification, especially around the distinction between Brahmans and non-Brahmans, in ways that can both be explained by historical process and be seen to shape the force of politics and history itself. But to attend to the historicity of caste, and to assert, as I do, that caste identities and antipathies have been dramatically transformed by colonial rule and modern history, brings with it the likelihood that in one or more of the contexts in which we write, this assertion will be understood as an apology for privilege.

### Philological Politics, Missionary Colonialism, and Tamil Cultural Discourses

The emergence of Tamil identity as non-Aryan and non-Brahman was, like so many other natural assumptions in Indian society, shaped under colonial rule and through colonial processes. But if the complex historical character of this process reflects the colonial instantiation of caste thinking more generally, the regnant Tamil categories seem to have a much clearer and more direct colonial origin. It is commonly believed that the categories of "Brahman" and "non-Brahman" were first constituted as racial and philological in the mid-nineteenth century by the Scottish missionary, the Reverend Robert Caldwell, using the denominations of Aryan and Dravidian.

When Caldwell first arrived in southern India, he found "the native converts sneered at by the governing race as 'rice Christians'; and disdained by the Brahmans and educated Hindus as a new low-caste, begotten of ignorance and hunger."[6] Robert Caldwell first went to India in 1838 as a nonconformist missionary, but after a few years switched allegiances to the Church of England, working for the Anglican Society for the Propagation of the Gospel, toward the end of his life becoming a bishop. Throughout his career he wrote yearly reports to the Mission Board back home, listing, as was common practice, the harvest in souls for each year, the ultimate index of missionary success. In the balance ledgers of salvation, the numbers not only remained frustratingly small and limited to specific areas, but reflected the overwhelming fact that for the most part only lower-caste Nadars and even lower "untouchables" converted to Christianity in any systematic way. Caldwell thought and wrote extensively about the question of conversion, defending the Church against critics who maintained, first, that conversion by the poor and downtrodden was motivated only by material interests and was as a consequence inauthentic and, second, that the failure to convert Brahmans rendered the missionary enterprise an absolute failure.

Caldwell admitted that the lower castes initially came to Christianity for protection and material help: "the natural outcome of the circumstances in which they are placed." He wrote, "I cannot imagine any person who has lived and worked amongst uneducated heathens in the rural districts believing them to be influenced by high motives in anything they do. If they place themselves under Christian instructions, the motive power is not theirs, but ours. . . . They will learn what good motives mean, I trust, in time—and perhaps high motives too—if they remain long enough under Christian teaching and discipline; but till they discard heathenism, with its debasing idolatries and superstitions, and place themselves under the wings of the Church, there is not the slightest chance, as it appears to me, of their motives becoming better than they are."[7] But Caldwell used this assertion to predicate a more general theory of conversion, in which he held that conversion was more than the acceptance of a new religion; it was the more radical inculcation of new possibilities and predispositions, a readiness for new beliefs as well as new forms of knowledge and morality. The Church, like Christ, would take whoever would come, for whatever reason, and then endow them with the means and the conditions for a new kind of life. Caldwell accepted that the task would be easier when more educated natives became converts to Christianity, and he resented the general antipathy and resistance of the higher classes. But he also developed a serious appreciation of the relation of knowledge and power, as well as of the ways in which cultural hegemony produced the terms on which knowledge and power would meet in colonial India.

When Caldwell died in 1891, he was recognized not only for his extraordinary success in building up the Tinnevelly Mission enterprise, but also for his impressive scholarly writing, including ethnographic work on certain caste groups in the south, a detailed history of southern India, and a pathbreaking philological work on the history and structure of Dravidian languages. Caldwell's first major publication was an ethnographic work on the toddy tapper caste of Shanars who lived in the southern portion of the Tamil country and became one of the principal foci of Caldwell's proselytizing efforts.[8] The book provoked a largely negative reaction from the educated members of the Shanar caste, who were upset in particular with Caldwell's assertion that the Shanars were non-Aryan.

Caldwell had argued that one of the principal reasons for the large number of Shanar converts to Christianity was that they were not under the sway of Brahmanical religion, an argument he felt was supported by claiming the authentic and autonomous racial identity of Shanars as original Dravidians. He had written that some among the wealthier Shanars imitated the Brahmanical ideas and rites held by the "higher classes of the Tamil people," but argued that for the most part "their connexion with the Brahmanical systems of dogmas and observances, commonly described in the mass as Hinduism, is so small that they may be considered votaries of a different religion."[9] He went on to anticipate the theory of Sanskritization, though in a far more critical light than M. N. Srinivas years later: "It may be true that the Brahmans have reserved a place in their Pantheon, or Pandemonium, for local deities and even for aboriginal demons; but in this the policy of conquerors is exemplified, rather than the discrimination of philosophers, or the exclusiveness of honest believers."[10] Indeed, Caldwell used this recognition to assert the fundamental autonomy of Shanar identity through religious practice, racial origin, as well as philological affiliation. He betrayed the usual missionary contempt for "native" religion, writing that "the extent and universal prevalence of their depravity are without a parallel. Where else shall we find such indelicacy of feeling, and systematic licentiousness."[11] But he saved his sharpest criticism for Brahmans and Brahmanism, arguing that the cultural elite of Hindu India was much more responsible for their depravity than the lower classes precisely because of their entitlement and education. He was therefore taken by surprise when these same Shanars whom he sought to defend and convert reacted with such vehemence that he was forced to withdraw his book from publication after a series of riots against it took place.

Nevertheless, Caldwell did not abandon his central thesis, instead generalizing it to apply to all Tamil non-Brahmans. In his *Comparative Grammar of the Dravidian or South-Indian Family of Languages*, first published in 1856, Caldwell predicated many of his earlier assertions on far more systematically presented historical and linguistic arguments. He had already suggested some of his fundamental philological convictions in the book on Shanars, in particular when he noted, "Every word in the Tamil language which denotes an image is of Sanscrit origin, and, as such, must have been introduced, with the worship of images, by the Brahmans." But now he extended this argument, proclaiming in his extraordinarily learned grammatical treatise not only the antiquity and autonomy of Dravidian culture, but that the language Tamil, the "most highly cultivated *ab intra* of all Dravidian idioms, can dispense with its Sanskrit, if need be, and not only stand alone, but flourish, without its aid." He further held that Brahmans had brought Sanskrit with them when they moved from the north to the south, along with a strain of Hinduism that emphasized idol worship. As he wrote, "Through the predominant influence of the religion of the Brahmans, the majority of the words expressive of religious ideas in actual use in modern Tamil are of Sanskrit origin."[12] Once again, the concerns of the missionary perhaps are nowhere more obvious than in this condemnation of Brahmanic religious influence, for in claiming the independence of the Tamils, he seemed also to claim their souls for Christian conversion.

Caldwell now clothed in impressive philological form his determination to prove the essential autonomy of Dravidian culture, language, and racial stock from the colonizing duplicity of Aryan Brahmans. He wrote that the Dravidians had occupied the southern portion of the Indian subcontinent sometime before the Aryan invasion. It was only well after the invasion that they were subdued by the Aryans, "not as conquerors, but as colonists and instructors." As he wrote, "The introduction of the Dravidians within the pale of Hinduism appears to have originated, not in conquest, but in the peaceable process of colonisation and progressive civilization. . . . All existing traditions . . . tend to show that the Brahmans acquired their ascendancy by their intelligence and their administrative skill." Caldwell further argued that "the Brahmans, who came in 'peaceably, and obtained the kingdom by flatteries,' may probably have persuaded the Dravidians that in calling them Shudras [members of the lowest of the four main castes] they were conferring upon them a title of honour."[13] But in fact, he continued, the Brahmans, as representatives of the Aryan race, made the Dravidian groups accept the appellation of what in the north was reserved for the servile castes. Dravidians had even, Caldwell maintained, accepted the falsehood that Tamil was inferior to and dependent on Sanskrit, the language of the Aryan race and of Brahmans in particular.

Caldwell's argument was made through a combination of historical speculation and philological conjecture. In particular, he correlated the autonomous survival of Tamil with his estimate of the limited number of Aryan colonists who actually settled in the south:

> If we should suppose that the Aryan immigration to Southern India consisted, not of large masses of people, but of small isolated parties of adventurers, like that which is said to have colonised Ceylon; if we should suppose that the immigrants consisted chiefly of a few younger sons of Aryan princes, attended by small bodies of armed followers and a few Brahman priests—the result would probably be that a certain number of words connected with government, with religion, and with the higher learning, would be introduced into the Dravidian languages, and that the literary life of these languages would then commence, or at least would then receive a new development, whilst the entire structure of their grammar and the bulk of their vocabulary would remain unchanged.[14]

Caldwell wrote that this was indeed the case, and that therefore it seemed reasonable to conclude that the Dravidians could throw off the shackles of the colonists. Here he articulated his extraordinary recognition of how conquest and colonization could work through a subtle combination of flattery and intimidation. He also used his theories of history and language to disparage the position of Brahmans in south Indian society, directly challenging their cultural hegemony.

Caldwell's dislike of Brahmans was matched by his dislike of caste, a sentiment that he shared with almost all the Protestant missionaries who worked in southern India in the nineteenth century. J. M. Lechler, writing from Salem in 1857, expressed a common conviction when he noted, "The greatest enemy that opposes itself to us and the gospel is that absurdity of absurdity and yet most clever masterpiece of Satan—Caste."[15] W. B. Addis, writing in 1854, noted his conviction that "idolatry will disappear from India before the system of Caste from its inhabitants."[16] Every missionary had hundreds of examples where the appearance of conversion was sustained until caste intervened: "Caste is an evil that sometimes lies a long time dormant, but revives when the individual comes in constant contact with it, or family, or other circumstances conduce to such an effect."[17] Caste was consistently seen as the primary enemy of conversion.

Caldwell's generalized antipathy to caste, however, has been received in Dravidianist ideologies principally in relation to the general critique of Brahmans, not as applying to caste divisions among non-Brahmans. Indeed, the critique of Brahmans has developed another kind of assumption in Caldwell's writing altogether, namely, that Brahmans and non-Brahmans were of different racial stock, that Dravidians were neither Indo-Aryans nor the original inhabitants of the subcontinent. Caldwell's articulation of the racial and historical basis of the Aryan-Dravidian divide was in fact perhaps the first European valorization of the Dravidian category cast specifically in racial terms, though he admitted the likelihood of considerable racial intermixture. At the same time, Caldwell was merely modifying conventional wisdom in his uncritical acceptance of an Aryan theory of race, in which Dravidians were seen as pre-Aryan inhabitants of India.

The Aryan theory of race, based as it was on William Jones's well-known "discovery" of the Indo-Aryan family of languages, had been developed by German comparative philologists in the 1840s and 1850s, and maintained that the speakers of Indo-European languages in India, Persia, and Europe were of the same culture and race.[18] While most Western writers on this subject ignored the racial equality this theory afforded Asian subjects of British colonial rule, Max Müller praised this common descent, though he lamented the demise of Indian civilizational genius in the medieval period. A number of Indian intellectuals used both Müller's praise and the general theory to claim equality and unity between Britons and Indians. Chief among these in the nineteenth century were Debendranath Tagore and Keshab Chandra Sen. Later nationalist leaders used "Aryan" less as a racial term than as a gloss for ancient Indian religious tradition. Dayananda Saraswati, Vivekananda, Ranade, and Annie Besant all urged in one way or another that the Aryan faith, which had united the north and the south in ancient times, be used once more to bring India together.

But in the Tamil country the theories of Aryanism, whether they linked or separated language and race, worked in most cases to do precisely the opposite. Frequently, British writers used the Aryan theory to justify a view of Dravidians as markedly inferior to Aryans. In the 1860s and 1870s Henry Maine and Meadows Taylor emphasized the barbarity and superstition of the early Dravidans, who "had infected ancient Hindu society and destroyed its pure Aryan features."[19] James Fergusson and R. H. Patterson took this argument one step further, arguing (in anticipation of Risley) that the caste system with its inbuilt racial suspicion and endogamous taboos made upper-caste Hindus more ambitious and progressive than they otherwise might have been, discouraging as it did intermarriage between Aryans and non-Aryans. Small wonder then that Caldwell's grammatical writings were particularly influential, given that they were written in a spirit of praise and respect both for the language Tamil and for the cultural inheritance of the south. But Caldwell's influence has had an extraordinary career in Madras, exceeding in many ways the influence of any other European ideological formulation in the history of British colonial knowledge on the subcontinent. Partly this was because of the emphasis on language, which subsequently became appropriated and inscribed in the deification of Tamil around the cult of the Tamil mother goddess.[20] But partly this was because, as I suggested earlier, Caldwell was the first to argue the dynamics and mechanisms of cultural imperialism, the operations of cultural hegemony itself.

Caldwell's historical and philological praise for Dravidian—read non-Brahman—culture in the south went against the grain of most orientalist assumption, even though it was by no means the only British expression of prejudice against Brahmans. This prejudice frequently grew out of the concern of certain British officials to dislodge the disproportionate reliance on Brahmans and "Brahmanical culture" in political, legal, as well as cultural domains (also reflecting some of the internal struggles for influence among orientalists distributed throughout areas and language competencies across the subcontinent). Burnell, Brown, and Ellis were all important nineteenth-century orientalists who were critical of Brahmanical domination in social and literary arenas as well as in the practice of Hindu law. The most vocal opposition to Brahmanic law was heard from one J. H. Nelson, an English judge and civil servant who failed to reach the Madras High Court at least in part because of his strenuous orientalist exertions and in particular because of his vigorous condemnation of Brahmanic influence. Nelson's central argument is summarized by Derrett: "A fantastic situation had developed in which the law of certain Sanskrit law books was being applied, as if it were their law and custom, to millions of people who had never been governed by any of their contents before, who were not in sympathy with their terror, and who were entitled to have their own customs applied to them."[21] Nelson saw the effect of British rule as not only reifying Brahmanic law in a general sense but also extending it to sectors of society that were totally unfamiliar with it.

Perhaps the strongest critique of Aryan influence came in an address delivered to the graduates of the University of Madras in 1886, when the governor of Madras, Mountstuart Elphinstone Grant-Duff, singled out the non-Brahman graduates—who made up only a quarter of the class—by saying, "You are of pure Dravidian race; I should like to see the pre-Sanskrit element amongst you asserting itself rather more." He went on, "The constant putting forward of Sanskrit literature as if it were pre-eminently Indian, should stir the national pride of some of you Tamil, Telugu, Cannarese. You have less to do with Sanskrit than we English have. Ruffianly Europeans have sometimes been known to speak of natives of India as 'Niggers,' but they did not, like the proud speakers or writers of Sanskrit, speak of the people of the South as legions of monkeys. It was these Sanskrit speakers, not Europeans, who lumped up the Southern races as Rakshusas—demons. It was they who deliberately grounded all social distinctions on *Varna*, Colour."[22]

Here Grant-Duff went well beyond Caldwell and Nelson, suggesting, for example (as Caldwell specifically did not), that the Sanskrit epic *The Ramayana* designated Dravidians as the race of demons who abducted Rama's chaste wife Sita, a theme picked up vigorously by E. V. Ramaswamy Naicker in later years. The deployment of racial epithets, and the specific comparison of Brahmans to colonial Britons, anticipates all too clearly the language of anti-Brahmanism as it developed in twentieth-century Tamil politics, as also the use by the British of the counterdemon Brahman to displace nationalist political sentiment into communalist ideology.

Nevertheless, not all British writers, even those who identified with the south, allied themselves so directly with the anti-Brahman cause, and residual prejudices about the inferiority of Dravidian culture continued to inform most official understandings of Tamil popular culture, social structure, and political aspiration. Colonial writings about Tamil religion invoked perhaps the most extreme version of racial and cultural division between Aryan and Dravidian traditions. W. T. Elmore, for example, in his *Dravidian Gods in Modern Hinduism*, wrote that Dravidian religion was connected with no literary tradition and no philosophical corpus: "The Dravidians are not a literary people, and their religion has no literature. There are no Vedas or other writings telling of their gods. Their history is contained in the somewhat confused legends recited by wandering singers who attend the festivals and assist in the worship." And Elmore goes rather further, asserting, "Comparing them with the ceremonies of Hinduism, [one] is inclined to feel that the Dravidian rites represent the very acme of immoral heathenism, while those of Brahmanic Hinduism have something of refinement and charm."[23] Such views can be found over and over again in official opinion commenting on such "pre-Aryan" and "Dravidian" rites as hookswinging, firewalking, and vow-taking associated with goddess cults. The anthropology of Edgar Thurston inscribed official opinion into anthropological wisdom; his *Ethnographic Notes on Southern India* drew material directly out of official debates about such matters as the possible suppression of barbarous rituals.[24] Thurston neglected to mention that the process of constructing colonial interpretations of popular cultural practices was the result of a complex negotiation between British concerns to regulate local cultural life and official policy not to interfere in "native religious practice." The negotiation was conducted through an official reliance on Brahmanic opinion and advice, solicited through the development of a discourse on values and civilization that built on the escalating interdependency of British and Brahman sensibilities about governmental responsibility and, more generally, the moral authority of the governing classes. In these long conversations, part of the production of new orthodoxies about the nature of Hinduism, the hegemony of Brahmans in a wide variety of everyday matters of life, and the shared values of secular Brahmans and enlightened colonials (in which, for example, the Theosophical society, or movement, in Madras played an incalculably important role), Tamil was ignored, and Dravidianism was reified, denigrated, and relegated to the place of illiterate superstition and native, non-Brahmanic popular culture.

During the late nineteenth and early twentieth centuries, an assumption of racial difference—of absolute racial difference between Aryan and Dravidian—was grafted onto this discursive fabric of cultural assumption and civilizational prejudice. Elmore, whose book on Dravidian religion in fact documents a wide variety of syncretic religious customs and traditions, anchors his historical argument on racial assumption: he begins his analysis of religion by pointing out that "when the Aryan invaders came to India they found another race in possession of the land—a race which they gradually subjugated, and to some extent assimilated. In South India, the Aryans are now represented almost exclusively by the Brahmans."[25]

The denigration of Dravidian religion—and the fact that such denigration tended naturally to tarnish a wide range of assumption about Dravidian culture, philosophy, and literature—provoked a number of reactions, reactions that frequently grew directly out of, even as they were in specific opposition to, the discursive formation of a dominant Aryan/Brahmanical civilizational complex in the Indian subcontinent. Indeed, neo-Saivism, a general intellectual and religious movement in the late nineteenth and twentieth centuries that reconstituted Saivism as the pre-Aryan religion of the south, cannot be understood apart from the history of Aryanism itself. Without in any way detracting from the impressive originality of the neo-Saivite movement, it is impossible to understand the movement in isolation from a recognition of the extraordinary strength and power of the British and Indian orientalist formations that made Brahmans, Sanskrit, Vedic sacrifice and Upanisadic speculation, Aryans and Aryanism synonymous with the privileged sphere of India's own civilizational genius and accomplishment.

The Dravidian renaissance entailed a multitude of intellectual, religious, cultural, and political activities from the late nineteenth century on. While Caldwell made philology a privileged domain for scholarly investigations into the glories, and autonomous history, of Tamil, U. V. Swaminatha Iyer's "discovery" of Sangam poetic texts gave the Tamil country a classical literature of its own that could claim the antiquity, the density, and the poesy of any great classical civilization. Characteristically, the most dramatic activities in the "Dravidianist" movement found issues of language, and specifically Tamil, at their core. Sumathi Ramaswamy has recently argued that the importance of the Tamil language, and language politics more generally, to the history of Tamil cultural nationalism hinged on the capacity of language to be central to a wide variety of cultural and political movements, at the same time that language could be used to unite a wide variety of potentially divisive identities and groupings. But, for reasons not difficult to discern both from the above account and the political issues at stake in cultural mobilization, the salience of Tamil also fed into the steady marginalization of Brahmans, and Aryanism more generally, from the core features of the Dravidian renaissance and its associated political movements. Ramaswamy has argued that despite the important role of Brahmans in the Dravidian movement and the rapprochement between certain areas of nationalist activity in the south and the key preoccupations of Dravidianism, Brahmans became increasingly inscribed as the internal other, foreigners who had oppressed and exploited the native population. In short, language politics could have been conducted without reference to caste politics, as occurred in other parts of India, but in part due to the narrative told above the two seemed linked almost from the start in the Tamil south.

### Nationalism and Tamil Cultural Politics

The nationalist movement directly spawned the most outspoken and dramatic critic of Brahmanism in the person of E. V. Ramaswamy Naicker. Naicker first achieved prominence in the movement when he led a *satyagraha* campaign in 1924 to secure the admission of untouchables into temples in Vaikom, in the old Travancore Princely State. Although Naicker seemed well on his way to becoming Gandhi's principal ally in the south Indian movement, he soon became disillusioned by what he felt were Brahmanic double standards. The immediate issues that led to his resignation from Congress in 1927 were the separate dining of Brahmans in a Congress-sponsored school, Congress's resistance to communal representation, and Gandhi's ideological adherence to the principles of *varnasharmadharma*, which seemed to Naicker to perpetuate, rather than, as Gandhi maintained, transform caste. Naicker went on to establish the Self-Respect Movement—a social reform association that stressed intercaste marriages, Brahman-free rituals, the uplift of women, and the philosophy of rationalism—and later the Dravidian Association (Dravida Karakam), the political movement that ultimately led to the founding of the offshoot political party, the Dravida Munnetra Karakam (DMK).

While organizing and popularizing the Self-Respect Movement, Naicker developed a sophisticated critique of Brahmanism in which he held that the basic ideas of Hinduism were unknown to the ancient Tamils. He used arguments drawn from Caldwell and other scholars, many European, to demonstrate that the names of Hindu gods and the terms of religious belief were Aryan and therefore foreign, and he expanded Caldwell's theory of cultural hegemony to suggest a comprehensive and deliberate use of caste and ritual by Brahman immigrants to subdue Dravidian warriors, merchants, and peasants. U. V. Swaminatha Aiyer's textual discoveries of early Tamil "Sangam" poetry were combined with the writings of missionary orientalists keen to show the racial and religious autonomy of southern India to buttress what became the most sustained and provocative of polemics in the history of Tamil political discourse. In one of his diatribes against religion, ironically inscribing Caldwell as a rationalist ancestor, he wrote, "The Self-Respecters contended that the Vellalas' eyes were partially opened to their cultural grandeur by the English Missionary Dr. Robert Caldwell, but still they remained under the spell of Smartaism, which could only be dispelled by the magic wand of the Self-Respect movement."[26] Perhaps one of Naicker's most exquisite polemics came in his retelling of the epic *Ramayana*, when he simultaneously echoed what was, by the late nineteenth century, growing British contempt for Brahmans and the products of Indian civilization, and transformed the epic into a story that acclaimed Ravana as the hero of the Dravidians who cruelly fell victim to the machinations of the Aryan invaders. But the Self-Respect Movement under Naicker also campaigned consistently against caste, arguing that the government should withdraw all subsidies for religious institutions and personnel, and advocate through legislation the creation of a genuinely caste-less society. While Naicker established new rituals and protocols for intercaste marriage, often repeating and updating reforms first introduced by Christian missionaries a century before, he also developed his philosophy of "rationalism." Translating and printing the works of Robert Ingersoll, Charles Bradlaugh, and Bertrand Russell through his Madras newspapers, Naicker turned his polemical target against Christianity, ridiculing the teachings of Christ and questioning the morality of Catholic priests.

Naicker echoed Caldwell in his concentration on the issue of language, which became a marker both for history and for race. Naicker had been a critical voice against the call, from Gandhi and other Congress voices, to install Hindi as the national language of India, but when this became official Congress policy with the establishment of the Congress Ministries of 1937, he began agitation on a much larger scale, borrowing again all the techniques and strategies of mass political mobilization introduced by Gandhi in the first place. Agitation around the imposition of Hindi, and the presumed discrimination against both the Tamil language and the Tamil people, led to the formation of the Dravidian Association in 1944, which became the base for Naicker's political and social movements for the rest of his life, despite the fact that he ultimately felt that language politics only distracted from the central salience of caste.

Naicker is perhaps best remembered for leading processions to protest the role of temples and priests in south Indian society, dramatically humiliating idols and priests by beating them with his slippers. In retrospect, his early enthusiasm for nationalism reveals certain deep continuities in his life, despite the usual charges about his quixotic impulsiveness. His first and most conspicuous political act had been to lead a satyagraha against the exclusion of untouchables from a high-caste temple. During this early campaign, he wrote, "They argue that pollution would result if we untouchables passed through the streets leading to the temple. I ask them whether the Lord of Vaikkom or the so-called orthodox Brahmans would be polluted by the presence of untouchables. If they say that the presiding deity at the Vaikkom temple would be polluted, then that could not be God, but a mere stone fit only to wash dirty linen with."[27] The rhetoric of this statement is directly reminiscent of much earlier bhakti critiques of Brahmanic ritualism in its emphasis on the contradictions of pollution concepts. But Naicker neither followed the path of bhakti nor used the reformist language of Christian missionaries and Hindu social reformers, instead embarking on a secularist political struggle that, unlike the sometimes linked but always constitutionally oriented Justice Party, named religion itself as the chief source of oppression.

Naicker was an impressive, complex figure, a kind of Rabelaisian Tamil alter ego for Gandhi; he rivaled Gandhi in his capacity to manipulate political symbols and gestures and reviled Gandhi by proclaiming his massive and carnivorous diet, his prowess in matters physical, his interest in the world of materiality. Also like Gandhi, he wrote and spoke prolifically with a tactical and strategic sense of political engagement that to his critics often seemed riddled with contradiction. He was particularly vehement, and yet ambivalent, on the subject of Brahmans. At times he called in symbolic rhetorical terms for the expulsion of Brahmans. At other times he made clear his friendship with individual Brahmans, most conspicuously C. Rajagopalachari, and specified that his concern was not about Brahmans but Brahmanism. But throughout his political career he played with the referential borders of the two allied terms, frequently blaming all the problems in the south on the Brahman Raj. And he did not shy away from the label communalist: as he noted, "If 97 percent of the people become alive to their rights and realize the absurdity of the claims of the so-called superior caste and that is called 'communalism,' I wish that we may always have that communalism as the cardinal principle of life."[28] Naicker continued to play an important role in post-Independence Tamil politics, though from the early 1950s on, as an increasingly independent figure at odds with many of his former followers and disciples.

The rhetorical politics of the Dravidian movement depended on a number of fundamental assumptions and classificatory logics. Brahmans and Brahmanism were synonymous with Aryans and Aryanism; Aryans were northern invaders—therefore Brahmans were as well. Elaborate historical anthropologies were constructed and unleashed to support these syllogisms and to sustain the view that Dravidians once had a great non-Brahman polity and civilization that had been destroyed by Aryan conquests and Brahman hegemony. C. N. Annadurai was one of the most effective propagandists of this view. In his book *The History of Eeelam*, he wrote:

> It was by saying that India is a single country that it was possible for the Aryans to make the land from the Himalayas to Cape Comorin their happy hunting ground and to be masters in the sphere of politics, teachers in the sphere of education, priests in the sphere of religion, lords of the earth in society and in the economic sphere to be people leading a pleasant time without toiling; and consequently a situation arose in which the people belonging to other races had to toil hard as servants and workers and became physical wrecks and languished. The best way of removing this tyranny is to divide the country so that a region may be assigned to each race.[29]

Some authors were even more explicit about the racial basis of the difference. M. Annalthango, in his *Mummurthigal Unmai Teriyuma?*, wrote that "Brahmans and Tamilians are different in dress, habits, ideas, general outlook and culture and cannot be regarded as belonging to the same race; the Tamilians should admit this fearlessly and draw a separate scheme for the advancement of their race and serve the Tamil race, the Tamil language, and the Tamil State."[30] He went even further, arguing explicitly that there had been no admixture of the blood of Tamilians and Brahmans, even though they share a mother tongue. He blamed Brahmans for keeping their women from non-Brahman men, despite his claim that Brahman women are notoriously "loose."

The rhetorical passion of the Dravidian movement deployed a large range of anthropological, historical, philological, and political arguments in denouncing Brahmans, north Indians, Aryans, and the Congress Party, among others. Race was one but by no means the only predicate of the Dravidianist critique. Nevertheless, the scientific certainty that Brahmans were Aryans and that Dravidians and Aryans were racially distinct underwrote much of the anthropological politics of the movement. Race became increasingly important because as an ascendant biological idea it made the ultimate argument about difference, inscribing into political discourse metatruths of biology that blended the legitimating apparatus of Western science with Tamil beliefs about blood and being.

So powerful was the separatist argument that many Tamil Brahmans have sought to refute their difference at the risk of their own ritual and social ontologies of identity. After Caldwell, philological scholarship became the principal terrain in which arguments about Brahman identity were made, with a number of authors vigorously contesting Caldwell's view that Tamil and Sanskrit are unrelated. R. Swaminatha Aiyar, for example, argued against "the current theory which assigns a remote antiquity to the development of the Dravidian languages and regards their structure as unaffected by contact with Aryan idioms."[31] The preface, by P. N. Appusamy, averred, "His labours should help promote national integration, by showing how, over two or three millennia ago, people living in different parts of India lived in linguistic amity taking freely from neighboring languages and thereby enriching their own."[32] Historical scholarship has often concerned itself with the character of Dravidian society before the Aryan invasion, the nature of Aryan influence, the rise of a varna caste system, as well as with a set of questions surrounding whether Tamil Brahmans came from the north or were recruited and converted within the south.

The power of race was that it naturalized a variety of claims about history, society, language, and identity. Despite the diminution in the significance of certain caste categories, and the powerful critiques of caste that Naicker and the Dravida Munnetra Karakam introduced to the Tamil scene, the power of race was also that it was grafted onto a structure of caste that was strengthened by colonial contradictions rather than weakened, that succumbed neither to the anguished critiques of missionaries nor the impassioned polemic of Naicker. Partly, this was because caste became a language of resistance for these movements; more substantially, this was because caste became the principal language for talking about society. In the south Indian case, caste became particularly vulnerable to racial grafting in part because of the specific history of colonial discourses on caste. The orientalist insistence on varna as the all-India scale for caste identity made it possible on the one hand to argue that caste was exogenous, on the other to sustain the racial identification of Dravidian with Shudra and Aryan with Brahman. At the same time that Dravidianist political ideology ostensibly argued against varna as a meaningful category for the south, the Tamil deviation from the varna system strengthened caste by opening it to a form of racial thinking that persists with caste to dominate political discourse to this day.

In southern India, the postcolonial present has been complicated by the double presence of the colonial other, figured most directly, and most conspicuously, in the Brahman (and by implication and association the north Indian, the Aryan). In a history that begins with the language of Caldwell in casting the Aryan as a colonial figure, we confront a postcolonial condition with a difference. And thus both colonialism and postcolonialism move offstage, to be replaced by a colonial theater of double mimesis, in which the Brahman plays the role—not quite, but well enough at some times and for some purposes—of the British colonial ruler. Only this part is played unwittingly, or rather played in the contradictory terms of the story I have told here, for it is the traditional Brahman cast by British orientalist and missionary frustration as the civilizational sign of recalcitrance that is most at issue, and yet that is perhaps less subject to the charge of colonial mimicry than the Dravidian movement itself. At the same time the Dravidian movement must accept an uncertain relationship to the history of the national freedom struggle. It cannot be easily recuperated with the transformational hopes Partha Chatterjee holds out for postcolonial nationalism when he writes, "Much that has been suppressed in the historical creation of post-colonial nation-states, much that has been erased or glossed over when nationalist discourse has set down its own life history, bear the marks of the people-nation struggling in an inchoate, undirected and wholly unequal battle against forces that have sought to dominate it."[33] For the struggle slid between the heroic progressivism of Naicker and his perhaps much too thorough provincialization of the national struggle.

While Naicker represents the most progressive strand of political thinking in the history of the Dravidian movement, and systematically rejected the deification of Tamil and the celebration of religious identities for Tamils, his relationship to other, more pervasive tendencies within the Dravidian movement, and even his canonization now in the most progressive expressions of Dravidianist political critique, raise at least some of the contradictory issues reviewed here. Naicker emphasized social reform and was consistently critical of caste as an institution; like his adversary Gandhi he worked throughout his life for the uplift of women and untouchables. But he also developed such a commitment to regional concerns and issues that his relationship to the nationalist movement, once he formally left it, surfaced only periodically, for example in relation to his brief flirtation with Communism and the Soviet Union in the late 1930s. In the present theoretical moment, those scholars interested in understanding contemporary Tamil politics are thus confronted by some particularly disturbing questions and difficulties. The postcolonial predicament in the Tamil country is embedded as much in a counternationalist as in a nationalist genealogy. Following from this, Tamil counternationalism participates in colonial categories without the mitigating justifications captured so well by Chatterjee. At the very moment that Tamil politics looks most colonial—that is, from the standpoint of colonial history, most familiar—it also appears most alien in relation to the history of nationalism itself.

### Coda: Toward an Anthropology of Audience

The tensions of appropriation are reflected both in the myriad contradictions that inhabit the world of colonial encounter in the first instance and in the multiple readings our critical accounts of colonial discourse and orientalist history receive once we move outside the context of the American academy. Tracing the reception of various interventions we can learn much about the contradictions of orientalist knowledge, social transformation, religious fervor, political provocation, cultural critique, nationalist mobilization, and postcolonial aspiration; we also learn about the hybrid transitivity between intention and effect, mimicry and mimesis; about how certain roles are taken on only to become impossible because they can never be played well enough; how other roles are thrust on us and become entrapments that cannot be thrown off; how yet other roles become available but then, for reasons beyond our control, turn tragedy into not just farce but melodrama, or worse, parody. In other words, we are confronted with the recalcitrance and the travesty of translation.

The story of Caldwell and his grammar is, of course, centrally about translation. A grammar is a kind of metatranslation, a code book that unlocks and translates the structure of a language into universal rules, forms, and features. For the British missionaries who went to India in the nineteenth century, the project of translation was fundamental, for it was the project of bringing the Gospel to the natives, of writing the Bible in native languages, of conveying universal truth in the particularistic settings of heathenism. By possessing a language, one could possess a people. But for Caldwell, the project of possession and translation involved creating a set of historical identities that both explained the difficulty of his own translation—namely the goal of conversion—and was designed to create the conditions for a cultural liberation that would replace one hegemony with another, one form of flattery and conquest with his own. Caldwell's grammar was about the repossession and redeployment of language: the exorcism of certain Brahmanic religious possibilities and the celebration of new, philologically purified identities that could now admit the instantiation of new utopias. That Christian utopia turned into (counter)nationalist politics was yet another effect of "colonial" translation.

These questions of (mis)translation, (mis)recognition, and appropriation double back and forth until we appreciate in new, and more nuanced, ways the difficulties of writing about the identities signified by language, race, culture, history, community, and biology. Perhaps we now confront the critical enterprise at its most vulnerable point, as we see language veer out of control at the moment we engage multiple audiences. I myself have had to learn why critical histories I have written can be read in south India as an apology for Brahmanism, since I have argued on previous occasions that caste is in large part a colonial construction, and that the specter of Brahmanism—at least as it presented itself to the anti-Brahman movement of Madras—was only genuinely produced in the colonial period. A critique of one form of colonialism runs aground on the dislocation of colonial figuration and critique within the political contexts of another colonial form or effect. Furthermore, to return to where I began in this essay, I have discovered that my work on caste has been used by some fellow scholars in India to argue against the implementation of the recommendations of the Mandal Commission, on the grounds that the use of caste for establishing the categories of positive discrimination will have the pernicious—colonial—effect of further strengthening caste as institution and ideology. Now colonialism is used as the negative measure for the postcolonial, one mistranslation justifying another. These examples illustrate how the historical anthropology of caste can work at such cross-purposes across the very domains we are so deliberately attempting to transgress and transform. And they remind us powerfully of the limits of critique, the likelihood that one position of privilege can suddenly turn into a position of vulnerability, that the claim to a higher ground of politics inevitably leads us to adjacent grounds where the "political" might look altogether different. Even as we continue to politicize our study of history, we must historicize (and, for that matter, anthropologize) the category of the political itself, engaging the difficulties of talking across politics (even as politics inexorably talks across us). But how to do this? The question of audience thus is linked to the question of location in ways that yield no simple answers. Where do we write? Why do we write? And to whom? And, to name a problem that appears with special force when revising a paper written for a conference a decade ago, what happens to debates, arguments, and interventions with the passage of time?

Even if this exploration of the dangers inherent in counter- or post-orientalist scholarship raises serious issues, it also reminds us forcibly of the prescience of Edward Said's original interventions around this question, interventions that continue after thirty years to educate and astonish us. Said's work was political in the best of senses, combining a keen theoretical understanding of the politics (and political history) of scholarship and the relationship between political commitment and critical insight. That these politics continue both to animate and confound our engagement with the history of orientalism is something Said not only anticipated but understood as the necessary condition of critical scholarship itself. It is in memory of Edward Said and his enduring legacy that I publish this fragmentary reflection — more than ten years after it was originally written — on the complicated politics, and history, of orientalism and its various legacies in southern India.

## Notes

1. See my *Castes of Mind: Colonialism and the Making of Modern India* (Princeton NJ: Princeton University Press, 2001).
2. See H. H. Risley, *The People of India* (London: Thacker, 1908).
3. For an overview, see Christophe Jaffrelot, *India's Silent Revolution: The Rise of the Lower Castes in North India* (New York: Columbia University Press, 2003).
4. For a more complete history of the origins of the philological argument that Tamil was a Dravidian language, fundamentally unrelated to Sanskrit and Indo-Aryan languages, see Thomas Trautmann, "Languages and Nations," unpublished manuscript.

5. See my "The Conversion of Caste," in *Conversion to Modernity*, ed. Peter van der Veer (New York: Routledge, 1996).

6. *London Times*, obituary, October 19, 1891.

7. Quoted in *Reminiscences of Bishop Caldwell*, edited by his son-in-law, Rev. J. L. Wyatt, Missionary, S.P.G., Trichinopoly (Madras: Addison, 1894), 190, 191.

8. Robert Caldwell, *The Tinnevelly Shanars: A Sketch of their religion, and their moral condition and characteristics, as a caste; with special reference to the facilities and hindrances to the progress of Christianity amongst them* (Madras: Christian Knowledge Society's Press, 1849).

9. Caldwell, *The Tinnevelly Shanars*, 17, 13.

10. Caldwell, *The Tinnevelly Shanars*, 59. For Srinivas's influential theory of Sanskritization, see his *Social Change in Modern India* (Berkeley: University of California Press, 1966).

11. Caldwell, *The Tinnevelly Shanars*, 59.

12. Robert Caldwell, *A Comparative Grammar of the Dravidian or South-Indian Family of Languages* (London: Trabner, 1856), 49, 51.

13. Caldwell, *A Comparative Grammar*, 109, 114, 117.

14. Caldwell, *A Comparative Grammar*, 577.

15. J. M. Lechler, letter to Church Board, Salem, dated January 13, 1857, box 10, archives of the Council for World Missions, South India, housed in the Library of the School of Oriental and African Studies, London.

16. W. B. Addis, letter to Church Board, Coimbatore, dated March 31, 1854, archives of the Council for World Missions, South India.

17. W. B. Addis, letter to Church Board, Coimbatore, dated January 6, 1852, archives of the Council for World Missions, South India.

18. See Thomas Trautmann, *Aryans and British India* (Berkeley: University of California Press, 1998).

19. J. Leopold, "The Aryan Theory of Race," *Indian Economic and Social History Review* 7 (1970): 281.

20. See Sumathi Ramaswamy, *Passions of the Tongue: Language Devotion in Tamil India, 1891–1970* (Berkeley: University of California Press, 1997).

21. J. D. M Derrett, "J. H. Nelson, the Forgotten Administrator-Historian of South India," In *Historians of India, Pakistan and Ceylon*, ed. C. H. Phillips (London: Oxford University Press, 1961), 365.

22. Quoted in Eugene Irschick, *Politics and Social Conflict in South India* (Berkeley: University of California Press, 1969), 281.

23. W. T. Elmore, *Dravidian Gods in Modern Hinduism: A Study of the Local and Village Deities of Southern India* (Madras: Christian Literature Society for India, 1915), ix.

24. Edgar Thurston, *Ethnographic Notes on Southern India* (Madras: Government Press, 1906).
25. Elmore, *Dravidian Gods*, 2.
26. Quoted in E. Sa. Visswanathan, *The Political Career of E. V. Ramasami Naicker* (Madras: Ravi and Vasanth, 1998), 357. The statement was made in 1929.
27. Visswanathan, *Naicker*, 43.
28. Visswanathan, *Naicker*, 238.
29. C. N. Annadurai, *The History of Eelam* (Madras: n.p., 1953), xxi.
30. M. Annalthango, *Mummurthigal Unmai Teriyuma?* (Madras: n.p., n.d.).
31. Swaminatha Aiyar, *Dravidian Theories* (Delhi: Motilal Banarsidas, 1975), 23, originally published in 1922.
32. P. N. Appusamy, preface to R. Swaminatha Aiyar, *Dravidian Theories* (Delhi: Motilal Banarsidas, 1975).
33. Partha Chatterjee, *Nationalist Thought and the Colonial World: A Derivative Discourse* (Minneapolis: University of Minnesota Press, 1995), 170.

# 10 | Taboo Memories and Diasporic Visions

## Columbus, Palestine, and Arab Jews

ELLA SHOHAT

Dr. Solomon Schechter [Cambridge expert in Hebrew documents a century ago] agreed to look at them, but chiefly out of politeness, for he was still skeptical about the value of the "Egyptian fragments." But it so happened that he was taken completely by surprise. One of the documents immediately caught his interest, and next morning, after examining [it,] . . . he realized that he had stumbled upon a sensational discovery. . . . The discovery has so excited Schechter that he had already begun thinking of travelling to Cairo to acquire whatever remained of the documents. . . . Schechter was fortunate that Cromer [the British administrator of Egypt] himself took interest in the success of his mission. The precise details of what transpired between Schechter and British officialdom and the leaders of Cairo's Jewish community are hazy, but soon enough . . . "they granted him permissions to remove everything he wanted from the Geniza [a synagogue chamber where the community books, papers, and documents were kept for centuries], every last paper and parchment, without condition or payment." It has sometimes been suggested that Schechter succeeded so easily in his mission because the custodians of the Synagogue of Ben Ezra had no idea of the real value of the Geniza documents—a species of argument that was widely used in the nineteenth century to justify the acquisition of historical artefacts by colonial powers. . . . Considering that there had been an active and lucrative trade in Geniza documents . . . and impoverished as they were, it is hard to believe that they would willingly have parted with a treasure which was, after all, the last remaining asset left to them by their ancestors. In all likelihood the decision was taken for them by the leaders of their community,

and they were left with no alternative but acquiescence. As for those leaders . . . like the elites of so many other groups in the colonized world, they
evidently decided to seize the main chance at a time when the balance of
power—the ships and the guns—lay overwhelmingly with England. . . .
Schechter . . . filled out about thirty sacks and boxes with the materials
and with the help of the British embassy in Cairo he shipped them off
to Cambridge. A few months later he returned himself—laden . . . "with
spoils of the Egyptians."—AMITAV GHOSH, *In an Antique Land*[1]

I begin my essay with a quotation from Amitav Ghosh's remarkable account
of the emptying out of the Jewish Egyptian Geniza archive, which by the First
World War was stripped of all its documents, which were then distributed
to Europe and America, with a large part of the documents going into private collections. There is nothing unusual about such a colonial raid of the
archive—in this case a very literal archive indeed. What is unusual, however,
is the ways the two groups of coreligionists, the European Ashkenazi Jews
and Sephardic Arab Jews, fell out on opposite sides of the colonial divide.
European Jews' closeness to Western powers permitted the dispossession of
Arab Jews, even before the advent of Zionism as a national project.

In this historical episode, the culture of the Egyptian Jewish community
was partially "disappeared" through the confiscation of its most sacred documents. At the moment of the Geniza removal, two years after its "discovery"
in 1896, Egyptian Jews had been for millennia a symbiotic part of the geocultural landscape of the region. The British Jewish scholars, like their non-
Jewish compatriots, cast a similarly imperial gaze at the Egyptian Jews, the
very people who produced and sustained the Geniza for almost a thousand
years, and whose remarkable achievement these scholars were engaging in
appropriating, but who the scholars describe as "aborigines," "scoundrels,"
whose religious leaders have the "unpleasant" habit of kissing other men
"on the mouth."[2] In a traumatic turn of events, the diasporization of the
Geniza anticipated by half a century the exiling of its owners. In the wake
of the Israeli-Arab conflict, especially after the British withdrawal from Palestine, and the establishment of the state of Israel in 1948, Arabs and Jews
were newly staged as enemy identities. If Ghosh's description vividly captures a moment when Arab Jews were still seen as simply "Arabs," colonized
subjects, with the partition of Palestine, Arab Jews, in a historical shift, suddenly become simply "Jews."

The historical episode described by Ghosh and its aftermath suggest that alliances and opposition between communities not only evolve historically but also that they are narrativized differently according to the schemas and ideologies of the present. And as certain strands in a cultural fabric become taboo, this narrativization involves destroying connections that once existed. The process of constructing a national historical memory also entails the destruction of a different, prior, historical memory. The archive of the Geniza was largely written in Judeo-Arabic, a language my generation is the last to speak; since the dispersal of its people from the Arab world, Judeo-Arab culture was disdained as a sign of *galut* (diaspora)—a negative term within Euro-Israeli Zionist discourse. The European discovery and rescue of the Geniza from its producers had displaced a long tradition in which Ashkenazi Jewish religious scholars had corresponded and consulted with the Sephardi religious centers of the Judeo-Islamic world. But since the Enlightenment, Eurocentric norms of scholarship have established typically colonial relations that have taken a heavy toll on the representation of Arab Jewish history and identity. In this essay I attempt to disentangle the complexities of Arab Jewish identity by unsettling some of the borders erected by almost a century of Zionist and colonial historiography, with its fatal binarisms of civilization versus savagery, modernity versus tradition, and West versus East.

### Toward a Relational Approach to Identity

Recent postcolonial theory has at times shied away from grounding its writings in historical context and cultural specificity. While innumerable post-structuralist essays elaborate abstract versions of "difference" and "alterity," few offer a communally participatory and politicized knowledge of non-European cultures. At the same time, however, the professionalized study of compartmentalized historical periods and geographical regions (as in Middle East studies and Latin American studies) has often resulted in an overly specific focus that overlooks the interconnectedness of histories, geographies, and cultural identities. In *Unthinking Eurocentrism* Robert Stam and I argue for a relational approach to multicultural studies that does not segregate historical periods and geographical regions into neatly fenced-off areas of expertise and that does not speak of communities in isolation, but rather "in relation."[3] Rather than pit a rotating chain of resisting communities against a Western dominant (a strategy that privileges the "West," if only as constant antagonist), we argue for stressing the horizontal and vertical links threading communities and histories together in a conflictual network. Analyzing the overlapping multiplicities of identities and affiliations that link diverse resistant discourses helps us transcend some of the politically debilitating effects of disciplinary and community boundaries.

The kind of connections we have in mind operate on a number of levels. First, it is important to make connections in temporal terms. While postcolonial studies privilege the imperial era of the nineteenth and twentieth centuries, one might argue for grounding the discussion in a longer history of multiply located colonialisms and resistances, tracing the issues at least as far back as 1492. Second, we propose connections in spatial and geographical terms, placing debates about identity and representation in a broader context that embraces the Americas, Asia, and Africa. We also argue for connections in disciplinary and conceptual terms, forging links between debates usually compartmentalized (at least in the United States): on the one hand, postcolonial theory associated with issues of colonial discourse, imperial imaginary, and national narrations, and, on the other, the diverse "ethnic studies," focusing on issues of minorities, race, and multiculturalism. The point is to place the often ghettoized discourses about geographies—"here" versus "there"—and about time—"now" versus "then"—in illuminating dialogue. A relational approach, one that operates at once within, between, and beyond the nation-state framework, calls attention to the conflictual hybrid interplay of communities within and across borders.

My subtitle, "Columbus, Palestine, and Arab Jews," already juxtaposes disparate entities to underline the ways in which nation-states have imposed a coherent sense of national identity precisely because of their fragile sense of cultural, even geographical, belonging. The formation of postcolonial nation-states, especially in the wake of colonial partitions, often involved a double process of on the one hand joining diverse ethnicities and regions that had been separate under colonialism, and on the other partitioning regions in a way that forced regional redefinitions (Iraq/Kuwait) or a cross-shuffling of populations (Pakistan/India, Israel/Palestine, in relation to Palestinians and Arab Jews). Given the minority/majority battles "from within" and the war waged by border-crossers (refugees, exiles, immigrants) "from without," Eurocentric historiography has had a crucial role in handing out passports to its legitimate races, ethnicities, nations. And in the words of the Palestinian Mahmoud Darwish's well-known poem "Passport" ("Joowaz sufr"),

"ʿAr min al ism, min al intima? fi tarba rabitʾha bilyadyn?" ("Stripped of my name, my identity? On a soil I nourished with my own hands?"). The same colonial logic that dismantled Palestine had already dismantled the "Turtle Island" of the Americas. Thus, the first illegal alien, Columbus,[4] remains a celebrated discoverer, while indigenous Mexicans "infiltrate" a barbed border every day to a homeland once theirs, while Native Americans are exiled in their own land.

Here, by way of demonstration of the relational method, I will focus on Sephardic Arab Jewish (known in the Israeli context as Mizrahi) identity as it intersects with other communities and discourses in diverse contexts over time. I will take as a point of departure the 1992 quincentennial commemorations of the expulsions of Sephardic Jews from Spain to argue that any revisionist effort to articulate Arab Jewish identity in a contemporary context that has posited Arab and Jew as antonyms can only be disentangled through a series of positionings vis-à-vis diverse communities and identities (Arab Muslim, Arab Christian, Palestinian, Euro-Israeli, Euro-American Jewish, Indigenous American, African-American, Chicano/a), which would challenge the devastating consequences that the Zionist-orientalist binarism of East versus West, Arab versus Jew has had for Arab Jews (or Jewish Arabs). Linking, de-linking, and relinking, at once spatial and temporal, thus becomes part of adversary scholarship working against taboo formulations, policed identities, and censored affiliations.

### Staging the Quincentenary

"Your Highnesses completed the war against the Moors," Columbus wrote in a letter addressed to the Spanish throne, "after having chased all the Jews . . . and sent me to the said regions of India in order to convert the people there to our Holy Faith."[5] In 1492, the defeat of the Muslims and the expulsion of Sephardi Jews from Spain converged with the conquest of what came to be called the New World. But while the celebrations of Columbus's voyages have provoked lively opposition (ranging from multicultural debates about the Eurocentric notion of "discovery" to satirical performances by Native Americans landing in Europe and claiming it as their discovered continent), the Eurocentric framing of the "other 1492" has not been questioned. Apart from some enthusiastic scholastic energy dedicated to the dubious pride in whether Columbus can once and for all be claimed as a (secret) Jew, expulsion events navigated on the calm seas of Old World paradigms. Furthermore, the two separate quincentenary commemorations, both taking place in the Americas, Europe, and the Middle East, have seldom acknowledged the historical and discursive linkages between these two constellations of events. To examine the relationship between contemporary discourses about the two 1492s might therefore illuminate the role scholarly and popular narratives of history play in nation-building myths and geopolitical alliances.

The Spanish-Christian war against Muslims and Jews was politically, economically, and ideologically linked to the caravels' arrival in Hispaniola. Triumphant over the Muslims, Spain invested in the project of Columbus, whose voyages were partly financed by wealth taken from the defeated Muslims and confiscated from Jews through the Inquisition.[6] The *reconquista*'s policies of settling Christians in the newly (re)conquered areas of Spain, as well as the gradual institutionalization of expulsions, conversions, and killings of Muslims and Jews in Christian territories, prepared the grounds for similar *conquista* practices across the Atlantic. Under the marital-political union of Ferdinand (Aragon) and Isabella (Castille), victorious Christian Spain, soon to become an empire, strengthened its sense of nationhood, subjugating indigenous Americans and Africans. Discourses about Muslims and Jews during Spain's continental expansion crossed the Atlantic, arming the conquistadors with a ready-made "us versus them" ideology aimed at the regions of India, but in fact applied first toward the indigenous of the accidentally discovered continent. The colonial misrecognition inherent in the name "Indian" underlines the linked imaginaries of the East and West Indies. (Perhaps not coincidentally, Ridley Scott's film *1492: The Conquest of Paradise* [1992] has orientalist "Ali Baba"–style music accompany the encounter with Caribbean "Indians.") India awaited its colonized turn with the arrival of Vasco de Gama (1498) and the Portuguese conquest of Goa (1510). If in the fifteenth century the only European hope for conquering the East—given the Muslim domination of the continental route—was via sailing to the West, the nineteenth-century consolidation of European imperialism in the East was facilitated by Europe's previous self-aggrandizing at the expense of the Americas and Africa. Thanks to its colonization of the Americas and Africa, Europe's modernization was made possible, finally allowing the colonization of North Africa (Maghreb) and the so-called Near East (Mashreq). "The Indian Ocean trade, and the Culture that supported it," writes Amitav Ghosh, "had long since been destroyed by European navies. Transcontinental trade was no longer a shared enterprise; the merchant shipping of the high seas was now entirely controlled by the naval powers of Europe."[7]

Although Moorish Spain testifies to syncretic multiculturalism avant la lettre, the reconquista ideology of Limpieza de Sangre, as an early exercise in European "self-purification," sought to expel, or forcibly convert, Muslims and Jews. The Crusades, which inaugurated "Europe" by reconquering the Mediterranean area, catalyzed Europeans' awareness of their own geocultural identity and established the principle that wars conducted in the interests of the Holy Church were axiomatically just. The campaigns against Muslims and Jews as well as against other "agents of Satan," heretics, and witches made available a mammoth apparatus of racism and sexism for recycling in the "new" continents. Anti-Semitism and anti-infidelism provided a conceptual and disciplinary framework that, after being turned against Europe's immediate or internal others, was then projected outward against Europe's distant or external others.[8] Prince Henry ("the Navigator"), the pioneer of Portuguese exploration, had himself been a Crusader against the Moors at the battle of Ceuta. Amerigo Vespucci, writing about his voyages, similarly drew on the stock of Jewish and Muslim stereotypes to characterize the savage, the infidel, the indigenous man as a dangerous sexual omnivore and indigenous woman as possessing an alluringly yielding nature.[9] In this sense, the metonymic links between Jews and Muslims—their literal neighboring and their shared histories—are turned into metaphorical and analogical links in relation to the peoples of the Americas.[10] The point is not that there is a complete equivalence between Europe's oppressive relations with Jews and Muslims and with indigenous peoples; the point is that European Christian demonology prefigured colonialist racism. Indeed, we can even discern a partial congruency between the phantasmatic imagery projected onto the Jewish and Muslim "enemy" and onto the indigenous American and Black African "savage" all imaged to various degrees as "blood drinkers," "cannibals," "sorcerers," "devils."[11]

One of the rare contemporary representations that expose ecclesiastic participation in genocidal measures, the Mexican film *El Santo Oficio* (The Holy Office, 1973) features the attempt by the Holy See to spread the Inquisition into the New World. Although the film focuses on the Sephardi *conversos*, it also shows that they are persecuted alongside heretics, witches, and indigenous infidels. Consumed by enthusiastic spectators, their burning at the stake is performed as a public spectacle of discipline and punishment, just as lynching was sometimes consumed as a popular entertainment by some whites in the United States. Screened at a Los Angeles ceremonial opening for a conference dedicated to the quincentennial expulsion of Sephardi Jews (organized by the International Committee—Sepharad '92) *El Santo Oficio* provoked strong emotions. Its documentation of Sephardi Jewish rituals practiced in secrecy and its visual details of torture, rape, and massacre were not received, however, in the spirit of the linkages I have charted here. The audience, consisting largely of Euro-American, Jewish, and a substantially smaller number of Sephardi American educators, scholars, and community workers, was eager to consume the narrative evidence of the singular nature of the Jewish experience. To point out the links between the Inquisition, the genocide of the indigenous peoples of the Americas, and the devastation of African peoples would be tantamount to promiscuously intermingling the sacred with the profane. In the reception following the film, Chicano waiters served food. The simplistic category of "them" (Spanish Christians), however, stood in remarkably ironic relation to the indigenous faces of the waiters, their presence suggesting that the charting of Sephardi conversos' history must be negotiated in relation to other conversos' histories.

The importance of rupturing the boundaries of these histories becomes even clearer in the actual intersection of diverse histories of forced conversions in the Americas. For example, the case of Chicano and Mexican families of part Sephardic Jewish origins suggests that at times the links are quite literal. Recent research by the Southwest Jewish Archives in the United States points out that Sephardic traditions remain alive in predominantly Roman Catholic Mexican-American families, although the family members are not always conscious of the origins of the rituals. They do not understand why, for example, their grandmothers make unleavened bread called *pan senita*, or Semite bread, and why their rural grandparents in New Mexico or Texas slaughter a lamb in the spring and smear its blood on the doorway. Revealing that some Chicanos and Mexicans are the descendants of secret Jews is a taboo that results in contemporary secrecy even among those who are aware of their ancestry.[12] The issue of forced conversions in the Americas and the consequent cultural syncretism implicates and challenges Jewish as well as Catholic Euro-indigenous institutions. The hybridity of Chicano and Mexican culture, however, does not necessarily facilitate the admission of another complex hybridity, one crossing Jewish/Catholic boundaries.

If the genocide of indigenous Americans and Africans is no more than a bit of historical marginalia, the linked persecutions in Iberia of Sephardi Jews and Muslims, of conversos and Moriscos,[13] are also submerged. The quincentennial elision of the Arab Muslim part of the narrative was especially striking. During the centuries-long reconquista, not all Muslims and Jews withdrew with the Arab forces. Those Muslims who remained after the change of rule were known as *mudejars*, deriving from the Arabic *mudajjin*, "permitted to remain," with a suggestion of "tamed," "domesticated."[14] The Spanish Inquisition, institutionalized in 1478, did not pass over the Muslims. Apart from the 1492 expulsion of 3 million Muslims and three hundred thousand Sephardi Jews, in 1499 mass burnings of Islamic books and forced conversions took place, and in 1502 the Muslims of Granada were given the choice of baptism or exile. In 1525–26, Muslims of other provinces were given the same choice. In 1566 there was a revival of anti-Muslim legislation, and between 1609 and 1614 came edicts of expulsions. In other words, the same inquisitional measures taken against the Jewish conversos who were found to be secretly practicing Judaism were taken against the Moriscos found to be practicing Islam, measures culminating in edicts of expulsion addressed specifically to Muslims. As a result, many fled to North Africa, where, like Sephardi Jews, they maintained certain aspects of their Hispanicized Arab culture.

This well-documented history found little echo in the events promoted by the International Committee—Sepharad '92, whose major funds came from the United States, Spain, and Israel.[15] Spain, which has yet to come to terms with its present-day racist immigration policies toward, among others, Arab North Africans, embraced its "Golden Age" after centuries of denial, while reserving a regrettable mea culpa only for the official spokespersons of "the Jews." As for all other representatives, including conservative upper-middle-class Zionist Sephardim, the elision of comparative discussions of the Muslim and Jewish (Sephardi) situations in Christian Spain was largely rooted, I would argue, in present-day Middle Eastern politics. The 1992 commemorations entailed a serious present-day battle over the representations of "Jewish identity" in terms of an East/West axis, a battle dating back to the nineteenth-century beginnings of Zionist nationalism.

### The Trauma of Dismemberment

Zionist historiography, when it does refer to Islamic-Jewish history, consists of a morbidly selective "tracing the dots" from pogrom to pogrom. (The word "pogrom" itself derives from and is reflective of the Eastern European

Jewish experience.)[16] Subordinated to a Eurocentric historiography, most quincentenary events lamented yet another tragic episode in a homogeneous, static history of relentless persecution. Not surprisingly, the screening of *El Santo Oficio* at the Expulsion conference elicited such overheard remarks as "You think it's different today?" and "That's also what the Nazis did to us. That's what the Arabs would do if they could" (a curious claim since the Arab Muslims had a millennium-long opportunity to install an inquisition against Middle Eastern Jews—or against Christian minorities—but never did). Such common remarks underline the commemorations' role as a stage for demonstrating (Euro-)Israeli nationalism as the only possible logical answer to horrific events in the history of Jews. The Inquisition of Sephardi Jews is seen merely as a foreshadowing of the Jewish Holocaust. In this paradigm, the traumas left by Nazi genocidal practices are simplistically projected onto the experiences of Jews in Muslim countries and onto the Israeli-Palestinian conflict.[17]

My point here is not to idealize the situation of the Jews of Islam, but rather to suggest that Zionist discourse has subsumed Islamic-Jewish history into a Christian-Jewish history while also undermining comparative studies of Middle Eastern Jews in the context of diverse religious and ethnic minorities in the Middle East and North Africa. On the occasion of the quincentenary, the Zionist perspective privileged Sephardi Jewish relations with European Christianity over those with Arab Islam, projecting Eurocentric maps of Christians and Jews as West and Muslims as East and ignoring the fact that at the time of the expulsion, syncretic Jewish communities were flourishing all over the Islamic Middle East and North Africa. Quincentennial events not only rendered the interrelations between Jewish conversos and indigenous conversos invisible, but also undermined the Sephardic Jewish and Muslim cultural symbiosis. The only Muslim country that received some quincentennial attention was Turkey, partly due to Sultan Beyazid II's ordering his governors in 1492 to receive the expelled Jews cordially. But no less important is Turkey's contemporary regional alliances, its national fissured identity between East and West. Unlike Arab Muslim countries, where expelled Sephardim also settled (Morocco, Tunisia, Egypt), Turkey has not participated in the Israeli-Arab conflict, nor in the nonallied embargo that has for decades regionally isolated Israel until the recent orchestration of Arab diplomatic recognition. Yet even in the case of Turkey, the quincentennial emphasis was less on Muslim-Jewish relations than on the voyages of refuge and, anachronistically, on the Turkish (national) as opposed to Muslim (religious) shelter.

In this rewriting of history, present-day Muslim Arabs are merely one more "non-Jewish" obstacle to the Jewish Israeli national trajectory. The idea of the unique, common victimization of all Jews at all times provides a crucial underpinning of official Israeli discourse. The notion of uniqueness precludes analogies and metonymies, thus producing a selective reading of Jewish history, one that hijacks the Jews of Islam from their Judeo-Islamic geography and subordinates it to that of the European Ashkenazi shtetl. This double process entails the performance of commonalities among Jews in the public sphere so as to suggest a homogeneous national past, while silencing any deviance into a more globalized and historicized narrative that would see Jews not simply through their religious commonalities but also in relation to their contextual cultures, institutions, and practices. Given this approach, and given the Israeli-Arab conflict, no wonder that the Jews of Islam, and more specifically Arab Jews, have posed a challenge to any simplistic definition of Jewish identity and particularly of the emergent Jewish Euro-Israeli identity.

The selective readings of Middle Eastern history, in other words, make two processes apparent: the rejection of an Arab and Muslim context for Jewish institutions, identity, and history as well as their unproblematized subordination into a "universal" Jewish experience. In the Zionist "proof" of a single Jewish experience, there are no parallels or overlappings with other religious and ethnic communities, whether in terms of a Jewish hyphenated and syncretic culture or in terms of linked analogous oppressions. All Jews are defined as closer to each other than to the cultures of which they have been a part. Thus the religious Jewish aspect of diverse intricate and interwoven Jewish identities has been given primacy, a categorization tantamount to dismembering the identity of a community. Indeed, the Euro-Israeli separation of the "Jewish" part from the "Middle Eastern" part, in the case of Middle Eastern Jews, has resulted in practically dismantling the Jewish communities of the Muslim world, as well as in pressures exerted on Mizrahim (Orientals) to realign their Jewish identity according to Zionist Euro-Israeli paradigms. Since the beginnings of European Zionism, the Jews of Islam have faced, for the first time in their history, the imposed dilemma of choosing between Jewishness and Arabness in a geopolitical context that perpetuated the equation between Arabness and Middle Easternness and Islam, on the one hand, and between Jewishness and Europeanness and Westernness, on the other.[18]

The master narrative of universal Jewish victimization has been crucial for legitimizing an anomalous nationalist project of "ingathering of the Diaspora from the four corners of the globe," but that can also be defined as forcing displacements of peoples from diverse geographies, languages, cultures, and histories, a project in which, in other words, a state created a nation. It has also been crucial for the claim that the "Jewish nation" faces a common "historical enemy"—the Muslim Arab—implying a double-edged amnesia with regard to both the Judeo-Islamic history and the colonial partition of Palestine. False analogies between the Arabs and Nazis, and in 1992 with Inquisitors, become not merely a staple of Zionist rhetoric but also a symptom of a Jewish European nightmare projected onto the structurally distinct political dynamics of the Israeli-Palestinian conflict. In a historical context of Sephardi Jews experiencing an utterly distinct history within the Muslim world than that which haunted the European memories of Ashkenazi Jews, and in a context of the massacres and dispossession of Palestinian people, the conflation of the Muslim Arab with the archetypical (European) oppressors of Jews downplays the colonial settler history of Euro-Israel itself.

The neat division of Israel as West and Palestine as East, I would argue, ignores some of the fundamental contradictions within Zionist discourse itself.[19] Central to Zionism is the notion of a return to origins located in the Middle East.[20] Thus it often points to its linguistic return to Semitic Hebrew, and to its sustaining of a religious idiom intimately linked with the topography of the Middle East, as a "proof" of the Eastern origins of European Jews—a crucial aspect of the Zionist claim for the land. And although Jews have often been depicted in anti-Semitic discourse as an alien "Eastern" people within the West, the paradox of Israel is that it presumed to "end a diaspora," characterized by Jewish ritualistic nostalgia for the East, only to found a state whose ideological and geopolitical orientation has been almost exclusively toward the West. Herzl called for a Western-style capitalist democratic miniature state, to be made possible by the grace of imperial patrons such as England or Germany, while Ben Gurion formulated his visionary utopia of Israel as that of a "Switzerland of the Middle East." Although European Jews have historically been the victims of anti-Semitic orientalism, Israel as a state has become the perpetrator of orientalist attitudes and actions whose consequences have been the dispossession of Palestinians. The ideological roots of Zionism can be traced to the conditions of nineteenth- and early twentieth-century Europe, as a reaction not only against anti-Semitism but also to the rapid expansion of capitalism and of European empire-building. In this sense, Israel has clearly been allied to First World imperialist interests, has deployed Eurocentric-inflected discourse, and has exercised colonialist policies toward Palestinian land and people.

The question is further complicated by the socialist pretensions, and at times the socialist achievements, of Zionism. In nationalist Zionist discourse, the conflict between the socialist ideology of Zionism and the real praxis of Euro-Jewish colonization in Palestine was resolved through the reassuring thesis that the Arab masses, subjected to feudalism and exploited by their own countrymen, could only benefit from the emanation of Zionist praxis.[21] This presentation embodies the historically positive self-image of Israelis as involved in a noncolonial enterprise and therefore morally superior in their aspirations. Furthermore, the hegemonic socialist-humanist discourse has hidden the negative dialectics of wealth and poverty between First and Third World Jews behind a mystifying façade of egalitarianism. The Zionist mission of ending the Jewish exile from the Promised Land was never the beneficent enterprise portrayed by official discourse, since from the first decade of this century, Arab Jews were perceived as a source of cheap labor that could replace the dispossessed Palestinian fellahin.[22] The "Jews in the form of Arabs" thus could prevent any Palestinian declaration that the land belongs to those who work it and contribute to the Jewish national demographic needs.[23] The Eurocentric projection of Middle Eastern Jews as coming to the "land of milk and honey" from desolate backwaters, from societies lacking all contact with scientific-technological civilization, once again set up an orientalist rescue trope. Zionist discourse has cultivated the impression that Sephardi culture prior to Zionism was static and passive and, like the fallow land of Palestine, as suggested by Edward Said,[24] lying in wait for the impregnating infusion of European dynamism. While presenting Palestine as an empty land to be transformed by Jewish labor, the Zionist "Founding Fathers" presented Arab Jews as passive vessels to be shaped by the revivifying spirit of Promethean Zionism.

The Euro-Zionist problematic relation to the question of East and West has generated a deployment of opposing paradigms that often results in hysterical responses to any questioning of its projected "Western identity." Zionism viewed Europe both as ideal ego and as the signifier of ghettoes, persecutions, and Holocaust. Within this perspective, the Diaspora Jew was an extraterritorial, rootless wanderer, someone living "outside of history." Posited in gendered language as the masculine redeemer of the passive Diaspora Jew, the mythologized *sabra* simultaneously signified the destruction of the Diasporic Jewish entity. The prototypical newly emerging Jew in Palestine—physically strong, with blond hair and blue eyes, healthy looking, cleansed of all "Jewish inferiority complexes," and a cultivator of the land—was conceived as an antithesis to the Zionist, virtually anti-Semitic image of the Diaspora Jew. The sabra, which was modeled on the Romantic ideal, largely influenced by the German *Jungend Kultur*, generated a culture in which any expression of weakness came to be disdained as *galuti*—that which belongs to the diaspora. Zionism, in other words, viewed itself as an embodiment of European nationalist ideals to be realized outside of Europe, in the East, and in relation to the pariahs of Europe, the Jews. Thus, the sabra was celebrated as eternal youth devoid of parents, as though born from a spontaneous generation of nature, as, for example, in Moshe Shamir's key nationalist novel of the 1948 generation *Bemo Yadav* (In His Own Hands), which introduces the hero as follows: "Elik was born from the sea." In this paradoxical idiosyncratic version of the Freudian *familienroman*, Euro-Zionist parents raised their children to see themselves as historical foundlings worthy of more dignified, romantic, and powerful progenitors. Zionism posited itself as an extension of Europe in the Middle East, carrying its Enlightenment banner of the civilizing mission.

If the West has been viewed ambivalently as the place of oppression to be liberated from as well as a kind of object of desire to form a "normal" part of it, the East has also signified a contemporary ambivalence. On the one hand, it is a place associated with "backwardness," "underdevelopment," a land swamped, in the words of 1950s propaganda films, with "mosquitoes, scorpions, and Arabs." On the other, the East has symbolized solace, the return to geographical origins, and reunification with biblical history. The obsessive negation of the "Diaspora" which began with the Haskalah (European Jewish Enlightenment) and the return to the homeland of Zion led, at times, to the exotic affirmation of Arab "primitiveness" as a desirable image to be appropriated by the native-born sabra. The Arab was projected as the incarnation of the ancient, the pre-exiled Jews, the Semite not yet corrupted by wanderings in exile, and therefore, to a certain extent, as the authentic Jew.[25] The Arab as presumably preserving archaic ways and rooted in the land of the Bible, in contrast to the landless ghetto Jew, provoked a qualified identification with the Arab as a desired object of imitation for Zionist youth in Palestine/Israel and as a reunification with the remnant of the free and proud ancient Hebrew.

This projection, however, coexisted with a simultaneous denial of Palestine. The role of archaeology in Israeli culture, it should be pointed out, has been crucial in disinterring remnants of the biblical past of Palestine, at times enlisted in the political effort to demonstrate a historical right to the "land of Israel." In dramatic contrast to Jewish archaeology of the text,[26] this idea of physical archaeology as demonstrating a geography of identity carries with it the obverse notion of the physical homeland as text, to be allegorically read, within Zionist hermeneutics, as a "deed to the land." And corollary to this is the notion of historical strata within a political geology. The deep stratum, in the literal and figurative sense, is associated with the Israeli Jews, while the surface level is associated with the Arabs, as a recent, "superficial," historical element without millennial "roots." Since the Arabs are seen as "guests" in the land, their presence must be downplayed, much as the surface of the land has at times been "remodeled" to hide or bury remnants of Arab life, and Palestinian villages, in certain instances, have been replaced with Israeli ones, or completely erased. The linguistic, lexical expression of this digging into the land is the toponymic archaeology of place-names. Some Arabic names of villages, it was discovered, were close to or based on the biblical Hebrew names; in some cases, therefore, Arabic names were replaced with old-new Hebrew ones.

### Parting Worlds, Subversive Returns

Yet, despite the importance of the idea of Return, it is no less important to see the Zionist representation of Palestine in the context of other settlers' narratives. Palestine is linked to the Columbus narrative of the Americas in more ways than would at first appear. The Columbus narrative prepared the ground for an enthusiastic reception of Zionist discourse within Euro-America. The Israeli-Palestinian conflict as a whole touches, I would argue, on some sensitive historical nerves within America itself. As a product of schizophrenic master narratives, colonial settler state on the one hand and anticolonial republic on the other, America has been subliminally more attuned to the Zionist than to the Palestinian nationalist discourse. Zionist discourse contains a liberatory narrative vis-à-vis Europe, which in many ways is pertinent to the Puritans. The New World of the Middle East, like the New

World of America, was concerned with creating a New Man. The image of the sabra as a new (Jewish) man evokes the American Adam. The American hero has been celebrated as prelapsarian Adam, as a New Man emancipated from history (that is, European history), before whom all the world and time lay available, much as the sabra was conceived as the antithesis of the "Old World" European Jew. In this sense, one might suggest an analogy between the cultural discourse about the innocent national beginning of America and that of Israel. The American Adam and the sabra masculinist archetypes implied not only their status as creators, blessed with the divine prerogative of naming the elements of the scene about them, but also their fundamental innocence. The notions of an American Adam and an Israeli sabra elided a number of crucial facts, notably that there were other civilizations in the Promised Land, that the settlers were not creating "being from nothingness," and that the settlers, in both cases, had scarcely jettisoned all their Old World cultural baggage, their deeply ingrained Eurocentric attitudes and discourses. Here the gendered metaphor of the "virgin land," present in both Zionist and American pioneer discourses, suggests that the land is implicitly available for defloration and fecundation. Assumed to lack owners, it therefore becomes the property of its "discoverer" and cultivators, who transform the wilderness into a garden, those who make the desert bloom.

In the case of Zionist discourse, the concept of "return to the motherland," as I have pointed out, suggests a double relation to the land, having to do with an ambivalent relation to the "East" as the place of Judaic origins as well as the locus for implementing the "West." The sabra embodied the humanitarian and liberationist project of Zionism, carrying the same banner of the "civilizing mission" that European powers proclaimed during their surge into "found lands." The classical images of sabra pioneers as settlers on the Middle Eastern frontiers fighting Indian-like Arabs, along with the reverberations of the early American biblical discourse encapsulated in such notions as "Adam," "(New) Canaan," and "Promised Land," have all facilitated the feeling of Israel as an extension of "us"—the United States. Furthermore, both the United States and Israel fought against British colonialism, while also practicing colonial policies toward the indigenous peoples. Finally, I would argue for a triangular structural analogy by which the Palestinians represent the aboriginal "Indians" of Euro-Israeli discourse, while the Sephardim, as imported cheap labor, constitute the "Blacks" of Israel.[27] (Taking their name from the American movement, the Israeli Black Panthers, for example, sabotaged the myth of the melting pot by showing that there was in Israel not one but two Jewish communities—one white, one black.) The manifest Palestinian refusal to play the assigned role of the presumably doomed Indians of the transplanted (far) Western narrative has testified to an alternative narrative in whose narration Edward Said has been in the forefront. The story of Sephardim—as the Jewish victims of Zionism—also remains to be heard.[28]

The same historical process that dispossessed Palestinians of their property, lands, and national-political rights was intimately linked to the process that affected the dispossession of Arab Jews from their property, lands, and root-edness in Arab countries as well as their uprootedness from that history and culture within Israel itself.[29] But while Palestinians have fostered the collective militancy of nostalgia in exile (be it *fil dakhel*, under Israeli occupation, or *fil kharij*, under Syrian, Egyptian, American passport or on the basis of laissez-passer), Sephardim, trapped in a no-exit situation, have been forbidden to nourish memories of at least partially belonging to the peoples across the river Jordan, across the mountains of Lebanon, and across the Sinai Desert and Suez Canal. The pervasive notion of "one people" reunited in their ancient homeland actively disauthorizes any affectionate memory of life before the State of Israel. Quincentennial events luxuriated in the landscapes, sounds, and smells of the lost Andalusian home, but silence muffled an even longer historical imaginary in Cairo, Baghdad, Damascus—and hid an even more recent loss. For centuries, both Muslim and Jewish poets eulogized Andalusia, referring to the keys they persisted carrying into exile. Yet, in contemporary Palestinian poetry, Andalusia is far from being only a closed chapter of Arab grandeur, for it allegorizes Palestine. In the words of Mahmoud Darwish's poem *"Al Kamanjat"* ("The Violins"):

> *Al kamanjat tabki ma'a al ghjar al dhahibina ila al andalous*
> *al kamanjat tabki ʿala al ʿarab al kharigin min al andalous*
> *al kamanjat tabki ʿala zaman daib la ya'ood*
> *al kamanjat tabki ʿala watan daib qad ya'ood.*

The violins weep with the Gypsies heading for Andalusia
the violins weep for the Arabs departing Andalusia.
The violins weep for a lost epoch that will not return
the violins weep for a lost homeland that could be regained.

But the parallelism between Andalusia and Palestine stops precisely at the point of reclaiming a Palestinian future.

The 1992 discussions of expulsion brought out the "wandering Jew" motif as perennially displaced people. But the Jews of the Middle East and North Africa, for the most part, had stable, nonwandering lives in the Islamic world. As splendidly captured in *In an Antique Land*, the Sephardim who have moved within the regions of Asia and Africa, from the Mediterranean to the Indian Ocean, did it more for commercial, religious, or scholarly purposes than for reasons of persecution. Ironically, the major traumatic displacement took place in recent years when Arab Jews were uprooted, dispossessed, and dislodged due to the collaboration between Israel and some of the Arab governments under the orchestration of Western colonial powers, who termed their solution for the "question of Palestine" as a "population exchange."[30] That no one asked either the Palestinians or the Arab Jews whether they wished to be exchanged is yet another typical narrative of Third World histories of partition. Sephardim who have managed to leave Israel, often in (an indirect) response to institutionalized racism there, have dislocated themselves yet again, this time to the United States, Europe, and Latin America. In a sudden historical twist, today it is to the Muslim Arab countries of their origins to which most Middle Eastern Jews cannot travel, let alone fantasize a return—the ultimate taboo.[31]

The commonalities between Middle Eastern Jews and Muslims is a thorny reminder of the Middle Eastern and North African character of the majority of Jews in Israel today. Not surprisingly, quincentenary events in Europe, the Middle East, and the Americas have centered on the Spanishness of Sephardi culture (largely on Ladino or Judeo-Español language and music), while marginalizing the fact that Jews in Iberia formed part of a larger Judeo-Islamic culture of North Africa, the Middle East, and the European Balkan area of the Ottoman Empire. Major Sephardi texts in philosophy, linguistics, poetry, and medicine were written in Arabic and reflect specific Muslim influences as well as a strong sense of Jewish Arab cultural identity, seen especially in the development of Judeo-Arab script,[32] used in religious correspondence between Jewish scholars across the regions of Islam, as well as in some specific local Jewish Arabic dialects. The Jews of Iberia had come from the east and south of the Mediterranean, some with the Romans, others largely with the Muslims; they returned there when they fled the Inquisition. Over 70 percent returned to the Ottoman Empire regions, while the rest went to Western Europe and the Americas.[33] Thus a historiography that speaks of a pan-Jewish culture is often the same historiography that speaks of "Arab versus Jew" without acknowledging Arab Jewish existence.

The erasure of the Arab dimension of Sephardim-Mizrahim has been crucial to the Zionist perspective since the Middle Easternness of Sephardi Jews questions the very definitions and boundaries of the Euro-Israeli national project. Euro-Israel has ended up in a paradoxical situation in which its "Orientals" have had closer cultural and historical links to the presumed Arab enemy than to the Ashkenazi Jews with whom they were coaxed and coerced into nationhood. The taboo around the Arabness of Sephardi history and culture is clearly manifested in Israeli academic and media attacks on Sephardi intellectuals who refuse to define themselves simply as Israelis and who dare to assert their Arabness in the public sphere.[34] The Ashkenazi anxiety around Sephardi-Mizrahi identity (expressed by both the Right and the liberal Left) underlines that Sephardi Jews have represented a problematic entity for Euro-Israeli hegemony. Although Zionism collapses the Sephardim and the Ashkenazim into a single people, at the same time the Sephardi difference has destabilized Zionist claims for representing a single Jewish people, premised not only on a common religious background but also on common nationality. The strong cultural and historical links that Middle Eastern Jews have shared with the Arab Muslim world, stronger in many respects than those they shared with the European Jews, threatened the conception of a homogeneous nation akin to that on which European nationalist movements were based. As an integral part of the topography, language, culture, and history of the Middle East, Sephardim have also threatened the Euro-Israeli self-image, which sees itself as a prolongation of Europe, "in" the Middle East but not "of" it. Fearing an encroachment from the East on the West, the Israeli establishment attempted to repress the Middle Easternness of Sephardic Jews as part of an effort to Westernize the Israeli nation and to mark clear borders of identity between Jews as Westerners and Arabs as Easterners. Arabness and Orientalness have been consistently stigmatized as evils to be uprooted, creating a situation where Arab Jews were urged to see Judaism and Zionism as synonyms and Jewishness and Arabness as antonyms. Thus Arab Jews were prodded to choose between anti-Zionist Arabness and pro-Zionist Jewishness for the first time in history. Distinguishing the "evil" East (the Muslim Arab) from the "good" East (the Jewish Arab), Israel has taken upon itself to "cleanse" Arab Jews of their Arabness and redeem them from their "primal sin" of belonging to the Orient. This conceptualization of East and West has important implications in this age of the "peace process," since it avoids the inherent question of the majority of the population within Israel being from the Middle East—Palestinian citizens of Israel as well as Mizrahi-Sephardi Jews. For peace as it is defined now does not entail a true democracy in terms of adequate representation of these populations, nor in terms of changing the educational, cultural, and political orientation within the State of Israel.

The leitmotif of Zionist texts was the cry to be a "normal civilized nation," without the presumably myriad "distortions" and forms of pariahdom typical of the *gola* (diaspora), of the state of being a non-nation-state. The Ostjuden, perennially marginalized by Europe, realized their desire of becoming Europe, ironically, in the Middle East, this time on the back of their own Ostjuden, the Eastern Jews. The Israeli establishment, therefore, has made systematic efforts to suppress Sephardi-Mizrahi cultural identity. The Zionist establishment, since its early encounter with Palestinian (Sephardi) Jews, has systematically attempted to eradicate the Middle Easternness of those other Jews, for example, by marginalizing these histories in school curricula and by rendering Mizrahi cultural production and grassroots political activities invisible in the media. However, Sephardi popular culture, despite its obvious shifts since the partition of Palestine, has clearly manifested its vibrant intertextual dialogue with Arab, Turkish, Iranian, and Indian popular cultures. Oriental Arabic music produced by Sephardim, at times in collaboration with Israeli Palestinians, is consumed by Palestinians in Israel and across the borders in the Arab world, often without being labeled as originating in Israel. This creativity is partly nourished through an enthusiastic consumption of Jordanian, Lebanese, and Egyptian television programs, films, and Arabic music video performances, which rupture the Euro-Israeli public sphere in a kind of subliminal transgression of a forbidden nostalgia. In fact, musical groups such as the Moroccan-Israeli Sfatayim (Lips) traveled back to Morocco to produce a music video sung in Moroccan Arabic against the scenery of the cities and villages that Moroccan Jews have left behind, just as Israeli-born Iraqi singers such as Ya'aqub Nishawi sing old and contemporary Iraqi music. This desire for a "return of the diaspora" is ironically underlined by what I would describe as a kind of reversal of the biblical expression: "By the waters of Zion, where we sat down, and there we wept, when we remembered Babylon."[35]

Arab Muslim historiography, meanwhile, has ironically echoed the logic of Zionist paradigms, looking only superficially into the culture and identity of Arab Jews both in the Arab world and, more recently, within Israel. Thus Ghosh, the visiting Indian anthropologist, notices what is otherwise unnoticeable: that in the Geniza's home country, Egypt,

> nobody took the slightest notice of its dispersal. In some profound sense, the Islamic high culture of *Masr* [Arabic for Egypt] has never really noticed, never found a place for the parallel history the Geniza represented, and its removal only confirmed a particular vision of the past. . . . Now it was *Masr*, which had sustained the Geniza for almost a Millennium, that was left with no traces of its riches: not a single scrap or shred of paper to remind her of the aspect of her past. It was as though the borders that were to divide Palestine several decades later had already been drawn, through time rather than territory, to allocate a choice of Histories.[36]

The amnesia of this recent history in most contemporary Arab culture has fed into an Israeli and Arab refusal of the hybrid, the in-between. Even Israeli Arab-Jews, such as the Iraqi-Israeli writer Samir Naqash, who to this very day writes his novels in Arabic, are rejected from membership in the Arab geocultural region; he is seen simply as "Israeli." The Jews of Islam thus today exist as part of a historiography in which our relations to the Arab Islamic world exist only in the past tense. Colonial partitions and nationalist ideologies have left little room for the inconvenient minority of Arab-Jews. Even the Geniza itself, presumably rescued from obscurity and decay at the hands of our own producers, has been used to support a nationalist narrative in which every text or fragmented document was deciphered for a Zionist transformation *megola le'geula* (from diaspora to redemption). The historiographical work of Euro-Jewish scholars such as S. D. Goitein and E. Strauss might have facilitated the entry of an Indian anthropologist such as Ghosh to the Indian Ocean world of a twelfth-century Tunisian Jewish trader, Abraham Ben-Yiju, who, unlike Ghosh, traveled in an era when Europe did not dominate the channels of scholarly communication. But the Geniza scholarship was shaped and used in a context of Zionist Enlightenment readings of the otherized Jews of the Levant, the very same Jews whose cultural practices made possible the Geniza scholarship of Western academic institutions. Within these asymmetrical power relations, it is the work of Euro-Jewish scholars that infused the colonized history with national meaning and telos, while, ironically, at the same time, Arab Jews were being displaced, and in Israel subject to a schooling system where Jewish history textbooks featured barely a single chapter on their history.

Today Mizrahim inhabit the pages of Euro-Israeli sociological and anthropological accounts as maladjusted criminals and superstitious exotics, firmly detached from Arab history that looms only as deformed vestiges in the lives of Israelis of Asian and African origins. Sociology and anthropology detect such traces of underdevelopment, while national historiography tells the story of the past as a moral tale full of national purpose. Such scholarly bifurcation cannot possibly account for an Arab Jewish identity that is at once past and present, here and there. Perhaps it is not a coincidence that the author of *In an Antique Land*—a hybrid of anthropology and history—ends up by splitting the subjects of ethnography and historiography, the first focusing on present-day Egyptian Muslims and the second on past Arab Jews. At the end of his book, Ghosh somehow stops his narrative at the very point where the subject of his historiography could have turned into a subject of his ethnography. Anthropological accounts of Ghosh's visits to Egypt are paralleled by his historiographical chronicle largely of the Judeo-Islamic world through the travels of Ben-Yiju. On his final trip to Egypt Ghosh notices Arab Jewish pilgrims from Israel coming to Egypt to visit the tomb of the cabbalist mystic Sidi Abu-Hasira, a site holy for both Muslims and Jews, with many similar festivities. Yet, for one reason or another, he ends up never meeting them. Perhaps Ghosh's missed rendezvous, his packing up and leaving Egypt precisely as the Arab Jews visit Abu-Haseira's holy site, is revelatory of the difficulties of representing a multidiasporic identity: the dangers of border-crossing in the war zone. So we Arab Jews continue to travel in historical narratives as imbricated with a legendary Islamic civilization. But as the postcolonial story began to unfold over the past decades, we suddenly ceased to exist, as though we have reached our final destination—the State of Israel—and nothing more need be said.

In contrast to the negatively connoted term "Orientals" (in the United States), in Israel "Orientals" (Mizrahim) signifies radical politics, evoking a common experience shared by all Asian and African Jews in Israel, despite our different origins. On the part of radical Sephardi movements, it also suggests a resistant discourse that calls for linkages to the East as opposed to the hegemonic discourse of "we of the West." The names of the 1980s movements

"East for Peace" and the "Oriental Front" in Israel, "Perspectives Judeo-Arabes" in Paris, and the "World Organization of Jews from Islamic Countries" in New York point to the assertion of the historical and a future interwovenness with the East. Sephardi Jews, along with Palestinians within Israel proper (Israeli Palestinians), compose the majority of the citizens of a state that has rigidly imposed an anti–Middle Eastern agenda. In a first-of-its-kind meeting between Sephardi/Mizrahi Jews and PLO Palestinians held at the symbolic site of Toledo, Spain, in 1989, we insisted that a comprehensive peace would mean more than settling political borders, and would require the erasure of the East/West cultural borders between Israel and Palestine, and thus the remapping of national and ethnic-racial identities against the deep scars of colonizing partitions. A critical examination of national histories may thus open a cultural space for working against taboo memories and fostering diasporic visions.

## Notes

This essay was presented as a lecture at the University of California Humanities Research conference "Beyond Orientalism" in October 1992. Parts of it have appeared in preliminary form in *Middle East Report*, no. 178 (September–October 1992), and *Third Text*, no. 21 (winter 1992–93). An earlier version was included in *Cultural Identity and the Gravity of History: On the Work of Edward Said*, ed. Keith Ansell-Pearson, Benita Parry, and Judith Squires (London: Lawrence and Wishart, 1997).

1. Amitav Ghosh, *In an Antique Land* (New York: Knopf, 1992), 89–94. Some of my comments on the book were made in a City University of New York Television conversation with Amitav Ghosh in March 1994. The conversation also included Tim Mitchell and was organized and moderated by Kamala Visweswaran and Parag Amladi.
2. Ghosh, *In an Antique Land*, 85, 93.
3. I thank Robert Stam for allowing me to use some "shared territory" from our book *Unthinking Eurocentrism: Multiculturalism and the Media* (London: Routledge, 1994).
4. See, for example, "Green Card," sculpture-installation by Inigo Manglano-Ovalle (1992).
5. Quoted in Jean Comby, "1492: Le Choc des Cultures et l'Évangélisation du Monde," *Dossiers de l'épiscopat français*, no. 14 (October 1990): 16.
6. See Charles Duff, *The Truth about Columbus* (New York: Random House, 1936).
7. Ghosh, *In an Antique Land*, 81.

8.  Jan Pieterse makes the more general point that many of the themes of European imperialism traced antecedents to the European and Mediterranean sphere. Thus the theme of civilization against barbarism was a carryover from Greek and Roman antiquity, the theme of Christianity against pagans was the keynote of European expansion culminating in the Crusades, and the Christian theme of "mission" was fused with "civilization" in the *mission civilisatrice*. See Pieterse, *Empire and Emancipation* (London: Pluto, 1990), 240.

9.  For details, see Jan Carew, *Fulcrums of Change: Origins of Racism in the Americas and Other Essays* (Trenton NJ: Africa World Press, 1988).

10. The indigenous peoples of the Americas similarly were officially protected from massacres by the throne only once they converted to Christianity.

11. The presumed "godlessness" of the indigenous people became a pretext for enslavement and dispossession. While Jews and Muslims were diabolized, the indigenous Americans were accused of devil worship. The brutalities practiced by official Christianity toward Jews and Muslims have to be seen, therefore, on the same continuum as the forced conversions of indigenous peoples of the Americas, who, like the Jews and Muslims in Christian Spain, were obliged to feign allegiance to Catholicism.

12. Pat Kossan, "Jewish Roots of Hispanics: Delicate Topic," *Phoenix Gazette*, April 14, 1992, section C.

13. Moors converted to Christianity.

14. Spanish Muslim culture in Christian Spain, like Sephardi Jewish culture, was expressed in Spanish as well.

15. On the history, see, for example, W. Montgomery Watt and Pierre Cachia, *A History of Islamic Spain* (Edinburgh: Edinburgh University Press, 1977); James T. Monroe, *Hispano-Arabic Poetry* (Berkeley: University of California Press, 1974).

16. This picture of an ageless and relentless oppression and humiliation ignores the fact that, on the whole, Jews of Islam—a minority among several other religious and ethnic communities in the Middle East and North Africa—lived relatively comfortably within Arab Muslim society.

17. For more complex analyses, see, for example, Ilan Halevi, *A History of the Jews: Ancient and Modern* (London: Zed Books, 1987); Maxime Rodinson, *Cult, Ghetto, and State: The Persistence of the Jewish Question* (London: Al Saqi Books, 1983); Ammiel Alacaly, *After Jews and Arabs: Remaking Levantine Culture* (Minneapolis: University of Minnesota Press, 1993).

18. See Ella Shohat, "Sephardim in Israel: Zionism from the Standpoint of Its Jewish Victims," *Social Text*, nos. 19–20 (fall 1988): 1–35.

19. For more on the question of East and West in Zionist discourse, see Ella Sho-

hat, *Israeli Cinema: East/West and the Politics of Representation* (Austin: University of Texas Press, 1989).

20. In the early days of Zionism, other "empty" territories were proposed for Jewish settlement; typically they were located in the colonized world. However, one of Herzl's famous proposals for settlement, Uganda, created a crisis for the Zionist Congress known as the Uganda crisis.

21. See Maxime Rodinson, *Israel: A Colonial-Settler State?*, trans. David Thorstad (New York: Monad Press, 1973).

22. See Yoseff Meir, *Hatnua haTzionit veYehudei Teman* (The Zionist Movement and the Jews of Yemen) (Tel Aviv: Sifriat Afikim, 1982); G. N. Giladi, *Discord in Zion: Conflict between Ashkenazi and Sephardi Jews in Israel* (London: Scorpion Publishing, 1990).

23. The phrase was used already in the first decade of the twentieth century by the early engineers (such as Shmuel Yaveneli) of "Aliya" of Jews from the regions of the Ottoman Empire. See Meir, *The Zionist Movement and the Jews of Yemen.*

24. See Edward Said, *The Question of Palestine* (New York: Times Books, 1979).

25. For a similar discourse addressed to Bedouins, see Smadar Lavie, *The Poetics of Military Occupation: Mezina Allegories of Bedouin Identity under Israeli and Egyptian Rule* (Berkeley: University of California Press, 1990).

26. See, for example, Jacques Derrida, "Edmund Jabès and the Question of the Book," in *Writing and Difference*, trans. Alan Bass (Chicago: University of Chicago Press, 1978), 64–78; George Steiner, "Our Homeland, the Text," *Salmagundi* 66 (winter–spring 1985): 4–25.

27. In recent years the term *sh'horim* (blacks) has also applied to the Orthodox religious Ashkenazi codes of dressing. I should point out that the sartorial codes favoring dark colors of centuries-ago Poland were never part of Sephardic Arabic culture. And over the past decade, since the massive arrival of Ethiopian Jews, the pejorative term "blacks" or *kushim* has been used against Ethiopian Jews.

28. I specifically address the relationship between the Palestinian and the Sephardi/Mizrahi questions vis-à-vis Zionism in my essay on Sephardi identity in Israel, entitled "Sephardim in Israel: Zionism from the Standpoint of Its Jewish Victims," a title referring to Said's essay "Zionism from the Standpoint of Its Victims" in Said's *The Question of Palestine*. Both have been republished in Anne McClintock, Aamir Mufti, and Ella Shohat, eds., *Dangerous Liaisons: Gender, Nation and Postcolonial Perspectives* (Minneapolis: University of Minnesota Press, 1997).

29. Neither Palestinians nor Arab Jews have been compensated for their lost property.

30. See, for example, Abbas Shiblak, *The Lure of Zion* (London: Al Saqi Books, 1986); G. N. Giladi, *Discord in Zion* (London: Scorpion, 1990).

31. Thus when, for example, the writer Shimon Ballas wrote the novel *Vehu Aher* (And He Is an Other) (Tel Aviv: Zmora Bitan, 1991) which partially concerned an Iraqi Jew who remained in Iraq after the dislodging of his community and who converts to Islam, he was vehemently attacked in a rush to censor the imaginary.

32. Jewish Arabic language was written in Hebrew script, but the script resembles very little the Ashkenazi Hebrew script that became a lingua franca since the revival of modern Hebrew and its spread through Zionist institutions. Today Sephardi prayer texts use the common Ashkenazi script, even when the prayer is in Judeo-Arabic, since the Ashkenazi script is known better today to most younger generations of Sephardim.

33. Most cultural expression in the Arab world, needless to say, was not in Ladino or Español. (In fact, it makes one wonder if this widespread misrepresentation of Arab Jewish history led Bharati Mukerjee to have her Iraqi Jewish protagonist, Alfie Judah, in *The Middleman* say that "old Baghdad," where "we spoke a form of Spanish," was "a good preparation for the Southwest."

34. For example, attacks on the Iraqi Israeli author Shimon Ballas after the publication of his novel *And He Is an Other* as well as on myself after the Hebrew publication of my book *Israeli Cinema: East/West and the Politics of Representation*, published as *Hakolnoa haIsraeli: Histpria veIdiologia* (Israeli Cinema: History and Ideology) (Tel Aviv: Breirot, 1991).

35. See Ella Shohat, "Dislocated Identities: Reflections of an Arab-Jew," Movement Research: Performance Journal 5 (fall–winter 1992): 8.

36. Ghosh, *In an Antique Land*, 95.

# 11 | Chinese History and the Question of Orientalism

ARIF DIRLIK

I consider below some questions raised by orientalism as concept and practice. These questions have their origins in Edward Said's *Orientalism*, published in 1978, which has had a lasting impact on Third World cultural studies in Europe and the United States.[1] Provocative as Said's book was in its
critique of orientalism as practice, its larger significance rests on Said's relentless demonstration of the intersection of historical interpretation, culture, and politics in Euro-American studies of Asia. I will argue, contrary to
critics of Said, that questions raised by this intersection are still very much
relevant to problems of historical interpretation of Asia in general, and China
in particular. On the other hand, I will suggest also that contemporary historiographical evidence calls for a recasting of the relationship between history, culture, and politics in a configuration that is significantly different than
Said's conceptualization of it in *Orientalism*. On the basis of this reconfigured understanding of orientalism, I will reflect by way of conclusion on the
possibilities of escaping the burden of orientalism in historical studies. As
orientalism as concept refers to the "Orient" as a whole, I should add that
in illustrating my arguments I will draw on evidence from the career of orientalism not just in the historiography of China but other histories as well.
Finally, I am concerned here not with specific historiographical questions,
but questions that are best characterized as metahistorical.

## Orientalism

To summarize very briefly in Said's own words:

> Orientalism . . . refers to several overlapping domains: first, the changing
> historical and cultural relationship between Europe and Asia, a relation-
> ship with a 4000-year-old history; second, the scientific discipline in the
> west according to which, beginning in the early nineteenth century, one
> specialized in the study of various Oriental cultures and traditions; and,
> third, the ideological suppositions, images and fantasies about a currently
> important and politically urgent region of the world called the Orient. The
> relatively common denominator between these three aspects of Oriental-
> ism is the line separating Occident from Orient and this, I have argued,
> is less a fact of nature than it is a fact of human production, which I have
> called imaginative geography. This is, however, neither to say that the di-
> vision between Orient and Occident is unchanging nor is it to say that it
> is simply fictional.[2]

Said's study was concerned almost exclusively with the second and the
third aspects of orientalism as it related to Western Asia, and drew upon the
work of prominent English and French orientalists to argue his thesis. A
central aspect of the work was to represent contemporary area studies as a
linear descendant of the orientalist tradition in Euro-America. Two guiding
assumptions of the argument are worth spelling out.

First, "one of the legacies of Orientalism, and indeed one of its epistemological foundations, is historicism, that is, the view . . . that if humankind has
a history it is produced by men and women, and can be understood historically as, at each given period, epoch or moment, possessing a complex, but
coherent unity." Said described this notion of historicism more precisely as
a "universalizing historicism," which placed different histories conceived as
"coherent unities" on a temporal scale.[3] Spatial differences were thereby rendered into temporal differences, and different societies were placed at different locations in a progressive temporality in which Euro-America stood at
the epitome of progress: "As primitivity, as the age-old antetype of Europe,
as a fecund night out of which European rationality developed, the Orient's
actuality receded inexorably into a kind of paradigmatic fossilization."[4]

Orientalist epistemology as it emerges from Said's analysis is also clearly culturalist, by which I mean a representation of societies in terms of essentialized cultural characteristics, more often than not enunciated in foundational texts. Culturalist essentialism is homogenizing both spatially and temporally. Spatially, it ignores differences within individual societies and, in the case of orientalism, differences between Asian societies, which are endowed with common characteristics that mark them as "Oriental." It is homogenizing temporally in substituting a cultural essence that defies time for culture as lived experience that is subject to temporal production and reproduction. Culturalism, in other words, nourishes off a de-socialized and de-historicized conceptualization of culture (as "organically and internally coherent, bound together by a spirit, genius, *Klima*, or national idea,"[5] which is the sense in which it appears in eighteenth-century European historicism, and also informs Said's use of "historicism") that suppresses relations both between and within societies in the production of culture as ongoing historical activity (which is informed by an alternative sense of historicism). Such culturalism is important to understanding why, in orientalism, so-called Oriental societies may appear at once as objects of admiration for their civilizational achievements, but also be relegated to the past as fossilized relics because, with culture substituted for history, they have no "real" historicity and, as Johannes Fabian puts it in a different context, no real contemporaneity, since their presents are but simple reproductions of their pasts.[6]

This epistemology, secondly, is bound up with questions of Euro-American power over the Orient. In *Orientalism*, Said singles out four preconditions without which orientalism "could not have occurred": European expansion, which brought Europeans into contact with other societies; the confrontation with other histories this contact necessitated, which culminated in comparative history; "sympathetic identification," which for some offered the only access to the panoply of alien cultures, "each permeated by an inimical creative spirit" (this, informed by, and informing, eighteenth-century historicism); and finally, "the impulse to classify nature and man into types" and to bring order into the profuse variety of experience that could no longer be contained in inherited conceptions of the world.[7] Expansion, we may observe, was the point of departure for the new epistemologies for reordering the world. Orientalism was an integral consequence of this process.

Orientalism, as part of this epistemological reordering of the world, is not a mere intellectual instrument of imperialism, it *is* "intellectual imperialism." For Said, orientalism is a "discourse" in the sense that Michel Foucault used that term: "Orientalism can be discussed and analyzed as the corporate institution for dealing with the Orient—dealing with it by making statements about it, authorizing views of it, describing it, by teaching it, settling it, ruling over it; in short, Orientalism as a Western style for dominating, restructuring, and having authority over the Orient."[8] It is important to underline here that, while Said is quite aware of the complex relationship between power and orientalism, he is adamant that orientalism does not merely serve or represent power, but is itself "a *distribution* of geopolitical awareness into aesthetic, scholarly, economic, sociological, historical, and philological texts"[9]—in other words, orientalism as discourse is an epistemology of power. As such, it is integral to a modern Euro-American cultural consciousness (and unconscious).

It is noteworthy that Said sets out to study in *Orientalism* this dimension of modern Euro-American culture, rather than the "Oriental" societies represented in it. In fact, one of his basic goals is to demonstrate how such representations of the Orient have silenced the "Orientals," and undercut their ability to represent themselves. His argument on orientalism, however, might not have been as compelling had he stopped here. *Orientalism* concludes not with condemnation or closure, but with a further set of questions: "How does one *represent* other cultures? What is *another* culture? Is the notion of a distinct culture (or race, or religion, or civilization) a useful one, or does it always get involved either in self-congratulation (when one discusses one's own) or hostility and aggression (when one discusses the 'other')?"[10]

Power, specifically Euro-American political power, is key to the argument Said presents on orientalism and configures the relationship between politics, culture, and history that structures his conceptualization of orientalism. Following the logic of the argument, we might expect a power shift in global relations to reconfigure that relationship, in which case orientalism may be consigned to the past as a manifestation of one specific period in the Euro-American relationship to the world. This is indeed one contemporary verdict on orientalism (not to speak of those who deny it altogether, past or present).

I would like to suggest here a contrary position: that far from being a phenomenon of the past, orientalism, and the culturalist epistemology that nourished it, are very much alive in the present, but not necessarily where Said located it, and in a reconfigured relationship between politics, culture, and history. The nature of this relationship is such, moreover, that it raises certain fundamental questions about Said's conceptualization of orientalism, its location and structure. One question that is of particular interest is: Is orientalism an autonomous product of Euro-American development, which is then projected upon the "Orient," or is it rather the product of an unfolding relationship between Euro-Americans and Asians that required the complicity of the latter in endowing it with plausibility? To mimic what E. P. Thompson said of classes, is orientalism a thing or a relationship? Let me offer some observations on contemporary self-representations before I return to this question and what it might tell us about the historical meaning of orientalism.

### "The Orientalism of the Orientals"

Said's argument in *Orientalism* may be open to criticism from a variety of perspectives, and it has received its share of criticism, especially from "Orientalists."[11] Whatever may be the merit or lack thereof of these criticisms, the central argument of the book is, in my opinion, indisputable: orientalism was an integral part (at once constituent and product) of a Eurocentric conceptualization of the world that was fully articulated in the course of the nineteenth century, that placed Europe at the center and pinnacle of development, and that ordered the globe spatially and temporally in accordance with the criteria of European development. Non-European societies were characterized in this reordering of the world not by what they had but by what they lacked—in other words, the lack of one or more of those characteristics that accounted for European development. Rather than provide contemporary alternatives to European development, they were perceived predominantly to be located at some rung or other of the ladder of development that Europe already had left behind. They provided Europeans with glimpses not of alternative presents, but of a past stage of European development, what has been described as "a theory of our contemporary ancestors."[12] The development of this new view of the world went hand in hand with the progress of European colonization and domination of the world.

While we may have come a long way since the nineteenth century, it is hardly arguable that Eurocentrism is already a thing of the past. Post–World War II modernization "theory," still fundamental to our views of the world, continues to bear strong traces of Eurocentrism. The difference is that it is now a surplus of history rather than a historical lack that defines the state of "premodern" non-European societies, what we call "tradition." It is the burden of the past in one form or another that marks a society as traditional, which impedes its ascent to modernity. In spite of radical challenges, including challenges from intellectuals from non-European societies, that modernity and tradition, or development and underdevelopment, may be different aspects of the same historical process, the conceptual isolation of the one from the other (of a developed "inside" from an undeveloped "outside") persists not just in the popular consciousness but in intellectual work as well. The "inside" now has come to include some non-European societies, which has created some problems for earlier versions of the modernization explanation, but arguably has contributed further to enhancing the power of the idea of modernization itself.[13]

The question I would like to raise here is whether orientalism was just the autonomous creation of Europeans, or whether it presupposed in its emergence the complicity of "Orientals." This is what I had in mind when I referred to orientalism above as possibly a "relationship." In *Orientalism* Said raises a number of questions that he does not pursue. These questions, brought to the surface, call for a number of qualifications with regard to the location, production, and consequences of orientalism that are, I think, fundamental to understanding orientalism and its place in modernity.

Said's *Orientalism*, as he is quick to acknowledge, is a study in Euro-American thought, and it has little to say on the question of how intellectuals and others in Asian societies may have contributed to the emergence of orientalism as practice and concept. And even if orientalism was a product of a European intellectual space, how did "Oriental" intellectuals respond to it, or receive it? Were the "Orientals" indeed as silent, or incapable of representing themselves, as Said's study suggests? How does "orientalism" and the whole question of a modern consciousness appear when we bring the "Orientals" into the picture, not as silent objects of a European discourse, but as active participants in its emergence? What bearing would such a reconstructed picture of orientalism have on the question of the relationship between orientalism and power? While Said is quite right in arguing that orientalism nourishes off an inside/outside (or Occident/Orient) distinction, moreover, is it possible that in the long run the consequence of orientalism is to call such a distinction into question?

First, the orientalists. Said notes that orientalism, by its very epistemological assumptions, called for "sympathetic identification" as a means to grasping an alien culture. I take this to imply that in the very process of understanding an alien culture, the orientalist needs in some measure to be "orientalized," if you like, which brings the orientalist closer to the Other while distancing him or her from the society of the Self. If only as specialist or expert, the orientalist comes not just to speak about but also *for* the Other. In a work on Chinese modernization, the editor Kurt Werner Radtke, presumably speaking for the contributors to the volume, writes that "the contributors, all intellectuals and China specialists, have in the course of their lives been affected by the process of sinification."[14] There is nothing peculiar about this except that, while we have no difficulty thinking of "Westernized Chinese," which is the subject of much scholarly attention, we do not often think of the "Sinified Westerner." If we do, the distinctions between self and other, or subject and object, crucial to the analysis of orientalism, become blurred though not necessarily abolished, as I will argue below. Suffice it to say here that examples of "orientalized Westerners" abound from the origins of orientalism to the present: from the Jesuits in China to Lawrence of Arabia, who sought to live as Chinese or Arabs; from William "Oriental" Jones, the founder of British orientalism, to the "sinified" contributors to Radtke's volume.[15] Their "orientalization" was what qualified the orientalists to speak for the Orient. To the extent that they were "orientalized," however, they themselves assumed some of the exoticism of the Orient, which on occasion marginalized them and even rendered them suspect ideologically at home. The latter inevitably raises questions concerning the relationship between orientalism and power.

Such suspicion may be a consequence of the fact that however "condescending" they may have been in their "veneration" of "Oriental" cultures (in Raymond Schwab's words), orientalists have been responsible also for introducing elements of Asian cultures into their societies, for their use of the "Orient" in self-criticism, as well as the critique of Euro-American modernity. French and German orientalists of the early nineteenth century called for an "Oriental Renaissance," which would make the "Orient" (understood in terms of India) instead of Greece and Rome the basis of a new departure in European history.[16] The use of the "Orient" in self-criticism is almost a discourse within a discourse of orientalism, from Montesquieu's *Persian Letters* and Oliver Goldsmith's *Citizen of the World* in the eighteenth century to

André Malraux's *The Temptation of the West* and radical U.S. intellectuals' critiques of the United States in the twentieth.[17]

Most revealingly, orientalism, itself a product of Eurocentrism, may even find service in the critique of Eurocentrism. A recent example of this is the notion of a "China-centered history" proposed by Paul Cohen and John Schrecker.[18] "China-centered history" as conceived by these authors is in keeping with the epistemological procedures of orientalism, especially in drawing a clear methodological line between Chinese and other histories, and arguing that Chinese history may be understood only in terms that are internal to it. Schrecker's *The Chinese Revolution in Historical Perspective* illustrates the approach by attempting to understand Chinese history over a three-thousand-year period in terms of the two Chinese concepts of *fengjian* and *junxian*. What is interesting about "China-centered history," however, is the authors' explicit positioning of themselves against Eurocentric histories of China. I will have more to say about this approach later.

Finally, as with the Oriental Renaissance, orientalism could serve as a critique of European modernity and a means to redirecting it. Such was the case with the Theosophical movement in the middle of the nineteenth century, which attracted the likes of Lafcadio Hearn in the United States.[19] Whatever these uses of the "Orient" may say about orientalism, they suggest also that orientalism played a transformative part in Euro-America.

A similar complexity attends the relationship of the orientalist to the "Orient." There is considerable evidence also that those in Asian societies did not necessarily perceive the orientalist as a vanguard of Euro-American power, to the extent that the orientalist was "orientalized" and could find acceptance in the society of the Other. The Jesuits are the classic example. In case they seem to belong to another age, we might adduce contemporary examples. In his recent proposal of a "Cultural China," Tu Wei-ming includes non-Chinese China specialists in the outer realm of his notion of a "Cultural China," the inner two realms consisting, respectively, of Chinese in China and Chinese overseas.[20] As if echoing his sentiments, *Sinorama* magazine in Taiwan published in 1991 a volume (compiled from earlier publications in the magazine) entitled *When West Meets East: International Sinology and Sinologists*.[21] Published in Chinese and English, the volume offers accounts of sinologists, all European with the exception of John King Fairbank, in order to, in the words of the publisher Yuming Shaw, see China through the eyes of others and "better appreciate ourselves." While the editors are by no means unaware of the connection between sinology and "trade and imperialism," the volume is on the whole quite laudatory of the part foreign sinology ("culture's other half") has played in globalizing Chinese civilization.[22]

Second, and even more complex, is the question of "the orientalism of the Orientals," of which the *Sinorama* collection is emblematic. While the Occident/Orient distinction, and orientalism as concept and practice, are of European origin, and the term orientalism has been used almost exclusively to describe the attitudes of Europeans toward Asian societies, I would like to suggest here that the usage needs to be extended to Asian views of Asia, to account for tendencies to self-orientalization that would become an integral part of the history of orientalism. We tend to view the Euro-American impact on Asian societies primarily as an impact of "Western" ideas and institutions on Asia. To the extent that orientalism had become a part of "Western" ideas by the early nineteenth century, the "Western" impact included also the impact on Asian societies of European ideas of the Orient. How Euro-American images of Asia may have been incorporated into the self-images of Asians in the process may in the end be inseparable from the impact of "Western" ideas per se. One fundamental consequence of recognizing this possibility is to call into question the notion of Asian "traditions," which may turn out, upon closer examination, to be "invented traditions," the products rather than the preconditions of contact between Asians and Europeans, that may owe more to orientalist perceptions of Asia than the self-perceptions of Asians at the point of contact.

One of the most fascinating examples of what I have in mind here is the so-called Bengal Renaissance, the rediscovery of Hindu traditions in the nineteenth century by Bengali intellectuals. British orientalism was to play the crucial part in the Bengal Renaissance by both authoring translations of and authorizing the rejuvenated study of ancient Hindu texts, which kindled the interest in these texts of Bengali intellectuals. In the process, a Hindu tradition was invented in the course of the nineteenth century in which orientalist interpretations of India played a significant part. Schwab's description of these textual interchanges is worth quoting at some length because of its relevance to the argument here:

Europe's knowledge of the Upanishads through Anquetil [-Duperron, Abraham-Hyacinthe] has as its origins a Hindu unitarian attempt. . . .

In 1665 the Mughal Prince of Delhi, Muhammad Dara Shikoh . . . wanted to compare the sacred books of all peoples in order to attain and adopt the ultimate truth. . . . Not satisfied with that and having heard of the Vedas, he summoned the ascetics of Banaras to instruct him in Brahmanical doctrine. For this occasion he ordered a remarkable version of the Upanishads made in Persian, the lingua franca of Asia at that time. It is this text that, in the following century, found its way to Anquetil through the efforts of Gentil and that Anquetil retranslated between 1776 and 1796, first into French and then into Latin, and published in 1801–2. As good historical fortune would have it, the same pandit-scholar who had been Dara's principal translator also became Bernier's most valuable instructor, and Bernier . . . brought a separate manuscript of the *Oupnek'hat* to France . . . the work that Dara had initiated impressed an important adept: it was this text which a century and half later fell into the hands of Rammohun Roy, and which he, in turn, translated and annotated in local dialects and English. It must be said that shortly after his birth the example of such parallels had been established by William Jones, who himself had become a student of Brahmans Radhakanta Sarman and Sarvoru Trivedi: the Hindus were moved by Jones' sincere desire to know their true beliefs. They soon became the pupils of their disciples, whose processes they adopted, beginning with the printing press, an instrument whose diffusion always rendered a critical spirit inevitable within a short time.[23]

The most famous product of the Bengal Renaissance would be Rabindranath Tagore, who in the early twentieth century was to emerge as a "missionary" of a pan-Asian civilization, distinguished from the "materialist" West by its spirituality. But it was not merely the tradition of the Bengal Renaissance that played a formative part in Tagore's thinking. He was also influenced deeply around the turn of the century by Okakura Kakuzo (himself a student at Tokyo University of Ernest Fenollosa), by the Theosophist Margaret Noble from Ireland (who helped Okakura with his influential book *The Ideals of the East*), and, as I noted above, by *Letters from John Chinaman*. Tagore, in turn, was to assume the role of a "missionary" of Asian civilization in Japan and China, where he exerted at least some influence on intellectuals such as Zhang Junmai and Liang Shuming, themselves involved in efforts to rejuvenate Chinese and Eastern cultures.[24] In the end, however, Tagore's messages of pan-Asianism and Asian spirituality were received more favorably in Europe and the United States, where they had originated in the first place, than in China or Japan (or, for that matter, India), all caught up in the contemporary concerns of national formation.

There are obvious differences between the Indian and Chinese encounters with Europeans, but similar processes are observable in the latter case as well. Unlike in India, where the Brahmanical texts were rescued from esoteric obscurity by British orientalists and made into the source of Indian civilization, Confucianism in China was state orthodoxy, and when Jesuits formulated their representations of China as a Confucian state, they no doubt had the benefit of drawing on the self-image of the bureaucratic elite. Nevertheless, the Jesuit "invention of Confucianism," as Lionel Jensen has described it, had the effect of codifying Confucianism as an emblem of Chinese society not just for Euro-Americans, but also for twentieth-century Chinese who drew not only on Chinese but also Euro-American scholarship in their own evaluations of China's past.[25] Benjamin Elman has suggested Jesuit influence in the emergence of textual criticism, which was to have a significant intellectual and political consequence in the interpretation of Confucianism during the Qing.[26] Where there seems to be little doubt concerning the Jesuit impact on the Chinese self-image is in the mapping of the world, of China, and of China's place in the world. Witek credits Matteo Ricci with coining the term Yaxiya, among others, which "presented to the Chinese . . . a unified conception of the world."[27] In a "ten-year project," Jesuits produced for the Kangxi Emperor the first comprehensive map of China. The Kangxi Emperor, according to Theodore Foss, was anxious to know "the extent of the empire," and especially to see a map of the Great Wall, a desire that was nurtured by a Jesuit advisor. The emperor's desire for control over his territories coincided in the project with the Jesuits' wish to fathom the extent of the realm that could be opened up to Christianity to produce the first map of China as a whole; in the process, local knowledges (Chinese maps of localities) were transformed into a map of the whole realm that became available to the Chinese at the same time as to the Europeans, and through the agency of the latter.[28] Arthur Waldron has provided us with a fascinating account of how "the myth of the Great Wall," invented by the Jesuits, would come to play a central part in Chinese nationalist consciousness at a later time.[29]

It is in the twentieth century, however, that Euro-American orientalist perceptions and methods become a visible component in the formulation of the Chinese self-image and Chinese perceptions of the past. The process was facilitated by the emergence of nationalism. Nationalism, once it has emerged, tends to project itself over both space and time, homogenizing all differences across the territory occupied by the nation, and projecting itself back in time to some mythical origin to erase the different temporalities of the past, so that all history becomes a history of national emergence. In the process, some trait or traits become emblematic of the nation, while others that are inconsistent with the national self-image are swept aside as foreign intrusions. In this metonymic reductionism, nationalism shares much in common with the culturalist procedures of orientalism, now at the scale of the nation.[30]

The Euro-American assault on imperial China both provoked the emergence of Chinese nationalism and, ironically, provided it with images of the Chinese past that could be incorporated in a new national identity.[31] While different political strands in Chinese nationalism focused on different aspects of the past and evaluated the historical legacy differently, metonymic reductionism has been apparent in the identification of China among liberals and conservatives with Confucianism, despotism, bureaucratism, familism, or even racial characteristics, all of them traceable to orientalist representations, or an unchanging "feudal" or "Asiatic" society, in a Marxist version of orientalism.[32] What was common to all was a rewriting of Chinese history with images, concepts, and standards drawn from a contemporary consciousness of which "Western" ideas, including the "imaginative geography" of orientalism, were an integral component. This consciousness was formed now not just by the circulation of Euro-Americans in China, as in the case of the Jesuits, but by the circulation of Chinese abroad.

This latter situation also has implied that the origins of our images of China's past have become increasingly blurred. A fascinating example is provided by the career of John King Fairbank, who has been held responsible for both the virtues and the woes of U.S. China scholarship. Fairbank's case is doubly interesting because he himself rejected European-style orientalism and played a major part in launching U.S. China scholarship in the direction of modern Chinese studies. A younger generation of scholars has accused Fairbank of promoting a Eurocentric "impact-response" view, which rendered Chinese into passive objects of Western impact. To be sure, Fairbank did place a great deal of emphasis on the ways in which Chinese tradition (perceived largely in terms of bureaucratic despotism) held China back, so that only the Western impact could provide the dynamic force of change in modern Chinese history. But how different were Fairbank's premises from those expressed in the following lines by a prominent Chinese intellectual in explanation of China's modern fate?

> First, we were lacking in science. In the competition between individuals or nations, what ultimately determines success or failure is the level of knowledge. The contest between scientific and non-scientific knowledge is similar to the contest between the automobile and the rickshaw. The basis of Western science was already established at the time of the Jia Qing and Dao Guang Emperors, when our ancestors were still writing eight-legged essays, and discussing Yin Yang and the Five Elements. Secondly, by the middle of the eighteenth century, the West was already using machinery to produce wealth and conduct war, whereas our industry, agriculture, transportation and military affairs followed the models of the Tang and the Song. Thirdly, the political visage of the West during the Middle Ages closely resembled that of the Spring-Autumn Period, while following the Renaissance it was more like that of the Warring States period. In the conflict for supremacy among the powers, Westerners cultivated a strong patriotism, and a deep national spirit. We on the other hand were stuck corpse-like in familism (*jiazu guannian*) and localism (*jiaxiang guannian*). So in the early years of the nineteenth century, though Western nations were small, their unity gave them a foundation of steel; our nation was big, but it was but a pan of sand, without power. In sum, by the nineteenth century, the Western world already enjoyed the so-called modern culture, while the Eastern world was still mired in the Middle Ages.[33]

The above is from the introduction to Jiang Tingfu's *Outline of Modern Chinese History*. Jiang had received his PhD in diplomatic history from Columbia University before he went back to China to establish the field of modern Chinese diplomatic history in Qinghua University. It was there that in the 1930s John King Fairbank as a graduate student worked with Jiang . In pointing to the strong parallelisms between Fairbank's and Jiang's views of modern China I do not wish to imply that Fairbank's views were shaped by Jiang's; if anything unites their views, it is a common origin in liberal interpretations of Chinese history. But the parallelisms do suggest the confounding of the origins in Europe or China of such views. By the twentieth century in particular, orientalist conceptions had no distinct spatial origin.[34]

This circulation of ideas is more than ever the condition of our understanding of China, which has led some to the conclusion that orientalism is no longer a problem. What I would like to propose instead is that what has changed is the power relationship between China and Euro-America, rather than the abolition of orientalism. On the contrary, the very transformation of power may have culminated in the reification of orientalism at the level of a global ideology. Orientalism, which earlier articulated a distancing of Asian societies from the Euro-American, now appears in the articulation of differences within a global modernity as Asian societies emerge as dynamic participants in a Global Capitalism.[35] In this contemporary guise, orientalism provides the site of contention between the conflicting ideological loyalties of an elite that is no longer identifiable easily as Eastern or Western, Chinese or non-Chinese.

The foremost example of this may be the appearance of "cultural nationalisms" in East and South Asia in the midst of the so-called globalization of Asian societies.[36] One aspect of this cultural nationalism, especially pertinent to Chinese societies, is the so-called Confucian revival. I have discussed this at length elsewhere, so I will summarize it very briefly here.[37] While the discussion of Confucianism among China scholars and Chinese intellectuals has never stopped, the intensive discussions of the 1980s do indeed mark this most recent phase as a "revival." The discussion this time involves not just China specialists or Chinese intellectuals, but state leaders, businesspeople, sociologists (such as Peter Berger), and futurologists (such as Herman Kahn). While in the past there has been a tendency to relegate Confucianism to the past, as an obstacle to modernization, this time around Confucianism is reaffirmed as a positive force in capitalist modernization, relevant not only to the experience of Chinese societies but to East Asian societies in general, and perhaps globally. Theoretically speaking, in its reversal of Max Weber's judgment on Confucianism, the "new Confucianism" seeks to refute orientalist evaluations of Confucianism. There is, however, no challenge to Weber's formulations on modernization per se: what Weber portrayed as inimical to the development of capitalism in China (Confucian values of harmony, familism, patrimonialism) is now reaffirmed as being eminently functional to capitalist development, at least in its present stage. Otherwise, the conceptualization of Confucianism is quite reminiscent of earlier orientalist conceptions of Confucianism as a de-socialized and de-historicized metonym for Chinese society; one advocate states that although Confucianism has a complex history, it may be used "loosely" as being "synonymous with Chinese culture."[38] Confucianism, moreover, has been "deterritorialized" from its Chinese sources to be rendered into a characteristic of East and Southeast Asian societies in general. Tu Wei-ming, whose name has been most closely associated with the Confucian revival, seeks to make Confucianism into a global philosophy (paralleling Christianity in Europe) that may be transplanted anywhere—from the United States to Africa. His efforts are quite reminiscent of the missionizing pan-Asianism of Rabindranath Tagore, and, as with Tagore, they ignore that the term "Confucian societies" disguises national appropriations of what may or may not be a common legacy of East Asian societies. But he is not alone in the undertaking. Political figures such as Lee Kwan Yew of Singapore and Prime Minister Mahathir of Malaysia have joined in a new chorus of "Asianism" against the West; in the case of the latter, obviously, it is Islam rather than Confucianism that is the point of departure. This, too, is consistent with earlier pan-Asianism, where different pan-Asianists projected upon Asia the different "characteristics" of their various national societies. Finally, these intellectual trends are clearly products of a contemporary circulation of intellectuals and ideas; Confucian revivalists, including Tu Wei-ming, readily cite Herman Kahn and Peter Berger as the "Western" authorities who have legitimized the "new Confucianism." On the other hand, the assertion of "Asian cultural differences" by Lee Kwan Yew, Mahathir Mohamad, and the People's Republic of China leadership, especially over issues of democracy and human rights, resonates with prevalent anti-Eurocentric sentiments in Europe and the United States.

In a different vein, one Chinese intellectual has explicitly reaffirmed the positivity of orientalism against Said's arguments. In *Occidentalism: Theory of Counter-Discourse in Post-Mao China*, Chen Xiaomei goes so far as to charge Said with a new kind of neocolonialism.[39] The "occidentalism" in Chen's title refers to Chinese reification of the "Occident," much like the orientalist "reifications" of the "Orient." Occidentalism is very much a mirror image of orientalism and, in Chen's usage, includes orientalism as a premise; the TV series *He Shang*, which is her point of departure, obviously combines "occidentalism" where the West is concerned with "orientalism" in its depictions of China. Chen, however, seeks to refute the connection Said establishes between orientalism and Eurocentric power, arguing that such representations carry different significations in different contexts. In the case of "occidentalism" (or orientalism, for that matter), she draws a distinction in the Chinese context between official occidentalism, which uses representations of the West to justify political repression at home, and antiofficial occidentalism, exemplified by *He Shang*, which serves as legitimation for resistance against oppression. The issue is not orientalism, in other words; the issue is the implication for power of orientalism in different social and political contexts.

Finally, I will mention as an instance of orientalism something that is very much bound with global exchanges and has received some critical attention among Chinese intellectuals: the reification of Chinese culture into a commodity, mainly in the cause of global tourism. Yang Congrong, from whose essay I have derived the title for this section, has pointed to the commodification of Chinese culture in theme parks, tourist brochures, and elsewhere that represents an "Orientalism of Oriental societies." In this case, culture is totally deterritorialized and placed in global tourist circuits, which now endow it with signification. The theme park is emblematic of the reification of culture in its spatialization of cultural artifacts, which derive their meaning from their positioning in the theme park rather than their locations in the complex geographical and social entity that we know as China. And the theme park comes to serve as a substitute for China, as in the Chinese state TV advertisement "You can see all of the four-thousand-year-old culture of China in half an hour in the Chinese culture theme park in Guangzhou." In this case, government and business collude in perpetuating a distinction between East and West so as to make an "exoticized" East more salable to a tourist industry to which East-West distinctions offer one more commodity for sale to consumers who are no longer identifiable clearly as "Eastern" or "Western."[40]

### Orientalism Reconsidered

Orientalism emerged historically in accompaniment with Eurocentrism.[41] The consequence of Eurocentrism historically was to erase the part that non-Europe had played in European development in the course of centuries of interaction and, on the contrary, to distance other histories from the European. The emergence of Eurocentrism also coincided historically with the establishment of Euro-American domination and colonialization of the world. Eurocentrism served the cause of colonialism by representing the world outside of Europe as "empty," at least culturally speaking, or backward,[42] defined in terms of "lack," and hence in need of European intervention. Europe had everything to give to the world; what it received in return were images of its own past—and the rightful material returns from its civilizing activity.

The "orientalization" of Asian societies not only erased the part they had played in "the making of Europe," but also the spatial and temporal complexities of these societies. The question of representation raised in Said's *Orientalism* is not the correctness or erroneousness of orientalist representation, but the metonymic reductionism that led to the portrayal of these societies in terms of some cultural trait or other, that homogenized differences within individual societies and froze them in history. Where the representation was extended to Asia as a whole, metonymic reductionism took the form of projecting upon Asia as a whole the characteristics of the particular society of the individual orientalist's acquaintance.

However individual orientalists may have responded to Asia, moreover, orientalism as *discourse* implied also a power relationship: Europeans, placed at the pinnacle of progress, were in a better position than the natives themselves to know what Asians were about, since they had the advantage of a more prodigious (and panoptical) historical hindsight. I noted earlier that orientalists did not just speak about Asia, they also spoke for Asia. While this points to perturbations within orientalism, it also raises the question of power: power to speak for the Other. The Oriental may speak about the past, of which he or she is an embodiment, but not about the present, in which he or she is not a genuine participant; this is especially true of the critical Oriental, who appears as a degeneration of the ideal type to the extent that he or she has learned to speak in the language of the present. Advocates of a "China-centered history" to whom I have referred above have suggested that contemporary Chinese, who have been touched by "Western" ideas and methods (especially Marxism, it seems), have lost touch with their own past and are at a disadvantage, therefore, in providing a truly China-centered history.

Where orientalism as articulated by Said is wanting, I think, is in ignoring the "Oriental's" participation in the unfolding of the discourse on the Orient, which raises some questions both about the location of the discourse and, therefore, its implications for power. I have suggested above that orientalism, regardless of its ties to Eurocentrism both in origin and in its history, in some basic ways required the participation of "Orientals" for its legitimation. And in its practice, orientalism from the beginning took shape as an exchange of images and representations, corresponding to the circulation of intellectuals and others, first the circulation of Europeans in Asia, but increasingly with a countercirculation of Asians in Europe and the United States.

Rather than view orientalism as an autochthonous product of a European modernity, therefore, it makes some sense to view it as a product of those "contact zones" in which Europeans encountered non-Europeans, where a European modernity produced and was also challenged by alternative modernities as the Others in their turn entered the discourse on modernity. I borrow the term "contact zone" from Mary Louise Pratt, who has described it as "the space of colonial encounters, the space in which peoples geographically and historically separated come into contact with each other and establish ongoing relations, usually involving conditions of coercion, radical inequality, and intractable conflict."[43] But the contact zone is not merely a zone of domination; it is also a zone of exchange, even if it is unequal exchange, which Pratt describes as "transculturation," whereby "subordinated or marginal groups select and invent from materials transmitted to them by a dominant or metropolitan culture. While subjugated peoples cannot readily control what emanates from the dominant culture, they do determine to various extents what they absorb into their own, and what they use it for."[44] We may note also that, in the contact zone, in the process of the very effort to communicate with the dominated, the dominant or the metropolitan culture goes through a language change, if to a lesser extent than the dominated.

The idea (and the reality) of the contact zone enables the explanation of some of the contradictions in orientalism that I have described above. The contact zone is a zone of domination because it does not abolish the structures of power of which it is an expression and to which it serves as a zone of mediation. But the contact zone also implies a distance, a distance from the society of the Self as well as of the Other. The orientalist, I suggested above, is "orientalized" himself or herself in the very process of entering the Orient intellectually and sentimentally. Same with the "Oriental," whose very contact with the orientalist culminates in a distancing from native society, where he or she becomes an object of suspicion, and who in the long run is better able to communicate with the orientalist than with the society of the Self (remember the quotation from Jiang Tingfu above). In some ways, it is this distancing from the complexities of everyday life in either society that facilitates the metonymic cultural representations that I have described above as a basic feature of orientalism—whether by the orientalist or by the self-orientalizing "Oriental." Is it very surprising that nationalism in China, which was as much a source of cultural reification as orientalism, was the production of intellectuals who were themselves products of contact zones, be they Chinese in China, Chinese intellectuals studying abroad, or Chinese overseas?

If locating orientalism in the contact zone modifies our understanding of the processes whereby orientalist representations are produced, the same location also reveals different relationships between orientalism and power. Chen Xiaomei's reminder that orientalism (or occidentalism) may have different meanings in different contexts is a valuable one, so long as we relocate the context of which she speaks not in "China," but in the contact zone of "Westernized" Chinese intellectuals. As Chen argues, occidentalism (the mirror image of orientalism) serves as the source of critique of an oppressive state ideology. But there is arguably another aspect to such self-orientalization. However closely orientalism may be tied in with Euro-American power historically, its contemporary manifestations are difficult to explain in terms of a past relationship between orientalism and Euro-American power. The Confucian revival of the past decade, I would like to suggest, is an expression not of powerlessness, but of a newfound sense of power, which has accompanied the economic success of East Asian societies, who now reassert themselves against an earlier Euro-American domination. In this sense, the Confucian revival (and other cultural nationalisms) may be viewed as an articulation of native culture (and an indigenous subjectivity) against Euro-American cultural hegemony.[45]

The challenge to Eurocentrism in the Confucian revival, within the context of a Global Capitalism, has had reverberations within a Euro-American context as well, raising questions about another fundamental premise of orientalism: the idea of an Occident with a unified culture. Interestingly, even as capitalism has emerged victorious over existing forms of socialism and global unity under a globalized capitalism seems a real possibility for the first time in nearly a century, new fissures have appeared that are expressed in the affirmation of cultural differences not just in Asia or what used to be the Second and Third Worlds, but within the First World itself. The notion of different "cultures of capitalism," to which I referred earlier, has been extended by some to differences among Euro-American societies themselves, as in work that identifies "seven cultures of capitalism," all but one (Japan) located in Europe and North America.[46] The contradiction may be a contradiction of proliferating "contact zones" under a globalized capitalism, which has been accompanied not by the abolition of but by a simultaneous proliferation of a national and ethnic reification of cultures.[47] The idea of a "West" is called into question in a Europe or North America striving for economic and political unification, just as claims to a Confucian zone runs aground on claims to national uniqueness in East and Southeast Asia.

The part that self-orientalization may play in the struggle against internal and external hegemony, and its claims to alternative modernities, however, must not be exaggerated. In the long run, self-orientalization serves to perpetuate, and even to consolidate, existing forms of power. Partha Chatterjee has observed that "nationalist thought accepts the same essentialist conception based on a distinction between 'the East' and 'the West,' the same typology created by a transcendent studying subject, and hence the same 'objectifying' procedures of knowledge constructed in the post-Enlightenment age of Western science."[48] Self-essentialization may serve the cause of mobilization against "Western" domination, but in the very process also consolidates "Western" ideological hegemony by internalizing the historical assumptions of orientalism. At the same time, it contributes to internal hegemony by suppressing differences within the nation.

Examples of the latter abound in contemporary cultural nationalisms. Most obvious is the use of "culture" to reject calls for "democracy" and "human rights," which is common to a diverse group, from Lee Kwan Yew to Mahathir Mohamad to the government of the People's Republic of China. While there is no denying that "democracy" and "human rights" as they are conceived are Euro-American in origin, and are often misused by the latter in the pursuit of power, their denial on the grounds of "cultural imperialism" also justifies oppression at home—and makes little sense when the regimes involved incorporate so much else that is also Euro-American in origin.

This "official Occidentalism," as Chen Xiaomei calls it, however, is only part of the problem. "Anti-official Occidentalism" may be just as complicit in oppression in its resort to self-orientalization as a protest against the oppression of the state. The essentialization and homogenization of the national terrain serves in that case as much as in the case of the state to disguise differences within the nation, including class, gender, and ethnic differences. I have suggested above that elites in Asian societies have been complicit all along in the production of orientalism. This may be more the case than ever in the past, as the idea of the nation has become problematic, and the nation difficult to define as a cultural entity, as globalization and diasporic movements of people complicate cultures and challenge state-defined national cultures with localized cultures. Culturalist essentialism, regardless of its origins in the state or with intellectuals, serves to contain and to control the disruptive consequences of globalization. This helps explain the simultaneous appearance of cultural nationalism with calls for economic globalization. In the works cited above by Harumi Befu, Yoshino Kosaku, Yang Congrong, and others, the authors all point to the part played by government and business in the production of "cultural nationalism." This has been the case also with the Confucian revival, in which Confucianism appears, on the one hand, as a dynamic ideological force in the development of capitalism and, on the other hand, as a value-system with which to counteract the disruptive effects of capitalist development.

While dissident intellectuals may employ occidentalism or orientalism to challenge existing hegemonies, internal or external, they often ignore this aspect of the problem. While *He Shang* in Chen Xiaomei's conception may serve the cause of the struggle against oppression at home, it is itself a product of dissident Chinese intellectuals of the "contact zone," who portray Chinese society from a privileged outside (as Chen admits) and render backward not just a reified native tradition but, with it, the people who are carriers of that tradition, thus a tendency among Chinese intellectuals in recent years to once again represent the "people" at large, especially the peasantry, not as an oppressed group but merely as carriers of "feudal backwardness."

While as an advocate of the revival of Confucianism someone such as Tu Wei-ming is quite different in his evaluation of China's past in terms of power relationships his position is revealing of a similar elitism that nourishes off his privileged status as a Westernized Chinese intellectual. In speaking of Cultural China, Tu has suggested that the creation of a Cultural China must proceed from the "periphery" to the "center," from Chinese overseas to Chinese in China (or, in terms of the metaphor used here, from the "contact zone" to China proper). In terms of Chinese societies, the center-periphery distinction suggests that "Cultural China" is to be created by the transformation of the centers of power by intellectuals from the margins with little or no power, as this is the configuration of power that the center-periphery model usually suggests. Viewed from a global perspective, however, the power relationship appears quite differently, because in that perspective, the periphery coincides with the centers of global power, while the "center" of Chinese society appears as the location of the periphery. "Diasporic Chinese," then, to the extent that they are successful in a global economy or culture, become the agents of changing China. But their very location suggests that they are no longer "Chinese" in any simple identifiable sense, but the products of the "contact zone," in which the West or the East, or the Occident or the Orient, are no longer identifiable with any measure of clarity. The assertion of "Chineseness" against this uncertainty seeks to contain the very dispersal of a so-called Chinese culture into numerous local cultures that more than ever makes it impossible to define a Chinese national culture. This strategy of containment is the other side of the coin to the pursuit of a "Chinese" identity in a global culture. If in the former case it may serve to counter a Euro-American hegemony, in the latter case it is itself an expression of establishing a cultural hegemony that denies the diversity of what it means to be Chinese. In this latter case, ironically, it is empowered by the very Euro-American hegemony that it seeks to displace.

Aijaz Ahmad has criticized Said for ignoring class relations in the emergence of orientalism.[49] Orientalism is not just a matter of continents or nations representing one another; it also entails class (or, for that matter, gender and ethnic) representations—not only in terms of who is engaged in representation, but how a society is represented. It was the upper-class upper-caste Brahmans who provided British orientalists with the texts of Hinduism, as well as their assumptions about Hindu spirituality. Jesuits in China, who were initially drawn to Buddhism as a means of entry into China, decided that Confucianism served better than Buddhism in the representation of China because their friends in officialdom pointed them toward the lifestyles of the elite. In our day, Confucianism may be subjected to different evaluations, which also suggest different relations of power within Chinese societies and between Chinese societies and the outside world. Recent experience also indicates that it is insufficient to conceive of orientalism simply in terms of Eurocentrism or nationalism. It is position in the capitalist structuring of the world that ultimately accounts for the changing relationships between orientalist discourse (Eurocentric or self-orientalizing) and power. Just as it was the apparent Chinese incapability to make the transition to capitalism that once condemned Confucianism to a defunct past, it is Chinese success in the world of capitalism that now enables its admission to the center of a global modernity as an alternative to Euro-American capitalisms—acknowledged as such even by the ideologues of the latter. Intellectuals who themselves have become part of a global elite (not to speak of the managers of capital) play a crucial part in the transformation.

Ironically, the self-assertiveness of "Orientals" under these circumstances would seem to represent not an alternative to, as they claim, but a consolidation of Eurocentric hegemony—or, more accurately, the hegemony of capital globally. As I noted earlier, orientalism was a product of capitalist modernization (and colonialism) in Europe, and the very notion of modernization incorporated orientalist assumptions as an integral premise. Where orientalism earlier represented the past of modernity, it is now rendered into one of its versions—but still without history. The cultural nationalisms of recent years, while they make claims to the uniqueness of essentialized national cultures, all share one thing in common: that the unique national culture is a force of modernization, more precisely, capitalist modernization. Rather than question capitalism with Confucian or other Chinese values, for example, the tendency has been to render it into a value-system conducive to capitalist development. While this has dislodged the claim that only Europeans had the value-system appropriate to capitalism and has asserted the possibility of multiple paths, the multiple paths are all contained within a teleology of capitalism as the end of history.[50]

Said suggested that the solution to overcoming orientalism may lie in the cultivation of a "decentered consciousness" that resists totalization and systematization,[51] something, I take it, along the lines of "multiculturalism." If my analysis based on the "contact zone" has any validity, this may not be sufficient, because orientalism itself may be a product of a consciousness already, if not completely, decentered. There is no self-evident reason why a decentered consciousness should not find relief in culturalist fundamentalism, or the reification of ethnicity and culture; the history of orientalism provides evidence of this strong possibility. Multiculturalism, ironically, may enhance tendencies to orientalism in its insistence on the cultural definition of ethnicity, which reifies cultural origins at the expense of the historicity of both ethnicity and culture.[52]

It seems to me to be more important to question the assumptions of capitalist modernity (not merely Eurocentrism), of which orientalism is an integral expression. To the extent that they have assimilated the teleology of capitalism, recent challenges to Eurocentrism (such as with the Confucian revival) have promoted rather than dislodged orientalism. What is necessary is to repudiate historical teleology in all its manifestations. This would entail the historicization of capitalist modernity itself, and the identification of alternative modernities, not in terms of reified cultures, but in terms of alternative historical trajectories that have been suppressed by the hegemony of capitalist modernity. It also requires questioning not just continental distinctions (Orient/Occident), but nations as units of analysis, since the latter also thrive on cultural homogenization and reification. It is necessary, I think, to restore full historicity to our understanding of the past—and the present—historicity not in the sense that Said uses "historicism" (that presupposes organically holistic cultures) but historicity that is informed by the complexity of everyday life, that accounts not only for what unites but, more importantly, for diversity in space and time, that is as undesirable to national power as it is to Eurocentrism. A thoroughgoing historicism subjects culture to the structures of everyday life rather than erase those structures by recourse to a homogenizing culturalism. This, of course, requires also that we conceive of alternative modernities that take as their point of departure not a reified past legacy, but a present of concrete everyday cultural practices where, as Yang Congrong put it, it is no longer possible to tell what is identifiably Chinese or identifiably Western.

## Notes

1. Edward W. Said, *Orientalism* (New York: Vintage Books, 1979).
2. Edward W. Said, "Orientalism Reconsidered," in *Literature, Politics and Theory: Papers from the Essex Conference, 1976–84*, ed. Francis Barker, Peter Hulme, Margaret Iversen, and Diana Loxley (London: Methuen, 1986), 211.
3. Said, "Orientalism Reconsidered," 223–24.
4. Said, "Orientalism Reconsidered," 215.
5. Said, *Orientalism*, 118.
6. Johannes Fabian, *Time and the Other: How Anthropology Makes Its Object* (New York: Columbia University Press, 1983).
7. Said, *Orientalism*, 116–20.
8. Said, *Orientalism*, 3.
9. Said, *Orientalism*, 12.
10. Said, *Orientalism*, 325.
11. I borrow this section's heading from Yang Congrong, "Dongfang shehuide dong fanglun" (The Orientalism of Oriental Societies), *Dangdai* (Contemporary), no. 64 (August 1, 1991): 38–53.

12. This argument is developed fully, if somewhat tendentiously, in J. M. Blaut, *The Colonizer's Model of the World: Geographical Diffusionism and Eurocentric History* (New York: Guilford Press, 1993). For "our contemporary ancestors," see p. 16.

13. The inside/outside distinction as a basic feature of Eurocentrism is developed at length in Blaut, *The Colonizer's Model.*

14. Kurt Werner Radtke and Tony Saich, eds., *China's Modernisation: Westernisation and Acculturation* (Stuttgart: Franz Steiner, 1993), 1.

15. *Orientalism* provides instances of such "orientalization." Also important for an account of many orientalists in Europe is Raymond Schwab, *The Oriental Renaissance: Europe's Discovery of India and the East, 1680–1880,* trans. Gene Patterson-Black and Victor Reinking, with a foreword by Edward Said (New York: Columbia University Press, 1984). Jonathan Spence, *To Change China: Western Advisers in China, 1620–1960* (Boston: Little, Brown, 1969), offers insightful portraits of Westerners involved in China whose activities provide insights into the workings of power at the ground level, as does Randall E. Stross, *The Stubborn Earth: American Agriculturalists on Chinese Soil, 1898–1937* (Berkeley: University of California Press, 1986). On the Jesuits, see Charles E. Ronan and Bonnie B. C. Oh, eds., *East Meets West: The Jesuits in China, 1582–1773* (Chicago: Loyola University Press, 1988), which contains a number of essays of great interest. For Lawrence, see his autobiography, T. E. Lawrence, *Seven Pillars of Wisdom* (New York: Dell, 1964), and for William Jones, see Garland Cannon, *Oriental Jones: A Biography of Sir William Jones (1746–1794)* (New York: Asia Publishing House, 1964).

16. Schwab, *The Oriental Renaissance.* What made the veneration condescending was the sense that India contained "the eternal in its present" (7). In other words, contemporary India was not truly contemporary, but showed Europe its own past. Nevertheless, the challenge to the earlier "Eurocentric" Renaissance is not to be ignored, and neither is the extension of the boundaries of the "inside" to include Asia.

17. Montesquieu (Charles-Louis de Secondat), *Persian Letters,* trans. and with an introduction by C. J. Betts (New York: Penguin Books, 1993); Oliver Goldsmith, *Citizen of the World: or Letters from a Chinese philosopher Residing in London to His Friend in the East,* in *Collected Works,* 5 vols., ed. A. Friedman (Oxford: Clarendon Press, 1966); André Malraux, *The Temptation of the West,* trans. and with an introduction by Robert Hollander (New York: Vintage Books, 1961); Edward Friedman and Mark Selden, eds., *America's Asia: Dissenting Essays on U.S.-Asian Relations* (New York: Vintage Books, 1971). It is important to underline that, as with the Oriental Renaissance, works such as Montesquieu's and Goldsmith's display an "ethnocentric cosmopolitanism," in other words, employ Asia to Euro-

pean ends. They also render Asians into caricatures of sorts. My concern here, however, is with pointing to varieties of orientalism and what this variety might imply for the connection between orientalism and power.

18. Paul Cohen, *Discovering History in China* (New York: Columbia University Press, 1984); John Schrecker, *The Chinese Revolution in Historical Perspective* (New York: Praeger, 1991).

19. Jackson Lears, *No Place of Grace: Antimodernism and the Transformation of American Culture, 1880–1920* (New York: Pantheon Books, 1981), 175–76. An interesting example of the utopianization of China as a refuge from modernity, written around the turn of the century, also in epistolary form, is Goldsworthy Lowes Dickinson's *Letters from John Chinaman* (London: R. Brimley Johnson, 1901), subsequently published in the United States in 1903 as *Letters from a Chinese Official: Being an Eastern View of Western Civilization.* This work spoke of the conflict between Eastern and Western civilizations and argued for the moral superiority of Chinese over Western civilization. What makes it interesting in this context is that it was one of the works that helped convince one important reader, Rabindranath Tagore (who was unaware of its English authorship), of the superiority of Asian over Western civilization. See Stephen N. Hay, *Asian Ideas of East and West: Tagore and His Critics in Japan, China, and India* (Cambridge MA: Harvard University Press, 1970), 34–35. Of Tagore and orientalism, more below.

20. Tu Wei-ming, "Cultural China: The Periphery as Center," *Daedalus* 120, no. 3 (spring 1991): 13. This was a special issue of *Daedalus,* "The Living Tree: The Changing Meaning of Being Chinese Today." Tu Wei-ming has recently initiated a new journal with the title Cultural China (*Wenhua Zhongguo*).

21. Wang Jiafeng (Wang Jia-fong) and Li Guangzhen (Laura Li), *Dang xifang yujian dongfang: Guoji hanxue yu hanxuezhe* (Taipei: Sinorama Magazine, 1991). This title, revealingly, conveys a sense of "going West to meet with the East." That this is the sense is confirmed by the editors' introduction, "A Sinological 'Journey to the West.'"

22. Wang and Li, *Dang xifang yujian dongfang,* 5, 29.

23. Schwab, *The Oriental Renaissance,* 246. For the Bengal Renaissance, see Atulchandra Gupta, ed., *Studies in the Bengal Renaissance* (Jadavpur, Bengal: National Council of Education, 1958); David Kopf, *British Orientalism and the Bengal Renaissance: The Dynamics of Indian Modernization, 1773–1835* (Berkeley: University of California Press, 1969).

24. Hay, *Asian Ideas.* It may be worth noting that another Indian intellectual and political leader, who would play an even more important part in asserting the contemporary relevance of ancient Indian values, Gandhi, first discovered the significance of those values and the texts in which they were embedded during his

years of education in London. In his case, in addition to the Theosophists, Europe-an intellectuals such as John Ruskin and Leo Tolstoy would play a significant role in his reading of these Indian traditions. See Mohandas K. Gandhi, *Autobiography: The Story of My Experiments with Truth* (New York: Dover, 1983), especially 59–61. In later years, in his critique of capitalist modernity and his pursuit of an alternative path for India, Gandhi did not hesitate to call on orientalist authorities to justify his advocacy. See the appendix to his *Hind Swaraj or Indian Home Rule*, revised ed. (Ahmedabad: Navajivan Press, 1921), 170–80.

25. Lionel Jensen, "Manufacturing 'Confucianism': Chinese and Western Imaginings in the Making of a Tradition," PhD diss., University of California, 1992. It is noteworthy that before they came to realize the importance of Confucianism through acquaintance with the Chinese scene, the Jesuits first attempted to enter China through Buddhism, no doubt on the basis of everyday encounters: "When they realized the low esteem in which Buddhism was held by the literati and saw the lifestyle and ignorance of some of the Buddhist monks, they adopted at the urging of some of their literati friends, the attire and lifestyle of the literati." See Joseph Sebes, S.J., "The Precursors of Ricci," in *East Meets West: The Jesuits in China, 1582–1773*, ed. Charles E. Ronan and Bonnie B. C. Oh (Chicago: Loyola University Press, 1988), 40.

26. Benjamin Elman, *From Philosophy to Philology: Intellectual and Social Aspects of Change in Late Imperial China* (Cambridge MA: Harvard University Press, 1984), 47, 62–63, 76.

27. John W. Witek, S.J., "Understanding the Chinese: A Comparison of Matteo Ricci and the French Jesuit Mathematicians Sent by Louis XIV," in *East Meets West: The Jesuits in China, 1582–1773*, ed. Charles E. Ronan and Bonnie B. C. Oh (Chicago: Loyola University Press, 1988), 71.

28. Theodore N. Foss, "A Western Interpretation of China: Jesuit Cartography," in *East Meets West: The Jesuits in China, 1582–1773*, ed. Charles E. Ronan and Bonnie B. C. Oh (Chicago: Loyola University Press, 1988), 209–51. See p. 223 for the Kangxi emperor and the Great Wall.

29. Arthur Waldron, *The Great Wall of China: From History to Myth* (Cambridge, England: Cambridge University Press, 1990).

30. Benedict Anderson, *Imagined Communities* (London: Verso Books, 1993), offers a stimulating critique of nationalism that incorporates the spatial and temporal implications of nationalism.

31. To my knowledge, Partha Chatterjee, in his analyses of Indian nationalism, has provided the most astute analyses of the problems presented by orientalism to national consciousness. See *Nationalist Thought and the Colonial World* (Minneapolis: University of Minnesota Press, 1993), and *The Nation and Its Fragments:*

*Colonial and Postcolonial Histories* (Princeton NJ: Princeton University Press, 1993).

32. The use of these various traits in representations of China is so commonplace that I will not attempt citation; some of the interpretive trends discussed below may serve as illustrations.

33. Jiang Tingfu, *Zhongguo jindaishi dagang* (Outline of Modern Chinese History) (Taipei: Jingsheng wenwu gongying gongsi, 1968), 4–5.

34. For the relationship between Jiang and Fairbank, see John King Fairbank, *Chinabound: A Fifty Year Memoir* (New York: Harper and Row, 1982), 85–90; Paul M. Evans, *John King Fairbank and the American Understanding of Modern China* (New York: Basil Blackwell, 1988), 50–51. What Jiang said in a lecture in England to returned students like himself is revealing: "We read foreign books and are engrossed in things in which the people have no interest. . . . [We can be] eloquent in the class room, in the Press in Shanghai and Beiping, even come to Chatham House and make you think we are intelligent, and yet we cannot make ourselves understood to a village crowd in China, far less make ourselves accepted as leaders of the peasants" (90). The statement may distinguish the Chinese intellectual from the foreign, even when they hold similar views.

35. See, for an example, Stewart R. Clegg and S. Gordon Redding, eds., *Capitalism in Contrasting Cultures* (Berlin: Walter de Gruyter, 1990).

36. See Harumi Befu, ed., *Cultural Nationalism in East Asia* (Berkeley: Center for Chinese Studies, 1993); Kosaku Yoshino, *Cultural Nationalism in Contemporary Japan: A Sociological Inquiry* (London: Routledge, 1992).

37. Arif Dirlik, "Confucius in the Borderlands: Global Capitalism and the Reinvention of Confucianism," *boundary 2* (forthcoming).

38. Hung-chao Tai, ed., *Confucianism and Economic Development: An Oriental Alternative?* (Washington DC: Washington Institute Press, 1989), 3. Ironically, Tai agrees with Said's thesis on orientalism, and sees the "Oriental alternative" of Confucianism as a means to counter Eurocentric orientalism. Not all those who write of Confucianism engage in this kind of reductionism. An example is Yu Ying-shih's *Zhongguo jinshi zongjiao lunli yu shangren jieji* (Modern Chinese Religious Ethic and the Merchant Class) (Taipei: Lianjing chuban shiye gongsi, 1987). While Yu subscribes to Weberian ideas of modernization, he offers a more nuanced analysis of Confucianism, which accounts both for change in Confucianism over time and for its different appropriation by different classes, in this case the merchants.

39. Chen Xiaomei, *Occidentalism: Theory of Counter-Discourse in Post-Mao China* (New York: Oxford University Press, 1994), introduction. See also her "Occidentalism as Counterdiscourse: 'He Shang' in Post-Mao China," *Critical Inquiry* 18 (summer 1992): 686–712.

40. Yang Congrong, "Dongfang shehuide dongfanglun." I may take note here of an important observation that Yang makes: "If we take the situation in Taiwan as a concrete example, it is very difficult in everyday life now to distinguish clearly what is typically Chinese culture from what is typically Western culture; but a clear distinction between Chinese and Western cultures seems to persist in people's minds. If they cannot refer something to a past that is no longer retrievable, then they insist on finding it in an inexhaustible West with an indistinct visage" (50). Yang describes the role the government and the tourist industry have played in the production of "Chinese culture," much to the denial of the complexities of the living culture of the present. A similar argument is offered by Allen Chun, "The Culture Industry as National Enterprise: The Politics of Heritage in Contemporary Taiwan," *Culture and Policy* 6, no. 1 (1994): 69–89. Both authors cite *Sinorama* magazine, cited above in connection with sinology, as one of the major organs of such "cultural production."

41. The emergence of Eurocentrism as an autonomous, self-contained development from ancient Greece to modern Euro-America has been examined incisively by Samir Amin, *Eurocentrism* (New York: Monthly Review Press, 1989), and Martin Bernal, *Black Athena: The AfroAsiatic Roots of Classical Civilization, Vol. 1: The Fabrication of Ancient Greece, 1785–1985* (New Brunswick NJ: Rutgers University Press, 1987).

42. Blaut, *The Colonizer's Model*, describes this as "the myth of emptiness" (15), which included the absence of working over the environment in European ways—in other words, living in harmony with nature.

43. Mary Louise Pratt, *Imperial Eyes: Travel Writing and Transculturation* (London: Routledge, 1992), 6.

44. Pratt, *Imperial Eyes*, 6.

45. This is very much the case with Tu Wei-ming's advocacy of a "Cultural China." See "Cultural China," 2.

46. Charles Hampden-Turner and Alfons Trompenaars, *The Seven Cultures of Capitalism: Value Systems for Creating Wealth in the United States, Japan, Germany, France, Britain, Sweden and the Netherlands* (New York: Doubleday, 1993). For an interesting take on this problem from an entirely different perspective, see J. G. A Pocock, "Deconstructing Europe," *History of European Ideas* 18, no. 3 (1994): 329–45.

47. I have addressed this question of "contact zones," or "borderlands," extensively in Arif Dirlik, *After the Revolution: Waking to Global Capitalism* (Hanover NH: University Press of New England for Wesleyan University Press, 1994). The notion of "borderlands" is quite pervasive in our day in all manner of cultural criticisms.

48. Chatterjee, *Nationalist Thought and the Colonial World*, 38.

49. Aijaz Ahmad, *In Theory: Classes, Nations, Literatures* (London: Verso Books, 1992), especially chap. 5.

50. Needless to say, this is not accepted universally and has produced predictions of new kinds of conflict in the world. The foremost example, by an influential U.S. political scientist, may be Samuel P. Huntington, "The Clash of Civilizations?," *Foreign Affairs* 72, no. 3 (summer 1993): 22–49. An example of a history-less Asia that is nevertheless modern is to be found in *Asian Power and Politics: The Cultural Dimensions of Authority* (Cambridge MA: Harvard University Press, 1985), by the distinguished political scientist and China specialist, Lucian W. Pye, with Mary W. Pye. Pye argues for differences among Asian societies, but differences on a common site marked by a culture of "paternalism and dependency." His argument is echoed by many an advocate of Confucianism. I noted Yu Ying-shih's study of Chinese merchants above as an example of a different, more historical approach to the problem of Confucianism and capitalism. It is necessary, in my opinion, to distinguish economic change from capitalist modernization. That Chinese society at different points had flourishing economic change does not imply that it was, therefore, headed for capitalism, just as the absence of capitalism does not imply that it was, therefore, stagnating. Such conclusions follow only from a hindsight application of the teleology of capitalism, as in the "sprouts of capitalism" idea in Chinese Marxist historiography.

51. Said, "Orientalism Reconsidered," 228.

52. Said himself has recognized these possibilities. See "Orientalism Reconsidered," 216.

# 12 | Profiteering Women and Primitive Communists

## Propriety and Scandal in Interwar Japanese Studies of Okinawa

ALAN S. CHRISTY

On March 16, 1939, six justices of the Naha District Court in Okinawa committed multiple acts of ethnology as part of a widely applied, but short-lived, experiment ordered by the Japanese Ministry of Justice. In 1937, responding to criticism that the centrally appointed judges of the district courts were trying cases in woeful ignorance of local customs and conditions (which might have supplied terms of mitigation?), the Ministry ordered all district courts to acquaint themselves with their districts by holding hearings on whatever issues of local import they deemed necessary. Most district courts held at least three or four such hearings, and many were on questions of local dialects or local industries (such as lumber, mining, and sericulture). The justices in Naha, however, held only one hearing, the transcript of which was entitled "On the Fishermen of Itoman and Their So-called Individualism."

At the time of the hearing, Itoman was a relatively prosperous fishing town a few miles south of the main Okinawan city of Naha. The association of Itoman with "individualism" originated in an essay by the Marxist economist and Kyoto Imperial University professor Kawakami Hajime, written in 1911 after a three-hour visit to the town. As we shall see, Kawakami's visit and article "branded" the town with a stigma that still festered twenty-eight years later, when the Naha District Court held its proceedings. The hearings, in effect, were a belated trial of Kawakami's claims, and the epistemological code that was employed to prove Kawakami's guilt (or, more precisely, Itoman's innocence) was ethnology.

My goal in this essay is to introduce to a non-Japanese-reading audience the basic outlines of Japanese studies of Okinawa in the first half of the

414

twentieth century. The reconsideration of orientalism that is undertaken by the essays in this volume offers a meaningful occasion to present what must appear to be an incredibly obscure body of texts to a nonspecialist audience. That is because I believe the Japanese discourse on Okinawa performed a significant function in articulating Japanese identity in an imperialist context.

Since Said, orientalism has come to be seen as indelibly linked with the colonialist project.[1] It was Said's contention that no matter how sympathetically, or deeply, orientalists engaged with their objects of study, by situating the European in the position of the dynamic knower and the Oriental in the position of the passively known, orientalism continually served the colonialist enterprise. In other words, even though a particular orientalist might harbor serious doubts about the propriety of colonial domination, his (and I mean this pronoun to be male) production of knowledge about the Orient performed domination in the epistemological domain. At the same time, for Said this was never simply an abstract concern. Instead, it was always ultimately grounded in geopolitical domination, because the orientalist was always backed up by the political, military, and economic domination of imperialism.

It is the relation between colonialism and orientalism that makes a discussion of Japan especially relevant to a reconsideration of orientalism such as the one in this volume. For while most students of the history of colonialism might find it initially jarring to think of an "Oriental" nation producing an "orientalist" discourse, many East Asian scholars have long felt dissatisfaction with Said's emphatic restriction of orientalism to the West. If orientalism was really about colonial power, and not just an essentialist failing of the West, then should we not give the case of Japanese colonialist epistemology a serious investigation?[2] I clearly believe we should, as I also believe that it is well past the time when scholars of the history and theory of colonialism should have begun to be as cognizant of the Japanese case in their scholarship as they are of the European and American cases. This also means that, as I believe the case of Japanese colonialism cannot be dismissed as merely brief and derivative, the case of Japanese "orientalism" cannot be easily filed away under the label "Orientalism, Others."

But in consideration of the limited space of an essay, let me truncate a review of Japanese colonialism and Japanese orientalism by asking what I think is the guiding question for such a task. What I would like to do is ask of Japanese colonial studies: What tasks did they have to perform? Japanese colonialism shared many features with Euro-American colonialisms, including a strong conviction of civilizational superiority. However, many proponents of Japanese empire also recognized that the racial differentiation between ruler and ruled was far less obvious in the Japanese case than in the European and American cases, according to racial paradigms of the time. To some, it was even nonexistent, since the Japanese Empire was constituted of the rule by Asians over other Asians. This meant that the racial categorization of colonial studies had to be significantly reworked. Not long after the acquisition of Taiwan (in 1895), Okakura Kakuzo struck the chord that would be picked up by colonial apologists when he wrote his most famous line, "Asia is One."[3] By the 1930s, Japanese colonial ideologues were insisting that Asian rule of Asians could not be considered colonialism. Instead, as they tried to argue at the League of Nations in defense of their puppet state in Manchuria, it was self-determination. Returning to my question above, this meant that Japanese colonial studies needed to establish the harmonious potential of racial affinities of the peoples incorporated into the Japanese Empire. At the same time, however, it was crystal clear that control of this empire was in Japanese, not vaguely Asian, hands. Thus, the more famous task of colonial studies was to guarantee that the Asian brotherhood was properly organized within a Japan-dominated hierarchy.

This may well have interesting comparabilities to the European conceit of universalism, a guiding assumption of both the right to rule and the inevitability of European domination. But the logic of Asian brotherhood arranged hierarchically necessitated a complex layering of ethnicity that maintained proximity to the core Japanese identity. With the Japanese Empire geographically concentrated, this ethnic hierarchy could be mapped onto space through a series of concentric circles radiating out of the home islands. While the range of circles could easily map the usual progressive-backward chronotope, the circles could also represent connections, or what Tomiyama Ichirō calls "spheres of contiguity."[4]

This is where Okinawa becomes important. Okinawa was the last territory to be absorbed into the modern Japanese state as a prefecture, in 1879. Prior to annexation, Okinawa was a semi-independent kingdom, known as the Ryūkyūs. While ranked the second most important kingdom in the Chinese tribute system, the Ryūkyūs were placed under the suzerainty of a Japanese domain when that domain, Satsuma, invaded it in 1609. From 1609 to 1868, the lords of Satsuma insisted that the Ryūkyūan royal government recognize its control by Satsuma, but maintained the fiction of Ryūkyūan independence so that it could tap into the lucrative trade that derived from the Chinese tribute system. The Ryūkyūs were the object of a brief international struggle from 1868 to 1879, when the Meiji state transformed the Japanese political landscape and sought to take over Satsuma's control of the island kingdom. Ryūkyūan aristocrats appealed to the Chinese for help in resisting the Meiji state's annexation, and the Chinese and Japanese governments engaged in troubled negotiations over the islands for most of the 1870s.[5] But the Meiji government brought the ambiguity of the islands to an end when Japanese troops removed the Ryūkyūan king from his palace, brought him to Tokyo, and made him a marquis in the Japanese nobility. At the same time, the royal government was folded, replaced by a government designated by the Japanese Home Ministry, and Okinawa prefecture was proclaimed. Okinawa thus became a part of the nation late, with a legacy of political difference and resistance and a tendency for most Japanese to see it as culturally affiliated with China, due to its prominent role in the tribute system.

In short, Okinawa, like Hokkaidō,[6] was a Japanese prefecture that was ruled like a colony and seen as culturally distinct from the main islands. From 1879 until it was conquered by the American military in 1945, Okinawa hovered in a gray zone between domestic politics (as a prefecture) and colonial rule. Indeed, in 1908, the Japanese legislature even considered a proposal to revoke Okinawa's prefectural status and place it under the Taiwan Government-General's administration. Which brings me to the issue at the heart of this essay. While this ambiguity was constantly addressed and experienced as a crisis of identity in Okinawa prefecture, it also made Okinawa extremely useful to the discourse on the Japanese Empire. At the geographical and imaginative border of the Japanese homeland, Okinawa could serve as a kind of discursive customs house, policing and regulating the traffic in and out of the home islands, but also enabling it. Okinawa could be the site that demonstrated the islands' uniqueness but also that naturalized relations with colonial others.

This, then, is the frame through which I shall introduce interwar Japanese studies of Okinawa. As I suggested in the opening paragraph, with my reference to ethnology as an epistemological code that could be used to "try" the veracity of statements about Okinawa, I believe that the Japanese discourse on Okinawa was dominated by ethnology to a degree that was unimaginable in other prefectures.[7] As I shall show, ethnology not only utterly displaced political economy, but it also constructed an image of Okinawa that restricted its meaning to the meanings it could have for Japanese. In other words, it made the prefecture a premier site of signification for what it meant to be Japanese.

By the time of the mock trial I mentioned at the outset, ethnology set the limits for what could be said about Okinawa. It was the "propriety" of my title. But just as using Okinawa to talk about Japan means approaching the subject from its margins, I would like to circle in on the proper domain of Okinawan studies by starting at their margins. That is, I would like to center my discussion on two "scandalous" texts on Okinawa, texts that had to be marginalized in order for proper Okinawan studies to commence. The first text is the infamous 1911 essay by Kawakami Hajime (1879–1946), "The Individualistic Families of Ryūkyū Itoman,"[8] that was ultimately subjected to trial. The second is a far weightier, far more carefully researched book by Tamura Hiroshi (1886–1945), *Studies of Ryūkyūan Communal Villages* (1927),[9] that was marginalized by neglect rather than attack.

### Stigma

Kawakami Hajime traveled down to Okinawa prefecture from Kyoto Imperial University in 1910 with a specific project in mind. A budding Marxist economist, Kawakami was going to Okinawa to gather material on a communal landholding system in Okinawa, known as the *jiwari* system, that had been abolished less than ten years previously. While there were features of this system that were specific to Okinawa, the village ownership and rotating cultivation of land that were the essentials of the system were common to many Japanese villages during the Tokugawa period (1600–1868). To that extent, a study of the Okinawan case could be of great relevance to understanding the recent Japanese past. But Kawakami had bigger fish to fry. He was engaged in a study of capitalism and he believed the jiwari system could give him comparative insights into what he called a "primitive communistic system."

As every researcher knows, unexpected diversions can suddenly appear in the field. Upon arrival in Okinawa, Kawakami contacted his friend Ifa Fuyū, an Okinawan with a degree from Tokyo Imperial University, who was quickly becoming the leading authority on Okinawan history for Japanese scholars. Ifa offered whatever help he could, but also suggested that while Kawakami was in the islands, he should take a short trip to a southern fishing town called Itoman to look into that town's unusual property customs. Kawakami was intrigued by Ifa's hints, so a few days after his arrival, the two traveled a dozen miles south of the main city of Naha, on the best road in Okinawa, to the town of Itoman.

Kawakami's "research" in Itoman consisted entirely of a three-hour interview of "a local man, Uehara Yoshikame," a man who was, in fact, an official in the Itoman town hall. Over a lunch at the White Silver Pavilion restaurant (the mere fact that Itoman had a restaurant struck Kawakami as a sign of its wealth), Uehara painted a picture for Kawakami of Itoman fisher families engaged in strikingly anomalous economic activities. As Kawakami's informant related, the fishing industry in Itoman had developed a division of labor in which the men went out to sea at night in dugout boats to fish and the women took the catch, on the men's return in the morning, and hustled up the coastline to sell the fish at the market at Naha. What was so peculiar about this was that, according to Uehara/Kawakami, the men "sold" the fish to their womenfolk at the beach when they came ashore. The women then sold the fish at market, most often at a price above that they paid the men, and then kept the difference as their profit.

Kawakami well knew that Japanese readers who were accustomed to a Civil Code that put all family property in the hands of the male head would be shocked by a system in which the men and women of the same household would engage in exchanges that resulted in a profit for the women. Moreover, Kawakami insisted that the women did not turn over their profits to their husband, or to a family account, but instead kept that money in a secret account (secret in location, not existence), apart from the family's. As if that were not shocking enough, Kawakami went on to insist that when children entered their money-earning years, they also kept their earnings apart from the family account (most family expenses were thus paid for by the father's earnings). Quoting a local saying with the approximate meaning of "The last person you could ever turn to for a loan is a relative," Kawakami presented an image of families in which every member of the household had his or her own income and rarely shared it with kin. In fact, when the main breadwinner, the male head, needed money to increase his capital investment in fishing (either to buy new nets or a boat), Kawakami told his readers, the man had to sign a loan agreement with the family member who provided the money. Many a divorce had come about, he suggested, because a man had failed to pay off his loan from his wife. As he informed his readers in the opening to his essay on this phenomenon, he had gone to Okinawa to do research into a communistic system and, instead, had found its exact opposite: extreme individualism.

Kawakami's explanation for the Itoman economy proved just as shocking as his description, for the reader who is grappling with this Okinawan oddity is suddenly transported, in the middle of the essay, to the southwest coast of Norway. The passage to Norway came in a book by a Frenchman, Henri de Tourville, *The Growth of Modern Nations: A History of the Particularist Form of Society.*[10] Kawakami presents de Tourville's work as a relevant, materialist study of the historical development of private property. In Kawakami's essay, de Tourville demonstrates how the concept of private property arose in Europe in specific geographical and climatological conditions, the kind that prevailed on the southwest coast of Norway. Peoples engaged in fishing in calm, warm waters off narrowly inhabitable coastlines backed by mountain ranges that cut them off from groups they had left behind, de Tourville insists, were the first, and only, ones in the world to develop the concept of private property at the heart of modern capitalism. Boldly, de Tourville insists that anyone anywhere in the world with a concept of private property is a descendant of these Norse fishermen. After walking his readers through de Tourville's text, Kawakami returns his readers to Itoman to note that the same geographical characterization could be made of Itoman. Clearly rejecting de Tourville's racist assumption equating private property with whiteness, Kawakami posits that the Itoman fishermen may provide an example of a parallel world historical phenomenon.

In the final section of his essay, Kawakami introduces the big picture question: Could the Itoman fishermen represent the real, native development of capitalism in Japan? The key, he suggests, may be to not look for capitalism in the accumulating production of the materials of daily life (that is, the capitalist is one who arises successfully from the ranks of laborers), but in the generation of surplus value. In the Itoman case, this meant looking at the economic functions of women, for they were the ones who generated a surplus that could become capital. Kawakami ends his analysis at a provisional stage, leaving much unsaid. But the essay teemed with implications, including the shocking idea that true capitalism in Japan may arise out of its most marginal places, from the hands of fishmongering women.

For a Marxist such as Kawakami, this could also imply that the Japanese transition to socialism, which would presumably begin in the most advanced area, could arise in Okinawa. Nowhere does Kawakami say this. But his notoriety in Okinawa began even before he returned to Kyoto to write his infamous essay on Itoman. As a prominent scholar from a top university, Kawakami was a major attraction for the elite of Okinawa. As a result, his schedule of research was peppered with commitments to deliver public lectures. All his plans in Okinawa came crashing down, however, after delivering his first talk. At a well-attended, and closely covered, talk Kawakami noted that many Japanese excoriated Okinawans for having a paltry sense of patriotism. Perhaps wishing to flatter his hosts, but also revealing his own hostility to the shrillness of Japanese nationalism since the Russo-Japanese War, Kawakami told his audience that he saw Okinawans' lack of patriotism as the sign that they were the hope of the future of Japan. In other words, Okinawans would show Japanese how to live without nationalism and the bigotry it naturally engendered.

Unfortunately, Okinawan elites, who were generally desperate for recognition from Japanese of their true and faithful commitment to the empire, responded with rage to Kawakami's claims. The day after his talk, the local newspapers condemned Kawakami for casting aspersions on Okinawan patriotism and demanded satisfaction. Within two days of giving his speech, the furor had reached such intensity that Kawakami immediately boarded the first ship off the island and headed home, never to return to Okinawa. His speech and essay were labeled by Okinawans the "Kawakami Insult Incident" and continued to fester for thirty-five years.

### Cobwebs

Tamura Hiroshi was a bureaucrat from Gumma prefecture in Japan who spent five years in the Okinawan prefectural government, from 1922 to 1926, four of those as chief of the Okinawa Prefecture Industrial Division. His sojourn in Okinawa coincided with some of the worst years of the post–World War I economic collapse. As a bureaucrat, his primary concern was engineering the recovery of the Okinawan economy. But in his free time Tamura was also a scholar-at-large, a man who was deeply interested in the economic historical problem of the evolution of property. During his five years in Okinawa, he threw himself into an investigation of the jiwari landholding system that Kawakami had originally intended to study. Over that time, he published several preliminary essays on the subject. But he finally managed to bring it all together shortly after he left for a post in northern Japan in a massive (five hundred pages), painstakingly documented and mapped book called *Studies of Ryūkyūan Communal Villages*. Tamura's manuscript was published by a new publishing house called Oka shoin (specializing in anthropology and ethnology) with the enthusiastic support of a powerful figure in Japanese ethnology, Yanagita Kunio.

From the beginning, however, the book was seen as anomalous. Just before accepting Tamura's manuscript, Oka had done very well with a book on archaic matriarchy in Okinawa by a young Okinawan researcher (and district court judge) named Sakima Kōei.[11] Calculating that the interest in Okinawa was high, Oka agreed with Yanagita's assessment that this was not really a book of ethnology, but figured that the wealth of detail would be useful to ethnologists. However, although Tamura's study had the backing of prominent scholars in Okinawan studies, the text sank into obscurity. One finds occasional references to his work in later studies of Okinawa, but no one took up his specific project or his methodology.

Tamura framed his study within a debate in the Western historiography of the evolution of property. As Tamura presented it, the debate at the time was over whether the origins of property could be found in "Primitive Communal Property" or "Primitive Private Property." The proponents of "Communal Origins," led by Lewis Morgan, argued that property originated as clan property. The development of the family meant the demise of the clan—and the rise of a more privatized form of property—but it also led to the rise of the village community that could limit family property or replace clan ownership with communal ownership. The proponents of "Private Origins," led by Jan Stanislau Lewinski, argued that property originated in monopolistic acquisition of territory, leading to gross inequities in the distribution of wealth. The communal body formed to check and redress this social imbalance and was therefore the engine of sociocultural progress. Through discussion of these debates, therefore, Tamura established at the outset an intertextual universe for his study consisting of Morgan, Lewinski, Lewis, Gomme, Maine, and Baeden-Powell, among others.

This intertextual terrain begins to look odd when Tamura moves into the main theses of his book: (1) that the history of property in Okinawa supported the Communal Origins theory and (2) that the history of property in Okinawa showed that Okinawa was purely Japanese. In other words, Tamura's text is tugging in two directions. On the one hand, Okinawa contributes evidence to a debate on the world historical stage, an argument that is smoothly consonant with his discussion of Western historiography. On the other hand, Okinawa is solely significant in its relation to Japan. It is this latter direction that develops as if the Western historiography he has gone through in such detail is suddenly irrelevant. More important, however, this is also the argument that gets the greatest emphasis in the book.

In terms of the first thesis, Tamura's story is of how clans (*munchū*) in archaic Okinawa were the original holders of property. As time passed and the clans grew in size, they became unable to sustain themselves. The clans then split into families, and the cooperative character of the clans was transferred to village communities. In evolutionary terms, therefore, property originated as a communal concept, slowly individualizing with the shift to family units, but always tempered by the resilience of the communal body.

The key question that links his first thesis to the second is the question raised by the Communal Origins theory of property: What is the origin of communities? Here Tamura examines three prevailing theories in Western historiography—a government origins, a racial origins, and a nature origins theory—and opts for a combination of race and nature.[12] Although recognizing the universality of evolution, Tamura also insists that racial unities and specific material conditions establish that each group travels its own particular path. (the specificities of race/blood and nature will outweigh universalist pulls in evolution).

Taken together, the Communal Origins theory and the Racial/Natural communities theories mutually support Tamura's overriding concern of establishing the pure Japanese-ness of the Okinawan case. They lay the ground for his portrayal of the Okinawan communal landholding system as being bound by relations of blood and arising from a spiritual life tied to specific places (in contrast to a nonlocalizable, universal notion of deity). This description perfectly matches his unexamined presumptions about community in Japan and smoothly subordinates Okinawa to the position of a particular case of a Japanese universal.

As we shall see below, Tamura's final portrayal is well within the bounds of "proper" interwar Japanese studies of Okinawa; in short, the Japaneseness of Okinawa is its sole meaning, its sole point of reference. But there is enough that is discomforting about Tamura's terminology and emplacement of his argument that later scholars of Okinawa ended up keeping his text at arm's length. By the mid-1930s, when a recognizable field of Okinawan studies was largely in place, references to Western historiography were almost totally absent, and even China was considered only so that it might be rejected as irrelevant.[13] Both Tamura's and Kawakami's intertextual worlds—populated by Morgans, Gommes, and de Tourvilles—are rejected by "proper" studies of Okinawa.[14]

But even more jarring to the later scholars was Tamura's use of the word *kyōsan* to signify "communal." Broken down into its constituent characters, the term can literally signify either common birth or common production. But while it had a firm place in academic terminology when paired with "village" to signify "communal villages," it was also the term that formed the core signifier of Communism: *kyōsan* (Communal) *shugi* (ism). Moreover, it was exactly the same as the word that the Marxist Kawakami had used to describe what he hoped to find in Okinawa. By 1927, when Tamura published his study, the term was already strongly linked to the Communist movement, and those writing about "community" had shifted to other terms, such as *kyōdōtai* (cooperative body) and *kyōdo* (native place). By 1939, in a political climate that was brutally intolerant of the merest whiff of Marxism, Kawamura Tadao could praise Tamura's research, but only bemoan the misunderstandings Tamura had caused with his "unfortunate" insistence on the word kyōsan.[15] Tamura's characterization of Okinawans as "primitive communists" (as the word was likely to be understood) was ultimately unpalatable (and potentially dangerous) to many Okinawans. It ended up relegating his book to exile, like an embarrassing, eccentric relative whose actions could either be explained (with difficulty) or, better yet, ignored.

### The Prosecution of Deviance

While Tamura's "mischaracterization" could be handled gently, Kawakami's attribution of "individualism" to an Okinawan town merited rougher treatment. Calling someone an individualist in interwar, and particularly wartime, Japan was akin to calling him a traitor (*hikokumin*). Although Kawakami had used the term in 1911, when there was still some room for public figures to associate themselves with the concept,[16] like all "slanders" the attribution had an uncanny ability to take a firmer hold of the popular imagination than did the rebuttals issued by Okinawans and their supporters. One likely reason for its durability was that Okinawans' existence on the border between home and colony in the Japanese social imaginary made them always suspect, more susceptible to slander than defense.[17]

Thus, we now return to the text with which I opened this essay: the mock trial of Kawakami's essay in the Naha District Courthouse in March 1939. It is not clear how Kawakami's text was chosen as the topic for the sole judicial investigation of local customs in Okinawa. Of all the hearings held by all the courts under the Ministry of Justice's program, it is the only one framed as a rebuttal (all the others have titles more appropriate to fact-finding commissions) in its very title, "On Itoman Fishermen and Their So-Called Individualism."[18] That alone suggests an Okinawan source for the choice of topic. Whatever its course into the courtroom, however, the hearing proceeded very much like a trial. One witness was called, the principal of the Itoman elementary school, Tamashiro Shōichi. A team of prosecutors led by Aoyama Shunsai and Shirakawa Ryūichi questioned him about Kawakami's essay, and the six judges of the panel cross-examined him, raising questions about Tamashiro's own representations of Itoman and its "purely Japanese great family system."

The transcript of the hearing gives a fascinating glimpse of the assimilative pressures brought to bear on Okinawans in imperial Japan. Although ostensibly this was a merely informational hearing, the exchanges between the Okinawan informant and his Japanese inquisitors from the bench quickly took on the flavor of a police interrogation. The key figure in this transformation was the witness, Tamashiro Shōichi. His position as school principal likely made him the most prestigious, if not only, representative of the national government in Itoman (apart from the police). In that position, Tamashiro represented the enlightening power of the state to other villagers. On the other hand, as we know from his surname, Tamashiro was himself Okinawan. Thus, while his position as school principal marked him as the local intellectual authority, capable of meeting the demands of the court for information, his identity as Okinawan placed him in the contradictory position of a representative of the local population to the state. Combining the two positions in his single person, Tamashiro's statements in the hearing embody both the desire for a harmonious joining of the two and the irrepressible suspicion that such a joining was impossible.

The hearing began with a thrust and parry. Deputy Prosecutor Shirakawa observed that Itoman fishermen were commonly believed to be individualistic. Tamashiro acknowledged that it was, indeed, a common perception, but he responded that this was a lie that was started by a discredited scholar based on shallow research. Far from being the truth, Itoman fishermen were, he insisted, "a community that faithfully maintains the extended familialism unique to Japan." From the first, therefore, the interlocutors established a pattern of accusation and defense. Although the transcript contains extended passages in which Tamashiro delivers mini-lectures on local life and customs, it is punctuated by questions about deviance. For most of the hearing, the objects of presumed deviance were the women of Itoman. They were the ones with private savings, made possible by exchanges over which they had the power of determination (price setting). This deviance from family law was presumed to lead to more fundamental cultural deviances, prompting Deputy Chief Justice Misaka Kinji to comment that "the women are in an extremely advantageous position." By the end of the hearing, the concerns about women's advantage revealed their ultimate significance when Prosecutor Shirakawa diverted a discussion of local religious beliefs to a bald expression of doubt: "Tell us about the Itoman woman's sense of chastity."[19]

Throughout the hearing, Tamashiro's primary strategy of defense was to argue for the authenticity of Okinawan membership in the Japanese Empire by keeping the focus on male activity in Itoman. Quickly deflecting questions about women's activities, he spent the bulk of his time describing the strength, valor, productivity, and righteousness of Itoman men, situating them at the heights of Japanese achievement. Notably, this strategy tried to resolve the conflicts in his dual position by representing the people of Itoman as already models of state enlightenment. But in the final minutes of the hearing, his strategy faced its strongest test as Justice Misaka called into question the racial status of the Itoman people: "It is often said that the Itoman people are physically large and that they are descendents of Westerners. What is your opinion of their race?"[20]

With this question near the end of the hearing, Misaka revealed the ultimate stakes in the judges' concerns about Itoman individualism. Combined with the obsessions about female virtue, the suspicion that the Itoman people were actually of Western descent signified that the justices took ethnic difference to constitute untrustworthiness. Tamashiro fended off this suspicion by (1) associating it with the deviance of the Marxist Kawakami and (2) explaining Itoman's physical makeup as equivalent to the state's goals of enlightenment. That is, Tamashiro dismissed racial difference and explained the "superiority" of Itoman physical stature as a result of nutrition and hygiene, two of the main features of state social engineering.

It is worth remembering that these suspicions were not voiced in a historical vacuum. In 1939, when the hearing was held, Japan was nearly two years into total war with China and six and a half years of endless crises on the expanding borders of empire. Domestically, Japan had long been engaged in an intense struggle over the meaning and character of Japanese society. In this struggle, the proponents of a unique world mission for Japan—one defined by the rule of a sacred emperor—had held the upper hand for at least a decade. Ideological struggle at home and crisis on the imperial borders dictated that if Okinawans were to avoid the imperial truncheon they would have to prove their unswerving fidelity, even authenticity, to Japaneseness. At the same time, Japaneseness was produced as the quality that guaranteed trustworthiness.

One final element is worth further discussion, however. In the wake of Kawakami's and Tamura's work, a new body of work on Okinawa was produced that avoided the pitfalls of both and thus constituted itself as proper and believable. It is to the character of that work that I turn in conclusion.

## The Coconut of Insight

The mainstream of imperial Japanese studies of Okinawa was dominated by two men, a Japanese ethnographer named Yanagita Kunio and an Okinawan historian named Ifa Fuyu. Together, but from significantly different positions, they established during the 1920s and 1930s the parameters of proper study of Okinawa in the Japanese context. While each held the other in high esteem, it is nevertheless important to not lose sight of their differences. It is their convergence, despite the differences, that made their constitution of the mainstream so secure.

Yanagita is remembered today as the father of Japanese folk studies; his 1910 collection of tales from a northern village is widely seen as its foundational texts.[21] Yet among specialists in his enormous oeuvre, many would concur with Fukuda Ajio's assertion that Yanagita's discipline of Japanese folk studies is constituted on the foundation of his work on Okinawa.[22] However, not all would agree for the same reason. In Fukuda's mind, Yanagita's interest in folk tales and folk lives took a significant turn toward disciplinarity when he wedded that interest to the question of the origins of the Japanese people. Like a good folklorist, Yanagita even had an origin myth for this interest. Late in life, he recalled a boyhood visit to southern Kyūshū to retrieve a lost memory of his interest in the South Seas. According to Yanagita, it was all due to a chance encounter with a coconut washed ashore on one of those southern beaches. The tropical fruit seemed out of place on that Kyūshū beach, but its mysterious presence suggested to Yanagita that if the coconut had managed to float unintentionally to the Japanese islands from the south, many people had managed to do so in the distant past. In other words, what Yanagita claimed to have latently discovered as a boy was the possibility that the ancient Japanese had not come to the islands from Korea and northern China, as was commonly assumed. Rather, the Japanese people may have come from Southeast Asia, always having been island people. Okinawa would play the key role in that theory as the nearest island to the south, where traces of that ancient migration might still be found.

Indeed, most of Yanagita's writings on Okinawa, particularly his foundational travelogue, *A Brief Account of a Journey to the South Seas* (1923), treat Okinawa as a repository of pretextual evidence of the ancient past of the Japanese people. Materials such as women's tattoos (arrow shapes on the back of the hands, which Yanagita took to be traces of archaic women's power to point in the direction of group migration), stone amulets, and yams played important roles as evidence. But most of all, Yanagita valued Okinawa as a "treasure house of language," where traces of the archaic language spoken in Japan, untainted by contamination with Chinese writing, could still be found in use in daily life. In Yanagita's work on Okinawa—which, in my opinion, did indeed work as a model for his more general work on the constitution of a Japanese cultural sphere—the islands served as the remainder of the archaic Japanese past still existing in the present day. In that sense, Okinawa was to serve not just as a space for the production of knowledge about authentic Japan. It was to do so by remaining frozen in the past. Yanagita's leading student, Orikuchi Shinobu, was to reveal this conceit as clearly as possible in his enthusiastic notebooks from his own fieldwork in Okinawa, undertaken in 1924, when he claimed that doing fieldwork in Okinawa was like "walking into the archaic past."[23]

Other scholars, such as Murai Osamu and Iwamoto Yoshiteru, however, see Okinawa as constitutive of Yanagita's folk studies in another, more overtly political way. Yanagita's early work in folk studies, such as his collection of tales from that northern town, were undertaken as a hobby while he pursued his career as a bureaucrat, primarily in the Ministry of Agriculture and Commerce. For Murai and Iwamoto, Yanagita's hobby was not a distraction from the labors of government, but were in fact meant to pursue lines of inquiry raised by his official duties. Most important, they observe that at the very moment that Yanagita produced his famous collection of fantastic tales of mountain deities and monsters from Tōno, he was officially engaged in the massive land survey efforts of the Japanese government attendant on their annexation of Korea. The land survey was meant to provide the Japanese government with a measure of the degree to which land in Korea could be expropriated for Japanese colonists, among other uses. To that extent, the land survey was a preliminary step toward the commingling of two different ethnic groups: the Japanese and the Koreans. It is in that context that Murai and Iwamoto situate the significance of Yanagita's early work in folklore, all of which was focused on the signs of radical heterogeneity that could still be located in Japan's own hinterlands. In a sense, his collection of folk tales about heterogeneity was undertaken as he contemplated the prospects for a future major engagement with heterogeneity in Korea.

After a decade of Japanese work on the Korean land survey (for which Yanagita was awarded a medal), however, the Korean people rose in a massive, sustained protest movement known today as the March First Movement. Murai proposes that the extent of Korean popular support for the protests, on the one hand, and the brutality of the Japanese military's response, on the other, were seen by Yanagita as an implacable repudiation of his youthful hopes for a peaceful encounter between the Koreans and the Japanese. Not coincidentally, in Murai's account, Yanagita gave up his career in the bureaucracy one year later, dedicating the remaining forty years of his life to transforming his private interest in folk studies into a new discipline. In doing so, as many observers have noticed, Yanagita's focus shifted from the traces of heterogeneity still found in Japan to a sustained search for the foundations of Japanese homogeneity. Not coincidentally, Yanagita's very first trip after abandoning his exalted status as official was to the forgotten islands of Okinawa, far to the south of all that had motivated and vexed him. On that trip, Yanagita found himself in a place of extreme heterogeneity (in part because contemporary Okinawan and Japanese are completely mutually unintelligible languages) within the domestic empire, and yet he could find nothing but evidence of homogeneity. Okinawa was not radically different, he assured his readers; it was radically the same, if one only knew how to dig beneath the surface. From that point on, Yanagita's brand of folk studies developed in part as a rejection of Japanese commonality with China and Korea, locating the sources of Japaneseness only to the south.

Yanagita's major associate in Okinawan studies was Ifa Fuyū, a scholar of tremendous breadth who nevertheless remained frozen in the Japanese academic scene as a regional specialist. Ifa's major contribution to the field was his groundbreaking work on the ancient history of Okinawa through the reconstruction and interpretation of its oldest texts, a collection of songs and poems known as the Omoro Soshi. As a native Okinawan, with the requisite linguistic expertise, Ifa was often relegated to the position of informant for Yanagita and his students. But in his own work he was just as ambitious as they were.

Having encountered Japanese prejudices against Okinawans in his youth (he was a leader of a school protest against a principal who viewed Okinawans as remedial students), Ifa was motivated in much of his scholarship by a desire to demonstrate to Japanese and Okinawan doubters the profundity of Okinawan cultural production. At first glance, this could appear to be the work of a cultural nationalist struggling against the depredations of a foreign power. Yet this project to excavate Okinawa on Okinawan terms was tempered by two significant frames. First, despite his intense engagement with the history of the Ryūkyūan kingdom, Ifa characterized its abolition by the Meiji state as an "ethnic liberation," in which a subgroup was finally freed to "rejoin its parents."[24] Second, by the late 1920s, after half a dozen years of engagement with Yanagita, Ifa adopted a significant change in nomenclature. Rather than refer to his object of inquiry as Ryūkyū or Okinawa (names that could be seen as self-referential), he began to call his object "the southern islands" (nantō). "Southern islands" is an appellation that contains a clear perspective. Okinawa is the "southern islands" only from the perspective of Japan. To call them that meant placing them permanently in the category of subgenus. The ultimate point of reference would remain Japan.

### Conclusion

Up until the end of World War II (and, frankly, well after) Yanagita and Ifa stood as the unquestioned masters of Okinawan studies. Having spent most of my space on moments of deviance, the topography of actual Okinawan studies may remain vague to many readers. But rather than delve into the arcana of Okinawan studies—the investigations of matriarchal religion, linguistic genealogies, or extended family system operations—I wanted to outline its larger tasks.

The cases of Kawakami and Tamura detailed in this essay were judged deviant primarily because they risked situating Okinawa ambiguously outside the Japanese sphere. In both cases, the study of Okinawa was undertaken as part of an inquiry into a world historical problem: the evolution of property. In both cases, this was manifested in an intertextual universe nearly monopolized by Western texts. Even though Tamura's ultimate goal was to argue for the uniquely Japanese character of the Okinawan case, his intertextual universe and terminological choice ("communistic villages") made possible serious misreadings of their works (the justices' question about the Western origins of Itoman fishermen in the case of Kawakami, and the common complaints about Tamura's use of the word "communistic"). The main point is that their ambiguity left Okinawa in a state of potential inauthenticity.

What Yanagita and Ifa sought to establish was a field of Okinawan studies in which the only conceivable reference was Japan. In their work, the authenticity or trustworthiness of Okinawa would be unquestionable because Okinawa was always already Japanese. Indeed, at certain moments, their work could be (and was) used to argue that it was the modern Japanese who had become inauthentic and that if Japanese sought a return to their true selves, they should turn to Okinawa for that source.[25]

A question remains as to the utility of this formation to colonial forms of knowledge. Setting aside for the moment the question of whether Okinawa was itself a colony, I proposed at the beginning of this essay that Okinawa served as an important discursive border crossing, regulating and enabling the linkage of domestic Japan to its colonial empire. At this point the question might be: How might a discourse on Okinawa, which tightly constrained all references to other societies, have served the needs of the Japanese Empire in its ideologies of cohesion and control?

On the one hand, the court hearing of 1939 reminds us that the suspicion of "infidelity" was impossible to eradicate. From the Okinawan perspective, that suspicion could only be cast off onto others. If Okinawans themselves were trustworthy, then there were others who were, indeed, not worthy of trust. They would presumably reside elsewhere in the empire since the condition of proof of Okinawans' faithfulness was their Japaneseness. In perpetuating the suspicion, by casting it elsewhere, the authentic Japaneseness of Okinawa sustained the colonial need to establish Japanese at the top of a colonial hierarchy.

On the other hand, the discourse on Okinawa—hinted at by Tamura but perfected by Yanagita and Ifa—was a model for working through apparent differences in order to arrive at deep convergences. Okinawan studies constantly struggled against popular perceptions of radical Okinawan difference. Moreover, these perceptions were not based on mere popular misinformation. Rather, they were often founded on practical realities, observable in differences in language and daily praxis, not to mention real nexuses of power. If the possibility of authentic assimilation could be found despite the clutter of images of difference, then similar operations could be undertaken in other regions of the empire. In many cases, such as the Pacific islands of Micronesia, Okinawans themselves would play the crucial roles of intermediaries.[26] Taken together, Okinawan studies played out the dual needs of colonial discourse in Japan: to establish Japanese leadership in an essentially homogeneous unit, ultimately known as the Greater East Asia Co-Prosperity Sphere.

But there is a risk of seeing these two possibilities as seamlessly coexisting because together they fulfilled the needs of a contradictory ideology of Japanese colonialism. Such are the risks of functional analyses. It is at this point that we must set aside function and remember the contests and struggles that can reside within any discourse. In this sense, I would argue, Okinawan studies also gives us a useful laboratory glimpse into the contradictions of Japanese colonialism itself. Yet, like the fascistic state that would arise from these contradictions, their coexistence within the same discourse could also offer to many the illusion of transcendence above contradictions, rather than their resolution through conflict.

## Notes

1. Edward Said, *Orientalism* (New York: Vintage Books, 1979).
2. Some might argue that since Japanese modernity was produced out of a nearly wholesale adoption of Western epistemology, then Japanese colonialism was still a basically Western project. This argument merits serious consideration, but it also has major drawbacks, not the least of which is the denial to Japanese of any agency in the making of their own empire. I believe the best approach is to see Japanese modernity as constructed out of an intense dialogue with the West. For a recent English-language presentation of this approach, see Alexis Dudden,

*Japan's Colonization of Korea: Discourse and Power* (Honolulu: University of Hawai'i Press, 2004).

3. Okakura Kakuzo, *The Ideals of the East with Special Reference to the Art of Japan* (Rutland VT: C. E. Tuttle, 1970).

4. Tomiyama Ichirō, "Colonialism and the Sciences of the Tropical Zone: The Academic Analysis of Difference in 'the Island Peoples,'" trans. Alan Christy, in *Formations of Colonial Modernity*, ed. Tani Barlow (Durham NC: Duke University Press, 1997).

5. While the main dispute was between the Japanese and Chinese, the Western powers were also briefly concerned with the transformation of the Ryūkyūs into a Japanese prefecture. Several had standing treaties with the Ryūkyūan kingdom (negotiated with approval from Satsuma), and the Chinese even tried to engage former President Ulysses S. Grant as a mediator in their dispute with Japan during his tour of East Asia after leaving office. George H. Kerr, *Okinawa: The History of an Island People* (Rutland VT: C. E. Tuttle, 2000).

6. For works on Hokkaido as colonial territory in modern times, see Richard Siddle, *Race, Resistance and the Ainu of Japan* (New York: Routledge, 1996); Shigeru Kayano, *Our Land Was a Forest: An Ainu Memoir* (Boulder CO: Westview Press, 1994); David L. Howell, "The Meiji State and the Logic of Ainu 'Protection,'" in *New Directions in the Study of Meiji Japan*, ed. Helen Hardacre and Adam L. Kern (New York: Brill, 1997); James Edward Ketelaar, "Hokkaido Buddhism and the Early Meiji State," in Hardacre and Kern, *New Directions in the Study of Meiji Japan*, ed. Helen Hardacre and Adam L. Kern. For a view of the colonization of Hokkaido that reaches further back in time, see Brett L. Walker, *The Conquest of Ainu Lands, Ecology and Culture in Japanese Expansion, 1590–1800* (Berkeley: University of California Press, 2001).

7. One could make the case that Hokkaidō was also dominated by ethnology, with the close association of Hokkaidō with the Ainu people in many Japanese minds. But a crucial distinction for me between the two prefectures is that Hokkaidō, climatically harsh as it was, also had a major role in the social imaginary as frontier, the open space where a new start was possible and where the developmental vigor of the Japanese people could be demonstrated. Okinawa, in contrast, was geographically tiny and economically insignificant, especially after the prefecture suffered a catastrophic economic collapse when the price of sugar, its main product, plummeted in 1920. Thereafter, Okinawa was a place people left behind to emigrate to other prefectures, other colonies, and other continents. While Hokkaidō was a place of becoming, Okinawa was a place with, to borrow a phrase from the Sex Pistols, "No Future." Ethnology, in Japan as elsewhere, was a discourse that specialized in "the Vanishing," as Marilyn Ivy has put it. For Japanese and Okinawans alike, it could function only as a sign of the past. Mari-

lyn Ivy, *Discourses of the Vanishing: Modernity, Phantasm, Japan* (Chicago: University of Chicago Press, 1993).

8. Kawakami Hajime, "Ryūkyū Itoman no kojinteki kazoku" (The Individualistic Families of Ryūkyū Itoman), in *Keizaigaku kenkyū* (Tokyo: Kyōritsusha, 1924).

9. Tamura Hiroshi, *Ryūkyū kyōsan sonraku no kenkyū* (*Studies of Ryūkyūan Communal Villages*) (Tokyo: Oka shoin, 1927).

10. Henri de Tourville, *The Growth of Modern Nations: A History of the Particularist Form of Society*, trans. M. G. Loch (New York: Longmans, Green, 1907).

11. Sakima Kōei, *Nyonin seijikō* (Tokyo: Oka shoin, 1926).

12. The first is what he calls the "tribute" theory, which he associates with Russian historians. Here the explanation is that governments make communities when they seek to levy taxes on large groupings of people rather than individuals. The second is the "racial" theory, in which migrating groups (the Aryans, in the literature he discusses) separate themselves out as a distinct unit from indigenous groups they encounter. The third is the "natural occurrence" theory, in which communities are seen as arising from a reciprocal relation between people and nature. Tamura, *Ryūkyū kyōsan sonraku no kenkyū*, 21–26.

13. Yanagita Kunio's seminal *Kainan shoki* (1923) is a great example of this. Yanagita began this profoundly important (to Okinawa studies) travelogue with a memory of being in Geneva as a member of the Japanese delegation to the League of Nations mostly to emphasize the impossible distance between Europe and Okinawa. As he recounts his travels through the prefecture, he continually encounters, then rejects as inauthentic, signs of Chinese cultural influence. For a close analysis of the text in English, see Alan S. Christy, "A Dream of Okinawan Assimilation: Yanagita Kunio's Kainan shoki," in *Productions of Culture*, ed. Robert Adams (Chicago: Center for East Asian Studies, University of Chicago, 1994).

14. A good measure of this rejection may be found in Kawamura Tadao's *Nanpō bunka no tankyū* (The Search for Southern Culture) (Tokyo: Sōgensha, 1939). Kawamura, a sociologist trained at the University of Chicago, where one would expect he would have inhabited a completely Western intertextual terrain, produced a major work on Okinawa not only bereft of non-Japanese references, but explicitly critical of both Kawakami and Tamura for textually situating Okinawa outside Japan.

15. Kawamura, *Nanpō bunka no tankyū*, 49.

16. For example, Sōseki Natsume, *My Individualism and the Philosophical Foundations of Literature*, trans. Sammy I. Tsunematsu (Rutland VT: C. E. Tuttle, 2005).

17. See Alan S. Christy, "The Making of Imperial Subjects in Okinawa," in *Formations of Colonial Modernity*, ed. Tani E. Barlow (Durham NC: Duke University Press, 1997) for a fuller description of the consequences of Okinawan liminality.

18. Ministry of Justice, "Itoman ryoshi to iwayuru kojinshugi ni tsuite," *Setai chōsa shiryō*, no. 18. The document is labeled "Not for public release" (bugaihi).

19. "Shihōshō chōsabu," *Setai chōsa shiryō*, no. 18, September 1939, 2.

20. Ministry of Justice, "Itoman ryoshi to iwayura kojinshagi ni tsuite," 22.

21. Yanagita Kunio, *The Legends of Tōno*, trans. Ronald Morse (New York: Japan Foundation, 1975).

22. Fukuda Ajio, "Kaisetsu," in *Yanagita Kunio zenshū*, vol. 1 (Tokyo: Chikuma Shobō, 1987).

23. Orikuchi Shinobu, "Okinawa saihō techō," in *Orikuchi Shinobu zenshū*, vol. 15 (Tokyo: Chūō Kōronsha, 1982).

24. Ifa Fuyū, *Koryūkyū: Ifa Fuyū zenshū*, vol. 1 (Tokyo: Heibonsha, 1974).

25. Yanagi Sōetsu, the main spokesman and theoretician for the Japanese folk craft movement, was one prominent proponent of this position. See, for example, Yanagi Sōetsu, "Okinawajin ni utauru no sho," in *Yanagi Sōetsu zenshū*, vol. 15 (Tokyo: Chikuma shobō, 1981).

26. See Tomiyama Ichirō, "Colonialism and the Sciences of the Tropical Zone."

SOURCE ACKNOWLEDGMENTS


"Orientalist Empiricism: Transformations of Colonial Knowledge," by David Ludden, is from *Orientalism and the Postcolonial Predicament: Perspectives on South Asia*, ed. Carol Breckenridge and Peter van der Veer. Copyright © 1993 by the University of Pennsylvania Press. Reprinted by permission of the University of Pennsylvania Press.

"The Command of Language and the Language of Command," by Bernard S. Cohn, is from *Colonialism and Its Forms of Knowledge: The British in India*. Copyright © 1996 Princeton University Press. Reprinted by permission of Princeton University Press.

"The Sociology of Islam: The French Tradition," by Edmund Burke III, is from *Islamic Studies: A Tradition and Its Problems*, ed. Malcolm Kerr. Copyright © 1980 by Undena University Press. Reprinted with permission.

"Scientific Production and Position in the Intellectual and Political Fields: The Cases of Augustin Berque and Joseph Desparmet," by Fanny Colonna. Translated by David Prochaska and Jane Kuntz. Originally published as "Production scientifique et position dans le champ intellectuel et politique. Deux cas: Augustin Berque et Joseph Desparmet," in *Le Mal de voir. Ethnologie et orientalisme: Politique et épistémologie, critique et autocritique*, ed. Henri Moniot (Paris: Collection 10/18, 1976), 397–415.

"The 'Passionate Nomad' Reconsidered: A European Woman in l'Algérie française (Isabelle Eberhardt, 1877–1904)," by Julia Clancy-Smith, is from *Western Women and Imperialism: Complicity and Resistance*, ed. Nupur Chaudhuri and Margaret Strobel. Copyright © 1992 by Indiana University Press. Reprinted with permission.

"The Unspeakable Limits of Rape: Colonial Violence and Counterinsurgency," by Jenny Sharpe, was originally published in *Genders* 10 (1991): 25–46. Copyright © 1991 by the University of Texas Press. All rights reserved. Reprinted with permission.

437

"Ethnography and Exhibitionism at the Expositions Universelles," by Zeynep Çe-lik and Leila Kinney, was originally published in *Assemblage* 13 (December 1990): 35–59. Copyright © 1990 by The Massachusetts Institute of Technology. Reprinted with permission.

"Taboo Memories and Diasporic Visions: Columbus, Palestine and Arab-Jews," by Ella Shohat is from *Performing Hybridity*, ed. Jennifer Fink and May Joseph (Minne-apolis: University of Minnesota Press, 1999), 131–56. Reprinted with permission.

"Chinese History and the Question of Orientalism," by Arif Dirlik, is from *The Post-colonial Aura: Third World Criticism in the Age of Global Capitalism*. Copyright © 1997 by Westview Press, a member of the Perseus Books Group. Reprinted by permission of Westview Press, a member of Perseus Books, L.L.C.

CONTRIBUTORS

EDMUND BURKE III is Professor of History at the University of California, Santa Cruz. He is the author of, among other works, *Prelude to Protectorate in Morocco, 1860–1912* (1976) and editor of *Islam, Politics and Social Movements* (with Ira M. Lapidus, 1988) and *Rethinking World History* (1993).

ZEYNEP ÇELIK is Professor in the School of Architecture at New Jersey Institute of Technology. She is the author of *Remaking of Istanbul* (1986), *Displaying the Orient* (1992), and *Urban Forms and Colonial Confrontations* (1997).

ALAN CHRISTY is Associate Professor of History at the University of California, Santa Cruz. He is completing a book, "Ethnographies of the Self: Japanese Native Ethnology, 1910–1945."

JULIA CLANCY-SMITH is Associate Professor of History at the University of Arizona. She is the author of *Rebel and Saint* (1994) and editor of *Domesticating the Empire* (with Frances Gouda, 1998).

BERNARD S. COHN taught history and anthropology at the University of Chicago. His publications include *An Anthropologist among the Historians and Other Essays* (1987) and *Colonialism and Its Forms of Knowledge* (1996).

FANNY COLONNA is Director of Research Emerita at the Centre National de la Recherche Scientifique. She is the author of, among other works, *Instituteurs algériens, 1883–1939* (1975), *Aurès/Algérie, 1954* (1994), *Les Versets de l'invincibilité* (1995), and *Récits de la province égyptienne (2004)*.

NICHOLAS DIRKS teaches in the Anthropology Department at Columbia University. His most recent books are *Castes of Mind* (2001) and *Scandal of Empire* (2006).

ARIF DIRLIK is Knight Professor of Social Science and Professor of History and Anthropology emeritus at the University of Oregon. He is the author of *After the Revolution* (1994), *The Postcolonial Aura* (1997), and *Postmodernity's Histories* (2000).

LEILA KINNEY is Administrator for Academic Programs, Comparative Media Studies, at MIT. She has published on early modernist painters, world's fairs, hybrid artistic genres, and new visual technologies in the nineteenth century.

DAVID LUDDEN teaches in the History Department at the University of Pennsylvania. His publications include *Agrarian History of South Asia* (1999) and *Early Capitalism and Local History in South Asia* (2005).

DAVID PROCHASKA teaches in the History Department at the University of Illinois, Urbana-Champaign. He is the author of *Making Algeria French* (1990, 2004) and *Beyond East and West* (with David O'Brien, 2004).

JENNY SHARPE is Professor of English at UCLA. Her publications include *Allegories of Empire* (1993) and *Ghosts of Slavery* (2003).

ELLA SHOHAT is Professor of Art and Public Policy and Middle Eastern Studies at New York University. She is the author of, among other works, *Unthinking Eurocentrism* (with Robert Stam, 1994) and *Taboo Memories, Diasporic Voices* (2006).

# INDEX

imperialism (*continued*)
  critiques of, 11–14; French critique
  of, 14–18; Marxist critique of, 13–14,
  19–20; orientalism and, 77
India, 363; 1857 uprising in, 31,
  214, 220–36; colonial, 75–97,
  102–46; communalism in, 334, 344;
  Rajasthan, 245–46, 249–52; Tamil,
  333–55
Indian Subaltern Studies Group, 12, 29
invented traditions, 392
Iraq War, 51
Islam, 292, 317, 322, 363–68, 374–75,
  378–79, 398; French sociology of,
  154–73
Islamic reform movement, 179, 181,
  187n7
Israel, 51, 359, 361, 367, 369, 372–80
Istanbul, 294, 317, 320
Itoman (Okinawa), 414, 419, 420, 425,
  426, 431

Japan, 41, 393–94, 402, 415, 425
Jesuits, 391, 394–95
Jews, Ashkenazi, 359
Jiang, Tingfu, 396, 401, 411n34
Jones, William, 24, 42, 76, 78–84,
  86–87, 90, 95, 110, 115–20, 143, 342,
  390, 393
Judeo-Arabic, 363, 375, 383n32

Kanwar, Roop, 250
Kawakami, Hajime, 414, 418–21, 424,
  426–27, 431
Kinney, Leila, 25–36
knowledge: colonial forms of, 2, 24,
  42, 46, 50–51, 415; about India,
  77–84, 86–88, 91, 93–94, 96, 102, 107;
  about Okinawa, 431
Korea, 429–30

Krauss, Rosalind, 274

Lacan, Jacques, 321
Lean, David, 217
Le Chatelier, Alfred, 157, 165–66
Lee Kwan Yew, 398, 403
Letourneux, A., 163
linguistic turn. *See* cultural turn
Ludden, David, 22–23
Lyautey, General, 204–6

Mahathir, Mohamad, 398, 403
Mandal Commission, 333, 403
Mani, Lata, 29–30, 54n16–17
Marx, Karl, 23, 36, 88–91, 225
Marxism, 91, 395, 400, 414, 418, 421,
  424, 426. *See also* imperialism,
  Marxist critique of
masculinism, 217, 337
Masqueray, Émile, 156, 164, 184, 186n4
metonymy, 42–43, 364, 395, 397,
  400–402
Middle East, 368–71, 375–77
Mill, James, 23, 89–90, 95
mimicry, 255, 282n37, 352–53. *See also*
  contact zone; hybridity
Minto, Lord, 129, 138
missionaries: in India, 337–47, 354
Mithad Efendi, Ahmed, 295
Mizrahim. *See* Arab Jews (Mizrahim)
modernity, 48–51, 337, 388–89, 391, 397,
  401–3, 405–6, 432
Moniot, Henri: and *Le Mal de voir*
  ("The Difficulty in Seeing"), 17
Montagne, Robert, 159, 161
Moriscos, 366
Morocco, 154, 157–59, 162–63, 165–67,
  367, 377
Moulin, F. J., 268–71
Mughal Empire, 102, 105–6, 108, 121

Müller, Max, 42, 342
multiculturalism, 406
Munro, Thomas, 78, 81–85, 86–89, 91, 95
Muslims. *See* Islam

Naicker, E. V. Ramaswamy, 336, 344, 347–57
Nana Sahib, 224, 232
nation, 361, 377, 380
nationalism, 11, 43–44, 344, 369–70, 372, 376–80, 394, 397, 402–3, 405–6, 421; and orientalism, 20, 40, 94, 97, 347–53
Nehru, Jawaharlal, 96
Nochlin, Linda, 33–34, 54n20
North Africa (*Maghreb*). *See* Algeria; Morocco; Tunisia
nostalgia, colonial, 248

occidentalism, 402–3
Okakura, Kakuzo, 416
Organisation Armée Secrète (oas), 246, 277
orientalism, 42, 47, 286, 292–97, 303, 305–10, 322n3, 335, 353, 355, 362, 369–70, 384–89, 394–407, 415; British, 22–24, 39, 392; critique of, 9–11, 45–46, 49; definitions of, 9–10; 75–76; French, 155; and gender, 28; and India, 82, 86–87, 89–97; and self-orientalization, 49, 392, 402–3; visual, 32–36. *See also* discourse; exoticism; Said, Edward
other. *See* alterity
Ottoman Empire, 292–94, 317, 375. *See also* Turkey
Ouled-Nail. *See* Algeria, Ouled-Nail of

Palestine, 51, 359, 361, 369–80

Paris, 287–88, 317
patriarchy, 286
Peirce, Charles, 254, 274
Persian, 104, 106, 110–12, 116, 118–19, 122, 125, 393
photography: colonial, 27, 33, 248–79. *See also* visual culture
picturesque, 34, 249–53. *See also* exoticism
Pinney, Christopher, 254
postcolonialism, 48, 248, 286, 320–21, 360, 379; and world history, 45–51
postcolonial studies, 46, 360–61; history and, 4–9
poststructuralism, 47, 248, 360
power, 287; orientalism and, 36–45, 387–89, 397, 398–402, 404. *See also* hegemony
Pratt, Mary Louise, 401. *See also* contact zone
Prochaska, David, 35, 197, 207n2

Quincentenary, 1492, 362–63, 365–67, 374–75. *See also* Columbus, Christopher

race, 27, 202, 215, 218–20, 221, 229, 235–37, 298, 351, 361, 364, 395, 416, 423, 426
Rani Lakshmibai of Jhansi, 228–29
realism, 34, 254, 271–75
Rennell, James, 78–81, 83–87
*Revue du Monde Musulman*, 165–66
Richard, Charles, 158, 161
Risley, H. H., 333
Roe, Sir Thomas, 103–4
Roy, Rammohun, 393
Ryūkyūs, 416-17, 430, 433n5

Said, Edward, 1–5, 10, 19, 27, 33, 36–37,

Milton Keynes UK
Ingram Content Group UK Ltd.
UKHW020813150924
448182UK00017B/204

9 780803 213425